1987

INTROD

Cultural Anthropology

Elmer S. Miller

Temple University

INTRODUCTION TO
Cultural
Anthropology

Prentice-Hall, Inc.
Englewood Cliffs, New Jersey

To Rosina and Lisa

Library of Congress Cataloging in Publication Data

Miller, Elmer S   1931-
    Introduction to cultural anthropology.

    Bibliography: pp. 373–382
    Includes indexes.
    1. Ethnology. I. Title.
GN316.M54   301.2   78-24083
ISBN 0-13-480236-5

Printed in the United States of America

10 9 8 7 6 5 4 3 2 1

Cover photo of Guatemalan Devil's mask by Luis Villota

Part-opening photo credits: Part One: George Rodger, Magnum; Part Two: Josef
Koudelka, Magnum; Part Three: Marylin Yee, *The New York Times.*

Chapter-opening photo credits: Chapter 1: Jacques Jangoux, Peter Arnold Photo Ar-
chives; Chapter 2: Stan Washburn, Anthro Photo; Chapter 3: Marc and Evelyne
Bernheim, Woodfin Camp; Chapter 4: Laima Druskis, Photo Researchers; Chap-
ter 5: Ken Hyman; Chapter 6: Fred A. Anderson, Photo Researchers; Chapter 7:
Katrina Thomas, Photo Researchers; Chapter 8: David Strickler, Monkmeyer;
Chapter 9: Paul Conklin, Monkmeyer; Chapter 10: Jen and Des Bartlett, Photo Re-
searchers; Chapter 11: Marc and Evelyne Bernheim, Woodfin Camp; Chapter 12:
Jason Lauré, Woodfin Camp; Chapter 13: Homer Sykes, Woodfin Camp; Chap-
ter 14: Y. Jeanmougin/Viva, Woodfin Camp; Chapter 15: Georg Gerster, Rapho/
Photo Researchers, Inc.; Chapter 16: Georg Gerster, Rapho/Photo Researchers,
Inc.; Chapter 17: Jim Cron, Monkmeyer.

Prentice-Hall International, Inc., London
Prentice-Hall of Australia Pty. Ltd., Sydney
Prentice-Hall of Canada, Ltd., Toronto
Prentice-Hall of India Private Limited, New Delhi
Prentice-Hall of Japan, Inc., Tokyo
Prentice-Hall of Southeast Asia, Pte. Ltd., Singapore
Whitehall Books Limited, Wellington, New Zealand

Outline

v

Contents

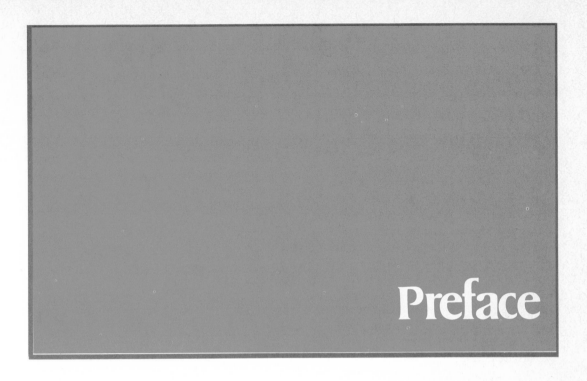

Preface

MANY students are first attracted to anthropology to satisfy their curiosity about ways of thinking and acting that are significantly different from their own. As they come to learn about the discipline, they discover that an equally fascinating subject is what human social groups everywhere share in common. It is a relatively simple matter to document human differences and similarities. To explain them intelligently is another matter. Recently anthropologists have become increasingly sensitive to the consideration that the conceptual tools and analytic categories they use to order a vast array of ethnographic information from all parts of the world are largely culture bound. That is, the questions raised by anthropologists in the field, and the data collected to answer them, are framed primarily in terms of Western understandings about the nature of reality. Students from Africa, Asia, and Latin America who have traveled to North American universities for training in anthropology have increasingly challenged some of its most cherished premises. Such challenges have provided a cross-fertilization that has served to revitalize the discipline during a period of serious self-reflection.

This text is written in such a manner as to introduce the basic findings of anthropology while calling into question some of its fundamental assumptions. The views of culture and of society presented here are broad enough to let the student make sense of our knowledge of the human experience yet restricted enough to systematize that knowledge. As a result, the student should come to recognize that our concepts of both culture and society are in fact analytic constructs rather than ultimate statements about reality.

General Plan and Organization

The book consists of three parts. Part One (Chapters 1–5) presents an overview of cultural anthropology together with general statements about methodology and theory. Part Two (Chapters 6–16) discusses the major topics generally covered in a basic introductory course. Each of these chapters is meant to be readable by itself, but the order provided is intended to give the reader an understanding of the key concepts by presenting them from various perspectives. Part Three (Chapter 17 and Epilogue) offers insight into some current directions in cultural anthropology with a view to recent concerns and practical problems. This organization has certain advantages, which can be summarized as follows.

Comprehensive Coverage

The 11 chapters of Part Two provide a comprehensive treatment of the major topics of current concern in cultural anthropology. In addition to the standard chapters on kinship and social organization, economics, politics, and religion, separate chapters are offered on such topics as social control, social stratification, ecology, and the arts. All of these topics are presented in such a manner as to demonstrate those conceptual approaches that have contributed most significantly to the subjects under discussion. Conflicting arguments are avoided except when they contribute directly to the understanding of the topic by disclosing differing premises and unique contributions.

Broad Conceptual Base

Chapter 3 offers a broad perspective on the concept of culture that takes into considera-

tion major theoretical approaches of contemporary significance. Nevertheless, a consistent and systematic view of culture integrates the chapter as well as the book. This view is based on a "mentalist" rather than a "materialist" approach, although the two are shown to be compatible depending upon what questions are being raised. The findings of major theoretical approaches can thereby be incorporated so that the student will have a solid foundation for later work.

Well-Balanced Content

The broad range of topics presented is also given balanced consideration in terms of geographic region and social type. Examples from traditional enthnographies are given along with others from more contemporary studies of Western societies. Most ethnographic work has been carried out in traditional, small-scale societies. The illustrations in this book reflect that balance while taking care to include the most recent work from other societies whenever possible.

Contemporary Approach

Rather than offer a separate chapter on culture change and the modern world, I have chosen to consider modernization at appropriate points in almost every chapter. Since culture is a dynamic process, its nature can be illustrated best by considering its workings in modern industrial states. In those areas in which little research has been carried out by anthropologists, I have tried to indicate the direction of future studies.

Readability

This is an introductory text for the beginning student in cultural anthropology. In order to aid understanding, I have taken care to present basic concepts with concrete examples in an easy-reading style. Even the supposedly dry topics of kinship and social organization, for example, take on interest when considered in terms of the organizing principles that govern our own social life. I have avoided professional jargon and extended debates as much as possible, particularly when they lead to dead ends rather than to constructive understandings.

Something New

The chapter on regional systems is perhaps the first of its kind in an introductory text in cultural anthropology. It represents an attempt to place the studies of complex societies and urban anthropology in the context of some very recent approaches in the discipline and thereby to inject new life into what rapidly have become old problems.

Learning Aids Within the Text

Illustrations

In few other subjects are good photographs as important as they are in cultural anthropology. A great deal of effort has been made in the preparation of this book to provide photographs that help the reader to see exactly what the text discusses, from generalities through specific ethnographies. At appropriate points specially designed illustrations make the substance of the text easier to grasp. The book contains about 30 charts, graphs, and drawings and over 100 photographs.

Chapter Summaries

Rehearsal is an important part of long-term learning. With this fact in mind, I have concluded each chapter with a summary of the major points that should be remembered from it.

Glossary and Bibliography

As each new important term is introduced in the text it is defined. A glossary at the end of the book redefines each term for the student, and a bibliography contains references to all of the material cited within each chapter.

Supplements to the Text

The text is supplemented by a study guide and workbook for the student and an instructor's manual and a test bank for the teacher.

The study guide is divided into four parts: a study outline; a list of key terms and concepts; a pre-test, consisting primarily of multiple-choice questions on the most important points covered in the chapter; and a study outline, consisting of questions of varied sorts that ensure that the reader has learned the material covered in the chapter at a greater depth. Immediate feedback is provided by having the answers to all questions provided in the margin of the workbook directly next to the question and by keying them to the page of the text on which the material appears, so that a reader who misses a question knows immediately where to look to rehearse the material.

The test item file consists of some 800 multiple choice questions; it is available, as is the instructor's manual, free upon adoption. The instructor's manual consists of an overview of each chapter, a group of resources for classroom discussion, a list of paper topics, and a film list keyed to appropriate sections of each chapter.

Acknowledgments

Cultural anthropology is a dynamic discipline moving in many directions at once. Traditional concepts are being questioned and new ones introduced at breathtaking speed. The challenge this presents to both author and publisher is being met increasingly by an approach in which editors and authors work together with writers and technical experts to produce a viable text in as short a time as possible. This text represents such a product. I wish, therefore, to acknowledge the efforts of those who have contributed so much to it.

Ann Torbert, manuscript editor, turned my sometimes rambling raw materials into their final form. Her quick grasp of key anthropological concepts, her eye for good style, and her ability to get all of us to work together made this book what it is.

Robert Fredericks assisted me in organizing the topics and in finding research materials to illustrate them. A staff of competent writers—Howard Cohn, Mary Pat Fisher, Marcia Golub, Carolyn Smith, and Marjorie Weiser—produced drafts that first Ann Torbert and then I rewrote and refined. The final version was also influenced by the thoughtful comments of reviewers, to whom I owe thanks: Ira Abrams, University of Southern California; Ann Buddenhagen, University of Massachusetts; Thomas Greaves, University of Texas at San Antonio; Robert Moorman, Miami Dade Junior College; Richard W. Stoffle, University of Wisconsin at Parkside; and Max W. Witkind, San Antonio College.

Stan Wakefield, anthropology editor at Prentice-Hall, supervised the reviewing process, and it was his efforts that brought me to the project in the first place. Ruth Kugelman provided the research base on which the book was begun. Patricia Quinn deserves special thanks as production editor for the efforts she made in giving the manuscript the attention it needed at crucial stages.

The contributions of technical experts must also include those of Cheryl Mannes, editorial assistant; Nancy Perkus, permissions editor; Alan Forman, photo researcher; Florence Silverman, art director; Marcia Schonzeit, copy editor; and Nancy Myers, manufacturing buyer. To each of these individuals I express my sincere thanks.

ELMER S. MILLER

INTRODUCTION TO

Cultural Anthropology

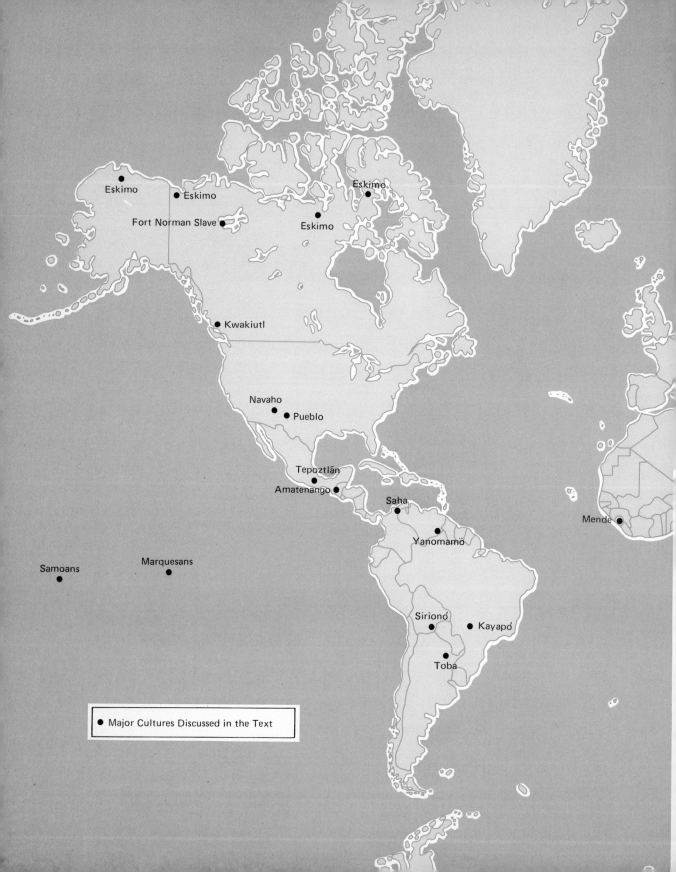

Eskimo

Eskimo

Fort Norman Slave

Eskimo

Eskimo

Kwakiutl

Navaho

Pueblo

Tepoztlán

Amatenango

Saha

Yanomamö

Mende

Samoans

Marquesans

Siriono

Kayapó

Toba

● Major Cultures Discussed in the Text

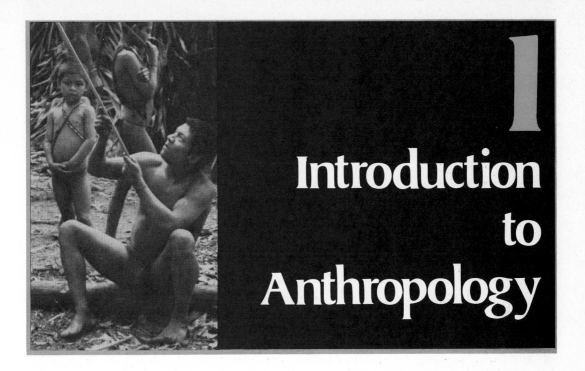

Introduction to Anthropology

P EOPLE have long been curious about the origins and nature of the human species. Many societies have developed beliefs about the creation of humans and their place in relation to the rest of the natural—and perhaps supernatural—world. The organized study of human beings—*anthropology*—has existed as a distinct field of inquiry for over 100 years. Only within the past few decades, however, has anthropology graduated from being a quaint subject that studied the "strange" artifacts and customs of little-known or remote peoples to a systematic attempt to explain human cultural and biological variability.

Modern communications and a world war that carried Westerners to far corners of the earth brought Western technology to isolated people and at the same time made Westerners aware that people once thought to be exotic are very much a part of the real world. As anthropology turned to questions of more direct significance to modern industrial life and adopted a more systematic, scientific approach to human social life everywhere, it acquired an established place among American academic disciplines that it had not had previously.

The Anthropological Approach

Anthropology is somewhat like sociology, history, human biology, and many other disciplines as well. What sets it apart from these ways of looking at humanity is its attempts at holism and relativistic comparison. It is an attempt to understand the origin, evolution, and present diversity of human biology and culture.

Anthropology is an immense subject. It is the most inclusive of any academic discipline, for it seeks to encompass not only all that is known about human beings around the world but also the history of their gradual evolution from small mammals that lived almost 70 million years ago. It covers all that is known of culture—the learned ideas and beliefs that characterize human groups as distinct from other primate groups—and of human biology as well. This takes anthropology through time and space into fields as diverse as paleontology (the study of fossils), anatomy, primatology, economics, archaeology, linguistics, genetics, religion, art, and political science, to name a few.

Anthropology tries to pull all this information together and organize it in some systematic fashion. For instance, anthropology makes inferences about the earliest humans by studying isolated living populations. It also compares the way of life of remote aborigines with that of urban city dwellers, and the behaviors of monkeys and other nonhuman primates with those of humans. It is this all-inclusive scope—called *holism*—that gives anthropology its unique character. Holism is an attempt to incorporate all of this knowledge into a meaningful understanding of humanity.

This claim of holism is more a goal than a reality, however. There is no overall framework—for example, no single theory of how culture works—that all anthropologists would happily use for explaining their data. Different kinds of anthropologists see things from very different points of view. Furthermore, increasingly specialized training has produced a generation of anthropologists who communicate primarily with those in their own subdisciplines. Still, the concept of culture ties together all anthropologists, whether they are interested in social relationships,

Anthropology studies populations throughout time and space—from the earliest humans to modern city dwellers—and attempts to incorporate knowledge of them into a meaningful understanding of humanity.
(Drawing by David Pascal)

linguistics, archaeology, or physical anthropology.

Traditionally, there was a continuum in anthropology, ranging from those who emphasized biology to those who emphasized culture. At one extreme were those who tended to view humans basically as biological organisms whose behaviors are largely determined by genetic and environmental factors. They analyzed human groups in the same terms by which other organisms are studied: inherited traits, local food supplies, climatic changes, and other features that affect biological survival. At the other extreme were those who saw humans as unique creatures who have asserted their independence from most biological factors by their genius for cultural solutions—houses to modify the effects of climate, tools for manipulating the environment, and political organizations to maintain social control. Today this division is not as important as it once was, since both physical and cultural anthropologists are using more of the same concepts and approaches. As we will see, the main subfields of anthropology continue to be informed by work done in the others, and attempts to integrate the whole field continue to appear.

Relativistic Comparison

In addition to holism, there is another unique aspect of the way anthropology looks at the human condition. This is *cultural relativism:* the attempt to understand and evaluate each cultural system in terms of its own internally consistent logic. Before the need for relativism was recognized, visitors to cannibalistic tribes, for instance, were appalled at their "immoral" practices. They were judging cannibals by their own society's moral code, by which it is unthinkable to eat human flesh. But later anthropologists made an effort to be less culturally subjective in their observations. They tried, for instance, to accept the fact that some cultures consider cannibalism acceptable behavior. Instead of condemning it, they tried to determine what functions cannibalism serves for the groups that practice it. *Ethnocentrism*—the tendency to judge other cultures by the standards of one's own culture—became the devil to be exorcised in every introductory anthropology course.

By the middle of this century, however, it became apparent that anthropologists could not completely free themselves from ethnocentrism. No matter how much they tried to immerse themselves in other cultures in order to understand them better, they were inevitably influenced to some extent by their own society's ways of looking at things. A certain amount of ethnocentrism seemed to be essential to the functioning of any social system, including their own. And in trying to explain their experiences to those back home, they found that they were obliged to translate them into terms which had significance in their own culture. Having to do so destroys the efforts to treat cultural systems in their own terms. Thus, anthropologists continually search for the most appropriate method of translating what they know about a culture into concepts that are meaningful in their own. Only by doing so are they able to offer insights into the operation of our own cultural system.

Another difficulty, which is potentially very serious, is that by attempting to explain objectively the function of practices which seem inhumane to us, anthropologists may seem to be approving them. Infanticide, for instance, can be explained in terms of its biological and social functions. To condemn the practice would require the kind of value judgment that anthropologists have long avoided. However, some anthropologists feel that they must make it clear where they stand on such matters. The question of how to do so without sacrificing relativism is a critical dilemma which anthropology has not yet resolved.

Anthropology and Other Disciplines

Anthropology occupies a central position in any liberal arts curriculum because it serves to link the humanities, natural sciences, and social sciences.

The *humanities* include art, languages, music, philosophy, and history. Anthropological research and interpretation extends into all these areas, often taking them into sectors of time and space that would not otherwise be described. In art, for instance, anthropology has contributed a great amount of information about the folk art of cultures outside Western traditions, as well as data on the role that art plays in society and culture. And in history, archaeology (a branch of anthropology) has pushed our understanding of extinct peoples back into the shadows of prehistoric times, before written records were kept.

The *natural sciences* upon which anthropology draws for some of its explanations include biology, ecology, chemistry, and geology. Chemical analysis, for instance, helps anthropologists figure out how old fossils and artifacts are. Geology contributes knowledge of the environments within which humans evolved. Ecology—the study of the relationships between living things and their environment—clarifies how human populations and the rest of nature influence each other. And biology is a rich source of concepts and information about human anatomy, physiology, variation, evolution, and behavior. The exchange is not just a one-way process, however. To these sciences, anthropology brings knowledge of how human activities have changed human biology. It also provides its special humanistic viewpoint—a fundamental concern for understanding and explaining human cultural differences.

Anthropology is most commonly listed as one of the *social sciences.* It deals with topics covered in a number of other social sciences—economics, psychology, sociology, political science, statistics, law, geography. Anthropology overlaps with geography, for instance, when it studies the links between culture and environment. It coincides with psychology—the study of individual behavior—when it looks at the relationship between culture and individual personalities and actions. And over and over again, anthropologists have pointed out that law, economics, and politics are parts of integrated cultural systems and cannot be fully understood unless the rest of these systems are described and explained.

Sociology cuts across some of the same territory as anthropology. But its subject matter is more limited, and its methods different. Traditionally, sociology has been concerned with Western societies, whereas anthropology studies societies and cultures everywhere in the world. Sociologists tend to isolate only certain influences on group behaviors—such as age, sex, income level, social status, and educational background. By contrast, anthropologists try to look at everything that may affect how people in a certain culture behave. This includes not only the factors listed above, but also the environmental setting, the group's survival strategies, its religious beliefs, its history and political organization, and so on. Sociologists run surveys with questionnaires and statistical samplings that reveal the relationships between certain variables (such as divorce, income, and educational level). By contrast, anthropologists try to figure out how a whole culture works by making in-depth studies. They may also compare features of one culture with those of others to see if there are any regularities in the ways humans tend to approach various facets of social life—sex, incest, adolescence, and so on (Fried, 1972). *Cross-cultural comparison* is one of the hallmarks of anthropology.

Subdisciplines

Anthropology is commonly divided into four subdisciplines: physical anthropology, archaeology, linguistics, and cultural or social anthropology. The major distinction traditionally has been between the first—the study of humans as biological animals—and the last—the study of humans as creatures who are unique because of culture. This is no longer necessarily the case, as we have seen. Archaeology is closely tied to cultural anthropology in its attempt to reconstruct life ways prior to written records. But it also works with fossil remains and biological concepts in reconstructing history. Linguistics is perhaps the most independent of the four subdisciplines because its body of data has distinct boundaries. As you will see, all of these branches are in a state of flux, revising their traditional methods to help them get at the heart of the questions that people are interested in today.

Physical Anthropology

Physical anthropology, the study of the biological aspects of human existence, was once a rather static science. Its nineteenth-century practitioners spent much of their time measuring people in the effort to group humans into races according to head shape and various other traits. The initial concern was to describe the variation of a few features in modern and ancient populations. Today, however, physical anthropology not only describes the variation of hundreds of features—from blood protein composition to limb length—but also encompasses the entire history and nature of human biological change. This new anthropology represents an enormous expansion in scope.

We can begin to make sense of the diversity of the field by thinking of physical anthropology as the study of the events and processes of human evolution. An event can be described as the appearance in the fossil record of any of the traits that characterize a species in different stages of its evolution. These events take place within a geological time frame and occur much more slowly than the events we read about in the papers. By placing thousands of fossils together in the correct time sequence, physical anthropologists have begun to reconstruct the history of our evolution.

An ideal picture of how we evolved would be complete in every detail, including a vivid

Physical anthropologist Donald Johanson uses an air scribe to clean sandstone from around the fossil skull of a child that lived 3 million years ago in East Africa. (David Brill © The National Geographic Society)

description of the climates, plants, and animals comprising ancient environments. The actual picture is far from ideal. Crucial periods early in the history of our evolution are almost completely unrepresented by fossils. For instance, during the period from 14 to 5 million years ago, our humanlike ancestors began to walk upright on their hind limbs. But we have no fossil leg bones or pelvises from this time. In fact, the known primate remains from this period are a single tooth. We do, however, have a fairly complete record of the human evolution during the past 3 million years. Geologists and a host of other specialists have developed techniques for determining prehistoric precipitation, geography, flora, and fauna. But for a complete understanding of how these features affected past human evolution, much more data must be collected.

The present is also a valuable source of clues to the past. By studying the anatomy and behavior of the other primates, physical anthropologists can reconstruct how fossil species (including the earliest humanlike creatures) probably moved and, to some degree, how they may have behaved together in social groups.

Physical anthropologists want to know more than what happened; they are also curious about *why* evolutionary events occurred as they did. They are interested in what evolutionary processes have been responsible for the events. The most important source of this knowledge is living human populations. Analysis of how the frequency of various physical traits in human groups is shifting in response to changing environments and cultural practices can provide analogies to evolution in prehistoric groups.

Physical anthropologists who study modern human variation face the problem of distinguishing environmental action on an individual during his or her lifetime—such as the effects on the body of growing up in a cold or a high-altitude setting—from those that are truly the result of inherited factors. Research-

ers must also separate the cultural influences on human biology from those of the natural environment. Cultural beliefs and values can shape the process of reproduction and therefore influence the course of evolution. Physical anthropologists have come to understand human variation as the consequence of enormously complex interactions with both the environment and culture.

The study of the interaction of biological and cultural factors has led to some unique contributions. For instance, Carleton Gajdusek, of the National Institute for Neurological Diseases and Stroke, won a Nobel Prize in 1976 for applying physical anthropological and epidemiological methods to the study of a progressive neuromuscular disease called kuru. The disease occurs among a group of New Guinea highlanders called the Fore. He found that kuru has a cultural component—the eating of uncooked diseased brains in the course of ritual cannibalism. The virus is then transmitted to those who eat the brains. Gajdusek discovered a genetic factor as well. Although cannibalism is a common practice among highland New Guinea peoples, the disease occurs only among the Fore highland groups. This fact suggested a genetic susceptibility to the disease. Gajdusek's discoveries are important because some progressive muscular disorders found in the West—such as multiple sclerosis—may also be studied in terms of the cultural and genetic factors involved.

Archaeology

Archaeology overlaps both physical and cultural anthropology. But it exists as a distinct discipline with its own subject matter and methods. It can be defined as the study of the history, life styles, and processes of change in prehistoric human cultures. For the most part, archaeologists examine what happened in human societies before they began to keep written records. Recreating what life was once

Archaeology students make a site survey at the Pyramid of the Sun, part of the monumental architecture of Teotihuacán, a city state that dominated much of Mesoamerica from about A.D. 200 to 500. Excavations at this site have added a great deal to our knowledge of the rise of cities and states. (Marilu Pease/Monkmeyer)

like in the dim past and understanding how it changed is like trying to put together an intricate jigsaw puzzle in which most of the pieces and the picture of the completed puzzle on the box cover are missing.

Generally working without written records, archaeologists use the most durable scraps of human activities as clues. Occasionally these are well-preserved buildings and implements. But more often, evidence consists of such objects as bits of broken pottery, flakes from ancient stone tool making, charred animal bones around an ancient hearth, and slight changes in vegetation or soil patterns caused by prehistoric farming. Archaeologists try to relate these material remains to the behaviors of the humans who left them behind. To do so, they systematically survey, dig up, date, classify, and then interpret the remains.

Interpretation of what went on in the past was once just a matter of organizing bones and artifacts into historical sequences. Long-inhabited sites with many layers built up over the years often reveal, for instance, that one kind of pottery was gradually replaced by another kind and then still another. Archaeologists were at first content merely to catalog these sequences. But in the "new archaeology," scientists analyze a variety of data as clues to the actual activities of the humans who left these traces. In following the spread of early human tribes, for instance, archaeologists analyze tools, indications of environmental conditions, and the remains of animal prey for information on the changing role of hunting.

Among other surprises, archaeologists have found that the appearance of tool-using humans in North America seems to have coincided with the disappearance of many large game animals. One hundred species of mammals—including mammoths, giant beavers, and giant ground sloths—suddenly became extinct about 10,000 years ago. In evolutionary terms, this was not long after the first humans seemingly made their way to the continent from the Far East, probably by way of a land bridge at the site of the Bering Strait. Were humans responsible for these mass extinctions? Had they developed hunting techniques—such as surrounding herds with fire or running them off cliffs—so wasteful that they wiped out their prey? Or was it something else—a major climatic change, perhaps—that killed so many so fast? We are not yet sure. The "Pleistocene overkill" theory is still under investigation, as are many other theories about how our ancestors lived from day to day and changed over the centuries.

To analyze and interpret their finds, today's archaeologists call on a battery of specialists. Analysts range from zoologists who examine deer antlers to determine what times of year a site was occupied to scientists who can tell from minute grains of pollen how old a site is, what kinds of plants once grew there, and what the climate was like. Interpretive models may also draw on the work of economists, ecologists, statisticians, geographers, cultural anthropologists studying modern primitive populations, and even physicists. Growing numbers of archaeologists are unearthing vast quantities of materials at sites around the globe, guided by a desire to find and record as much data as possible before the evidence is destroyed by advancing industrial civilization. The result is a dynamic field undergoing explosive growth. We now know far more about how humans once lived than we did even a few years ago.

Linguistics

Thanks to the work of linguists, scientists who study language, our understanding of this central aspect of social life is also increasing. Anthropological research into language is expanding in many directions at once.

Some anthropological linguists are busy recording languages that will soon become extinct because they are spoken in vanishing cultures. Others are trying to find ways in which all languages are similar. These findings may suggest something about humans' basic capacity for using vocal symbols to communicate with each other, as well as the fundamental structure of the human mind. Other linguists focus on differences, rather than universals, in languages. These, they think, reveal fundamental differences in the ways people of various cultures perceive life. Some languages, for instance, have no way of expressing neat divisions of time into past, present, and future, as ours does. Our vocabulary and grammar reflect a linear view of time—and perhaps an obsession with it—that is by no means universal. People of other cultures are obsessed with other kinds of details. Indians* of northern Canada, for instance, have not 1 word for

*In this text we will use the term *Indian* to identify aboriginal peoples in the New World—in North, Central, and South America. We do, however, recognize the fact that some people prefer various other terms—especially *native American*. We choose *Indian* from among the list of possibilities as the one term that applies everywhere in the New World.

cultures work. For anyone patient enough to record and analyze its intricacies, language is a rich source of information about everything from the patterning of kinship relations to how other domains of culture are perceived (Fried, 1972).

Cultural Anthropology

The fourth subdiscipline, cultural anthropology, is the most familiar of the branches, the one which people usually think of when the word "anthropology" is mentioned. But, given its diversity, it is also the hardest of the four to define.

Cultural anthropologists themselves do not all agree on what it is they are studying. Culture—one of their principal subject matters—is variously defined as a worldwide striving toward "civilization" through the accumulation of practices and beliefs; a unique pattern of beliefs that shapes personalities in each society; a local system of ideas and practices that are functionally integrated; an unconscious structure that generates ideas and behavior; a system of shared symbols that come into play in social interactions; and a system by which people adapt to their environment. Cultural anthropologists work with the concepts culture and society. Those who focus on the interaction of individuals, and the institutions such interaction creates, sometimes stress their particular focus by referring to themselves as social anthropologists. In this text, the emphasis is on culture as an idea system, but the concept of society is absolutely essential to all of the chapters dealing with social organization, such as kinship and marriage, non-kin groupings, and politics and leadership.

Underlying most definitions of culture is the basic assumption that groups of people—Samoans, Americans, members of an Eskimo tribe—come to share a set of understandings about how their society works and how one should behave in it. These un-

Anthropological linguists study the form and use of spoken language, as well as nonverbal systems of communication that are characteristic of various social groups. (Klaus D. Francke, Peter Arnold Photo Archives)

"ice," as we do, but at least 13. Since it is important to them to know whether a stretch of frozen water will support a foot traveler or a dog sled, they are careful to categorize these kinds of ice in their verbal communications (Basso, 1973).

However linguists approach it, language is a key element in the study of culture. Fieldworkers obviously need to know a people's language before they can learn much about them. Models developed for the study of language can also be used to study how whole

Cultural anthropologists study people's understandings about how their particular society works and how to behave in it. Here, the men of a Hoti Indian family in Venezuela inspect the bamboo used to make blowguns with which they will hunt monkeys and birds, and boys of the Ibo of Nigeria dance around a masked figure at their New Year festival. (Jacques Jangoux, Peter Arnold Photo Archives; Peter Buckley, Photo Researchers)

derstandings in turn affect the ways in which people behave—how they choose marriage partners, build houses, organize politically, procure food, communicate, worship, divide labor, maintain social control, express themselves in art, and so on. Since these beliefs and behaviors may be quite different from one group to another, anthropologists usually see them as products of the local culture rather than as basic aspects of human nature. In each society, though, members tend to accept their own way of looking at things as the norm. In the United States, for example, we "know" that older people need to be retired (and thereby lose the opportunity to contribute their knowledge and skills to society). But in some other societies, the aged are respected for the knowledge and wisdom they have developed over the years.

Collecting information about "strange" practices was the central concern of an-

thropologists during the early years of the discipline. This concern frequently appeared to be separated from any understanding of one's own culture. The information they gathered fascinated and amused the folks back home. But today a crisis of sorts is facing the field: there are very few "unknown tribes" left to describe. The cultures of many peoples are rapidly becoming extinct. In some cases, contact with Westerners has introduced diseases for which their bodies have no built-up immunity. Measles, tuberculosis, smallpox, mumps, and other introduced diseases have decimated many primitive* tribes. And as more technologically advanced peoples have pushed into the environments that once sus-

*We use the term *primitive* here to indicate, in general, nonliterate peoples who live without permanent dwellings and by means of simple technology—hunting and gathering of food.

tained them, hunting-and-gathering tribes have been relegated to the most barren settings or resettled in communities that are inadequate for their needs and desires. This disruption of their traditional life style and food supplies has created severe vitamin and mineral deficiencies and, in some cases, destroyed their social structure. As a result of such pressures, the aboriginal population of Australia, for instance, plummeted from 250,000 at the turn of the century to no more than 40,000 today (Lévi-Strauss, 1967).

Elsewhere, though, formerly primitive populations are reproducing rapidly and becoming part of a growing and restless third world. In Latin America, Asia, and Africa, people are increasingly aware of the more technologically advanced nations and of their own lack of power and material wealth. They resent being the objects of anthropological studies, and they express ambivalent feelings about Western technology and ideologies.

To deal with the first crisis—that of extinction of primitive peoples—cultural anthropologists are speeding up their attempts to gather information while they may. Data on how the remaining primitive tribes live provide invaluable clues to the primitive life ways of ancient humans. Observation techniques are therefore being sharpened and made more systematic in the urgency of capturing this information before it is lost forever. At the same time, however, many anthropologists are turning to the study of the far more numerous urban cultures.

The second crisis has serious implications for world harmony. Third world cultures feel that anthropologists from technologically advanced nations are more interested in maintaining the status quo than in helping them develop and join the rest of the political and economic world. This feeling is due to the fact that the study of colonial peoples by anthropologists often stresses traditional systems rather than situations of change and unrest resulting from colonial administration. In the face of this distrust—and of the extinction of their other subjects—many Western anthropologists are turning to a study of their own culture instead. When they do so, they find it hard to maintain anthropology's traditional distinction between the anthropologist and the group being studied. Instead of the perspective of a culturally alien observer trying to be a participant, studies of Western culture have the peculiarly self-reflective point of view of participants who are trying to be observers.

French anthropologist Claude Lévi-Strauss (1967) suggests another alternative: invite third world anthropologists to come study us. This solution might reveal things about our own "strange" customs that are hard for those of us who have grown up with them to see. It might revise anthropology's established use of alien peoples as subjects and permit a more meaningful interaction with the third world.

The fact that there are so few isolated peoples also requires another change in cultural anthropology as it was practiced in the past. Traditionally, in-depth studies described a single social group, in and of itself. But such isolated pictures no longer reflect the whole situation. In Brazil, for example, even the most remote Indian tribes in the Amazon jungle have been affected by the new trans-Amazonian highway and by the policies of government agencies appointed to deal with Indian societies. They also are influenced by the influx of commercial enterprises that have begun to exploit the natural resources of the region. When anthropologists describe village life in these remote areas, they can no longer ignore the effect of these regional influences. This methodological problem is even more acute in the developing countries. There, the lives of people whose parents or grandparents were members of more isolated cultures are now touched more directly, not only by regional economic and political developments but by world events as well. As a result, it is increasingly important that analyses of cul-

The telephone booth in the marketplace in Jedda, Saudi Arabia, is a relatively new addition, one that is indicative of the modern communication systems that are becoming regular features of developing nations all over the world. (Kent Reno, Jeroboam)

tural systems take into account the wider social systems in which they are encapsulated.

Although the days of describing remote tribes are coming to an end, anthropology is needed now more than ever before. All over the world, modern communication systems are bringing a flood of information about other cultures to mass audiences. Anthropologists' perspective and knowledge of these cultures can help to interpret the information and build understanding between peoples. There is also hope that in coming to understand other people better, we will learn something about ourselves—perhaps that our behaviors are to some extent the result of local choices rather than inevitabilities of human nature or of the "right" way of doing things.

In addition to serving the public, anthropologists are also in demand by international organizations. As the third and fourth worlds begin to organize and assert them-

selves, the major powers need to learn more about these people's life ways, heritages, and points of view. Cultural anthropologists' new studies of urban cultures may also contribute to programs of development and planning.

Instead of being simply a science *of* humanity, anthropology is becoming a science *for* humanity. In all its branches, anthropology is being drawn into the serious questions of the day—the effects of unequal distribution of wealth, of genetic engineering, of loss of cultural identity, of technological impact on the environment, of racial strife, of sex-role stereotyping. Instead of simply observing and describing interesting details of the human scene from afar, anthropologists are becoming aware of the serious implications of their research for people's lives. Sensitive topics are now being handled with greater care than they once were. The American Anthropological Association, for instance, is very concerned about information collected by anthropologists and how it is disseminated to the public. The result may be a science that is at the same time more systematic and more humane.

Summary

1. Anthropology is the study of everything human—from our biological origins to how our cultural systems influence our behaviors.

2. Anthropology cuts across the entire liberal arts curriculum, taking other disciplines into sectors of time and space that might otherwise be neglected; it studies people from all times and in all places. It also distinguishes itself from the subjects it overlaps by its *holism* (all-inclusiveness) and its *relativism* (considering people in terms of their own cultures). But some of its own branches and points of view do not mesh well with each other. And in some serious matters, anthropologists feel that they must reveal their value judgments.

3. There are four main branches of anthropology: physical anthropology, archaeology, linguistics, and cultural anthropology.

4. Physical anthropologists traditionally studied a limited range of biological variations in living human populations. But now they study as well the events and processes by which humans have evolved.

5. Archaeologists study extinct human cultures. Using durable fragments of human activities as clues, they devise theories about how people behaved and changed before they began to keep written records.

6. Linguistics—the study of languages—has been adopted by some anthropologists as a way of understanding how cultures work. The language that a people uses may reveal many features of their social life.

7. Cultural anthropologists generally study the understandings about human life and the external world that people in every human group learn from those around them. This understanding—that is, culture—tends to shape everything they do, as well as their beliefs and attitudes. Cultural anthropologists have traditionally studied the "strange" (to us) ways of "exotic" peoples. But today the cultures of these remote and primitive peoples are vanishing as they are touched by the industrial world. The focus of anthropology is, therefore, shifting to urban cultures elsewhere and at home.

PART ONE

Perspectives on Cultural Anthropology

2

Observations and Inferences

ANTHROPOLOGISTS study both the characteristics that all humans share and those that are unique to a specific social group. Shared characteristics include such phenomena as kinship and language use. Unique aspects of these phenomena are, for example, the clan organization of the Bororo Indians of Brazil and the jargon of Americans talking over citizens band (CB) radio. Anthropology considers people from all times and places, from the earliest apelike human ancestor to the baby born this morning, from isolated hunters and food-gatherers of the Amazon to professionals in large urban centers.

Cultural, or social, anthropology concerns itself with living populations. It examines the beliefs and practices that make social life possible. These features—religious beliefs, political, economic, and legal institutions, arts and crafts, to name a few—comprise the *culture* of a particular society or population. The

next chapter will discuss this key concept in detail.

Another key concept utilized by anthropologists is that of *society*. This term refers to a group of human beings that is organized in various ways in order to accomplish common purposes. The notion of society calls attention to the interaction of humans in various social settings, whereas culture refers to the common bond of understanding that makes such interaction possible. In this chapter we look at the methods and techniques used by cultural anthropologists in their work. To discover the patterns of organization within a society, its development and change, and its relations with other societies, cultural anthropologists have adopted various techniques of observation, description, comparison, and analysis. These techniques enable researchers to record in detail the various practices they observe. Anthropologists use their recorded data to compare what they have learned with the

17

findings of other observers of the same culture. They also compare the features of one culture with those of other cultures.

Ethnography and Ethnology

The collection of information on societies and cultures by anthropologists is called *ethnography*. Anthropologists must often spend months in the field observing and interacting with their subjects of study. They provide detailed descriptions—*ethnographies*—of the activities, values, and thought of a given social group. *Ethnography* literally means the "de-scription of a people." It records in careful and minute detail the social and cultural phenomena observed by the anthropologist in the field. Although such phenomena may be of interest in themselves, anthropologists are primarily interested in the relationships and patterns that exist among them. It is these patterns that are disclosed through the analysis and interpretation of ethnographic accounts. Anthropologists analyze these accounts by seeking out the patterns in the activities they describe, and they then compare these patterns with those of different cultures. *Ethnology* is the study of culture on a comparative basis. Ethnology traditionally has been considered more theoretical in nature than ethnography. Because ethnography is usually a slow process and less theoretical in orienta-

Different observers attach different interpretations to the same set of phenomena. (Twohy)

tion than ethnology, it has in the past been held in lower esteem by many cultural anthropologists who preferred the theoretical side of the discipline. Recently, anthropologists have come to understand that ethnography and ethnology are not completely separate activities, but, rather, interrelated and even interdependent stages in a single process of investigation.

Differences in Observation

Anthropologists cannot begin their fieldwork without some background in theory, since theory enables them to classify and interpret what they see. It is important, though, that anthropologists be as aware as possible of their theoretical preconceptions. Above all else, they must be prepared to abandon any theoretical framework that does not fit the facts discovered in fieldwork. They must also be aware that other observers, with different theoretical views, may disagree completely about the meaning of the same set of phenomena. An example will serve to illustrate this point.

A classic instance of differing interpretations is found in the studies of the Mexican village Tepoztlan published by Robert Redfield (1930) and Oscar Lewis (1951). Redfield, who visited Tepoztlan in 1926, believed that the character of tribal and peasant societies is completely different from that of modern urban communities. According to Redfield's theory, tribe members and peasants—the inhabitants of folk communities—have direct contact with one another, feel strong group solidarity, and behave in predictable and "traditional" ways. Modern city dwellers, on the other hand, he believed to be less friendly, more isolated from their fellows, and less likely to act in predictable ways. Because of his preconceptions, Redfield's study, *Tepoztlan – A Mexican Village,* offers a harmonious picture of rural existence in which social life is seen as peaceful and well integrated.

Oscar Lewis visited Tepoztlan in 1943 to see firsthand the workings of the folk community that Redfield had described. He published his observations in *Life in a Mexican Village: Tepoztlan Restudied* (1951). What Lewis found, however, was a village seething with personal tension and discord. Lewis's conclusions were so different from Redfield's that other scholars wondered at first how the Tepoztlans could have changed so radically in only 17 years. The change, anthropologists soon realized, was not so much in the people as in the opposing perspectives of Redfield and Lewis. One looked in Tepoztlan for a peaceful folk community, the other for the problems of daily life. Tepoztecan society, like all societies, was sufficiently complex to contain both harmony and stife, integration and conflict.

To imagine any observer as a mere recording eye and ear, then, is misleading. Every observer inevitably colors what he or she sees according to personal background, education, interests, beliefs, and values. In fact, it has been pointed out that the topics treated in ethnographic accounts, as well as the manner in which they are analyzed, frequently reflect the prevailing intellectual climate of a given period. British anthropologists, for example, emphasized integration and conflict resolution during a colonial period when these topics were on the minds of people in administrating nations. Thus, an ethnographic record cannot be separated from the ideas and theories that influence a particular fieldworker. The more clearly fieldworkers identify their own premises and beliefs—for themselves as well as for their readers—the more clearly their observations will be understood for what they are—observations from a particular perspective.

Alien Observers

When cultural anthropologists engage in fieldwork, they are generally aliens or outsiders in a society that may not share their inquisitiveness about local beliefs and practices. Anthropologists' special interests, after all, are shaped by the values of their own cultures. These values and understandings in turn influence the manner in which social and cultural phenomena are perceived.

For example, when living among the Toba Indians of northern Argentina in the late 1950s, the author noticed that the villagers reacted with great excitement to an early manufactured satellite that passed overhead. The villagers were divided as to its significance, but all agreed that it was a powerful sky spirit carrying a message or omen that could be interpreted only by a shaman (a religious and medical specialist). After a long discussion of the object, several Toba asked the author what he thought the "sky being" was. He confidently explained that the object had been placed in orbit from the earth by a powerful machine and carried the message of extraordinary technological achievement. His companions, however, were unconvinced by this explanation and stuck to their original story. Furthermore, they pressed their visitor until he acknowledged that the "sky being" did appear to be a moving star and that he could not prove that it had not been set in motion by a powerful shaman who could also interpret the meaning of its heavenly trajectory.

Both the author and his Toba companions had seen the same phenomenon, but each had interpreted it differently. The anthropologist, familiar with aerospace technology, recognized an orbiting satellite. The Toba, accustomed to magical signs and omens, detected the presence of a sky spirit. Conditioned by different traditions and bodies of knowledge, each saw, in effect, a different object. This disagreement between the anthropologist and the Toba Indian villagers was due, at least in part, to the vast differences between them in culture and education. But anthropologists themselves, although they may share similar backgrounds, cultural systems, and educa-

tions, sometimes draw opposing conclusions from virtually identical phenomena, as did Redfield and Lewis.

In the course of doing fieldwork, anthropologists frequently revise and reformulate their field of inquiry. Unexpected developments or discoveries make such modifications virtually unavoidable. But the changes themselves are always limited to a degree by what the ethnographer already understands—that is, by his or her own culture and education. This is the dilemma: anthropologists attempt to record living societies in all their diversity, but the record is ultimately made in terms and categories that have meaning primarily for members of their own culture, and especially for those who have studied anthropology. In an attempt to make sense out of what he or she observes, the anthropologist discovers that one's own ready-made categories often do not fit the field data. For some anthropologists, therefore, the most enduring and central aspect of fieldwork is not the encounter with another culture nor the data collected but deeper insights into one's own culture that often follow. Having acknowledged this problem and its challenge, we should stress that ethnography nonetheless forms the foundation for all work in cultural anthropology.

Ethnographic Fieldwork

Early Fieldwork

When anthropology emerged as a discipline in the late nineteenth century, the influence of evolutionary theory was encouraging the belief that human existence had followed a pattern of "progress" from lower to higher forms of life. Social scientists believed that there existed orderly "stages" of cultural evolution, from more simple to more complex forms. The main goal of anthropology, they thought, was to reconstruct the patterns of development in technology, kinship, and religion. They assumed, too, that so-called "primitive" societies found today represent remnants of an earlier stage of human social development. So, early anthropologists were interested in the collection of data on so-called "primitive" cultures which would exemplify early stages in this pattern of progress. One of the best known early anthropologists was Sir James Frazer. The research that Frazer undertook in 1887 consisted of sending a questionnaire to missionaries and colonial administrators around the world. It was entitled *Questions on the Manners, Customs, Religions, Superstitions etc. of Uncivilized or Semi-Civilized Peoples.* Frazer apparently did not use much (if any) of the material that was sent to him (Leach, 1961). Instead, as he wrote some years later,

I made a practice of noting in a book the passages of authors who seemed to me of particular significance in their descriptions of the manners and customs, the beliefs and practices, of the various races of men, especially of those races of backward culture, an understanding of whom is of special importance for a knowledge of our race. (Frazer, 1938, p. vii)

Although early anthropologists such as Frazer catalogued and recorded the customs of exotic peoples, they made no attempt to see these customs as part of a consistent whole in which single activities could be understood in relation to others within a system. The materials collected were analyzed from an armchair position rather than from firsthand observation in the field. Perhaps for this reason, the interconnections of cultural phenomena were more readily ignored.

In contrast to early evolutionists, prominent anthropologists in America such as Franz Boas (1858–1942) and Alfred Kroeber (1876–1960) stressed the study of particular societies over specified periods in order to construct their cultural histories. Boas and Kroeber studied chiefly North American Indian groups whose cultures had been drastically altered and sometimes threatened with extinction by the European settlers of the New World. They attempted to record in detail the features of these cultures. Their desire, of course, was to record for posterity those cultures before they lost all resemblance to their original forms or disappeared altogether. But by the time early culture-historians such as Boas and Kroeber began their work, the changes were in some instances already so great that it was possible to find only a handful of individuals who could recall the traditional practices and beliefs. These informants were chosen because their ages or social positions suggested that they could describe fully and accurately the earlier social and cultural life of their people. But they were sometimes unreliable or misleading. Led more by the inclinations of the informants than by the shape of the culture they thought they were preserving, anthropologists often accumulated fragmented accounts of language, folklore and mythology, ritual, technology, and political systems; but these accounts also rarely if ever reflected the full range of a people's thought and activity.

Modern Fieldwork: Participant Observation

Bronislaw Malinowski's research in the Western Pacific during World War I marked a radical development in the nature of ethnographic research and laid the foundation for modern anthropological fieldwork. Malinowski firmly believed, as did Boas, that ethnographers must take up residence among the subjects of their study and learn the native language. They must not only participate in daily activities but also learn to act as members of the community insofar as possible. This method, which came to be known as *par-*

ticipant observation, is now accepted as a prerequisite to responsible fieldwork. Only by moving into a local community, involving oneself in the daily life of the people, learning the language, and settling down for a period of months can the ethnographer begin to recognize the ordinary but vital texture of village life. Living with the people themselves helps the fieldworker to overcome the suspicions of his or her hosts and to be tolerated (if not accepted fully). As Malinowski remarked about the attitude of the Trobianders to him: "as they knew that I would thrust my nose into everything, even where a well-mannered native would not dream of intruding, they finished by regarding me as part and parcel of their life, a necessary evil or nuisance" (1922, p. 8).

An anthropologist "going native"—in tennis shoes. (Napoleon Chagnon, Anthro-Photo)

Malinowski gave attention to every detail of social life, stressing the patterns in the behavior observed. In place of the loose, fragmentary data that had been a feature of earlier work, modern fieldworkers consider the structure and function of social and cultural phenomena. They conceive of cultures and societies as complex wholes in which the patterns of relationships, and not merely isolated phenomena, must be studied. Despite the fact that recent fieldwork has gone beyond Malinowski in precision and completeness, he is recognized as having pointed the way to modern fieldwork methodology.

Thus, modern fieldworkers recognize that the object of study is not the *place* itself (the village, settlement, or city neighborhood) but *what happens within it*—the events of daily life, the development and expression of values and attitudes. Anthropologists choose one place rather than another because they believe it to be a promising source of information about the processes in which they are interested. Obviously, not every village or every society offers the same sort of data in equal abundance and richness. For this reason, choosing a place of study is important. If one wished to investigate the relation between national political parties in the United States and local factionalism, one presumably would not go to a Mennonite community, whose members neither vote nor participate in national politics.

It is important to note, too, that the gender of the fieldworker can be a factor in terms of establishing rapport and collecting information. It is difficult to believe that any male could have collected the data that Margaret Mead did on child rearing in the Pacific or have been privy to the kinds of activities that Elizabeth Fernea (1975) reported in her study of women in Morocco. On the other hand, female anthropologists sometimes find it difficult to acquire information from males who are not accustomed to communicating with women on given topics.

Measures of Fieldwork

The task of ethnographers continues to be to observe everything that occurs in the social life of a people, their public transactions, and their personal dealings, together with their comments on them. Ethnographers must record their observations systematically and clearly. To ensure credibility of their observations, anthropologists have been concerned with problems of reliability and validity. *Validity* is the degree to which observations actually record what they are intended to record. To illustrate, Pelto (1970) offers the example of a door-to-door interviewer soliciting intimate details about respondents' sex lives. The information gathered in this way is not likely to represent accurately real behavior and would therefore lack validity if presented as data about sexual practices. If the responses were said to reveal the ways in which people answered questions on a sensitive subject, however, their degree of validity might be quite high.

Reliability, on the other hand, is the degree to which the result of an experiment or a set of observations can be obtained on another trial by a second experimenter or observer. If repeated door-to-door interviews produced similar sets of responses to questions about respondents' sex lives, the observations would have high reliability (Pelto, 1970). The responses may be reliable without being valid, if, for example, the respondents lied consistently to all interviewers.

Use of Informants

In many instances, the most dependable ethnographic descriptions are characterized by high degrees of both validity and reliability. This correlation is easier to obtain when informants describe ideal behavior—how things ought to be. High degrees of validity and reliability are more difficult to achieve when in-

Individual informants are the primary source of field data. Here, a village chief in Kenya is interviewed by a fieldworker. (Georg Gerster, Rapho/Photo Researchers)

formants describe real behavior—the ways things actually happen. In such cases, there is a strong likelihood that the researcher's data will be less reliable, since an informant may not trust the fieldworker completely and may consciously mislead him or her. Many times, this misdirection is not deliberate, since native descriptions often are rationalizations of a given activity. Other times, in order to satisfy the anthropologist's desire to learn about some unobserved custom, informants may pretend to remember more than they actually do. Informants continue to be the primary sources of data in fieldwork, but it is crucial to avoid depending too heavily upon too few, unconfirmed sources. Pelto and Pelto (1973) mention one ethnographer who interviewed a single Ingalik Indian for 500 hours. This informant may have been a remarkably knowledgeable person—or simply a great storyteller. For this reason, one must question the reliability of information until it is confirmed by more than one member of a society. Experienced ethnographers learn to confirm whatever information they record by checking it with other informants who, by virtue of the positions they hold or have held, can comment on the activities in question.

Whatever the limitations of informants in specific instances, their necessity to fieldworkers is beyond question. They help teach fieldworkers to speak the local language; to master native skills; and to behave in appropriate ways. Without such instruction, a stranger might linger indefinitely on the fringes of society, unable to gain acceptance. One's first informants are often marginal members of the society themselves and therefore more easily approached and more eager to give information. They may be, for this reason, less initiated into the inner workings of the group than others closer to the center. But with the introduction provided by initial informants, anthropologists usually soon establish rapport with others in the group. They may sometimes even achieve this access unaided, if they are already adept at some important local skill. Freilich (1970), for example, reports his quick acceptance by his Creole subjects in Trinidad because he was adept at cricket: "The British had introduced cricket to Trinidad, and the sport was popular with young and old. My knowledge of the game soon brought me into contact with Mr. Ed . . . [whose] house was a hang-out for many of the Creole peasants. . . . After cricket practice we would all stop at Ed's house." Anthropologists frequently find that they can collect valuable information at such informal gatherings. One's simple observations of who is present and who is absent in themselves provide insights into local relations and groupings or, more important, into changes in them.

Field Data

Maps, Inventories, and Census

One of the major problems encountered in the early stages of fieldwork is simply one of settling into the society—setting up housekeeping and some sort of work schedule, finding one's way around the community, learning the language and the daily routine of the people—not to mention the physical adjustments to changes in temperature, food, and water. From the beginning, most anthropologists keep diaries in which they note as many details of each day's events as possible. They try to record only what they have observed and not to generalize about their experiences. Eventually, of course, many small items from these diaries work their way into broader understandings. Therefore, the writer tries to omit nothing, no matter how poorly or incompletely he or she may understand an observation. For example, when the author had returned home from Argentina and was in the process of analyzing his field data on Toba religious leaders, he found references in his diary to places and dates that proved helpful in separating out distinctive attitudes of various Toba communities toward their leaders. In fact, a chance comment about the action of one chief led to a major reconsideration of the widely held distinction between religious and political leaders.

While ethnographers are still relatively unfamiliar with their subjects and as yet unable to speak the native language, they usually take the opportunity to collect certain information about the local community. They gather data that are easy to compile without much fluency in the language or help from native* infor-

---

*To anthropologists, the term *native* refers simply to indigenous people, those belonging to the region. Thus, natives may be primitive people living in the wild, or the most sophisticated urban dwellers, depending on what region is the subject of fieldwork.

vegetable gardens — creek — vegetable gardens — "Druze" — "Christians" — grove — bridge — spring — spring — terraces

N

☑ Christian household
☐ Druze household

A map drawn in the course of fieldwork in a Lebanese village shows physical features of the area, as well as the religious affiliation of households. A census of who lived in the "Druze" (a Moslem sect) and in the "Christian" parts of the village showed the inaccuracy of the native model of the village as rigidly divided on the basis of religion. (Robert W. Fredericks)

mants but which will be useful later in interpreting other materials. This early period is very often spent in mapping the physical features of landscape and habitat and making inventories of material goods. Among the physical features the ethnographer would note are the locations and types of fields and forests and sources of water—streams, springs, or wells. In the local community itself, the anthropologist would record the presence of paths and streets, the arrangement, density, and construction of buildings, and the like.

Inventories of material goods also can be extremely informative. They can reveal differences—by local standards—between the more and the less materially successful members of the community. Some of the items that an anthropologist might consider in an inventory of material goods are house style; materials used in house construction; source of water and lighting (if any); amount and kinds of furniture; numbers of animals owned; landholdings; means of transportation; tools; food; clothing (Pelto, 1970). By plotting this data, the fieldworker discovers not merely who is rich and who is poor, but also how different individuals and groups live and are employed. An inventory also can highlight what equipment is technically useful and what items are connected to status and prestige in that society. Since people sometimes enjoy showing off their possessions, taking inventory can often serve as a pleasant introduction of the ethnographer to the community.

In addition to maps and inventories, anthropologists use photography as a means of collecting field data. Photographs and films themselves often serve as documents of anthropological fieldwork. In recent years, anthropologists have sought professional assistance in filming ceremonies and other types of social interaction. These films have proved to be useful not only for descriptive purposes but also when analyzing aspects of social interaction. Some people, in fact, consider use of photography in fieldwork a specialized subfield of the discipline, which they call *visual anthropology*.

Once the ethnographer can speak easily to the people under study, he or she customarily attempts to take a census of each household. The purpose of the census is to map, among other things, the residence patterns of individuals, recording changes of residence throughout their lives. The age, marital status, and education of each member and his ownership of land or other property or forms of wealth also are recorded.

At this point the fieldworker usually proceeds to collect data on kinship and marriage. Such work frequently begins with the collection of genealogies (descent charts). In some societies, genealogies provide insights into the entire social system. Anthropologist Napoleon Chagnon discovered in studying the Yąnomamö Indians of Venezuela and Brazil that "accurate genealogies are fundamental to an understanding of Yąnomamö social organization, intervillage political relationships and past history. . . . [Genealogical]

In an area where the supply of water is a problem, Irven DeVore and a Bantu interpreter measure the amount of water used in a day by a group of !Kung bushmen hunters. (Stan Washburn, Anthro-Photo)

data have constituted the most important single source of information on many different aspects of the culture" (1974, p. 89).

In recent years, anthropologists have begun to include a number of other items in their census. To shed light on the problems of food production and distribution, for example, some fieldworkers have recorded the number of individuals who participate in the production of food, the length of the working day, seasonal variations in the routine of food production, the number of years men and women are thought capable of contributing to food production, and other related factors. Consumption goods are weighed and measured in each household in order to determine how much value a given household places upon accumulation rather than consumption.

When the community under study is too large to be canvassed completely by direct interviews and surveys, different methods are required. In this case, the ethnographer must master the techniques of sampling. They will ensure, as far as possible, that the data collected and conclusions reached are representative of the community as a whole and the groups within it. To generalize from data carelessly compiled can lead to serious distortion—and sometimes has done so. Despite the fact that anthropologists have moved increasingly to the study of urban communities, it does not mean necessarily that they are always working with large populations. In fact, many of their studies continue to be with small groups, such as skid-row drunks or minorities of one sort or another.

Whether the community is large or small, however, there are many reasons to collect reliable quantitative information. Mitchell (1967) provides an example of marriage between clans. If two clans have no preference for intermarriage, the incidence of marriage between members of the clans would be determined by the number of eligible marriage partners. If the anthropologist finds there are more intermarriages than chance would dic-

tate, he or she has discovered a preference for interclan marriage. If there is less intermarriage than chance would dictate, one may have discovered an aversion to interclan marriage. Thus, quantitative data may reveal the patterning of certain phenomena. Demographic features—birth and death rates, frequency of marriage and divorce, age distribution, and kinship categories—may reveal the basic organization of a community. When a report of the fieldwork is written up, demographic features are often used to support the fieldworker's analysis of the social structure.

Organizing and Using Field Data

From this discussion, we have seen what kinds of material anthropologists gather in the field and the sequence in which they are collected. We have yet to learn how they go about organizing their data into categories or framing questions about these materials. In compiling a genealogy, for example, how do anthropologists identify particular members of a kinship group? Should they use the native categories and terms or kinship categories from their own culture? Should they attempt to formulate a uniform, comprehensive system that permits them to describe and analyze not only the kinship system under study but other kinship systems as well and to compare one system with another? From whose point of view should anthropologists attempt to view a kinship system—or any other social phenomenon—the natives' or their own? Will one's own categories hold any meaning for the natives? Anthropologists who enter the field with their survey questions already rigidly drawn up sometimes find that the natives cannot make sense of the questions and are unable to answer them since the questions seem irrelevant.

Even when anthropologists agree about terminology, disagreement may arise over its application. For example, two surveys of residence patterns on Truk, an island in the North

Pacific, done only 3 years apart by John Fischer (in 1944) and Ward Goodenough (in 1947), differed considerably. Goodenough's results indicated that Truk residence was overwhelmingly *matrilocal,* meaning that when a couple married, the groom moved to or near the home of his bride's parents. Fischer, however, found the residence pattern to be *bilocal,* meaning that the couple lived with or near either the husband's or the wife's parents. Fischer found that although in more than half the cases residence patterns were matrilocal, another third of the newlywed couples lived at or near the home of the groom's parents (a residence pattern termed *patrilocal*). After comparing their divergent findings, Goodenough concluded that the differences arose "from an honest difference in how to interpret the data" (1956, p. 24). That is, Goodenough and Fischer did not agree on what was a case of patrilocal residence. Goodenough himself stated that they had probably "been working in practice with somewhat different concepts of residence" (p. 24). He further concluded that all too often anthropologists do not routinely gather enough census data to permit them to identify residence patterns with any degree of certainty.

In the 1950s, *ethnoscience,* or cognitive anthropology, emerged as an approach to studying other cultures. It claimed that by employing the language categories of native speakers, one could identify the native—or insiders'—points of view. Ethnoscientists argued that a valid description of a society could be made best by a fieldworker who learned to speak the native language fluently and to understand its terms (such as those of kinship or residence) well enough to behave in a local setting as if he or she were native to it. Social behavior, according to the ethnoscientist, should always be studied from the point of view of the native, and the categories applied to the social activities should always be native categories. Ideas should never be imposed by anthropologists upon their material; ideas should be allowed to surface from within by means of procedures attuned to native thinking and terminology. Although this approach is relatively recent, its origins can be traced back half a century to the writings of Edward Sapir, a culture-historian. Sapir warned of the pitfalls of externally describing cultural behavior:

It is impossible to say what an individual is doing unless we have tacitly accepted the essentially arbitrary modes of interpretation that social tradition is constantly suggesting to us from the very moment of our birth. Let anyone who doubts this try the experiment of making a painstaking report of the actions of a group of natives engaged in some form of activity, say religious, to which he has not the cultural key. If he is a skillful writer, he may succeed in giving a picturesque account of what he sees and hears, or thinks he sees and hears, but the chances of his being able to give a relation of what happens in terms that would be intelligible and acceptable to the natives themselves are practically nil. He will be guilty of all manner of distortion. His emphasis will be constantly askew. He will find interesting what the natives take for granted as a casual kind of behavior worthy of no particular comment, and he will utterly fail to observe the crucial turning points in the course of action that give formal significance to the whole in the minds of those who do possess the key to its understanding. . . . Forms and significances which seem obvious to an outsider will be denied outright by those who carry out the patterns; outlines and implications that are perfectly clear to these may be absent to the eye of the onlooker. It is the failure to understand the necessity of grasping the native patterning which is responsible for so much unimaginative and misconceiving description of procedures that we have not been brought up with. It becomes actually possible to interpret as base what is inspired by the noblest and even holiest of motives, and to see altruism or beauty where nothing of the kind is either felt or intended. (Sapir, in Mandlebaum, 1949, pp. 546–547)

The declared aim of ethnoscience has been to discover and employ the cognitive processes by which members of a society organize and understand their own knowledge of the world.

Critics of this approach make the point, as we have, that the anthropologist's overall theoretical framework controls much of his or her mode of observation. They also point out that although the native models of reality may often offer insight into their social life, this view cannot be relied upon to explain all its aspects. The native view often fails to illuminate important relationships and processes; at times native explanations even obscure or distort aspects of social *processes*.* Anthropologists frequently find, for example, that such explanations may serve to mask tension or conflict between individuals or groups. More frequently the anthropologist finds that the natives' purpose is *opposed* to that of the anthropologist, which is to make clear the patterning of relationships and the cultural processes involved. Nevertheless, because native explanations often point to the most significant aspects of a phenomenon, they do frequently offer valuable clues to the anthropologist. Among the Toba, for instance, it is widely believed that a man will lose his ability to hunt if a menstruating woman touches his bow or arrows. One adult male, in particular, insisted that he had lost his luck as a hunter because his wife had handled his weapons during her menstrual period. Further analysis of the culture demonstrated that hunting was one of several activities where male and female roles were clearly differentiated. Hunting was the domain of males, and women were expected to have no association with it. The Toba explanation served to perpetuate this separation of roles. Furthermore, it turned out that the male in question had never been a good hunter; his complaint was an excuse to cover his own ineptitude.

*Anthropologists use the term *process* to refer both to the internal mechanisms within a society that provide the impetus for its peculiar character (one society might stress competition while another might value cooperation), and to the conditions of culture contact that produce change.

Inference

Generalizing from Observations

In any ethnographic study, generalizations are based on hundreds or, more often, thousands of observations of the practices of a single social group. As the anthropologist begins to identify behaviors and attitudes that seem to form a pattern, he or she begins to make tentative inferences about possible relationships. The anthropologist quickly tests these hunches against further observations in order to confirm the tentative conclusions. In this manner he or she begins to make generalizations and to discover patterns.

We should note, however, that the anthropologist usually arrives in the field with a specific problem in mind and maybe even a proposed solution as well. In order to meet the requirements of a degree and to acquire funds to do fieldwork, the anthropologist has already defined a problem and considered its theoretical and methodological implications. It would be misleading, therefore, to imply that the problem under study is derived strictly from observations in the field.

Finding Patterns. The simplest level of generalization involves the description of a single pattern or regularity found to exist in the social life of people under study. Sometimes ethnographers document these patterns with supporting field data. More commonly, they simply state the patterns as fact, with little or no documentation. The next task is to link a pattern with others in order to show how they are interrelated.

Thus, when anthropologists are able to make firm generalizations about one or more aspects of the social life of a group, they are tempted to create a pattern of generalizations based on those key points, and then to make other related generalizations from them. This method is logical, but it can lead to problems. For example, the anthropologist may have dependable data from a single culture about the patterning of relations among kinspeople but less information about the patterning of relations within voluntary associations (groups of people not related by kinship but united by common interest). The anthropologist may wish to offer a generalization that will link the patterning of relations in these two groups. But he or she may not be able to decide whether to regard voluntary associations as a pattern similar to, and perhaps derived from, the kin groups in the society, or as a reaction against such groups. If the anthropologist stresses similarities, he or she might suggest that voluntary associations derive from or attempt to simulate kin groups. If he or she stresses differences, the logical inference might be that voluntary associations arose in reaction to the demands of kinship (Cohen, 1970).

The manner in which anthropologists go about generalizing from field data continues to be an important matter for debate in the discipline. The problem can best be illustrated by a specific example.

Marriage in the Middle East. The example concerns marriage relations in Middle Eastern societies. In many of these societies, marriages between the children of brothers (or those classified by the society as the children of brothers) is widespread. Anthropologists call these unions *patrilateral parallel-cousin marriages,* and considerable attention has been paid to them in the literature. Many anthropologists conducting research in these societies act as if there were no other forms of marriage practiced. By ignoring all other forms of marriage, they imply that everything one needs to know about marriage is exemplified by patrilateral parallel-cousin marriages.

Hilma Granqvist (1931), a Danish anthropologist, was one of the first to study marriage relations in the Middle East. In her analysis of the social life of a Palestinian village, she does mention that several forms of marriage are practiced, but she considers in her study only those marriages between persons classified as patrilateral parallel-cousins. Accounting for 47 percent of the marriages in the village, this is the most prevalent form, although of course more than half the marriages are not between such cousins. According to Granqvist, the popularity of patrilateral parallel-cousin marriages is rooted in the desire to keep the ownership of land and other property within the family. Since, in these societies, property is inherited through one's father, if a man's daughters marry his brothers' sons, then their inherited property remains within the kin group. This one factor—the desire to keep property, particularly land, within the family—is, to Granqvist, solely responsible for determining the preference for marriage forms in the village.

This is a questionable explanation at best. Critics point out that the loss of property through women who have married outside the kin group would, in many cases, be balanced in the long run by property gained through women from other groups who married into it. Regardless of such criticisms, what is important for our purposes is the methodology used by Granqvist to construct her patterns of generalization. First she listed all forms of marriage practiced in the village. She then isolated the one form—patrilateral parallel-cousin marriage—that was statistically most common. Finally she identified the single feature—namely, the retention of property by the kin group—shared by all cases of such marriages. In other words, Granqvist looked only for similarities among the group of marriages, not for point of contrast or differences.

A study of marriage relations among the Bedouin of Cyrenaica (Libya) by Emrys Peters (1963) reveals a different approach. The Bedouin economy has been primarily pastoral.

Thus, the rights to pasture lands and sources of water have been of great value to the Bedouin. Peters points out that one of the major social distinctions the Bedouin make is between *patrons* and *clients.* Patrons may claim the use of pasture and water as rights, whereas clients may not. Although both patrons and clients practice the same forms of marriage, the social implications of marriage between patrilateral parallel cousins are quite different for patrons than they are for clients. When a patron marries within his kin group, he increases his access to pasture and water by virtue of his wife's rights in the kin group. He therefore is able to increase the size of his animal holdings. Clients have no rights of access to pasture and water, and therefore they cannot increase the size of their herds and flocks by marrying within their kin group. On the basis of this one difference, Peters proceeds to construct a pattern of generalizations that has implications in many fields of activity, showing the differences in potential of kin-group marriages for patrons and for clients. In particular, Peters shows that patrons are able to exchange access to pasture and water for political loyalty. Clients cannot make transactions of this kind since they have no rights in the resources they use.

By examining differences as well as similarities, Peters has revealed a pattern through which he can make sense of patrilateral parallel-cousin marriage among both patrons and clients. He is able also to use the pattern to illuminate a number of other fields of activity and, in the process, show some of the implications of this marriage form throughout Bedouin social life. In contrast to Granqvist and most other anthropologists who have written on marriage in the Middle East, Peters does not dwell upon a single marriage form exclusively. Through his analysis, he sheds light on the total pattern of marriage among the Bedouin. Again, had Peters looked only at similarities, he would have ignored many important features of Bedouin social life.

In looking at patterns of social behavior, anthropologists consider the ways in which various activities interrelate. A yearly festival is the only occasion these Moroccan nomads have for a marriage ceremony. Their entire tribe meets once a year, at which time young people are married off, camels are traded, and divorces are available. (Stephanie Dinkins, Photo Researchers)

The Comparative Method

A major approach in anthropology has been *cross-cultural comparison,* or what has come to be termed the comparative method. There is, in fact, no single comparative method but a series of them. In the nineteenth century, anthropologists demonstrated the development of societies by comparing selected aspects of culture according to their relative degrees of sophistication. Thus, among means of transportation, for example, the horsecart might be judged more advanced than the sedan chair but less advanced than the stagecoach. The belief in ancestor spirits was considered more advanced than the belief that all natural phenomena are inhabited by spirits (animism) but less advanced than the belief in one supreme being (monotheism). Such comparisons of separate elements were measured along a scale from more simple to more advanced.

In the twentieth century, the comparative method came to mean comparing instances of culture change within a specified geographical area. In American anthropology, this involved studies of North American Indian communities; in British anthropology, the focus was mainly on African societies. In 1954, in an address to the Association of American Anthropologists, Fred Eggan proposed a method he called *controlled comparison*. To Eggan, this meant making comparisons between similar social groups or similar cultural types. He suggested, for example, first comparing the lineage structures of Australian aboriginal tribes and then comparing these findings with the results of a similar study of the Indians of Southern California, whose social structure resembles that of the Australian aborigines. Still further comparative studies could be made with other similarly organized groups. This method has not been widely used, but it demonstrates the range and variety of the comparative method.

A more ambitious version of the comparative method was introduced by George Peter Murdock, who in 1937 initiated the Cross-Cultural Survey, later converted into the Human Relations Area Files (HRAF). The purpose of HRAF is systematically to gather information on every known human society and to arrange the data in categories that permit anthropologists to take a single element of one culture and compare it with its counterparts throughout the world. For example, habits of dress, marriage customs, or table manners could be examined and compared for every society for which there is information. Already a *World Ethnographic Sample* has been compiled, based upon a representative sample of cultures and using the available data. This sample can provide information for cross-cultural study of any anthropological topic. It is to date the most ambitious attempt to organize ethnographic data on a global scale.

One achievement of the quantitative studies that have come out of uses of the *World Ethnographic Sample* has been to identify a group of elements that occur together in a number of cultures and to ascertain what principles link them. For example, Guy Swanson (1960) found that monotheistic beliefs tend to originate in societies with a hierarchy of three or more independent social groups. Witchcraft was found to be prevalent in societies in which sovereign social groups interact without legitimate mechanisms for social control. Such comparative studies have been criticized for trying to compare incompatible data, but their findings often are provocative.

Structural Models

In their continuing attempts to compare social phenomena, anthropologists have shifted their attention increasingly from the level of observable social behaviors to the level of models. A *model* is a system of relations that is thought to be parallel to, or a simulation of, a set of relations under study. It can be thought of as a kind of analogy. There are many types and varieties of models used in anthropology. The most characteristic feature of a model is its reduction of a state of affairs to the most simple and logically determined level. This simple and logical state can then be reapplied to more complex and elusive aspects of social life in order to generalize on their nature. A model must satisfy certain requirements. First, it must be a system composed of interdependent parts, so that a change in one element will cause changes in the other elements. Second, it should enable one to predict what will happen if one or more elements of the model are modified. Third, the model as constructed should explain all the observed social phenomena (Lévi-Strauss, 1953). Once an anthropologist has constructed a model, he or she will usually compare it to other similar models, letting the relationships of one social structure shed light upon another. It is the structural similarity that is sought, rather than a similarity of content in terms of data. Those who construct structural models for the comparative analysis of social phenomena are called *structuralists*.

Two major types of structuralists are found in anthropology. The first type, represented by the works of Radcliffe-Brown and his students, finds structure at the same level as observable social interaction. These structuralists look at social interaction and infer from it a model that may account for the activities concerned. A different type of structuralist approach is found in the writings of Claude Lévi-Strauss, who derives his models not from conscious social activities but from logical properties associated with the human mind. The kind of structure sought by Lévi-Strauss is found in unconscious reality, which cannot be discovered by observation but can be demonstrated by models that are used to uncover structure. The underlying structure can be called upon to interpret social relations as they appear at the level of observation. Thus, Lévi-Strauss took attention away from the *content* of social relations to focus on their underlying structure.

Microcosmic Models and the Bigger Picture

Anthropologists have been largely content in the past to confine their observations and inferences to the local community. In other words, they have taken a microcosmic approach to their fieldwork. In the microcosmic approach, the local community, be it a camp or village, is considered to be the entire society in miniature or, conversely, the society is thought to be no more than the local community much expanded. Not only is the local community treated as "typical" of other communities in the society, but it is also believed somehow to "typify" the society itself. The problem with this approach is that it is extremely unlikely that the local community is representative of anything except itself.

Thus, generalizations about the larger unit tend to be meaningless. It is therefore extremely difficult to imagine a case in which the microcosmic approach would be sufficient to explain the variation within a single society.

The chief shortcoming of the microcosmic approach is that it has led some anthropologists to believe that the focus of their study is more or less isolated, capable of being studied in and of itself as a complete system. They assume that every important influence on the beliefs and practices of the community under study is to be found within the physical limits of the community. Any outside influences that clamor for description are given "secondary" status or, in some cases, no status at all. But no social unit, no matter how small, simple, or seemingly isolated, is bounded in such a clear and absolute fashion. The boundaries of any community are ill defined and constitute merely thresholds of intensity in kinds of interaction. For example, when the Argentine government required military training of all aboriginal populations, it opened up contact

Few cultures today remain untouched by either urban society or tourists. Here, Western tourists watch a New Guinea ceremonial dance. (Philip Jones Griffiths, Magnum Photos)

with the broader society that had far-reaching implications. Young men who had stayed close to their native communities now had the opportunity to go to new places and have new experiences. Were one to study the Toba without taking into consideration government policies toward Indians, the resulting enthnography would be limited in scope and devoid of valuable information necessary to understand life among the Toba.

Cultural anthropologists now recognize that events and activities outside the boundaries of the local community influence what happens, or what people think and do within it. What at first glance appear purely local activities and ideas cannot be fully interpreted without reference to regional, national, and even global frameworks. When anthropologists insist upon too narrow a focus, they necessarily limit the validity of their findings. Growing acceptance of this viewpoint makes current anthropology more realistic and illuminating and facilitates its relevance to pressing problems and issues of the day.

"Truth" in Anthropology

We have discussed the methods of cultural anthropology—fieldwork involving participant observation, the use of informants, compilation of field data and their comparative analysis—and have noted the problems of some aspects of anthropological method. But we have still not answered the question of what constitutes "truth" in anthropology. Lévi-Strauss (1968) has suggested that anthropological truth may not be "factual evidence" of the sort to be found in the natural sciences but may "consist in a special kind of relationship between the observer and the observed" (p. 351). One resemblance between modern anthropology and the natural sciences, however, may explain why data collected as recently as the early twentieth century often no longer seems adequate or valid. Just as advances in the natural sciences have rendered invalid a great quantity of early theory and experimental data, so have advances in anthropology robbed many earlier observations of their "truth." In some cases, the questions themselves are no longer relevant. Nevertheless, much of what early anthropologists accomplished continues to serve as the basis for new developments in the field. As Lévi-Strauss has written, "in anthropology, as elsewhere, progress will never result from destroying what has been previously achieved but rather from incorporating the past of our science into its present and future, enriching the one with the other and turning the whole process into a lasting reality" (p. 352). Every piece of work in anthropology is limited—by the constraints of the situation, the shortsightedness of the observer, lapses in the field, and the limits of the age. Multiple observers, working together or at different times, can improve the quality of our knowledge and understanding, but they can never tell us all there is to know. In other words, because issues and interests change from period to period, we may approach but never arrive at the "truth." Every student of anthropology realizes that his or her work offers only partial and fleeting insights into the nature of cultural phenomena. There will always be new ideas to consider, as well as new ways of looking at what we think we already know.

Summary

1. *Ethnographers* observe in detail the social and cultural life of a people. To accumu-

late material for their ethnographies, they usually live with their subjects of study for a time. During this period they observe, question, and even adopt the customs of the people. *Ethnologists* analyze the information gathered, looking for patterns, processes, and signs of change. These findings are subsequently compared with other ethnographies in an attempt to contribute to a larger understanding of humankind. The dilemma faced by anthropologists is that they seek to comprehend an alien social and cultural system, but their own categories of understanding influence the degree of comprehension possible. No matter how effective their adaptation, they always remain "marginal natives."

2. Modern ethnography begins with the work of Malinowski. Earlier fieldwork was often fragmentary, misleading, and based upon unreliable reports. Malinowski insisted that fieldworkers make long, patient, and thorough studies, taking notice of the smallest aspects of social life. Modern ethnographers are *participant observers,* living among their subjects, speaking their language, and gathering facts in order to discover the underlying patterns of their society and culture.

3. The ethnographer aspires to make descriptions that are not only detailed but *valid* and *reliable* as well. A valid scientific observation is one that records the facts it claims to record. A reliable observation is one that can be repeated by other experimenters or observers. The most useful observations possess high degrees of both validity and reliability. While informants are a major source of data for the anthropologist, they sometimes can be unreliable.

4. Mapping is useful for recording the physical landscape and residence patterns. Genealogical data and a census of individual households help the anthropologist learn about social status, size of population, occupations, and ownership of land and other property, among other things. Some anthropolo-gists fail to collect quantitative data, but such data have proven valuable to most researchers.

5. *Ethnoscience,* or cognitive anthropology, claims that observers should adopt the natives'—or insiders'—perspective. Categories, ideas, and judgments should emerge from the phenomena observed and not be imposed on them. Critics of ethnoscience argue that this is an impossible aim.

6. Every ethnography makes many generalizations based on thousands of observed acts. A single generalization signifies very little, so anthropologists often relate one generalization to another. A *pattern method* of generalization permits the anthropologist to show the relationship of a number of social and/or cultural phenomena. Any pattern should consider differences as well as similarities between the elements of comparison. To ignore differences may lead to distorted or misleading conclusions.

7. There are many applications of the comparative method. One early use involved studying cultural change in a single geographic area. Through *controlled comparison,* anthropologists study only groups or elements that show strong social or cultural similarities. The Human Relations Area Files (HRAF) were developed so that anthropologists could compare cultural phenomena around the world. Structuralist anthropologists make their comparisons based on models of social structures derived from what they have observed in the field. Some models are at the level of observable social phenomena; others at the level of the unconscious workings of the human mind.

8. A regional perspective is gradually replacing the microcosmic approach to field work. According to the microcosmic approach, a single community can be considered a miniature version of an entire society. The observer may thus confuse the focus of study, the local community, with the true point of study—the patterns of interaction in the community. Anthropologists are coming to agree

that no single place should be studied in isolation.

9. Anthropological truth is hard to define, because the "truth" of anthropology may "consist in a special relation between the observer and the observed." That is, it may be more experiential than factual in nature. The truth itself is so complex that there can be no final, definitive statement about cultural phenomena.

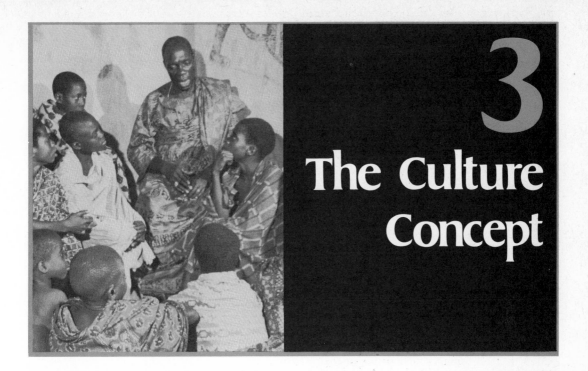

3

The Culture Concept

WHAT does the word *culture* suggest to you? Is it a special quality you can somehow develop by visiting book-lined studies, opera halls, and museums? Can you "catch" culture by listening to Mozart, studying poems, or appreciating paintings? According to anthropological definitions of culture, none of these activities is necessary—we all have culture already by virtue of having been raised in a society. We express culture in such everyday activities as eating, shopping, and going to school. For *culture,* to an anthropologist, is something shared to a large extent by everyone in a particular society, something we learn from each other and from past generations, something that influences how we think and act. It refers to that which is learned and shared, in contrast to what is genetically transmitted among humans. When it comes to applying the concept of culture to actual situations, however, anthropologists find themselves in fundamental disagreements.

The history of cultural anthropology can be seen as a series of attempts to define and use the concept of culture. On each definition, different anthropologists have built very different ways of examining the human condition. In this chapter, we describe eight major theoretical approaches in anthropology by looking at how the concept of culture is defined in each of them.

From Speculation to Science

Attempts to understand and explain the nature of human existence and behavior are probably as old as humankind itself. For as long as written records have been kept, people have speculated about the origins of their institutions and their relationship with the outside world, each other, and supernatural beings. In the classical civilizations, they often credited supernatural beings with creating social institutions and beliefs. The ancient Egyptians, for instance, created elaborate myths to explain the facts of the human condition in terms of intervention by the gods. It was Osiris, for example, who taught people how to grow crops and trees and who gave them the gifts of wisdom and appreciation for the arts. He made laws that enabled humans to live together harmoniously, explained the origin of the earth and humanity, and taught people about the gods and how they were to be honored (Colum, 1930). The Mesopotamians, on the other hand, thought the gods had created humans to do their earthly chores. A cosmic council was said to have chosen a human king and charged him with establishing social order on earth. Social phenomena—such as laws, kinship patterns, or food getting—were thus considered human-made features of life and not the work of gods (Wright, 1960).

Such explanations increased over the years. It was not until the late nineteenth century that the study of humanity was clearly defined as a science, a methodical attempt to explain the human condition through the use of theories (White, 1949). A theory, according to Freeman (1968), is simply "the expression of a series of hunches about which things go together in the world of our experience" (p. 193). An anthropologist might, for instance, suspect and demonstrate a relationship between a group's treatment of certain animals and the group's religious beliefs. The treatment of cattle in India and the position of cattle in Hinduism is a case in point.

A basic problem in formulating theories is knowing where to look to find the things that fit together. There are so many things we might observe about people—a person's hairdo, one's depression over turning 40, the choice of clothing, the arrangement and presentation of food, a country's treaty-making practices—that to generate theories we have to focus on only those phenomena that will tell us most about human behavior in society. This was difficult until someone suggested how to limit the field of inquiry.

Edward B. Tylor first did so in 1871, by defining the subject matter for a new science of humankind. He called it "culture." The science he fathered became known as anthropology. Ever since then, anyone who has proposed a different way of looking at human behavior has begun by redefining this subject matter. This is why we have so many definitions of culture today: different theorists have chosen to focus on different aspects of the human condition. Although the variety of approaches is confusing, each has contributed to our total understanding of humanity.

Culture as Evolutionary Progress

Tylor set forth his classic definition of culture in the first sentence of his 1871 book, *Primitive Culture:*

Culture, or civilization . . . is that complex whole which includes knowledge, belief, art, morals, law, custom, and any other capabilities and habits acquired by man as a member of society. (1958, p. 1)

Learned Behaviors

One of the key words in Tylor's definition is "acquired." It focused attention on the aspects of human behavior which can be traced to social learning rather than to biological heredity or individual experience. According

Culture consists of socially learned understandings. Elements of culture include the stories and myths people learn and how they learn them; the clothes they wear; the kinds of art with which they are familiar; the social groups in which people participate; the buildings in which they live and work, and their furnishings. (Marc and Evelyne Bernheim, Woodfin Camp; Alan Harbutt, Magnum)

to Tylor, the biological facts of the human condition—such as cutting teeth and having the urge to eat—are not the sorts of things anthropologists should study. But *learned* ways of expressing these biological features—customs and beliefs surrounding the eruption of the first tooth, for instance, or the use of chopsticks or silverware or other eating utensils—are. Likewise, the characteristics that individuals develop from their own unique experiences—the fear of worms, for instance, or the ability to play the piano—are not cultural phenomena unless they can be shown to be socially transmitted to a large segment of the population.

Culture, then, for Tylor, consisted of such things as knowing how to make a dug-out canoe (knowledge); feeling that supernatural beings are aware of your every move (belief); painting designs on clay pots (art); thinking it acceptable to cheat in order to gain personal advantage (morals); forbidding a community to enter into economic transactions on Sunday (law); and sharing the first piece of wedding cake with your spouse when you marry (custom).

The Complex Whole

Another important part of Tylor's definition is the phrase "complex whole." It suggests that culture traits are not isolated, random characteristics, but instead that they bear some kind of relationship to each other. A group's size, for instance, might bear a complicated relationship to its ways of obtaining food, its kinship practices, and a number of other social arrangements as well. The idea that culture traits form a "complex whole" foreshadowed the later notion of culture as an integrated system of related elements.

The Notion of Progress

Tylor's emphasis on socially learned characteristics and his notion of culture as a complex

whole still provide the general framework for the science of anthropology today. But his tendency to equate the term *culture* with *civilization* and to view human history as progress is no longer accepted.

In Victorian England, Tylor was immersed in a society that saw progress everywhere—in advancing industrial technology, increasingly enlightened politics, an ever-expanding economy. Swept up by the general feeling that life was getting better and better, Tylor looked at what was known of the history of humankind and saw in it an evolutionary progression from primitive existence to the peak of civilization—his contemporary England. As he saw it, all human groups were moving in the direction of increasingly rational thought and practical behavior, though some had progressed farther than others.

This notion of evolutionary progress gave Tylor a way to organize his thoughts about culture. Another evolutionist writer, L. H. Morgan, had proposed that humankind was moving upward through three stages: savagery, barbarism, and civilization (1877). The traits in a "savage" society included small groups, simple tools made of wood, stones, or bones, and a hunting and gathering mode of subsistence. Progress into the "barbaric" stage was to have been heralded by the development of either agriculture or animal raising. People in this stage were thought to live in settled villages, to establish political institutions, and to begin to build things from metal. The onset of the "civilized" stage, Morgan proposed, was signaled by the use of writing. Along with the advent of writing, there developed trade with other societies, formal government and courts of law, specialization in occupations, and the growth of social classes (Freeman, 1968).

Leslie White: A Return to Evolutionism

Since Tylor, in particular, saw humankind as progressing toward a state of civilization, he thought of culture in the singular. To him, culture was something all humans shared, though some had more of it than others and were therefore more "cultured." Anthropologists gradually dropped this notion, preferring to study the differences among groups as just that: differences, not lags in development. But the notion of culture as evolutionary progress in humanity as a whole reappeared in the middle of the twentieth century, in the writings of Leslie White.

Symboling. To White, author of the influential book *The Science of Culture* (1949), culture is:

a distinct . . . class of phenomena, namely those things and events that are dependent upon the exercise of a mental ability, peculiar to the human species, that we have termed "symbolling." . . . Culture consists of material objects, . . . acts, beliefs, and attitudes. . . . It is an elaborate . . . organization of . . . ways and means employed by . . . man in the struggle for existence and survival. (1949, p. 363)

By "symbolling," White meant people's use of symbols, such as words, to represent the things in their experience. With symbols, people can pass on knowledge and beliefs without having to use the actual things they are talking about as demonstrations. A mother can, for instance, tell her daughter the "proper" way to act toward her husband-to-be without producing the fiancé and acting out mock domestic scenes.

Through the use of symbols, people also give meaning to their experiences. In some societies, for instance, a woman may see her fiancé as a symbol of love and companionship; in others, he may symbolize authority, protection, and material security. This possibility of differing interpretations of the facts of social existence allows considerable variations in world views.

Progress as Energy Harnessing. To explain the development of variations in the ways people in different societies live and think, White returned to Tylor's view of history as evolutionary progress. All people, he thought, are moving toward the same goal through adaptation; some have simply gone farther than others. Like Tylor, White therefore asserted that we can think of all cultures as composing a single unit—the culture of humankind—and trace its development from the past to the present.

When White did so, he found evidence that human progress depended not on such things as writing or legal codes but primarily on a technoeconomic factor—the harnessing of energy. Culture, to White, was a system for capturing energy to aid people in the "struggle for existence and survival." He stated that the increased harnessing of energy represents progress because it produces changes that enable people to adapt themselves more efficiently to their environment.

The earliest human groups, according to White's theory of the history of culture, depended on human energy alone. Averaging the contributions of children, men, and women, including the aged, this would probably amount to only about 1/20th of one horsepower per person. Fire might have been used for warming the body, cooking, and scaring away wild beasts, but it was rarely used as a substitute for muscle power.

Whereas the most primitive groups subsisted solely on wild plants and animals, the domestication of crops and herds gave people greater control over nature and released a considerable amount of human energy for what White called "culture building" (1949, p. 371). Within a few thousand years (a relatively short period compared to the hundreds of thousands of years of slow and limited development during the Stone Ages), cultures mushroomed into great civilizations. From China to Egypt to Mexico, cities and empires replaced small-scale, isolated social groupings. Progress in industry, art, and knowledge was rapid. There were huge engineering projects,

PYRAMIDES AEGYPTIACÆ

A. Die grösse Pyramide, woran 360000 Menschen 20 Jahr gearbeitet B. Die andere, welche etwas weniger im Umfange hat C. Die kleineste, in welche, wie in die andere gar kein Eingang ist D. Das überbliebene von dem Colossalischen Sphynx E. Deßen sonst vollkomne Gestalt. Ansan.

A La plus grande des Pyramides, qui a eté l'ouvrage de 360000 hommes pendant 20 Ans. B. La seconde, qui a un peu moins de circonference C. La plus petite, qui a nulle ouverture, comme la Seconde. D. Le reste du Sphynx Colossal. E. Le Sphynx dans sa forme entiere. Ansan.

Culture historians believe that domestication of plants and animals released human energy that led to the development of the great ancient civilizations of China, Mexico, and Egypt. (From the collection of Dr. N. T. Gidal, Monkmeyer)

great architectural efforts, and impressive accomplishments in the arts. Writing, mathematics, astronomy, and medical science appeared and developed.

But after this mushrooming of the great ancient civilizations on the basis of agriculture and animal husbandry, progress reached a peak and then leveled off or, in some areas, even declined until about 1800 A.D., when a new way to harness energy was found—the engine. With this advance, others quickly followed. Population increased; cities and political units expanded in size and scope; wealth accumulated; and the arts and sciences developed more rapidly than ever before.

Writing in 1949, White speculated that the new harnessing of atomic energy might start humanity on a fourth great spurt of culture building.

Today when it is apparent that the high control and utilization of energy can be counterproductive, in that it can destroy the very environment that provides humankind with its basic means of subsistence and survival, the notion of progress is considered much more problematic. The idea of culture as a single thread of development could not withstand intensive scrutiny, and it had to be replaced with a more flexible and relativistic approach.

Culture as Historical Processes

An argument against looking at culture in terms of progress appeared around the turn of the century in the works of Franz Boas; he has sometimes been labeled the father of American anthropology. He replaced the evolutionists' sweeping generalizations about the history of culture as a whole with ways of examining specific cultures which are still apparent in American anthropology (Stocking, 1974).

Boas felt that anthropologists did not yet have enough information to develop general theories about culture. He argued that the "laws" that govern cultural change can only be discovered by intensive investigations of the histories of specific cultures. In his words,

before we can build up the theory of the growth of all human culture, we must know the growth of cultures that we find here and there. . . . We must, so far as we can, reconstruct the actual history of mankind, before we can hope to discover the laws underlying that history. (1898, p. 4)

To put this plan into practice, Boas chose to search out detailed histories of human groups in a limited geographical region. He first studied the northern regions of Asia and North America which bordered the Pacific Ocean. His goal was to figure out whether people on either side of the Bering Strait had contacted and influenced each other and, if so, what kind of historical processes had been at work in shaping these cultures.

Diffusion and Integration of Traits

Boas's North Pacific expedition came up with these results: at some time in the past, there was probably considerable contact be-

tween the East Siberians and the Indians of British Columbia, because a number of the same complex myths were found on both sides of the ocean. These myths were *not* found in the Eskimo tribes which had later migrated into the area, forming a wedge between the other two groups (Lowie, 1937).

In painstaking plotting of the distribution and elaboration of the myths, Boas found evidence of two important historical processes: diffusion and integration. *Diffusion* is the spread of culture traits—such as the use of shredded bark in religious ceremonies or the presence of nature-spirits in myths—from one group to another by historical contacts. *Integration* is the modification of these borrowed elements to fit the local cultural, social, and environmental contexts.

Indians of the Great Lakes area, for instance, tell of a terrible flood that occurred long ago. According to one version of the myth, several animals escaped in a canoe and tried repeatedly to dive under the flood waters to bring up some mud. One of the animals, a muskrat, was at last successful in dredging up a bit of mud, and it expanded magically to form the earth. This tale has been found throughout a large area, including the Mackenzie River Basin in Canada, the Great Lakes watershed, the mid-Atlantic and southern parts of the United States, and several places on the Pacific Coast. But in each area, it is told somewhat differently. The Cherokee, for instance, say that in the beginning all the animals were in the air. Nothing existed below them but a great spread of water until a little water beetle and a water spider began to dive under the water to bring up some mud, thereby forming the earth. While the earth still was soft, a buzzard flapped its wings about the new land and created mountains.

According to Boas's analysis, this account of the creation of the earth was carried from one tribe to another by the process of diffusion. He argued that the spread of the myth by diffusion is more likely than its having developed independently in all these different societies. As it diffused throughout the various areas it was altered to fit each group's unique characteristics through the process of integration (Boas, 1940). We could probably account for the spread of the St. Nicholas legend from Russia (where he is a patron saint) to the United States (where he is a kindly symbol for merchants) by the same two processes in much the same way.

The Uniqueness of Culture

The process of integration, Boas felt, ties cultural traits into a coherent, though changing whole. This whole and the circumstances that have formed it may differ considerably from one group to the next. Each must therefore be studied in its own terms, rather than be compared with a single standard of comparison. For instance, Tylor looked at various societies to see how they measured against Victorian English standards. But his approach did not provide a way to understand a society that emphasized other standards. If a society considers capacities such as the power to heal the sick or to obtain the blessings of divine beings more important than the ability to grow more food than the people need, then traits in that society should be considered as choices based on spiritual beliefs rather than as failures to make technological progress.

Boas and his students thus came to view a given culture as the result of specific, often complex, historical processes. Instead of considering human culture as a whole, they focused on specific cultures in order to better understand how they had developed. Evolutionists had thought of culture as a series of stages (such as savagery-barbarism-civilization or humanpower-domesticated plant and animal power-fuel power-atomic power). Anthropologists who followed Boas saw culture as a number of historically molded units. They approached these cultural units as integrated

wholes that could be evaluated and understood in terms of their own internal principles.

Cultural Relativism

It was in this context that the twentieth-century American view of *cultural relativism* emerged and took shape. Cultural relativism is the principle that all cultural patterns are equally valid. It takes form in the attempt to understand other cultural systems in their own terms, not in terms of one's own cultural beliefs. Sometimes this is not easy because the practices one encounters (such as human sacrifice or infanticide) may seem so different from the fundamental ideas or practices of one's own culture. For example, when the author first traveled among the Toba of Argentina, he was shocked to discover that the food items that he had taken with him in the jeep were not considered his personal property. Upon arriving at a settlement, he was informed by the Toba host that times were hard and that there was no food on the premises. "That's no problem," announced a Toba companion who had requested a ride to the community, "we have bread and oranges in the jeep. Brother Elmer, how about getting them some." Not only had the author lost control over his emergency food supply, but he was being ordered about by someone who had begged a ride from him in the first place! Further experience in the community made it clear when it was acceptable to horde food and when one was obligated to share, as well as when it was advisable to follow or to contradict the advice of a colleague. By withholding judgment, the author was able to learn about an elaborate system of food sharing and about the expression of opinion, which provided an important background for interpreting Toba behavior.

Although the historical view of culture contributed some important insights into the nature of the human condition, it failed to provide a clear-cut rationale or a coherent theoretical approach that could guide the discipline through the twentieth century. Failing to find generalizing principles at the level of unique cultures, it turned increasingly to the individual and to psychological processes to account for cultural phenomena. This led to the development of the culture and personality approach that will be discussed subsequently. The concept of society was underdeveloped and largely ignored by the historical approach.

Culture as Functionally Related System

While reaction in America to a nineteenth-century evolutionary view of culture was changing into concern with the details of individual cultures, opposition to Tylor's approach was taking a different course in England. There, anthropologists stopped trying to re-create the history of humankind, either as a whole or in pieces. Instead, they thought they would learn more by looking at living societies and cultures, analyzing them as systems in which every relationship or institution has a function and is understood as a part of the larger whole that is society. Two principal proponents of this *functional* or *structural-functional* approach were Bronislaw Malinowski and A. R. Radcliffe-Brown.

Malinowski viewed culture as an instrument for fulfilling human psychological and biological needs, such as reproduction, nutrition, comfort, and safety. For him, certain cultural institutions—such as those involved in obtaining food—exist to satisfy these basic needs. Others, he argued, satisfy the secondary needs that arise from them. The primary need for bodily comfort, for instance, may be transformed by one culture into a need for the manufacturing of inner-spring mattresses and upholstered furniture.

While Malinowski looked at cultural phenomena as mechanisms that meet individual needs, Radcliffe-Brown focused on the needs of society. To him, the purpose of any social relationship was to ensure the integration and stability of the social structure that formed the basis of society. He equated a society or social system with the total ensemble of social relations, the social structure that he saw as observable in the everyday life of a people.

Structural Principles

Radcliffe-Brown's chief interest was in discovering certain fundamental principles that contribute to the coherence of society, such as the divisions of people on the basis of generation and sex, or the closeness of sibling groups. This kind of analysis has become quite sophisticated, with studies that try to uncover the mechanisms that allow societies to maintain their structure, even though maladaptive. Of the two, Radcliffe-Brown's influence has been more persistent and extensive.

S. F. Nadel (1960), for instance, has demonstrated that witchcraft in four African societies is a mechanism that allows tensions between people occupying certain social roles to continue, without disrupting the social structure. Among the Nupe people, for instance, witches are always women; their victims are invariably men. The sex antagonism this reveals—with evil intentions ascribed to females and kindly ones to males—can be explained as a result of tensions built into the relationship between Nupe husbands and wives. The women are usually better off financially than their husbands, which the men consider to be contrary to the traditional way of things. Among the Nupe, it is often the mother, rather than the father, who puts up the bride price that their son needs in order to marry. She also finances big feasts and pays for the children's education. Women often earn their income as itinerant traders. To do so, they may leave their children when they are 4 or 5 years old, refuse to have any more children, and accept the image of having loose morals which is associated with the trading profession in Nupe society. Men deeply resent these reversals of what they feel are the proper sex roles, but they are helpless to change them. Their hostility toward domineering and independent women, resentment of their own powerlessness, and wishes of having the upper hand, Nadel argues, are transformed into witchcraft beliefs in which men are both the victims of women's immorality but also the only ones who can develop the magical power to block their witchcraft.

In another group, the Mesakin, the tensions that cause witchcraft beliefs seem to revolve around older men's envy of younger men's virility and youth. The Mesakin divide male adolescence and adulthood into three highly formalized age classes. The first class includes all prepuberty boys. The second class consists of boys who have reached puberty and is characterized by the right to engage in certain sporting contests. The third class occurs around age 24; at that point a man is considered to be already old and is grouped with physically old men.

The first sporting contest, which is allowed when a boy reaches puberty, is an occasion of much celebration among the Mesakin. It is expected that the boy's uncle will honor the occasion with an important gift—an animal from his herd. According to the descent rules of the Mesakin, the boy will some day inherit this herd; thus, the animal given at puberty is a sort of anticipated inheritance. The demand of the inheritance while the older man is still very much alive aggravates the existing tension between the young boy and the uncle. Having a relative old enough to claim the inheritance is a pointed reminder of growing

old. The older man, therefore, refuses to give the inheritance, and the young man is expected to take it by force. Quarrels over the inheritance are common, and if any misfortune befalls the youth, the older man is suspected of having used witchcraft against him. Accusations of witchcraft are frequent, and it is always the older man who is accused. According to Nadel (1952), the witchcraft beliefs of the Mesakin are obviously related to the stress that Mesakin society puts upon men as they age and to the hostility of the older men toward the younger.

What purpose, then, do witchcraft beliefs serve in these situations? Some theorists might say that they channel social hostilities into outlets that are relatively harmless, thus enabling society to continue functioning in as much harmony as possible. But Nadel points out that witchcraft beliefs, instead, fan these hostilities, adding to the stresses in society by causing bloody acts of revenge. They deflect tension from the real cause of the problems—in Nupe, for instance, the marital and economic situation; in Mesakin, the failure to distinguish between social old age and physical old age. The function of witchcraft beliefs in these societies, then, is to control social conflict but not to resolve it, since the conflict is rooted in the very structure of society. According to Nadel, witchcraft beliefs

enable a society to go on functioning in a given manner, fraught with conflicts and contradictions which the society is helpless to resolve; the witchcraft beliefs thus absolve the society from a task apparently too difficult for it, namely some radical readjustment. (Nadel, 1960, pp. 418–419)

In functionalism, the focus of research shifted from the concept of culture to that of society. It also shifted from that of history and change to that of static equilibrium. Not only did functionalism fail to account for change, it also failed to explain how any supposed system came to be what it was claimed to be. Since any social phenomenon was explained in terms of its relationship to another one, there was no logical place to begin and end the systemic analysis. Its reasoning appeared to be circular. Society and culture were treated as mirror images of each other, and no dynamic interaction between the two concepts was proposed.

Culture as Personality Configuration

At the same time that the structural-functional approach was taking form in England, the students of Boas in the United States were coming around to a similar view of culture as an integrated system. Compared to the British, though, they gave more attention to the limitless possibilities for cultural variations and put more stress on the psychological reasons for differences between cultures.

Cultural Diversity

The classic example of this approach is to be found in *Patterns of Culture* (1934) by Ruth Benedict, a student of Boas. She pointed out that the various aspects of social life—concepts of ownership, relations of production, trade, sexual activities, religious beliefs and rituals—may be endlessly varied and combined into different patterns. Each culture selects only certain elements for its pattern and emphasizes some more than others. As Benedict wrote, "one culture hardly recognizes monetary values; another has made them fundamental in every field of behavior . . . . One builds an enormous culture superstructure upon adolescence, one upon death, one upon after-life" (Benedict, 1934, p. 22).

Typical Personality Patterns 47

The basis for variations in cultural patterns, Benedict decided, lies not only in history or the functioning of social institutions but also in the temperament of a people. A whole society, she wrote, may develop a typical pattern of emotions and attitudes, or what she called a personality configuration. For instance, people in one culture might tend to be aggressive, passionate, and proud, whereas those in another might typically be easy-going, loving, and modest. Benedict held that such personality configurations determine which cultural elements will be selected, rejected, or modified to be integrated into the cultural pattern of a society. According to Benedict, you cannot really understand a culture unless you are aware of the underlying pattern that holds everything together. To illustrate this point, she explained the contrasts between two American Indian groups on the basis of their personality differences.

The Pueblo and Plains Patterns. Benedict used two personality configurations borrowed from the Greek tragedies to describe the two groups of Indians. She characterized one group, the Pueblo Indians, as "Apollonian," and the other group, the Plains Indians, as "Dionysian." The "Dionysian" character of the Plains Indians was expressed in excess, frenzy, and heightened individual experience. To achieve supernatural power, for instance, men of the Plains tribes subjected themselves to terrible tortures—slicing skin off their arms, cutting off fingers, swinging from poles by straps run under their shoulder muscles, denying themselves food and water, among others. They sought religious ecstasy in trances induced by fasting, cactus beer, peyote, or marathon dancing, sometimes with snakes. This tendency to value excesses was expressed in other customs as well, from abandoned mourning behaviors to violent reactions to adultery.

The "Apollonian" character of the Pueblos stressed moderation and cooperation in all things, according to Benedict (who has been accused of ignoring evidence to the contrary to make her point). For instance, their funeral rites were simple and undramatic; disagreements were handled without violence; and initiation of boys into manhood was supportive rather than humiliating. Whereas a Plains Indian husband would react violently to his wife's adultery and cut off part of her nose, a Pueblo husband would respond mildly to such a discovery. Pueblo institutions allowed easy divorce, and adultery might simply be seen as the first step in this direction.

Although some of the same cultural elements can be found in both Pueblo and Plains tribes, Benedict argued that these elements were used differently according to the temperamental type around which each culture was integrated. Fasting, for instance, supposedly was used by the Plains Indians to produce visions. The Pueblo peoples fasted, too, but primarily to purify themselves for religious ceremonies (Benedict, 1934). However, subsequent investigation has shown this observation to be oversimplified and superficial.

The French "National Spirit." This search for an integrating principle or personality type below the level of cultural expression has been used to understand technologically developed, diversified cultures as well as simpler ones. Edward Sapir, for instance, analyzed French cultural institutions as embodiments of what he called the French "national genius": "clarity, lucid systematization, balance, care in choice of means, and good taste. . . [but also] overmechanization, . . . emotional timidity or shallowness, . . . exaggeration of manner at the expense of content" (Sapir, 1949, p. 312). Among the cultural traits Sapir

traced to this French national spirit are the formal nature of classical French drama and the tendency to intellectualism in French art, philosophy, and literature. Other attempts to capture national character have been equally vague and impressionistic. For this reason, national character studies have come to be abandoned completely.

Psychoanalysis of Cultures

Scholars associated with this approach to culture, known in anthropology as the "culture and personality school," turned increasingly to psychology and psychiatry for descriptions and explanations of how various configurations developed. Often, explanations were sought in early childhood experiences that were thought to be typical. Tight swaddling of Russian infants, for instance, was said to produce manic-depression in Russian adults (Gorer & Rickman, 1950). Strict toilet-training of Japanese babies was pinpointed as the cause of compulsiveness in the Japanese national character (LaBarre, 1945). Anthropologists who took this approach began to see whole cultures as sick personalities. The Kwakiutl of British Columbia, for instance, with their obsessive potlatches (ceremonies in which large quantities of various possessions are given away or destroyed to enhance status) were considered to be "megalomaniac"; the magic-stressing Dobus of New Guinea were thought to be "paranoid" (Benedict, 1934). Such characterizations have not proved to be particularly useful; consequently, they have been largely abandoned in the discipline.

Much as the functionalist approach to society made culture a mere reflection, so the configurationist approach to culture viewed society as generated by culture patterns. Instead of deriving culture from social interaction, the nature of society was derived from cultural configuration. In either case, no means was provided for considering the manner in which the variables in society and culture might operate independently of each other.

The personality configuration approach to an understanding of culture focused on the *emotions* that were thought to be characteristic of a people. We will now turn to three twentieth-century approaches that are based, instead, on the *ideas* that characterize a culture. The first of these views culture as a cognitive system.

Culture as Cognitive Systems

In the "cognitive" approach, cultures are defined as systems of knowledge—the things that people have to know or believe in order to behave in ways that are acceptable to their group. Nowhere, except perhaps in asylums, do people perceive their world as completely disorderly and meaningless. The reason is that in all societies, children are taught how to view their experiences and how, on the basis of these views, to interact with one another. In our society, for instance, a child learns that certain pieces of green paper are valuable and can be used in exchange for material goods and that a funeral is an occasion calling for dark clothes, sober looks, and soft speech. Although people within our culture may not agree precisely on these matters, they agree with each other more than they agree with people from another culture who may, for instance, find in death an occasion for shouting and dancing.

For cognitive anthropologists, these ready-made models of reality are what constitute the local culture. They feel that if one can discover the models that a people use to interpret their experiences, one can begin to explain their various patterns of behavior (Scheffler, 1970). In this view, culture does

not consist of customs, habits, or any other forms of concrete behavior, but of the concepts that lie behind them. It is the cognitive models people use for "perceiving, believing, evaluating, communicating, and acting" that constitute culture (Goodenough, 1970, p. 99).

Native Categories

Anthropologists using the cognitive approach try to discover native ways of thinking as a means of understanding the various activities of a society. Rather than approach an alien culture with predetermined categories—such as upper, middle, and lower socioeconomic classes, a classification system based on our own money-oriented way of thinking—they try to discover the classification systems that natives themselves use to order their experience of the world. On the Pacific island of Tikopia, for instance, all spatial relationships are perceived in terms of the classification system "inland" and "seaward," since the island is so small that people can hear and often see the sea from any point on it (Firth, 1963). A Tikopian might say, "It's on the seaward table," rather than, as we might, "It's on the table to your right," or "It's on the table against the east wall." Notions of left and right, north, east, south, and west are part of our geography system, but not of theirs.

To discover the classification scheme of a culture, cognitive anthropologists often focus on its language. While they admit that analysis of language does not yield everything to be learned about native ways of thinking, they feel that as its main communication device, language, should reveal a culture's most important cognitive features (Frake, 1974). An important part of their fieldwork therefore consists of formal interviews that are designed to reveal the language categories and subcategories that people carry in their heads.

For instance, those of us who get our food from grocery stores and supermarkets might walk through the woods seeing only "trees" and "plants." But an ethnographer's observation and questioning of a tribe that subsists by hunting and gathering wild foods will reveal that these people perceive their natural environment in quite different terms. The Wanindiljangwa, who live on an island near Australia, can name and identify over 120 kinds of trees and plants that are either edible or otherwise useful. This is what they "see" when they walk through the woods. In addition to perceiving vegetation as useful or nonuseful, they also classify the useful things differently than our botanists do. To the Wanindiljangwa, living things are divided into four categories: things in the air (a group which includes not only birds but also insects, bats, and flying foxes), things in the sea, land animals, and trees and plants (Brain, 1976).

From Categories to Behaviors

Once anthropologists have painstakingly elicited the details of a native classification system, they still cannot predict what behaviors natives would think appropriate unless they know how these categories are combined and applied in different situations (Basso, 1973). For example, hunters and gatherers do not grab every useful plant they see. Whether they pick something probably depends not only on whether it is considered edible but also on other factors, such as whether it is considered ripe for harvesting, how much food they already have, whether the food is a choice item not often found, and whether it is for an ordinary meal or a ceremonial one.

The jump from drawing out native linguistic categories to understanding what ideas govern which behaviors is a big one (Keesing, 1974). So far, cognitive analysts have only been able to map the classification systems necessary to operate successfully in a few rather limited situations. Frake (1961), for instance, has carefully analyzed how the

Subanun (of the Philippines) categorize and diagnose human illnesses. Of the 186 named disease categories of the Subanun, Frake concentrated primarily on skin diseases. He argued that the disease categories were mutually exclusive, and despite occasional confusion in diagnosis, the Subanun considered the categories discrete. He subsequently extended his study to include ecology and settlement patterns (1962), social interaction (1964a), and religious behavior (1964b).

In another case, Basso (1973) has carefully analyzed the 13 labels the Slave Indians of northern Canada give to different kinds of ice. He has also identified the situational variables that determine whether the Indians would consider trying to travel across the ice. These variables include the mode of travel—walking in canvas shoes or snowshoes, traveling by dog sled—and the speed at which they need to travel.

After much questioning and the playing of a game by which the Slave fathers teach their sons what different kinds of ice "mean," Basso learned how to define types of ice as the natives do. "Tevu," or "hollow ice," for example, is ice that is more than 4 inches thick, is neither melting nor cracking, but has large air pockets under the surface. Considered strong enough to support a man on foot or snowshoes, it might not be safe for a dog sled and would be carefully checked if this were to be the mode of travel.

The cognitive models that have been constructed thus far are still too limited to provide any general understanding of why people in a specific culture behave as they do in even the most basic, everyday situations. Rather than pursue broader research, cognitivists are trying to determine how people in a particular culture separate what is relevant in their experiences from what is irrelevant; how they code information; how they anticipate events; and how they evaluate and choose among possible courses of action. In doing so, cognitive anthropologists are gathering data toward some long-range goals. They hope to contribute to anthropology an understanding of the relationships among language, cognition, and behavior; a way to make useful cross-cultural comparisons by discovering universal principles that classify the outside world; and descriptions of what a person must know in order to behave appropriately in any given culture (Frake, 1961).

Some anthropologists have pointed out that it is a big step to assume that the formal properties of a cultural code reveal the workings of the human mind. Burling (1964) has also argued that the total number of alternative analyses of any given cultural domain is so great that no single analysis can be considered definitive. In the cognitive approach, culture is again the dominant analytic concept, and it is assumed that social relations are generated by the cognitive system.

Culture as Structural System

While cognitivists analyze native cognitive processes to discover universal similarities in the ways people of various cultures construct categories of understanding, "structuralists" also look for universal principles of thought. Despite obvious differences in ways of life from one culture to the next, structuralists believe that the minds of people in widely different circumstances function according to the same basic structural principles. According to French anthropologist Claude Lévi-Strauss, the most prominent of the contemporary structuralists, the thought processes of people in simple societies are as complex as those of people in more "advanced" societies. For Lévi-Strauss and most structuralists, in addi-

tion to being constrained by the mind, social relations are also confined by the ecology in which a society is found. As such, they cannot be said to be either purely mental or purely material phenomena.

Lévi-Strauss's writing and his theories are not always easy to communicate to introductory students. But in general, he feels that cultural elaborations—kinship systems, myth, music, art, and so forth—are merely superficial elements that can be analyzed to find the underlying structural properties of the human minds that produce them.

Oppositions

One of the basic structural principles Lévi-Strauss identified is that of contrasts in a natural world that is often changing and random (Keesing, 1974). The difference between nature (which is random, changing, meaningless) and culture (which imposes order and meaning on experience) is itself one of the contrasts people in all societies have noticed and worked into their mythologies and ways of behaving. Other such universal contrasts, or oppositions, include life/death, male/female, animal/plant, individual/group, and friend/enemy.

These contrasts may not be perceived as clear black-and-white oppositions. For instance, we do not divide the people we know into only two groups—great friends and great enemies. But oppositions give us a scheme for sorting out and classifying our experiences (Lévi-Strauss, 1963). You may think of your acquaintances as falling along a continuum that runs from best friend to worst enemy. Most of them probably fall somewhere in between, but it is the friend/enemy contrast that gives you a way to organize your perceptions of them.

Edmund Leach (1970) used traffic signals to illustrate the structuralist notion that relations which exist in nature are repeated in the formation of cultural phenomena. He points out that the colors red and green are universally seen as opposites of a sort (except by those who are colorblind), because of the differences in their wavelengths and intensity. The human brain interprets these colors as oppositions, even though the color spectrum is a continuum rather than a series of distinctly different colors. Red and green are then transformed to another set of opposites: danger/safety. In our own culture, for instance, red is given the value of a danger sign: traffic lights, hot water taps, live electric wires, and debit entries in account books. A similar pattern appears in other cultures as well. Leach suggests that seeing the color red as a danger signal may have something to do with the association of red with blood. In any case, the use of green to mean "go" and red to mean "stop" in our traffic lights shows how relations which exist in nature are transformed into cultural phenomena patterned on those same relations.

Unconscious Logic

To a structuralist, then, the task of cultural analysis is to identify the structural principles that underlie the cultural elaborations of a people. Since people are largely unaware of these principles, which operate mostly on an unconscious level, asking them to describe their ways of perceiving and classifying things does not do much good. Lévi-Strauss recommends, instead, techniques such as analysis of myths or language to discover the hidden logic behind them. The object is to break down the particular social phenomena in order to reconstitute them in a way that shows the rules by which meaning is produced from raw perceptions of the natural world. Here linguistic models serve as a guide for analyzing the messages of myths.

The logic by which Lévi-Strauss moves from basic structural principles to various expressions of cultural behavior and vice versa has not been easy for anthropologists to duplicate. Perhaps his greatest contribution has been to open anthropology to a range of considerations that it might otherwise have ignored. Here, again, the distinction between society and culture is insignificant in terms of analysis.

Culture as Symbolic Systems

A third approach to culture as ideas has been proposed by a group of scholars who treat cultures as fundamental systems of shared symbols and meanings. This point of view is most clearly expressed in the works of American anthropologist Clifford Geertz.

According to Geertz, anthropologists can use observable public events as their subject matter. Whereas Lévi-Strauss looks at cultural phenomena as isolated puzzles to be deciphered by finding their underlying structure, Geertz holds that more meaning can be extracted from these phenomena if they are examined in the broader context of social life. He finds culture not in people's heads but in public scenes of social interaction. Geertz tries to figure out what is going on in such events as sheep raids, cockfights, mass festivals, and priest-consecrating ceremonies.

In such situations, Geertz holds, people both tell and learn something about themselves. They are expressing, through symbolic acts, various themes in their social life. At a Balinese religious festival, for instance, Geertz thinks the people are acting out a friendly feeling of spiritual unity despite their differences in earthly status and interests. This symbolic meaning is shared by the actors but may not be readily apparent to an outside observer. What a native observer might see as a mere contraction of the eyelid, for instance, might be a wink full of meaning for two mischievous conspirators (Geertz, 1973).

Interpretation and Explanation of Social "Texts"

How, then, can an anthropologist make any sense of the puzzling behaviors of people of another culture? According to Geertz, to get at the meaning behind socially established patterns, an anthropologist can interpret them as "texts" of a sort, models of and for reality and social interaction. Using social action rather than printed words, anthropologists try to read a "text" over the actors' shoulders to see how they interpret it. This involves *thick description*—understanding the meaning of social patterns to those who take part in them. The term *thick description* refers to the fact that a single activity may consist of various layers of meaning. Different messages may be conveyed at different layers. Thick description means calling things "conspiratorial winks," if that's what they mean to the actors, rather than "contractions of the eyelid." The second step is explanation—trying to see overall themes in thickly described events, what it is that they demonstrate about the culture and perhaps about social life in general.

The Balinese Cockfight. To illustrate how this works, Geertz (1973) presents a lengthy analysis of Balinese cockfights, important social events which the ruling Javanese have tried unsuccessfully to outlaw. Geertz sees the fights as complex embodiments of many themes in the Balinese view of life. For one thing, the roosters are obvious masculinity symbols; their male owners passionately identify with them. But in their mindless rage when fighting, the birds are also symbols of animality, the dark natural powers that so many Balinese customs are designed to thwart. Infants, for instance, are not allowed to crawl since this behavior is too animal-like; the chief puberty rite consists in filing the

child's teeth to keep them from looking like animal fangs; and emotions are kept under careful control. Identification with one's rooster thus has something of the fascination with the forbidden about it. After winning one of these bloody struggles, a victorious bird owner goes home not only with the loser's carcass but also with what Geertz calls "a mixture of social embarrassment, moral satisfaction, aesthetic disgust, and cannibal joy" (1973, p. 421).

Because of these ambivalent feelings, those watching a cockfight do so in utter silence, constrained by an elaborate system of rules handed down through the generations. There are no disputes. An extremely well-trusted, solid citizen acts as umpire. Under his direction, the violence of what the roosters are doing to each other takes place in a carefully ordered human setting.

There is a great deal of intricate betting. Large sums of money are wagered by the birds' owners and their supporters in even-money "center bets"; lesser sums are exchanged in unbalanced side bets. The fact that the center bets may involve up to about 200 times as much money as an average worker earns in a day makes the game highly risky but also deeply fascinating for the participants. Since they have bet well over their heads, the Balinese feel that more than money is symbolically at stake. What they really stand to gain or lose, temporarily, is their social status. Bets thus oppose people who are opposed in social life, either those of different descent groups within a village or even a whole village against another.

Despite the dramatic clashes taking place on all these levels at a cockfight, nothing really happens to anyone except the birds. People humiliate each other, but only symbolically. No person gets killed, or castrated, or turned into a beast, or raised or lowered in social status. No one even becomes dramatically richer or poorer, because cockfights take place every few days and the roosters are matched

Geertz saw cockfights as multilayered "texts" that revealed important patterns in Balinese social life. (Elizabeth Reeve, Magnum)

so evenly by convention that exchanges of money tend to even out over a period of time.

According to Geertz, the cockfight takes a number of themes in human life—masculinity, status, rivalry, pride, loss, chance—and focuses them in an ordered social structure. This structure neither heightens nor relieves the passions evoked by these themes. But it gives the participants a chance to see them for what they really are. Emphasis on prestige, for instance, is everywhere apparent in Balinese customs. But only in events like the cockfight, Geertz writes, are the emotions upon which the social hierarchy rests revealed in their true colors.

Enveloped elsewhere in a haze of etiquette, a thick cloud of euphemism and ceremony, . . . they are here expressed in only the thinnest disguise of an animal mask. . . .
Jealousy is as much a part of Bali as poise, envy as grace, brutality as charm; but without the cockfight the Balinese would have a much less certain understanding of them. (Geertz, 1973, p. 447)

Discontinuity

All cultures, Geertz feels, can thus be approached as collections of "texts" (like the cockfight) that demonstrate to people what their emotions look like when expressed collectively, though symbolically. Geertz holds that these texts do not always fit together neatly to form a coherent whole. Contrary to those who try to explain cultures as higly integrated sets of elements, Geertz sees cultures and cultural symbols as disconnected, and often contradictory (Keesing, 1974).

It was Geertz who called attention to the useful distinction between the social and cultural aspects of life, suggesting that they may be treated as "independently variable yet mutually interdependent factors" (1957, p. 33). In making this conceptual distinction, Geertz proposes that culture be viewed as "an ordered system of meaning and symbols, in terms of which social action takes place," and that society refer to "the pattern of social interaction itself" (1957, p. 33). It is this distinction between symbolic meanings (which allow humans to interpret their experience and guide their actions) and social structure (which analyzes the form social interaction takes) that makes symbolic anthropology an engaging enterprise.

Culture as Adaptive Systems

The last definition of culture circles back past all the other definitions based on ideas or emotions, all the way to Tylor and the biological notion of evolution. Anthropologists taking this approach look at cultures as expressions of people's adaptation to their environmental setting. Julian Steward, who is usually credited with developing this contemporary approach to cultural analysis, calls it *cultural ecology*. Since we will later devote a whole chapter to cultural ecology, we will merely outline its main ideas here.

When he studied the aboriginal cultures of the North American Great Basin Area (which includes present-day Nevada and parts of the surrounding states), Steward began to focus on what he called the *culture core*. This consisted primarily, in each society, of the economic and subsistence activities that seemed most directly involved with making it possible for the people to survive in their particular environment. The culture core in one group, for instance, might be its use of hunting and gathering to extract food from the environment, plus a number of other cultural elements—such as group size and political organization, or lack of it—that can be seen as functionally related to this adaptation. To understand the reasons for these core activities as well as the secondary elements that are related to them, Steward held that one has to understand in detail features of the environmental setting.

As Keesing (1974) has pointed out, there is a great range of opinion today among those who view cultures as adaptive systems. But they do hold in common at least four ideas about how cultures develop and why they change:

1. Cultures are systems for relating human groups to their environmental settings.
2. Culture change is largely a means of adaptation, a process by which individuals respond to changing conditions in order to function in a given environment.
3. Most central to cultural adaptation are technology, subsistence activities, and means of organizing the society for production.
4. The ideas that dictate cultural behavior —such as religious beliefs—may have adaptive purposes, too, such as controlling population growth or keeping people from overexploiting and thus destroying their environment.

The Cattle Complex

As an example of the kind of interpretation the cultural ecology approach can yield, con-

Cultural ecologists have explained the cattle complex of East Africa as an adaptation to the harsh environment of the area. (Yoram Lehmann, Peter Arnold Photo Archives)

sider the so-called "cattle complex" in Africa. There, it appears that a number of tribes lovingly raise cattle for seemingly nonutilitarian purposes. Cattle are normally neither eaten nor used to pull things. Though they supply milk and are occasionally killed for ceremonial feasts, they are more often considered a means of displaying status, validating weddings, making friendship contracts, and providing a legacy for one's sons.

In the past, these uses have been explained simply as an expression of a reverence for cattle. But a number of recent researchers have found that the value placed on cattle keeping can be explained as an adaptation to the East African environment.

For one thing, agriculture is impractical in the mountainous areas of irregular rainfall where people keep cattle instead of growing crops. Keeping animals that can be moved from one sparse grazing area to another gives people a way to utilize the available plant energy without being hampered by the possibility of localized water shortages and danger-ous insect infestations. The animals are thus able to follow the rainfall and may graze over an area as large as 500 square miles in the course of a couple of years (R. Dyson-Hudson & N. Dyson-Hudson, 1969).

Energy stored in the cattle is then used selectively for adaptive purposes, with each cattle owner offering his neighbors at least one meat feast a year. The immediate consumption of a whole steer prevents spoilage of fresh meat in the absence of refrigeration, sets up reciprocal obligations which will later help feed one's own family, and enhances community cooperation. One support of this explanation is found in the fact that meat feasts are likely to take place when other foods are in short supply. These adaptive functions may be hidden beneath a maze of cultural elaborations and may not even be suspected by the cattle keepers themselves. A Karimojong boy, for instance, "is given a specially named male calf to identify himself with, to care for and to decorate, to commemorate in song at dances and beer parties, and to incorporate into the style of his most formal name as an adult" (R. Dyson-Hudson & N. Dyson-Hudson, 1969). Cultural ecologists can demonstrate that such cultural elaborations have developed and persisted because of the value of cattle for the survival of the people (Netting, 1971).

The concerns of anthropologists who take an adaptational approach focus primarily upon the material nature of human existence. Thus, the approach provides an important balance to those that concentrate on ideas and mental activities. It also ties in with investigations of hominid evolution and ethological research which relates culture to biological processes. It integrates the subdisciplines of physical anthropology and archaeology with cultural anthropology better than do the idealist views of culture.

Designs for Living and Designs for Research

These eight approaches to the concept of culture by no means exhaust all the possibilities. In their book *Culture, a Critical Review of Concepts and Definitions* (1952), for instance, A. L. Kroeber and Clyde Kluckhohn discuss more than a *hundred* views of culture that have been advanced. Each one is significant because it has shaped (1) the questions posed in research, (2) the inferences the researcher makes about data collected, and (3) the results obtained. Many of the old definitions—such as those based on a view of culture traits as genetic variations—are no longer in use today. But those at which we have looked represent an overview of most of the ways of looking at culture that are found in contemporary anthropological studies.

It would be nice, for the sake of organizing the large body of cultural information, if we could somehow combine all the definitions of culture and say that all anthropologists are

dealing with essentially the same subject matter. But it is not possible to follow this strategy very far, since some definitions vary greatly in what aspects of human social activity they emphasize.

Some approaches are obviously more compatible than others. The adaptive and evolutionary views, for instance, fit together fairly well since both emphasize the material conditions of human existence. These two approaches are characteristic of the materialistic view of culture that we discussed earlier. The structural-functional and evolutionary approaches are also compatible, since both are concerned with systems of cultural characteristics—cultural elements that influence one another—and they both search for cause-and-effect relationships. Although structuralists stress stable patterns while evolutionists stress change, there is little basic conflict between the two approaches (Freeman, 1968). The cognitive, structural, and symbolic approaches are consistent with the idealist view of culture. They all stress the mental processes behind cultural forms.

Although some approaches are compatible, great differences remain. In writing textbooks, as in designing research, anthropologists must therefore choose from the available definitions instead of trying to synthesize them. In this book we treat culture as "designs for living,"* the conscious and unconscious understandings that natives use to interpret their experiences and to guide their actions.

Using the Native Model: Designs for Living

Of what value to us is the native's understanding of his or her experiences? As we pointed out earlier, the native's conscious models of reality tend to be poor ones for an anthropologist to rely on in *analyzing* society

---

*The expresssion "designs for living" was coined by Clyde Kluckhohn. See Kluckhohn & Kelly (1945).

and culture. They are intended, as Lévi-Strauss points out, neither to explain nor comprehend social phenomena but rather to "perpetuate" them. However, Lévi-Strauss also notes that native models may provide substantial "insights into the structure of the phenomena" (1963, p. 282). The idea that the anthropologist must begin with native concepts of things in order to arrive at an anthropological understanding of them is very old and well established in the discipline. Thus, native models provide some of the basic materials for any anthropological analysis; without them, no reconstruction of a cultural system would be possible.

Every functioning member of a society carries in his or her head a design for living which is similar to that of others in the society. These behavioral expectations do not need to be shared fully in order for a human society to operate efficiently. They must be shared sufficiently, however, so that people can understand and communicate with one another (Wallace, 1961). People in our society, for instance, share the assumption that property disagreements that cannot be resolved by discussion must be settled in courts of law. The opponents may differ in their interpretation of the law. But they can communicate with each other better than if one believed in settling property disputes by gunfight, or if one did not believe in property ownership at all. It is these areas of mutual understanding—such as belief in a judicial system and in private ownership of property—that the anthropologist seeks to discover in his or her fieldwork.

Choosing an Anthropological Model: Designs for Research

Every textbook has a bias that is reflected in the materials chosen for presentation and the manner in which they are discussed. Since the purpose of an introductory text is to offer an overview of the discipline, however, it is important that the student be introduced to a variety of conceptual approaches. The important thing is to make sure that the bias of the approach in question is clearly stated. Unfortunately, not all case studies in anthropology do this. While some anthropologists rely on native models for basic raw material, some fail to get beyond this raw material in their analysis. The preference in this text is to select studies in which anthropologists have removed certain elements from the native model and clearly regrouped them according to one or more of the analytic models described before, that is, models constructed by the anthropologists themselves. Among these, those works written from an idealist view of culture will be relied upon most heavily.

Separating cultural phenomena from the observable flow of social life frees us to see relationships between different kinds of activities (between food getting and religion, for instance) that are not apparent in the everyday life of a people. It allows us to move beyond the interpretations and justifications for their actions put forward by the natives themselves to find explanations that are not apparent to them. It is this reorganization and reinterpretation of raw data that we refer to here as "designs for research."

In some cases, one will find that the same social phenomena have been studied through more than one analytic model. The potlatch ceremony of the Kwakiutl Indians of the Pacific Northwest, for example, is on first sight a ceremony in which the chief wantonly destroys or gives away many of his possessions to an assortment of invited guests. This puzzling practice has been explained by Ruth Benedict according to her personality configuration approach as an expression of megalomania, a mental disorder characterized by delusions of grandeur, wealth, and power. She interpreted the destruction and giveaways as ostentatious attempts on the part of a chief to prove that he is wealthier and superior to his guests (Benedict, 1934).

Other anthropologists have come up with different explanations of the potlatch as they fit it into different analytical models. Some, for instance, have analyzed it in terms of environmental adaptation. They have suggested that the practice could be seen as an adaptation to changes in the food supply. Food shortages existed periodically in all parts of the region, but not necessarily at the same time. The real function of the potlatch, according to this model, was to redistribute food, to spread it out more equally within the tribe. Anthropologists who came up with this interpretation acknowledged that the Kwakiutl drive for prestige certainly had something to do with it. But for them, prestige was a secondary basis for the potlatch—one which had developed and lasted because it motivated people to keep having potlatches—rather than as the primary one (Suttles, 1960).

The choice among analytic models and the explanations they suggest is sometimes difficult. But anthropologists usually try to choose research designs that allow them to understand the most social phenomena. Can the adaptational approach to the cattle complex, for instance, account for the fact that herds are often so large that they overgraze their range, for the timing of meat feasts, for the characteristics of the pastoralist personality? Often a combination of perspectives provides the most insights and the most interesting studies. In Gregory Bateson's classic study *Naven* (1936), for example, we find the analysis of a New Guinea tribe from three points of view. Bateson analyzed the Iatmul ceremony in terms of (1) its social structure, as understood by structural-functionalists; (2) its cultural structure, much as cognitivists would see it today; and (3) its personality structure, as elaborated by Benedict and Mead.

Whichever approach anthropologists choose, the concept of culture is the key analytic tool that allows them to interpret and compare their data with that from other so-cieties. The very ambiguity of the term, which sometimes frustrates beginning students of anthropology, turns out to be a major strength for those who pursue the discipline. It permits them to systematize their understanding of the social patterns they are studying from several perspectives. And in seeking to understand others, they place themselves in a better position to understand themselves, to pose relevant questions about their own social life and their own view of the world.

Summary

1. The age-old attempt to explain the human condition became a science in 1871, when Tylor set forth a definition of culture as a complex whole that is learned and passed on to succeeding generations. Tylor tended to view culture as a universal effort toward a "civilized" condition. In the end, he identified culture with civilization.

2. The Victorian view of culture as evolutionary progress was echoed in the twentieth century by White. He saw in human history a pattern in which the increased harnessing of energy leads to advances in all other spheres of social life.

3. Boas rejected these sweeping generalizations about human history, preferring to concentrate instead on what could be learned about the histories of specific cultures. Each culture is uniquely shaped, Boas thought, by historical processes such as the *diffusion* and *integration* of traits and should not be judged by standards developed in another culture.

4. Malinowski and Radcliffe-Brown defined culture as *functionally integrated systems.* In such systems, each institution has a purpose and is related to other institutions. Malinow-

ski tended to see institutions as satisfying individual needs, whereas Radcliffe-Brown thought their function was to keep the social structure intact.

5. Benedict emphasized the seemingly unlimited diversity of cultural phenomena. She felt that each society had developed a typical *personality configuration* which could be seen as the integrating principle behind its elements.

6. The *cognitivists* define culture as a system of categories. They try to uncover native models for classifying the things they experience. They do so in order to see how people of the culture perceive life and how they make decisions about how they should act.

7. Lévi-Strauss seeks to reduce the apparent discontinuities of society and culture to underlying *structural* invariants. He looks for universal features in the way the human mind works. Among the unconscious mental structures he has found in all cultural systems is the fact that people think in terms of oppositions and contrasts.

8. Geertz and others have defined culture as *symbolic systems.* They feel that people in a society share an understanding of what their actions mean. These meaningful behaviors are most clearly expressed in public performances, where people are acting out social dramas that express the basic themes in their social lives.

9. An eighth definition of culture comes from *cultural ecologists,* like Steward, who see it as an *adaptive system.* They focus on a core of activities that are most closely linked to survival and on the cultural features that support the basic adaptation of people to their environment.

10. In this book, the term *culture* will be used in two ways. On the one hand it will refer to the models of and for experience shared by a particular social group. These can be thought of as *designs for living.* On the other hand, the term *culture* must also be recognized as an analytic tool used by anthropologists to understand social life on a comparative basis—their *designs for research.* The two ideas are intricately intertwined, of course, since native designs for living can only be grasped by non-natives through the designs for research constructed by social analysts.

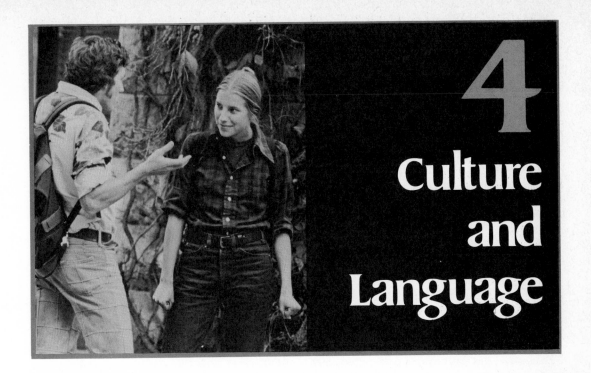

4
Culture and Language

LANGUAGE, more than any other attribute, distinguishes human beings from other animals. In many cultures, a child is considered fully human only when he or she has begun to speak. Then the child is given a name and initiated into truly social existence. All physically normal humans possess the innate capacities to learn to speak and to communicate through language. The structure of the vocal tract and the physics of sound wave activity are the same among all peoples and in all places. Differences between the sound systems of one language and another are the result of factors other than the speakers' ability to produce sounds. A classic joke among linguists concerns a British couple who adopted a French baby and then proceeded to study the French language so they would understand the child when she began to talk. In fact, any human being can learn to utter the sounds of any human language.

Language is the most characteristic pattern of behavior that distinguishes one social group from another and is often considered the primary mark of its identity or its connection to other similar groups. For example, we consider as "Latin America" all those countries south of the United States in which Romance languages are spoken, despite the cultural differences among them. People who speak the same language are thought to be able to communicate with one another. Although this is not always true, certainly little communication of any consequence is possible between two people who cannot understand each other's languages. Several languages, however, can coexist within a single group, even if its members do not all speak every language.

The purpose of this chapter is to show how an investigation into the nature of language contributes to our understanding of the nature of culture. Since language is the primary means by which humans communicate with each other, it becomes the primary target for understanding how designs for living are understood and shared among humans. In order to show this, we will first consider how anthropologists have viewed the relationships of language and culture. Next we will look at the structure of language and its unique representational quality. Finally, by placing language in a broader area of communication, which demonstrates that not all language is coded in linguistic form, we will discover the extent to which models for analysis of language also contribute to the analysis of culture.

The Relationship of Language to Culture

Linguists and anthropologists agree that human language and culture are closely related, although they disagree as to the nature and extent of these relationships. Both culture and language, after all, are the results of human activity and are expressions of the human mind. If they were not related at all, we would have to conclude, with Lévi-Strauss (1963), that there is no connection between what goes on in the mind from one level to another. If this were true, the consequences would be disastrous not only with regard to the connection between language and culture but also for the entire fabric of beliefs and activities that we think of as culture.

People in some societies talk a great deal, even making a cult of conversation or communication and recording much of what is said or written. Our own society is one such group. In contrast, other social groups speak very little and then only in specific contexts that require it. Spoken language in those societies may be for the purpose of instruction, indoctrination, or the performance of rituals.

Nevertheless, every society requires language for its existence. Other animals possess social organization—families and larger groups such as herds or colonies—but only human beings are able to formulate, prescribe, and compel obedience to rules governing incest, marriage, divorce, inheritance, and many other areas of social life by means of speech. Without language, human beings could not have developed political, economic, or religious traditions. They would be unable to transmit their beliefs and values, bodies of law, knowledge and literature, ceremonies and social customs. These require the use of symbols, the ability to employ abstractions for absent or nonmaterial things. For example, it is not unknown for other animals to make

Writing is a more mysterious communication system in some cultures than it is in ours. Here, a Moroccan letter writer records a message. Although the woman may not be able to read what is being written for her, her posture and attention convey the importance the communication has for her. (Joel Gordon)

what can be called spontaneous use of tools. Apes have been observed to grasp at a stick lying nearby in order to reach for a more distant object or to pick up a rock to break the hard shell of a piece of fruit. But only humans have shown the capacity for setting the stick aside in order to use it again in the future. To plan in this way requires the ability to abstract the general or symbolic utility of the stick from its immediate usefulness—in other words, to get the idea of the stick's potential value as a tool.

Language Independent of Culture

Language, then, makes the development of culture possible. But the question persists: Is language itself a part of culture or is it an external, independent phenomenon? Many linguists have preferred to analyze language with reference neither to its social nor to its cultural context. Leonard Bloomfield's example is sometimes quoted to illustrate how the linguist narrows the focus to exclude social context from what he or she studies: "If a beggar says 'I'm hungry' to obtain food and a child says 'I'm hungry' to avoid going to bed, then linguistics is concerned just with what is the same in the two acts" (in Hymes, 1974)—that is, with the statement "I'm hungry." According to this view, what is in the speaker's mind when speaking is largely irrelevant to the linguist.

When we reflect upon how we ourselves communicate—how a speaker gets meaning across to an audience, for instance—we realize that in order to express our private thoughts, feelings, and experiences we must often use terms that do not quite seem to fit. For example, when a speaker uses the word "house," he or she may be referring to a specific idea of house quite different from anything the listeners have ever thought of by the term. Nonetheless, in order to speak and be understood, the speaker will simplify his or her private sense of things, will

throw whole masses of experience together as similar enough to warrant their being looked upon—mistakenly, but conveniently—as identical. This house and that house and thousands of other phenomena of like character are thought of as having enough in common, in spite of great and obvious differences of detail, to be classed under the same heading. (Sapir, 1921)

Even the most personal utterance is conveyed through words that do not depend upon the speaker's thoughts for their meanings. Speakers express meaning in large measure only by making use of the concepts that are available in language.

Individual words or concepts alone, of course, do not constitute language. In order to make ourselves fully understood, we must string our words together in patterned units. Some linguists, notably Noam Chomsky, suggest that the pattern or structure of a given language results chiefly from "factors over which the individual has no conscious control and concerning which society may have little choice or freedom" (1965). Although individuals are free to say many things, they are not free to choose just any form in which to express a given utterance. For example, in English we can say, "John smoked a pipe," but not "A pipe smoked John." No individual speaker is free to choose his or her own patterns, except at the risk of being misunderstood or speaking nonsense.

Correspondence of Language and Culture

Most contemporary anthropologists no longer accept the view that culture and language are completely separate phenomena. They do not believe that either culture or language can be studied in isolation. Anthropological linguists have come to see that language tells us a great deal about culture itself. Malinowski (1935) asserted that the chief role of language was to take active part in human behavior and not to serve merely as a vehicle for the expression of thought. Most anthropologists have come to agree with this statement. They see that a speaker not only makes a statement about something, but performs an action—that is, does something—as well. To illustrate, we may return to Bloomfield's remark cited earlier. The little girl who says "I'm hungry" in order to put off going to bed may be appealing to her parents' good natures, challenging their authority, or struggling to cope with fear of the dark. The beggar's identical remark may be an attempt to protest his misery, or it may be a bid for a handout.

Language, then, is one of a number of codes that each culture uses in order to communicate. Its unique status as the means by which many—if not all—phenomena in a culture are expressed and understood does not place it outside the confines of the culture. Quite the contrary. The presence of language and its service in every area of culture from law making to love making point to the critical role of language in cultural life. The words we speak when we are introduced to someone for the first time express our culture as surely as do our customs of shaking hands upon meeting and parting, standing when we are introduced, and keeping a comfortable distance from people we are not intimate with.

Benjamin Lee Whorf, a student of Edward Sapir, made a number of bold, original speculations about the interrelations of culture and language. Whorf's work refined in many ways the work of Sapir and Boas. Boas, especially, asked how cultural behavior is a cognitive classification of experience. He left as an open question the extent to which these classifications are conscious or unconscious. Whorf proposed that in any language, speakers would be most aware of word categories and unaware of the way in which linguistic structure shaped their understanding of their experience. His theory, called the *Sapir-Whorf hypothesis,* was that the grammar of any language is not merely a way of speaking about the world but that it embodies a model of that

world as well. Whorf believed that language reflects the way in which speakers of the language perceive and think about the world. Whorf compared a number of the features of Western languages (which he referred to as Standard Average European) with those of the Hopi language. He discovered, for example, that the great stress on nouns as things in Standard Average European (SAE) encouraged a quantitative view of time. An SAE speaker says, "ten days"; a Hopi says, "until (or after) the tenth day." The Hopi view of time is of "becoming later and later," whereas the SAE view is of a series of units. An illustration of the SAE view is the film portrayal of the passage of time as a series of leaves torn from a calendar (Whorf, 1956). Whorf concluded that cultural and environmental influences in Hopi society interacted with Hopi linguistic patterns "to mold them, to be molded again by them, and so little by little to shape the Hopi world-outlook" (1956, pp. 157–158). The relationship between language and culture, as Whorf saw it, was bidirectional.

Current inquiry by anthropological linguists often involves the attempt to place language in the cluster of various elements that figure in communication and to clarify the functions of language within the cluster. Dell Hymes (1974) has shown that a study of a community and all its means of communication reveals the frames of reference of its speakers. For example, the !Kung Bushmen of the Kalahari Desert customarily belittle the size and worth of the game they kill, despite their dependence upon the game for subsistence. They explain their behavior as intended to discourage arrogance among those who supply meat to the community. An uninitiated outsider, however, would think their behavior very odd, indeed. It seems calculated to deny !Kung hunters the recognition and gratitude due them for their service to their fellows (Lee, 1969). No account of !Kung language habits that ignored their economy and their belief that the hunter must be kept humble could hope to make sense of their speech.

Most contemporary anthropologists see the relationship between language and culture as one of correspondence. But they stop short of suggesting that either one influences the other. Instead, they see the two as moving along parallel tracks. There is correspondence, not because there is any certain connection between the two, but because both language and culture are creations, largely unconscious, of the human mind.

Language Is Culture

A third view about the relationship of language to culture suggests that the two do more than parallel each other—that, basically, language *is* culture. People who hold this view focus their study on the functions of language.

One function of language is the referential, the act of describing or telling about something. But few statements are merely referential. Michael Silverstein (1977) has recently called attention to a second (and to him, more important) kind of meaning in language, its indexical function. Indexing reveals through speech the culturally understood contexts of speaking and its purposes: the roles and social positions of speakers and hearers, the setting and the occasion of a communication, the purpose of a statement, and so forth. The fact that the referential function is essential to a communication explains why so much attention has been given it in linguistic analysis. But context-defining functions are important as well.

Influenced by the work of Roger Brown (1957; 1970), many scholars point out that in order to understand any statement containing a personal pronoun, we must know something about the speaker, the audience, and the social situation. Silverstein (1977) illustrates this with the English sentence *You went away happy,* which might be spoken to one or more persons, to its equivalent in French. If the French speaker is addressing more than one person, he or she uses the plural pronoun *vous.* In speaking to only one person, there is a choice between *tu* and *vous,* depending upon the age, social status, and degree of intimacy between speaker and listener. Furthermore, the full meaning of the sentence would not be clear to anyone who did not also know all these things. This distinction is a feature of many languages, including German, Russian, and Spanish. English usage is simpler because the singular *thou* has disappeared, and the plural *you* now is used in all cases. Nevertheless, English is capable of indicating this sort of distinction, though perhaps in a less formal way: an English speaker decides whether to address someone by first name or title (for example, Mr., Ms.) on much the same grounds as the French speaker chooses *tu* or *vous.* Other languages are a great deal more complicated. Geertz (1960) shows the elaborate indexical system of the Javanese speaker who must control many levels of style including words, phrases, and grammatical patterns, to show deference to the listener and to the topic of discourse. The delicacy with which a speaker does this, on the other hand, shows his or her own social status.

Other indexing devices include accent and vocabulary. Whether a person intensifies or minimizes an accent that relates to a particular region or social class, for instance, depends on the status of the audience relative to the speaker. Secretaries sometimes take on an "upper-class" accent when doing business on the telephone, but abandon it when doing something less publicly self-conscious, such as ordering lunch. Or a famous ballplayer may emphasize his street dialect when giving a clinic in his old neighborhood, to make himself seem more like a "regular guy." Individuals also are likely to choose different words in communications with different people—your peers versus your grandmother, for example —even when the message to be communicated is the same. Thus, linguistic behavior is seen as an inseparable part of cultural behavior.

The Structure of Language

Language is the medium through which human thought is expressed. The medium of language, in turn, is sound; sound constitutes the basic element of speech. *Phonology,* the study of human speech sounds, is generally subdivided into two parts: *phonetics,* the study of speech sounds from a physiological point of view, and *phonemics,* the manner in which sounds are used to communicate meaningfully in a given language.

The Sound System

Phonemics deals with the sets of sounds employed by speakers of specific languages. It does so by identifying *phonemes*—distinctive but meaningless sounds heard by native speakers of a language. Each language has a limited number of phonemes, usually 30 to 50, and each phoneme represents a single sound in that language. Infants younger than 12 months of age seem to produce in their babbling the sounds heard in various human languages, including pronunciations from languages that English speakers find difficult. As babbling continues, children begin to reproduce the sounds of the language they hear around them. They eventually limit themselves to the sounds of their own languages and cease to produce "foreign" sounds.

The phonemes of various languages are so different that adult speakers who pronounce effortlessly every phoneme of their own language may have trouble pronouncing or even distinguishing phonemes lacking in their native tongue. For example, [th], as in *thin,* and [th], as in *then,* are recognized and pro-

nounced without difficulty by most speakers of English. Both these sounds, however, are missing from the phonemics of French. A speaker of French attempting to speak English will likely pronounce them as [s] (thin/*sin*), [z] (then/*zen*), or [d] (then/*den*). This appears less astonishing, perhaps, when we realize that there are dialects of American English with the same kind of phonemic system. A visitor to a working-class bar in an American city might hear one of the regulars tell the bartender to "trow da bum out" when a patron grows unruly.

Various sounds are produced by the different positioning of the lips, teeth, and tongue. Different kinds of articulation identify the way in which a sound is produced. They include stops, fricatives, resonants, and vowels. *Stops* are produced by momentarily blocking the flow of air, as in the sounds *p* or *b*. *Fricatives* require impeding the flow of air, but not completely shutting off its passage; the sounds *v* and *th* are examples of fricatives. *Resonants* require a partial obstruction of the air flow (as in *m* and *w*). *Vowels* are produced without obstructing the passage of air at all.

To determine all members of the phonemic inventory for a given language, the phonologist looks for *distinctive features*. These are the differences in sound that speakers recognize unconsciously in minimally different words, called *minimal pairs*. English *pat* and *bat* constitute such a minimal pair. Both [p] and [b] are stops, produced when the flow of air through the vocal tract is momentarily impeded by compressing the lips, but [p] is voiceless, whereas [b] is voiced. To produce a voiced sound, the vocal chords must vibrate as air passes through the throat. When the sound is voiceless, the vocal chords do not vibrate. By such analysis we discover that voicing is a distinctive feature in English.

In order to identify the truly distinctive features in a language, we must pay attention to *complementary distribution* of sound. Several sounds in a language may differ from one another, but speakers of the language may treat them as a single phoneme because they never contrast in the same sequence of sounds. For example, [p] in *pine, spine,* and *sip* is a single phoneme, although it is pronounced differently in each case—aspirated, unaspirated, and unreleased, respectively. But because each [p] sound occurs in a unique environment (aspirated when it falls initially; unaspirated after an *s;* and unreleased as the final sound), these phonetic differences are ignored by the normal speaker of English. We therefore speak of only a single /p/ phoneme.

Discussing the phonemes of a language and their rules for sequencing, we find that the sound system of any language is systematic and regular, and that languages conform to similar principles. In addition, linguists formulate rules to account for the way language is structured into larger units of meaning. These rules are known as the *grammar* of a language.

The Grammatical System

The study of grammar has traditionally been divided into two parts: morphology and syntax. *Morphology* analyzes the combination of *morphs*—the smallest units of meaning in a given language—into words. *Syntax* is concerned with the rules for combining words into larger units of meaning, such as phrases or sentences.

The more we study grammatical systems, the more we realize that the structure of language does not consist of letters, words, and sentences, since parts of words, or morphemes, are frequently directly meaningful parts of whole sentences. For example, the sentence "The girl loves baseball" may be altered to "The girl love*d* baseball." There is but one simple difference in sound between these two sentences, yet this difference changes the meaning of the entire sentence.

Morphology and syntax share several important linguistic processes: selection, arrangement, and modification. We select the words we use in a sentence from the appropriate word groups; we arrange them in a meaningful order; and we modify the forms or pronunciation as necessary to their surroundings. In a language such as English, in which the normal word order of the sentence is subject-verb-object, speakers select nouns or nounlike words for subject and object and arrange them before and after the verb. Speakers modify the form of a word as well as the pronunciation when the grammatical surroundings require it. In the sentence "We like him," for example, *him* is a modification of *he* and in that position is pronounced [im] rather than [him]. Examples of morphological selection include the adding of affixes (prefixes or suffixes), as in *pre*pay or pay*check*. Morphological arrangement often also involves affixes. We say *mouth*piece and piece*meal,* for example, and not piece*mouth* or *meal*piece.

Instead of attempting merely to define morphemes, we can now give an inventory of the possible types of morphemes:

1. A single sound, like the plural morpheme *-s* in *cat-s*
2. A single syllable, like *child, girl,* and *-ish,* in *childish* and *girlish*
3. Two or more syllables, as in *aardvark, crocodile,* or *salamander*
4. No sound (zero-form), as in the plural of *sheep* and the past tense of *hit*

Different morphemes may be represented by the same sound, as in the plural *boys* and the possessive *boy's.* The sounds that constitute a morpheme in one place may not do so in another. The unit *-er,* designating a doer, is a morpheme in *singer* and *fisher,* but not in *butcher.* In the word *nicer, -er* is not a morpheme at all. In other cases, the same morpheme may be presented by different sounds. *Sign* and *signature* are examples of this class of morphemes.

Transformational Grammar. These observations about grammar tell us a good deal about how the words and sentences we speak may be classified. They do not tell us how every normal speaker develops the ability to "create" such a wide variety of sentences. The theory that we learn to speak by imitating what we hear others say, although undoubtedly partly true, fails to account for a speaker's ability to utter a vast number of sentences that do not resemble anything he or she has previously heard. *Transformational grammar* attempts to account for the phenomenon of creative language use.

Transformational grammar was introduced by Noam Chomsky, whose own research in descriptive linguistics was unable to offer any clue as to how speakers learn to use language in a creative way. Of course, no speaker is totally conscious of the system of grammar he or she has mastered, and every speaker, in practice, makes frequent errors. Those errors, though, are much less frequent than is usually supposed (Labov, 1972). Further, they often support the notion of linguistic competence, as when a child gives the past tense of *buy* as *buyed* instead of *bought*.

The key elements in Chomsky's theory of language are found in his idea that every sentence consists of both a surface structure and a deep structure. The *surface structure* of a sentence corresponds to the sounds we hear. An example of surface structure may be shown by the sentence "A wise man is honest." (See Figure 1.) The *deep structure* represents the underlying meaning of the sentence, which is more abstract than the surface structure. (See Figure 2.)

Every English sentence or surface structure is generated according to the rules of a deep structure found in English grammar. The relationships between deep and surface structure—the ways in which one can be "translated" into the other—are explained by rules called *grammatical transformations*. A set of "rewrite rules" breaks the units of the deep

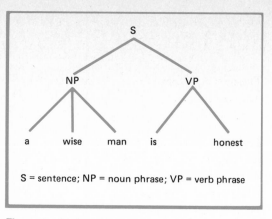

S = sentence; NP = noun phrase; VP = verb phrase

Figure 1 Surface structure

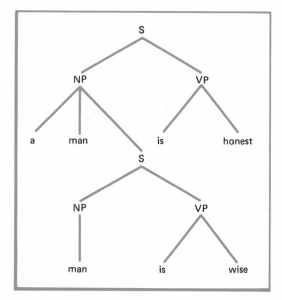

Figure 2 Deep structure

structure into noun phrases and verb phrases. Then appropriate operations, such as replacement, deletion, inversion, or negation, are performed to result in the surface structure. In Figure 2, for example, we saw the following noun and verb phrases:

$$\underbrace{a\ man}_{\text{NP}_1}\quad \underbrace{[man\ is\ wise]}_{\text{NP}_2 \qquad \text{VP}_2}\quad \underbrace{is\ honest}_{\text{VP}_1}$$

The first operation that occurs is a replacement of NP_2 with *who:*

> *a man who is wise is honest*

The next transformation is the deletion of *who is,* thus:

> *a man wise is honest*

The final operation is an inversion, which completes the transformation from deep to surface structure:

> *a wise man is honest*

Universal Grammar. Chomsky's theory of *universal grammar* or *linguistic universals* has been called his most daring speculation about the nature of language. This theory, which he concedes exists thus far only in the barest outlines, asserts that all known languages "rest on the same basic principles" and that children are born with knowledge of these principles (Chomsky, 1965, 1972). Universal grammar is thought to be a substructure of rules or properties common to all languages. Two such "universal" properties are the processes of negation *(I do not like beets)* and interrogation *(Do you like beets?),* which exist in all human languages (Elgin, 1973). The ability of children to learn any language to which they are exposed early in life and to emerge as creative users of the language despite a limited exposure to it, lends strong support, in many linguists' opinion, to the theory of universal grammar.

The Semantic System

Semantics, the study of meaning, is of greater interest to anthropologists who study human thought and communication than any other area of linguistics. One of the reasons that Chomsky's work was of such interest to anthropologists is that his first notion of underlying structure was close to semantics, or logical structure. Hence, it served as a window on human cognition, independent of culture or language use in communication. Semantics may also be the most elusive area of linguistics. Just as we often disagree about the "meaning" of a single statement, so there is considerable disagreement about what is meant by the term *meaning* itself. To anthropologists, meaning refers not merely to the lexical (or "dictionary") sense of words or morphemes. It also includes knowledge agreed upon by speakers of a language about the objects and events signaled by language. This knowledge may not be shared equally by all speakers of the language, but a sufficient amount of meaning is shared in order for members to communicate.

An analogy may help explain the anthropologist's view of semantics. Almost everyone has had the experience of going to a party with a friend and finding that most of the people present—except yourself—know each other very well. They may all have been in the same school or neighborhood or office, and they have a number of acquaintances and experiences in common. Eventually—despite efforts to include you—conversation will turn to people or events about which the members of the group share knowledge: "Sandy lost 50 pounds." "Can you believe that Sam is office manager?" You know the lexical meanings of the words you hear, but you do not have sufficient knowledge to understand their significance. Did Sandy weigh 120 or 230 before the weight loss? Did Sam start his career in the mail room, or is he the boss's son-in-law?

The anthropologist faces the same problem of interpretation when trying to make sense of meanings in alien cultures. Meaning includes the lexical meaning of vocabulary items, as well as situational and expressive components in native statements. For the anthropologist, the object of inquiry is more important than Sandy's weight or Sam's career path. Semantics concentrates on the aspects of language most closely associated with thought processes. The anthropologist seeks to discover the entire system of ideas that exists behind the statements he or she records. Thus, it is an area of primary concern to cognitive anthropologists, who attempt to identify underlying meaning systems of various cultures.

Sociolinguistics

From what we have discussed to this point in the chapter, it is clear that language is a social phenomenon. Language is learned only within social communities. Children raised in isolation, for example, do not learn to speak, although the *capacity* for learning language appears to be carried by the genes. The study of language use within a speech community is generally called *sociolinguistics*. Scholars have often suggested other terms to describe this research. A few of these terms—including "the ethnography of speaking" and "the sociology of language"—may express more clearly, perhaps, the particular focus of the field.

Sociolinguistics studies the variety of languages within speech communities, the elements of those languages, and the relationships and differences among them in usage and structure. The ways in which people actually speak is of great importance, although sociolinguists search for specific varieties of language rather than for particular speech patterns of individual speakers.

The diversity of language within a speech community is a mark of the social and cultural diversity of the community itself. The various languages therein may represent differences of national, geographic, or ethnic origin; economic or educational status; occupation; or personal interests. The range of possible languages within a single community, therefore, may often be considerable. But what emerges in speech is not at all a Babel of competing tongues. Each speaker selects from his or her own repertoire according to the hearer, the size and social makeup of the group, the setting, the topic of discussion, and many other factors (Fishman, 1970).

For instance, high-school friends or old army buddies who meet after many years of separation may automatically revert to the language of their old neighborhood or teenage or service slang. Yet when their spouses, who share none of these things from the past, approach to be introduced to these old friends, the group inevitably returns to a more standard, less specialized language.

Sociolinguistics seeks to discover the makeup of speech communities and to measure the interactions of subgroups with the larger community and with each other. Sociolinguistics also analyzes the speech event itself in the fullest possible context. It is here that the term "ethnography of speaking," introduced by Dell Hymes (1971b), has its greatest relevance. Just as the anthropologist describes and analyzes a number of social phenomena, so the sociolinguist must describe and analyze the use of language in its social context. Hymes points out that the sociolinguist must pay as much attention to the social behavior of speakers as to what they say. This social behavior includes the functions as well as the structure of language; the speech act as performance and as information; and the impact of speakers upon language and social life. The participants in speech events must be considered: senders and receivers, speakers and hearers, even messengers. Language itself can be seen in the kinds and forms of communications, verbal and nonverbal, and in the attitudes and meanings that may be conveyed. Above all, Hymes stresses the importance of "socially constituted linguistics"—identifying social functions, analyzing their influence upon the actual workings of language, and placing language in the larger context of social action (1971a, 1974).

Sociolinguists study how language is used in various social contexts. One area of study is the sacred quality of language used in communicating religious belief. Here, Indian boys are being taught from the Koran. (George Rodger, Magnum)

The work of William Labov falls squarely in this area. His work depends upon actual speech over a period of time for its data. Labov focused on everyday speech in an effort to observe directly the shifting of styles by speakers responding to changes in social context and topic, and the degree of monitoring performed by speakers upon their own speech. He thus attempted to reveal the processes by which variation arises in a community's speech and how it is absorbed into the language.

In addition to these contributions, Labov improved the means by which linguistic data are gathered. In particular, he found solutions to what is called the Observer's Paradox. The paradox is that the very presence of the observer inhibits the speech of the subjects, although the observer's chief purpose is to find out how people normally talk. One solution is to arrange definite breaks from the interviewing, during which the subject relaxes and assumes that he or she is no longer being interviewed. Another solution is to introduce topics that involve the speaker in strong emotions or dramatic incidents. Labov cites as a successful example the question, "Have you ever been in a situation where you were in serious danger of being killed?" People answering this question almost always seem to shift style from the careful, conscious style they use when being interviewed to common, everyday language (Labov, 1972). It should be noted that Labov's linguistic methods have a sociological flavor, since he relies on the statistical manipulation of large bodies of linguistic data.

Sociolinguists use the superior data now available to identify subtle attitudes held by speakers toward their languages. For example, a given speaker may be ambivalent about the language of her ethnic ancestors. She may be proud to speak it among her family and close friends but embarrassed by using it among relative strangers. Values associated with various languages are themselves not fixed, but change in response to many personal, social, and demographic factors (Fishman, 1970).

As we have seen, the most useful way of viewing the relationship between culture and language is to view the two as intricately linked phenomena. Linguistic behavior of all sorts is part of cultural behavior more generally. We have looked at the properties of language that are shared with culture. But human beings are by no means the only animals capable of communicating with others of their own kind. We will now turn to animal communication studies to consider what relationships might exist between human language and that of other animals.

Language and Communication Studies

Human Speech and Animal Communication

Anthropologists study the languages of animals and the capacities of animals to learn human language in order to understand more fully the fundamental nature of language. Humans have long believed that only they possess language and that language is what distinguishes our species from the beasts. Yet we now know that other species are also highly intelligent, with sophisticated systems of communication. Ours is a single, extremely refined form of a general system of languages.

Much of the research in animal communication has focused on the capacity of animals to learn human language, and much of this work has been done with chimpanzees. In captivity, chimpanzees have learned to understand clas-

sifications and to sort pictures into classifications: fruit-vegetable, young-old, small-large. They also show the ability to classify the same object in more than one way. For example, they can recognize a watermelon as *fruit* in a fruit-vegetable grouping, and as *large* in a small-large grouping. Chimpanzees can learn not only the names of members of a class of objects but also the names for the classes of objects themselves (Premack & Premack, 1972).

The earliest attempts to teach chimpanzees human language were made in the 1930s and 1940s. The chimps were raised with human families and did learn to understand a large number of words. But, they did not learn to speak. A chimpanzee named Vicki did manage to combine several sounds and pronounce what seemed to be human phoneme combinations—such as the words "mama," "papa," and "cup"—with apparent human meaningfulness. But it has been demonstrated that apes lack the physical means of making human speech sounds. More recent experiments have therefore switched to sign languages. Washoe, a female chimpanzee, learned over 80 finger and hand signs by the time she was 4 years old. Her use of these signs, moreover, showed that she understood the concepts behind them. For example, after learning the sign for "open" with reference to a particular door, she then applied it to other doors. She finally applied it to other objects—drawers, jars, and the like.

Sarah, a chimpanzee in the laboratory of Ann and David Premack, has acquired a vocabulary of 130 terms using pieces of plastic of various shapes and colors. She can read and write in the language, selecting from pieces representing "apple," "banana," "red," "give," "color of," "pail," and many others. In addition to sentences like "Red color of apple" and "Mary give raisin Sarah," she was also able to read, write, and act upon utterances such as "Sarah insert apple pail banana dish" (Sarah inserts apple in pail and banana in dish). This was an important test, because it showed that Sarah understood the component structure of the sentence. She did not confuse either member of the pair "apple pail" with "banana" or "dish" of the other pair, although the terms were lumped together. And she realized that the verb ("insert,") and the subject ("Sarah") applied to both of the pairs in the sentence.

Sarah's achievement—the development of vocabulary and mastery of the elements of sentence organization—is impressive. She achieved a competence in language roughly equivalent to that of a 2-year-old child. Despite her obvious skills, it is not yet known whether she is able to use her plastic-word language to store information or to solve problems otherwise beyond her grasp. If Sarah were able to think "apple" without requiring that an apple be present, she would possess a crucial element of human language use: the ability to think and talk about things that are not actually there. Further studies may reveal whether chimpanzees can learn to do what human beings take for granted—to talk about absent friends, a trip one is looking forward to, or even things that are imaginary or fictional (Premack & Premack, 1972).

The language that Sarah learned was a very simple one, and it was necessary to teach her more directly and persistently than would have been necessary with a human infant. Each phase of instruction had to be broken down into simple steps. But, according to the Premacks, Sarah learned a simple form of human language. Moreover, the system that was used to teach Sarah has been employed in teaching brain-damaged people to speak, suggesting that Sarah's capacity to communicate may merely be weaker than—but not different from—that of humans. She would not have learned without being taught, but neither do human children who are completely isolated learn to speak. Future research will continue to explore the fascinating boundary between human language and the languages of animals.

In recent years, researchers have focused not only on language but on other signaling systems as well. They concluded that any one of these systems can be studied in the context of the others. As a result, nonlinguistic communication has become an area of growing interest. Two fields of study—proxemics and kinesics—focus on codes of nonlinguistic communication that exist in various human groups.

Edward Hall has studied the ways in which various societies use physical space. This field, called *proxemics,* borrows concepts from ethologists, who study territoriality among animals. The focus of proxemics is wide ranging; it considers how humans use space in such matters as architecture, furniture arrangement, interpersonal distance, listening behavior, and notions of privacy. Hall has found that space can be organized either to be conducive to communication or to produce "solitarity" (Hall's word for the state of being alone). A library in which people sit together at tables to study, for instance, tends to encourage more communication than does a library with individual carrels for reading and study. Hall found that notions of physical space differ by culture: "An Arab colleague has noted, for instance, that his small paneled recreation room was "cozy" to German friends but had just the opposite effect on Arabs, who found it oppressive" (Hall, 1968, p. 91).

Understanding proxemic distinctions is important in encounters with people of cultures different from one's own. Interpersonal distance, especially, tends to be dynamic and to vary widely from culture to culture. Latin Americans typically engage in more eye contact during conversation than do Americans; our tendency to let our eyes wander often seems to them like lack of attention (Hall, 1968). Also, two Latin American individuals engaged in serious conversation seem to talk

A subject for study in proxemics—spacing of telephones in our society and our attendant notions of privacy. (Kent Reno, Jeroboam)

chin to chin. The amount of space between them is significantly less than the space between two Americans would be. Proxemics reveals that items such as eye contact, posture, voice loudness, amount of physical contact, and personal space between speakers engaged in conversation are ingredients by which various groups measure interpersonal distance.

Other researchers, principally Ray Birdwhistell, have studied body movement and gesture as means of communication. This field, called *kinesics,* relies heavily on linguistic models. Just as linguists reduce speech sounds to morphs, so kinesicists seek to reduce body motion to least perceptible units, called *kines.* For example, Birdwhistell identifies brief raising and lowering of the eyebrows as a kine. He argues that differences in high or low eyebrow placement among various regional and economic groups can be identified. Many Englishmen, he asserts, position their eyebrows high; Americans tend to associate such

eyebrow position with a look of surprise. Kinesics has argued that brow and scalp behavior, facial expression, and posture—like spoken language—are learned behaviors that communicate messages, and thus form an important part of culture.

Metacommunication

In virtually all societies, spoken language is the official communication system, but features other than spoken language may determine the way we understand the social effectiveness of language. By placing language in a broader context of communication, anthropologists call attention to messages that are communicated beyond the confines of what is normally considered language. Messages may be communicated not only by language but by gesture, expression, tone of voice, and spatial movement. Such nonlinguistic messages put a "frame" around another

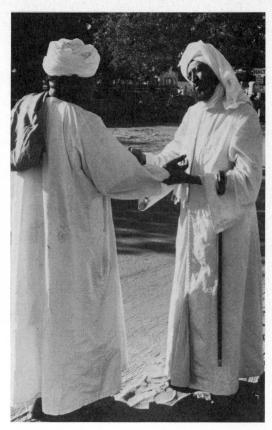

How we interpret extralinguistic messages depends on the system of nonverbal "language" by which we communicate. These, like spoken language, are learned behaviors that differ in various cultures. (Laima Druskis; Carl Frank, Photo Researchers)

message to tell the receiver how to interpret it. For instance, one's tone of voice and facial expression can tell a listener whether the statement "Thanks a lot" is an expression of gratitude or a sarcastic expression of displeasure. Gregory Bateson coined the term *metacommunication* to refer to a message that tells the receiver how another message is to be understood.

Metacommunications are different from nonlinguistic elements of communication studied in proxemics and kinesics in that metacommunications accompany spoken language. They are, therefore, so tied to the spoken message that they would have little or no meaning without it. Unlike proxemics and kinesics, they cannot be studied as a *system* of communication, but only as an adjunct to it.

Uses of Language and Linguistics in Anthropology

The three views introduced earlier of the relationship of language to culture—language independent of culture, the correspondence of language and culture, and language as culture—can be seen in anthropological studies of language over the years.

The study of language has been an important feature of the practice and development of anthropology, especially of American anthropology. From its first use as a means of analyzing the history and nature of American Indian tribes, the linguistic method has served the broader aims of the study of culture. The work of early anthropologists was primarily to classify peoples according to their language, race, and/or culture. Since then the scope of anthropology has broadened considerably. As linguistics developed, the range and number of its contributions to cultural anthropology multiplied.

The contribution of language to the earliest anthropological work can hardly be said to have been linguistic in nature. As we have said, cultures were classified according to the languages their members spoke. But language was considered to be independent of culture. It was merely convenient to the researcher to have some knowledge of native languages. Such knowledge served to help the anthropologist gain admittance to and a degree of acceptance by the people being studied. Once anthropologists began to collect ethnographic data, however, the great advantage of competence in native languages became obvious. Fieldworkers who spoke directly to the people they studied had a great advantage over those who were forced to work through interpreters. They could gather data more easily, were likely to collect superior data, and were in a position to validate their findings.

Linguistic methods began to play an active part in anthropological research when interest turned to native languages as cultural entities and not as mere conduits of information. Anthropologists saw that the grammar of a language and its terminologies could reveal a great deal about the world view and patterns of thought of a culture. Earlier studies, ignoring the language itself, often had failed to

penetrate these. More recent studies have focused specifically on all aspects of native grammars, both for linguistic purposes (to learn more about the nature and structure of languages) and anthropological ends (to see, for example, how the tense structure of a language affects the perceptions of speakers of that language) (Hymes, 1971).

Contemporary anthropologists are aware of the difficulty of discovering the underlying principles of organization of the cultures they study. Formerly, native informants were assumed to be qualified sources of reliable information about their social institutions. But it is now understood that though a member of a culture is an invaluable source of information, he or she cannot be depended upon to explain the culture as a system. Just as a competent speaker of a language may not know the grammatical rules governing use of that language —except implicitly—so a native may have little knowledge of the rules governing the social life of his or her people.

Other recent research has stressed the usefulness of language as a model for other cultural systems. The organization of various cultural phenomena may be seen as similar to a language, possessing a vocabulary and a grammar. In the study of kinship, for example, one begins with the terms of kinship and then passes on to its "grammar," the rules that regulate various areas of kin behavior, such as marriage, inheritance, roles within families, and so forth. The conduct of these processes and their interactions constitute the "syntax" of the system. As anthropology has matured from a discipline concerned chiefly with taxonomy (the classification of terms and features) to one that observes and analyzes the complex process of interaction among related elements, the models of language and grammar have been of great value.

Although linguistic models may be useful, not all cultural phenomena are organized in the way that language is. We have seen that language is closely bound up with many of the other cultural phenomena anthropologists study. It can be a valuable model for analysis of many of these phenomena. But not all data collected in fieldwork can be interpreted or analyzed by means of methods modeled on linguistics. Anthropologists therefore look for appropriate cultural entities, those that can be organized according to their distinctive features and analyzed according to rules. Although their value is great, linguistic models are only one of the tools essential to anthropological research.

Summary

1. Language is the distinguishing attribute of human beings and a precondition of human society. Since language is a primary means by which humans communicate, it is the prime target for understanding how cultural designs are understood and shared.

2. Linguists and anthropologists agree that human language and culture are closely related. They do not agree on the nature and extent of the relationship. Linguists tend to see language as an independent phenomenon, separate from social or cultural context. According to this view, the function of linguistics is to describe a statement, but not to explain its meaning. Most contemporary anthropologists, on the other hand, see the relationship between language and culture as one of correspondence. Because both are creations, largely unconscious, of the human mind, they parallel each other. The *Sapir-Whorf Hypothesis*—that language reflects the way in which its speakers perceive and think about the world—is an example of the correspondence view. A third view suggests that language *is* culture, that linguistic behavior is inseparable from social context and cultural behavior.

3. Sound is the medium through which language is expressed. *Phonology* (the study of sounds) consists of *phonetics* and *phonemics.* Each language possesses a limited number of *phonemes,* the distinctive but meaningless sounds heard as the same by native speakers of a language. Children learn to use only the distinct sounds of their language, although their babbling consists of many sounds that are foreign to an adult speaker's phonemic system.

4. From an analysis of speech sounds, phonologists formulate rules that govern the ordering of language into meaningful units. This set of rules for a particular language is its grammar. Grammar is divided into morphology and syntax. *Morphology* analyzes the combination of *morphs* into words. *Syntax* deals with the rules for combining words into phrases and sentences. Morphology and syntax share the processes of selection, arrangement, and modification. *Transformational grammar,* introduced by Chomsky, attempts to explain how speakers develop linguistic competence and become creative users of language. Sentences consist of *surface structure,* corresponding to the sounds we hear, and *deep structure,* representing the underlying structure by which meaning is generated. Grammatical transformations change deep into surface structure. *Universal grammar,* according to Chomsky, is the set of rules or principles governing all languages that explains basic resemblances between languages as well as the child's ability to master any language.

5. *Semantics* is the study of meaning; it involves attempts to define "meaning" and classifies kinds of meaning. Semantics is of special interest to cognitive anthropologists because it concentrates on aspects of language most closely associated with thought processes.

6. *Sociolinguists* study language use within a speech community. Topics of interest to sociolinguists are the varieties of languages within speech communities, the elements of

those languages, and the relationships among them to usage and structure. Speakers select language according to their audience, the setting, and the topic of discussion.

7. Anthropologists study animal communication in order to understand more fully the nature of human language. Chimpanzees have learned to communicate with humans using simple vocabulary and basic sentence structure.

8. Two fields of study—proxemics and kinesics—focus on codes of nonlinguistic communication in human groups. *Proxemics* studies the ways in which various groups use physical space. *Kinesics* studies body movement and gesture as means of communication.

It has found that such things as brow movement, facial expression, and posture—like spoken language—are learned behaviors.

9. Some messages are transmitted beyond the confines of what is normally considered language. A message that tells the receiver how another message or behavior is to be interpreted is termed a *metacommunication*.

10. Language has always been important to anthropology, but early research ignored the cultural elements of language. When language was seen to be related to culture, anthropological interest in it increased. Recent research has employed the categories and methods of linguistics as one of a number of tools by which to analyze cultural phenomena.

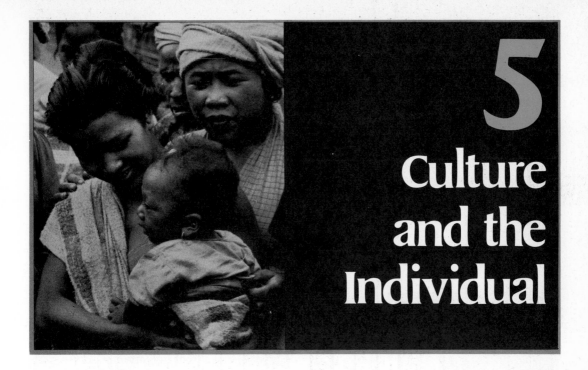

5
Culture and the Individual

IT has been said that every human being is in some ways like every other human being, in some ways like some other human beings, and in some ways like no other human being (Kluckhohn & Murray, 1962). Although each of us is an individual with a distinct personality, it is clear that most of us agree on what are desirable personality characteristics, many of which we share. Our general sharing of such values as outspokenness and competitiveness makes us quite unlike inhabitants of Acoma Pueblo or Soviet Armenia. Indeed, our very insistence upon "rugged individualism" is a characteristic that would be quite alien, if not downright revolutionary, in a Pueblo Indian or an Armenian.

We saw earlier that culture involves understandings about life experiences shared by members of a human social group. In their inquiries into the designs for living of human groups, anthropologists deal directly with the individual participants in a given culture, whose activities are expressions of the cultural system. Of course, no one individual can express every aspect of a cultural system. Nor is any single member capable of knowing or communicating all the designs associated with that system. However, most people are able to understand their own society sufficiently well to function within it as "normal" members. A Navajo sheepherder, for example, does not have the knowledge that the singers in his culture who heal the sick through elaborate song cycles and traditional sand-painted designs possess, but he is able to explain many of their functions in his community as well as his understanding of interactions with them.

The relationship of the individual to society is the subject of this chapter. This field of investigation has traditionally been known in anthropology as "culture and personality." More recently, the term *psychological anthropology* has come into use. Psychological anthropology analyzes culture as expressed in the actions, thoughts, and feelings of its individual members.

The Concept of Personality

Personality may be thought of as the organized response patterns within every human being. These patterns shape the actions,

Personality is molded by an infant's earliest experiences as well as by the cultural designs of the group in which he or she lives. (Ken Heyman)

thoughts, and feelings of the individual in various situations. Within each individual, these patterns are more or less consistent with each other throughout life.

Personality directs us to act, think, and feel in certain ways. It is our particular style of facing and dealing with life events. Because one's personality is generally predictable, it allows us to say confidently, "If such-and-such were to happen, I would do thus-and-so." Each of us can be reasonably certain whether we would stand up and fight; cope with an emergency; evade an issue; prefer science fiction films or romantic novels; and so on. In these and countless other details we hourly acknowledge the consistency of personality. We do so also in our expectations of others' behavior, in such expressions as "She's the kind of person who . . . ," or "He's always doing things like that."

Personality may be thought of as the substantially consistent "blueprints" within each of us that allow us to respond to the world around us in predictable ways. This definition parallels our definition of culture as the designs that allow individual members of a group to interact with one another in expected ways. Cultural designs are, of course, intersubjective in nature and, in existence, well before the birth and development of any individual. They are themselves significant factors in the development of every human personality. Culture is, however, only one of the determining factors in the formation of personality.

We do not know at what age human personality is formed—6 months, 6 years, and every age before, between, and after have all been advanced by one authority or another. There is, however, general agreement that some aspects of personality are set very early in life, long before one is able consciously to do anything much about them. Although personality may be modified somewhat throughout life, our earliest experiences are influential in personality formation. "As the twig is bent, so is the tree inclined," goes an old saying—

and so the starting point for our discussion is those elements that go into bending the twig. In addition to culture, other significant factors in personality development include physical characteristics, environment, and the life experiences that are unique to every individual.

Physical Factors and Personality

Human physiology is surely one of the most obvious contributors to the formation of personality. It involves two aspects of biological characteristics: inherited physical and mental capacity on the one hand, and the health and functioning of the human organism on the other. Physical factors in personality thus include everything from the age, sex, and complexion of the individual to various endocrine disorders (such as diabetes) and other biochemical malfunctions. Mental attributes, too, are factors in personality. Personalities of the gifted, the talented, the average, and the retarded all reflect their inherent abilities. They reflect, as well, the extent to which peoples' capacities are utilized, recognized, frustrated, or looked down on in their cultural setting.

Clearly, the appearance of an individual's body has an influence on personality. However, body build is not evaluated equally in all cultural systems. In American culture today, obesity is considered unattractive (and unhealthy) in adults. Elsewhere in the world—and even at an earlier time in the United States—stoutness may be prized as a sign of prosperity and considered esthetically pleasing. So strong is the link between appearance and personality that some people reshape their physical characteristics to fit cultural norms and values. Certain traditional Polynesian cultures prized obesity, and the ruling class was force-fed to meet the standards for royal plumpness. Other physical characteristics that mold personality, and that may be subject to differential cultural appraisal, include health and strength. Consider, for ex-

Body build is evaluated differently in various cultures. Sumo wrestlers in Japan are honored for their size, as are some professional athletes in our own society. (Fred Mayer, Woodfin Camp)

ample, a girl with a healthy constitution and athletic bent in Victorian England, when daintiness and inactivity were the fashion for females.

An early study of the relationship between physiology and personality was done by W. H. Sheldon, who took detailed measurements and made tests on Harvard students and other American males. Sheldon assigned his test subjects to three categories on the basis of body build and claimed that there was a consistent personality within each category. Thin individuals (ectomorphs) were likely to be nervous, introverted, and have skin ailments and insomnia. Husky, muscular men (meso-morphs) were usually energetic, lively, and athletic. And heavyset individuals (endomorphs) tended to be extroverted, lazy, and luxury-loving (Sheldon, 1940 and 1942). Similarly, E. A. Hooton correlated the body builds of convicts with the kind of criminal activity in which they had been involved. He found that, for example, short, heavy men were more likely than tall, thin ones to have engaged in crimes of violence such as assault and sex offenses (Hooton, 1939).

This type of evidence, however, has been fragmentary and inconclusive. Yet there is no doubt that some inherited traits do play a significant role in personality development and expression. As Kluckhohn and Murray express it, "biological inheritance provides the stuff from which personality is fashioned and . . . determines trends and sets limits within which variation is constrained" (1962, p. 57).

Environment and Personality

Folk wisdom or "common knowledge" has long believed that physical environment and climate shape personality. It has been suggested that people raised in the tropics are likely to be slow-moving, indolent, uninventive, and unambitious, whereas mountain dwellers are energetic, tough, and individualistic. No careful research has been carried out to support or disclaim such impressions, but individuals in every clime have been found with abilities and characters different from those proposed by such theories. Today it is generally accepted that such notions are without foundation.

Nevertheless, it *is* recognized that physical environment does influence human personality in specific ways. For example, the environment provides the materials for human handcraft or other production—from rocks, grasses, lumber, cave walls, and ocher for making paints to diamonds, petroleum, and

uranium. Technology allows for the use of these materials. Thus, human occupations, choices, and the utilization of human abilities (with all of their implications for personality) are clearly dependent upon the facilities provided by, or nonexistent in, a particular setting.

But the most important influence of the environment on human genetic potential is nutritional. The environment, of course, provides the materials for human diet. It has been shown that individuals whose diets lack key nutrients never achieve their maximum growth or optimal body functioning. In addition, they are likely to succumb to illness more frequently, to experience illness more severely, and to recover less completely than individuals with good nutrition—all factors which affect personality. Further, prolonged lack of various nutrients is itself a cause of disease. Dietary deficiency diseases are characterized by personality change as well as physical deformities.

Arctic Hysteria. Cross-cultural studies of nutrition are beginning to illuminate the role of minerals and other dietary factors in personality development. The outbursts of agitated behavior known as Arctic hysteria have recently, for example, been shown to be related in part to calcium deficiency. Arctic hysteria takes the form of wild running to and fro, screaming, and even convulsions. Such behavior occurs with significant frequency in Greenland, Lapland, Siberia, Alaska, and other polar areas. There, as Foulks (1972) has shown, the distinctive environment is responsible in several ways for limited calcium intake and use. For one thing, the irregular alternation of daylight and darkness directly interferes with the body's use of calcium, which is needed for the functioning of the central nervous system. In addition, the lengthy winter and the cold climate, requiring heavy and extensive body covering much of the year, allow only a minimal amount of solar ultraviolet radiation to reach the Eskimo's body. Ultraviolet light is required by the body for vitamin D production and utilization, which in turn affects the body's use of calcium (Foulks, 1972). And not least, the Arctic environment further limits the available natural food sources of calcium.

But environmentally produced calcium deficiency is not the sole cause of Arctic hysteria. Eskimos now live less in igloos and more in wooden shacks heated by coal stoves. In the wooden shacks, the heated air is not humidified, as it was by the melting and dripping of the frozen igloo walls. This change resulted in an increase in respiratory infections among the Eskimos. One consequence of such infections was that many individuals had chronic middle ear disease, symptoms of which include central nervous system disorders that may resemble Arctic hysteria. The introduction of a cash economy has led to the purchase of inexpensive starchy foods, bringing such dietary changes as an increase in carbohydrate intake and a corresponding decrease in the protein and mineral content of their food. And as part of the Eskimo cultural tradition, there was a social model for hysteria. In contests held during certain festivals and in the institution of shamanism, frenzied behavior similar to that of Arctic hysteria was considered appropriate (Foulks, 1972). Thus, Arctic hysteria as a personality trait has been shown to be the product of both environmental and cultural influences.

Personal Experiences and Personality

Without any doubt, personality owes much to factors and events particular to the individual. Every person has a unique history, composed of experiences that are never exactly like those of anyone else. This holds true even for identical twins brought up in the same household. One twin is older than the other, even if only by minutes; one may weigh less or be otherwise less sturdy or healthy than the other, and perhaps thus get more caretaking attention from parents; one may have a better appetite and consequently get more affection from the parent; and so on. Recent studies have shown that not only whether one is male or female but also aspects of the family into which one is born—such as age and the educational, occupational, and socioeconomic levels of one's parents—all contribute to the uniqueness of individual development. Then, too, there is the contribution to personality of the character and severity of illnesses and the age at which these occur. Similarly, we may have our share of those experiences labeled "traumatic"—a serious accident, hostility on the part of peers, the death or departure of a parent or other close family member.

Cultural norms and social conditioning may work to equalize certain types of experiences, but they cannot succeed in erasing or "normalizing" all of them. For example, Operation Head Start has attempted to provide enrichment for very young children from so-called "culturally deprived" backgrounds; months or years of psychotherapy may rid an individual of the aftereffects of a traumatic series of events. Yet the original experience can never be removed after the fact. The individual may learn in various ways to minimize or control its effects, but once experienced, an event or situation has been an influence.

Personality, as an organization of forces within the individual, is the cumulative result of all the factors just discussed. But of them all, culture is by far the major influence on the formation of any given personality. The rest of this chapter discusses in detail the cultural factors in personality development. First, we will survey contrasting views of personality to get some perspective on the studies that will follow.

Contrasting Views of Personality Formation

There are a number of different ways of looking at how personality is formed. Salvatore R. Maddi (1968) describes three major ones: conflict theory, fulfillment theory, and consistency theory.

Conflict Theory

The *conflict theory* of personality formation states that personality is formed as a result of constant conflict between the desires or instincts of the individual and the constraints imposed by society. Freud's articulation of the gratification/punishment principle is a statement of the conflict theory of personality formation. According to this view, the natural human instinct for gratification is inevitably curbed and frustrated when it comes up against the needs or demands of other persons in society; the individual must constantly compromise and adjust. All children learn sooner or later, for example, that food is not always promptly or adequately available on demand; that the rights and needs of others must be considered and respected; that bodily functions must be controlled. Freud believed that this process of adjustment is accompanied by varying degrees of frustration, repression, guilt, resentment, and anxiety, with consequent effects on personality. In response, all individuals develop self-protective personality mechanisms. These mechanisms may be healthy (such as the substitution of an acceptable activity for one that is taboo), or neurotic (such as ascribing to others unacceptable tendencies one cannot acknowledge in oneself).

Fulfillment Theory

Fulfillment theory, on the other hand, holds that conflict is not continuous but, rather, a periodic occurrence, and that the main stimulus to personality development lies within the individual. According to this point of view, all living things strive to realize the full measure of their genetic potential. For humans, self-actualization always requires the approval of others (one's family, for example, or community) and of the self as well. We develop a positive self-image in response to the image of ourselves reflected from others. The lack of a positive self-image is profoundly disturbing to the individual and severely interferes with his or her functioning within various reference groups (possibly resulting in a mental breakdown). The fulfillment model of personality formation is the theoretical foundation for the collection of current therapies and related activities known as the Human Potential Movement. In general, it emphasizes ways for the individual to become free from the influences of others in order to achieve optimal self-realization.

Consistency Theory

In contrast to both of these views of personality formation, *consistency theory* emphasizes the continuity of life experiences; each experience is filtered through the world view built up by the individual on the basis of prior experience. Personality within each individual, then, is largely consistent, since the individual processes new information and events in terms of the outlook that has resulted from the sum of past experience. The consistency model is based on the need of individuals for organization of various feelings and attitudes into one integrated and harmonious personality.

However, consistency theorists recognize that personality formation is a lifelong process and that an individual may well encounter situations and information that are inconsistent with his or her earlier personality construct. When this happens, the individual may experience anxiety to a greater or lesser ex-

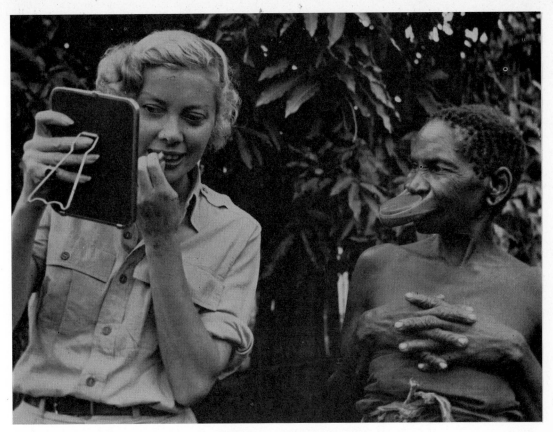

Contact with other cultures introduces experiences and behaviors that may be totally different from one's own. Here, a Pygmy woman watches the application of lipstick with bemused fascination. (Monkmeyer)

tent. If the inconsistency is sufficiently significant, the individual may be driven to a reappraisal of his or her situation and world view, leading perhaps to changes in outlook and personality. We sometimes hear of a person whose life took a different course after a specific event or as a result of a new influence. Such dramatic reversals can be due to changes in the society as well as to events unique to the individual. The phrase *cognitive dissonance* has been applied to a situation in which an individual's outlook or self-image comes up against an opposite or inconsistent experience. In a sense, all of us experience cognitive dissonance as we go from one stage of life to the next. The role dependencies of childhood

must give way to the responsibilities of adulthood and the various roles associated with it. The individual's personality makes the adjustment during the transition period of adolescence (and, in more complex societies where assumption of the full adult role is delayed, in young adulthood).

Barnouw (1973) notes that each of these three theoretical views of personality formation takes a different attitude toward the relationship between personality and culture. For conflict theorists, culture is an inhibiting, controlling factor. Some of them hold that cultural complexity increases human frustration and that people in simpler cultures are less likely to develop neuroses. For fulfillment theorists, culture provides the means by which self-actualization can take place and human needs be fulfilled. The consistency model takes a more balanced view of the role of culture, making it neither an adversary (as in the conflict model) nor a primary determinant (as in the fulfillment model). Rather, culture is seen as an ever-present, but essentially neutral, factor. It is there to shape one's interactions with other individuals (Barnouw, 1973).

Of the three theories, the consistency view best fits the approach of this text. Just as the individual must integrate new developments into a preexisting personality structure, so too cultures attempt to incorporate new influences with minimal dislocations. The consistency of culture provides security within which the individual can develop. At times, inability to integrate new developments may result in what is called *culture shock*. This is a psychological response to an unfamiliar culture and is characterized by disorientation, anxiety, and sometimes mental breakdown, depression, or even suicide. But the formation

of personality is a lifelong process, and most individuals in most cultures learn to integrate their accumulated experiences so that their self-image is not too incompatible with reality.

However, the other points of view about personality formation are also relevant to our purposes. The conflict model has been the starting point for the development of psychoanalytic theory. It underlies, as we shall see, studies that emphasize the role of childhood training in personality development and national character. Similarly, aspects of fulfillment theory underlie assumptions about the relationship of individuals to their society, as we shall see in our examination of role theory.

Socialization and Enculturation

The primary focus of psychological anthropology has been directed to the question

Socialization involves learning skills that enable one to function as a competent member of society. The Hoti Indians of Venezuela learn spear throwing at an early age by playing a game in which they throw spears through a hoop. (Jacques Jangoux, Peter Arnold Photo Archives)

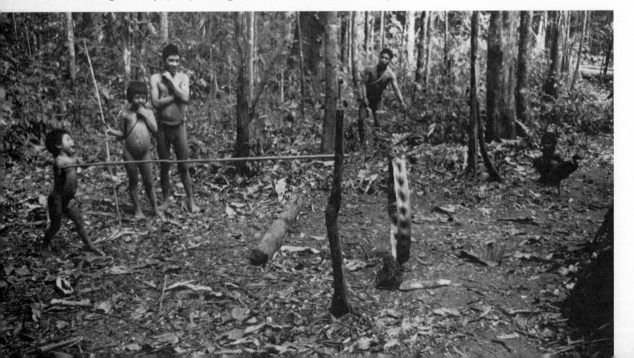

of how a personality type characteristic of a given culture is continually recreated in each generation. The means by which the individual learns in the earliest years to become a functioning adult within a specific society and culture has been called both "socialization" and "enculturation." These terms involve essentially the same processes—absorption of a culture's values, world view, life styles, and skills. However, there is an implied shade of difference. *Enculturation* refers to the process whereby individual members of a society acquire the characteristics of a given culture, learning its language and generally acquiring competence in the culture. *Socialization* refers to the more general process whereby someone new to a society learns to function as a member of that society; it includes the learning of social roles such as that of wife or elder, and of occupational roles, whether through example or through more structured training, as in school.

In real life, of course, both processes happen together and are inseparable. "Socialization" is used most frequently by sociologists and psychologists and comprises all aspects of learning to grow up, including control of bodily functions, learning to relate to others, assuming adult responsibilities, and so on. Many anthropologists, on the other hand, tend to prefer "enculturation" because it comprises total learning of cultural expectations and does not imply undue emphasis on social roles. In this text both terms are used interchangeably.

Role Theory and Socialization

The nature of society's influence on individual identity is the subject of *role theory*. The pioneering work of social psychologist George Herbert Mead in the early part of this century laid the foundation for role theory. Mead's research and teaching established that identity is socially constructed and sustained. Children first learn the social roles of their group from those individuals with whom they deal most intensively—parents, siblings, other close relatives, teachers, and peers. Mead termed this important group of people *significant others*. After a while, the child discovers that the social roles learned from significant others are also those recognized by members of the society at large. This more distant and less intimate entity takes on a character of its own. It becomes a person's mental representation of the expectations of society; Mead termed it the *generalized other*. Referring to the generalized other enables a person to see things from the perspective of his or her entire group. Mead showed that a child takes on an image of self during the same time that he or she forms opinions about society. By combining the demands of significant others and of the generalized other, the child develops an image of self and comes also to understand the social roles that exist in his or her particular society.

Within every culture, identifiable social roles are assigned on the bases of age, sex, and occupation. Individuals learn what is expected of them by patterning their behavior on *role models*. These models are provided by members of the society who are already engaged in the role the individual can expect to assume. Regardless of what society one lives in, the criteria of age, sex, and occupation serve to create role models. In every society, those members of the next older age group provide models for behavior. Seven-year-old children get their notions of what it will be like to be 12 by observing the behavior and experiences of 12-year-olds, just as 12-year-olds watch teen-agers for an understanding of what is to come. As we shall see in a later chapter, some societies have clearly demarcated age categories in which certain defined roles and behavior

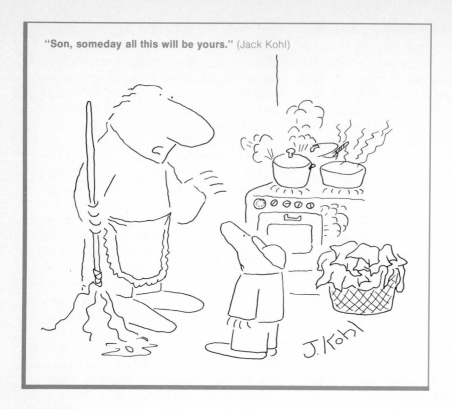

"Son, someday all this will be yours." (Jack Kohl)

are prescribed. Individuals also pattern behavior on the basis of sex. In most societies, girls pattern after their mothers, boys after their fathers. Sometimes other adult men or women may also serve as models. Among the Haida of British Columbia, for example, a boy will live with, learn from, and model his behavior after that of his mother's brother (Murdock, 1934). Similarly, observed occupations may serve to shape behavior. Children may not know exactly what the work connected with a particular occupation is like on a day-to-day basis. But they do form general notions of the roles connected with such occupations as medical/religious practitioner (doctor and witch doctor, clergy and shaman), political leader, teacher, housewife, farmer or herder, artisan. Occupational role models define not only roles available in a particular society but also expected relationships among various people.

Childhood Determinism

Whereas G. H. Mead's work focused on the influence of social roles on identity, Freud's theories of personality formation emphasized the encounter between infant and early childhood instincts and the necessary restraints imposed by society through parents and other caregivers in the socialization process. Freud stressed in particular the influences of weaning, toilet-training, development of various sexual inhibitions and controls, and the resolution of oedipal feelings.*

*The oedipal conflict is the child's early attachment to the parent of the opposite sex, and concurrent resentment or hostility toward the parent of the same sex. These feelings must be resolved through identification with the same-sex parent in order for the child to progress to an adult relationship with a member of the opposite sex.

Our culture is so familiar with the notion that childhood training shapes adult personality that we easily accept the idea as a basis for our study of culture and personality. This general approach is known as *childhood determinism*. In emphasizing the early stages of life as crucial to personality formation, Freudian theory has been a stimulus to anthropological studies of child training in diverse cultural settings. Field studies and theoretical analyses have examined the role of early experiences in shaping adult personality. One type of inquiry looks at differences in enculturation processes in various societies. It attempts to answer the question, "How do children learn their culture?" A second kind of study is concerned with the influences of child-care practices on the sequence of human development. It addresses the question, "How do infants in different cultures develop in comparison to one another?" A third approach focuses on the correlations between childhood training practices and adult personality with the question, "What traits in adult personality can be attributed to experiences in one's childhood?" A fourth type of study relates child-rearing practices to other aspects of a specific culture. It considers the question, "What child-rearing practices reflect general patterns of a particular culture?" (Bourguignon, 1973). The key research projects that are described below are studies that examine these various aspects of the connections between culture and personality.

Margaret Mead: Enculturation and Child-Care Studies

Margaret Mead was among the first anthropologists to organize field research centering on a specific problem, in contrast to earlier studies which had attempted to be all-encompassing in scope.* Her first study dealt

*This discussion is based on Barnouw (1973), pp. 129–147.

with the constraints and limitations imposed by culture on adolescents. In this study, published as *Coming of Age in Samoa* (1928), Mead posed the question, "Are the disturbances which vex our adolescents due to the nature of adolescence itself or to civilization?" In Western cultures, adolescence is generally characterized by emotional tension, intergenerational conflict, and rebellion against authority. Mead intended, through comparison of different cultures, to discover whether these characteristics were due to physiological changes occurring at puberty. If so, Mead reasoned adolescence should present similar problems in all places and at all times, regardless of how different the cultures might be.

Mead found that on the South Pacific island of Samoa adolescence was very different from the tension-ridden experience she had known in the United States. Instead, for various social and cultural reasons, it was a period of relative calm, stability, and even intergenerational cooperation. Moreover, Mead felt that the social interactions of adolescent Samoans generally were characterized by a high degree of casualness and ease. She found that even premarital sexual relationships were accepted in Samoa as a natural part of adolescence, since the individuals involved did not invest a high degree of emotion in these relationships. In this study, as in the two that followed it, Mead showed that characteristics of personality are not a simple and inevitable consequence of biological processes common to human beings in all places and at all times. They are, instead, influenced by various social and cultural factors. Mead's work here illustrates the second inquiry of field research mentioned above, focusing on the ways that cultural differences influence personality development.

Mead's next effort was a pioneer work in the influence of childhood training on personality development. Here, she was concerned with the upbringing of children among the

Manus of the Admiralty Islands off the coast of New Guinea. In *Growing Up in New Guinea,* Mead (1930) observed that Manus children were not closely supervised by adults. Except for being instilled with a certain respect for property, they were left pretty much to their own devices. Among the Manus, children lived in a world populated by their peers. They spent most of their time in play and had few responsibilities and little contact with their elders. When they were young

the adults give the children no storytelling pattern, no guessing games, riddles, puzzles. The idea that children would like to hear legends seems quite fantastic to a Manus adult. . . . Where we fill our children's minds with a rich folklore, songs which personalize the sun, the moon, and the stars, riddles and fairy tales and myths, the Manus do nothing of the sort. (M. Mead, 1930, pp. 125, 130)

Mead concluded that the imagination and creativity we tend to associate with childhood must be cultivated through adult guidance and instruction. Without such a pattern for fantasy, this tendency will be kept from manifesting itself. Here Mead called attention to the beneficial side of our social tradition, which can be seen not only as a constraint but as thought-provoking and creativity-inspiring as well.

Mead's third study compared three tribes in New Guinea—the Arapesh, the Mundugumor, and the Tchambuli—which, though living within the same general area, were significantly different in many aspects of their society and culture. In particular, Mead focused on the influence of culture on sexual roles and attitudes; she found that personality is not sex-linked, but culturally derived. In *Sex and Temperament in Three Primitive Societies* (1935), Mead discussed the evidence that led her to state that "many, if not all, of the personality traits which we have called masculine or feminine are as lightly linked to sex as are the clothing, the manners, and the form of head-dress that a society at a given period assigns to either sex" (p. 280). Sexual roles and attitudes, she concluded, are not biologically determined.

Although a number of questions have been raised about Mead's research, her studies remain landmarks in the field of culture and personality. They emphasize the importance of cultural influence on personality formation. As she concludes, "the differences between

Margaret Mead doing fieldwork in Bali in 1957. (Ken Heyman)

individuals who are members of different cultures, like the differences between individuals within a culture, are almost entirely to be laid to differences in conditioning, especially during early childhood, and the form of this conditioning is culturally determined" (1935, p. 280).

Basic Personality, Modal Personality, and Childhood Training

The concept of basic personality structure was articulated by Abram Kardiner as a means of relating childhood training to adult personality in a specific culture. *Basic personality structure* consists of the cluster of tendencies common to the personalities of all individuals who shared early childhood experiences as a result of being brought up in the same culture. Kardiner was a psychoanalyst who came into contact with Edward Sapir, Ruth Benedict, Ralph Linton, Cora Du Bois, and other anthropologists of the so-called "culture and personality school" in a seminar at Columbia University in the 1930s. He came to see traditional Freudian ideas of personality formation as strongly tied to Western society and theorized that other societies might have different ways of dealing with problems of personality.

Kardiner believed that some life experiences naturally have more impact than others. Those that are most responsible for disciplining, restricting (inhibiting), and gratifying the child he termed *primary institutions.* They consist of family and kinship arrangements; institutionalized activities associated with feeding, weaning, and sex training; and subsistence patterns. Primary institutions shape basic personality structure. *Secondary institutions* are those that serve the "needs and tensions" generated by the primary ones; that is, those through which basic personality structure is expressed. They include taboo systems, religion, the arts, mythology.

For anthropologists, Kardiner's approach

has proved both problematic and useful. A basic limitation is, as Singer (1961) points out, the lack of adequate proof of causal connections among child-rearing practices, personality traits, and forms of culture such as art, religion, and folklore. The approach has been useful to anthropologists because it looks at both cultural institutions and personality traits common to members of a society. It has prompted anthropologists to do studies using various psychoanalytic techniques and has led to other productive concepts.

Foremost among these was the notion of modal personality proposed by Kardiner's colleague, Cora Du Bois (1944).* *Modal personality* consists of the characteristics or tendencies shared by *most* members of a given culture. In a field study that was exceptionally thorough and, at that time, novel, Du Bois spent a year in general ethnographic inquiry on Alor, an Indonesian island. She followed this by psychologically oriented research. In this second phase, Du Bois obtained detailed life histories and materials such as the drawings of children, and she administered various projective tests to the people of Alor.†

When her field research was completed, Du Bois submitted the various psychological materials to a number of specialists, including Kardiner. They analyzed them independently of one another, and without knowledge of the cultural background of the people tested. So

*This discussion is based on Barnouw (1973), pp. 153–162.

†Projective tests present subjects with a visual stimulus—inkblots, for example, in the Rorschach tests. In response, without cues from the test administrator, subjects must express freely what they see or think is happening. Their responses are categorized by psychoanalysts according to the personality traits they indicate. Because the range of projective test responses has been standardized within contemporary American-European culture, a built-in culture bias can skew the interpretation of results from subjects with non-Western cultural backgrounds. One must understand the culture very well for a useful interpretation to be made. For this reason, projective tests are seldom used in anthropological research at the present time.

striking was the correspondence between the findings of the various specialists that Du Bois was convinced that each specialist, herself included, was correctly describing some general tendencies of Alorese personality.

Du Bois found that, among the Alorese, the sexual divison of labor was an important influence on personality development from infancy on. Men spent their time in such economic transactions as the exchange of pigs and ceremonial goods; women were the main producers of food and spent most of their time in its cultivation and collection. They spent so much time and energy in this activity that they had to leave their infants at home with a relative. Du Bois argued that for this reason, young children experienced various forms of stress, which multiplied as their lives proceeded. The initial stress took the form of oral frustration when the infant was left to be nursed by women other than the mother. Often a child simply was deprived of milk because no other lactating women were available; the child waited to nurse until the mother returned at day's end. Other frustrations followed when, after a year or so, the child began to walk and was no longer carried about, thus losing the security of physical contact with a caregiver. Feeding continued to be highly irregular as the child grew older. These frustrations were compounded by the custom of teasing, in which mothers showed preference for the children of other women or either parent pretended aggression toward the child. Du Bois felt that, as a result, the world appeared threatening to Alorese children. Consequently, she did not find it at all surprising that before the age of 5 or 6, children often throw rather intense and long temper tantrums.

During adolescence, Alorese boys and girls followed different sets of daily activities. Boys gathered together for idle play or, at times, intermittent periods of work in the fields; girls joined their mothers in most of their activities. Courting began toward the end of adolescence.

Marriage seemed to be a very tense relationship among the Alorese, who divorced an average of twice during a lifetime. As Du Bois saw it, this tension derived from the conflicting feelings of love and hate toward their mothers that Alorese males developed in early childhood. These attitudes were then transferred to their wives. A man, continuing to seek nurturance and other forms of attention, continued to be frustrated; the wife, like the mother, did not have time to satisfy his needs and desires. Men were consequently much given to jealousy and continued feelings of inadequacy. Du Bois was told, interestingly, that a man's wife should have the qualities of a mother, and she recorded instances when analogies between wives and mothers were drawn. The specialists analyzing her data noted suspicion, apathy, insecurity, and lack of emotional involvement among the personality traits of the Alorese (Malefijt, 1974). Through her wide-ranging research techniques, the evidence amassed by Du Bois seems to support the conclusions she and her consulting specialists reached, even though, as Du Bois is well aware, factors other than child training are also involved in shaping the modal personality of any culture. Furthermore, the agreement among the analysts of the Alorese data may have been as much a reflection of their common cultural understandings as it was of the situation on Alor.

National Character Studies

During World War II, the need arose to know more about the people of several nations, both enemies and allies. This need presented something of a problem because field study was not possible under wartime conditions. Nor were subject societies the "primitive" societies studied by ethnologists in the past but, for the most part, modern nations.

Under the guidance of Margaret Mead, Ruth Benedict, Geoffrey Gorer, and others, anthropological culture and personality study methods served as a starting point for the development of new techniques for analyzing "culture at a distance" (M. Mead & Metraux, 1953).

The techniques used for indirect culture study included interviewing former residents of or visitors to the nation under study; analysis of the history, economy, and geographical setting of the nation; and the careful inspection of such cultural materials as films, paintings, sculpture, architecture, literature, and speeches (Singer, 1961).

Of the national character analyses made during World War II, Ruth Benedict's classic study of Japan, *The Chrysanthemum and the Sword* (1946), is an outstanding example using the culture pattern (or configuration) approach. Earlier we looked at Benedict's notion that cultures are more or less consistent clusters of themes or patterns. This view was described as configurational theory. Child rearing is one of the patterns in the overall cultural configuration. It constitutes the means of communicating the configuration to the next generation. Benedict ascribed the themes running through Japanese culture and the personality traits of Japanese adults to early child-training practices, including teasing and strict toilet-training (Singer, 1961).

But in configuration theory, other cultural patterns combine with child rearing to influence personality. Attention has been called, for example, to the common characteristics or themes of interpersonal relationships in a culture. Relationships between interacting groups or individuals may be complementary, eliciting opposite behavior—dominant/submissive, for example—from both parties. Or they may be symmetrical, with both parties responding similarly to one another. Gregory Bateson (1942), for one, conceives of national character in terms of patterns in interpersonal relations; national

characters differ according to combinations of specific themes in a given culture. For example, the Balinese seem to combine dependence, exhibitionism, and high status; Europeans seem to combine high status with social service (Singer, 1961).

National character can be seen as an element in a circular system of personality formation. Parents and child constitute a "mutually interactive system" (Singer, 1961, p. 48) with the parent responding to the child and in turn stimulating responses from the child. Other cultural patterns also have circular interactions wtih the individual. So, configuration theory moves beyond linear or direct causal relationships in its view of childhood training and adult personality. As Mead has written, in a circular system "the method of child rearing, the presence of a particular literary tradition, the nature of the domestic and public architecture, the religious beliefs, the political system, are all conditions within which a given kind of personality develops" (M. Mead, 1951).

Child Rearing and Culture Patterns: The Six Cultures Study

In the 1950s a vast quantity of ethnographic material was being assembled in the Human Relations Area Files at Yale University. Because the raw data had been accumulated over a long period of time by different researchers using different methodology, there were gaps in this cross-cultural record. Although it was the most comprehensive correlation of cultural material ever undertaken, the Human Relations Area Files contained only occasional material on child rearing and often sketchy descriptions of childhood experience. Because of such deficiencies, John W. M. Whiting devised an outline to guide field researchers, whose resulting studies would then be comparable. The result is known as the Six Cultures Study.

Each of six teams trained in the Whiting

approach studied a community of from 50 to 100 families, concentrating in each on a group of 24 mothers and their children between the ages of 3 and 10. The research reports were to follow a specific outline: the first part contained detailed descriptions of specific ethnographic material—ecology, kinship, architecture, and so on—and the second part focused on maternity and child-rearing practices. An aim of this coordinated cross-cultural survey was to identify any recurring correlations that might exist between specific child rearing practices, childhood experiences, and cultural institutions.

The materials from the six cultures were sorted according to comparable categories of data. Observations of children's behavior, for example, sorted out into two quite separate clusters. One cluster consisted of groups emphasizing cooperation; the second cluster was characterized by individualism. Children in the first, or Type A, group offered more support and help; children in the second, or Type B, cultures more often sought help and allowed themselves to be dominated. Other similarities in the Type A cultures included subsistence farming as the economic basis, along with lack of economic role specialization, egalitarian social organization, and lack of buildings for purposes other than dwelling. Type B cultures, on the other hand, were more complex and were characterized by a cash economy, division of labor, some class or caste hierarchy, specialized buildings, and a centralized political organization (Barnouw, 1973).

Because of the standardized and detailed methodology employed in the Six Cultures project, it has produced some of the most useful culture and personality studies. Research using Whiting's approach has continued in other cultures. Further, the material has proved fruitful for additional analysis and speculation about the applications of some of the findings to problems in American society. For example, the influences that produce the typical male aggressive-hostile personality

among the Gusii of East Africa have been compared to studies showing that the "macho" culture of lower-class American males was related to their growing up in predominantly female households, lacking effective male role models (Barnouw, 1973).

All of the approaches to personality formation discussed in the preceding pages have in common an emphasis on childhood experience as a determinant of adult personality. They also consider the accompanying role of culture in making certain possibilities available, restricting other opportunities, and generally providing the framework for the development of the individual. But childhood experiences, as some anthropologists have pointed out, can have a paradoxical relationship to adult personality. A society may raise its children in so permissive a manner as to "be ideal from a Freudian point of view" (Barnouw, 1973, p. 34) and yet wind up with neurotic, anxiety-ridden adults. Some would argue that we have seen this happening in postwar United States where permissive child-rearing practices apparently created an institutionalized counterculture that was, in its determination to undermine the establishment, exactly counter or against the previously prevailing cultural themes. Making a similar point, Wolfenstein (1955) has shown that the tension experienced by children in France under rigid behavioral restrictions and enforced hard work in school and other training for adulthood, nevertheless somehow produces adults with characteristic *joie de vivre*.

Altered States of Consciousness

Consider the following statements:

A Zuni woman remarks, "Sometimes when I have to paint a pot, I can't think what design to put on it. Then I go to bed thinking about it all the time. Then when I'd go to sleep, I dream about designs." (Bunzel, 1929/1953, p. 270)

The bandstand was only a foot high but when I went to step down it took me a year to find the floor, it seemed so far away. I was sailing through the clouds, flapping my free-wheeling wings, and leaving the stand was like stepping off into space. Twelve months later my foot struck solid ground with a jolt, but the other one stayed up there on those lovely clouds. . . .I was up in a plane, soaring around the sky, with a buzz-saw in my head. Up and around we went, saying nuts to Newton and all his fancy laws of gravitation (sic), but suddenly we went into a nosedive and I came down to earth, sock. . . .When I went back to the (band)stand I still heard all my music amplified, as though my ear was built right into the horn. (Mezzrow and Wolfe, 1946, pp. 71–77)

A Polar Eskimo can become a shaman only if he has received a call, which he recognizes when he sees or hears a spirit. He then undergoes certain supernatural experiences, receives his own familiar spirit and learns how to use it. His power as a shaman will come from this spirit or *tornguang,* which may be an animal or nature spirit or a human ghost. When healing the sick, the shaman speaks to his familiar spirit in a dialect unintelligible to onlookers, sings a spirit song, and dances about wildly. The shaman trembles, groans, and works himself into an ecstatic state during which the *tornguang* is commanded to recover the lost soul of the patient so that he will become well. (Murdock, 1934, p. 217)

These passages describe three different altered states of consciousness—dream, trance, and spirit possession, respectively. Different cultures deal with these experiences in different ways and attribute varying degrees of significance to them. The same behavior that in one cultural context is interpreted as conferring leadership ability may be seen elsewhere as abnormal. What is acceptable in an Eskimo shaman would indicate to people in our society a need for medical help. The drug-induced experience described in the second paragraph above was within the social norms of a cultural subgroup, American jazz musicians. Such hallucinations would be terrifying to the vast majority of other Americans.

Bourguignon (1972) has organized altered states of consciousness into a continuum with REM (Rapid Eye Movement) sleep during which dreams occur at one end and possession trance at the other end. Hallucination and vision trance fall at the midpoint. (See Figure 1.) Other altered states of consciousness occupy various positions on the same continuum. Daydreaming, for example, falls between sleep dreaming and trance. Glossolalia (or "speaking in tongues") approaches very near to possession. Altered states are frequently considered to be the work of forces or even beings outside one's self (Bourguignon, 1972). Culture provides the framework within which these states are experienced. For

Figure 1 Altered states of consciousness. (Adapted from Bourguignon, 1972, p. 424)

At a religious festival in Brazil, a woman is possessed by a spirit. Where possession is culturally sanctioned, it generally becomes a public performance. (Jacques Jangoux, Peter Arnold Photo Archives)

example, the Bagobo of Malaya believe they have two souls, a good or right-hand soul, and a bad or left-hand one. It is the left-hand soul that often leaves the human body and wanders about having adventures that are experienced as dreams or nightmares (L. W. Benedict, 1916/1953).

Possession, of course, is the ultimate altered state in which an individual is apparently taken over or inhabited by an external force. In traditional Jewish folklore, it is believed that a *dybbuk* (the soul of a dead person) can appropriate the body of a living person; in Christian belief, witches are said to be possessed by a devil. Ritual exorcism to get rid of the invading spirit is the prescribed solution to both of these cases of negative possession. Illness is often believed to be the result of possession by evil forces.

But ethnographically speaking, most examples of possession, as with the Eskimo shaman described above, are seen culturally as positive forces. They are believed to enable the one so possessed to deal with the supernatural forces that cause illness or some kind of social crisis. Modern Western societies view as psychopathological the behaviors associated with possession. It should be noted that where possession is culturally sanctioned, it becomes a public performance, as well as a ceremony. When it takes place, possession reinforces the cultural norms that prescribe it in the first place.

Trance, hallucination, or visionary states are a different kind of consciousness alteration, characterized by relatively inactive outward behavior and a great deal of internal activity. Such states are often experienced as the self looking on at the adventures of another self. Many peoples use a two-souls explanation for this, in which one soul is believed to part from the body temporarily; the remaining soul is an inactive observer. The person in trance may stare into space or go through normal activities in slow motion. The person in trance seems "spaced out," "not there," or to use the phrase spawned by the drug culture of the 1960s, "on a trip." Trances can be induced by suggestion, as is done in hypnotism; by a large variety of drugs; or by subjecting the body to severe stress.

Hallucinations can be auditory, visual, kinesthetic, or olfactory. The hallucinatory experience of "Mezz" Mezzrow described at the beginning of this section had several of these elements; it was induced by his first experience with marijuana. Use of natural plant substances to induce hallucinations is widespread; in the Americas, especially in Mexico, peyote and mescal have been widely used.

Among the Crow and other Plains Indians, visions are considered of prime importance. They are the source of songs and rituals; of designs to be painted on tepees or shields; of contents to put into a medicine bundle; of wealth, prestige, and success in warfare and hunting. Therefore visions are sought by all, but they do not come to everyone. Most try to bring them on by rites of self-torture intended to win the good will of the spirits (Murdock, 1934).

Even an ordinary dream can be induced, as the Zuni potter quoted at the beginning of this section would agree. So would the American woman who, about to begin psychotherapy, read an article about psychiatric uses of dream material. Concerned because she seldom dreamed, she fell asleep—and next morning was able to recall vividly a complex dream to present to her analyst.

Dreams occur to every human being (and to nonhuman animals as well). Research over the last two decades has established that sleep consists of repeated cycles composed of definite stages: light sleep, deep sleep, and REM (Rapid Eye Movement) sleep. It is during the REM stages of sleep that dreams occur; the eye movements observed in sleep laboratories signal that the sleeper is literally watching the events that constitute a dream. Dreams have always held great fascination and are often accorded significance. They are often considered to foretell the future or to reveal something hidden, such as the source of illness or the identity of a witch. Dreams are also believed to confer special powers on the dreamer.

Although anthropologists have often recorded dreams—in particular those dealing with religion or other aspects of supernatural power—few studies have been specifically directed to this subject. Since Freud, the studies that have been done have focused on psychoanalytic aspects of dreaming. Freud saw dreams as wish fulfillment, providing release for the individual who has consciously to restrict behavior during waking hours. He believed that the latent content, or the symbolic meaning, of the images and events experienced in the dream represent the real longings and needs of the subconscious. The latent content, unique for every dreamer, has to be interpreted in the context of the individual's psychic history.

The Iroquois have a very similar concept. They believe that the symbolic content of dreams must be translated by specialists who can see into "the depths of the soul."

One of the techniques employed by these Iroquois seers to uncover the latent meanings behind a dream was free association, a technique employed by psychiatrists today. . . . The Iroquois still pay attention to hints given in dreams when they have to choose a curing ceremony, select a friend, or join a particular association; they still bring their more vivid dreams to a clairvoyant, usually a woman, for interpretation. (Farb, 1968, pp. 103–104)

The actual content of dreams appears to be culturally determined. In several hundred dreams collected among the Hopi, the water serpent was a frequent motif. This serpent is a fertility figure and, as such, has obvious sexual import; but it is also a deity controlling social antibehavior including gossip, quarreling, physical aggression, and sexual misconduct (Eggan, 1966, pp. 260–261).

The cultural content of 149 dreams collected by Sharp from 43 men and 8 women of the Yir Yoront of Australia was analyzed by Schneider into four categories: sexual intercourse, aggression, death, and dreams of whites and white culture. In the dreams with sexual content, the sex partner of the male dreamer was usually from the group considered by the society as an appropriate source of mates. When this was not the case, the dreamed sexual activity was interrupted and "the magnitude of the interruption correlates with the strength of the prohibition of sexual relations" (Schneider & Sharp, 1969, p. 51). In the aggression dreams, the dreamer was the target of aggression in 56 percent of cases and the instigator in only 19 percent. The mother's brother and the dreamer's elder brother were usually the aggressors, in dreams as in real life. Death dreams and cultural contact dreams likewise reflected realistic situations. Bourguignon remarks that "the correspondence between cultural reality and the manifest content of these dreams, taken as a group, is striking" (Bourguignon, 1972, p. 407).

Cultural patterning of dreams is not alien to twentieth-century America. Many adults, for example, dream of being back in college and taking a test for which they did not prepare adequately; they vividly reexperience the anxiety of this stressful situation, which may reflect current feelings of anxiety or helplessness. The important point is that although dreams, trances, spirit possession, and other kinds of altered consciousness are highly individualistic experiences, they are shaped in a cultural context. They express certain social norms and are interpreted according to cultural values. In some cultures, as we shall see below, altered states have provided opportunities that may lead to social action and change.

Anthropologists are particularly interested in the relationships between culture and altered consciousness. What altered states of consciousness characterize a given society? Which individuals are likely to experience them? What use or interpretation are these experiences given? And what can cross-cultural comparisons of these phenomena add to our knowledge of human psychic and behavioral capacity? These are questions for further research and study.

The Individual and Culture Change

Every individual is born into a society with its characteristic designs for living, but everywhere these designs are subject to change. Among the agents of change are the actions of individuals. Every society contains people who deviate from the norm, but what is considered deviant behavior varies from one culture to another. Often it is the deviant who tries out new ideas, establishing a movement toward possible change in the designs of a particular culture.

Deviance frequently is rejected at first, but subsequent events may make the deviant acceptable. Noah, Moses, Jonah, Jesus, and Joan of Arc are all examples within the Judaeo-Christian tradition of visionaries (literally) whose experiences led them to undertake missions with both spiritual and pragmatic components. All of these prophets were at first seen as deviants, scorned and "without honor in their own land." Eventually they were accepted in a leadership capacity by significant numbers of their fellows (and/or posterity). However, some deviants are so charismatic, and make their appearance on the scene at a moment so crucial in the life of their society, that they capture the imagination of followers. These leaders serve as the focus of social movements aimed at promoting change in the social or cultural system. Jesus and Moses, for example, after initial setbacks, were able to influence people on a significant scale through their charismatic leadership. Mohammed is another example of how a prophetic leader changed the direction of social life to a significant extent.

A more recent example of the role of an individual who contributed to culture change is Wovoka, a Paiute from Nevada who became known as the Indian Messiah. In the 1880s, his message of peaceful response and even submission to white domination promised the eventual resurrection of all Indian people, who would then live on the earth in peace, following their old ways of life. Wovoka, while recovering from an illness, had had a revelation vision during an eclipse:

When the sun died, I went up to heaven and saw God and all the people who had died a long time ago. God told me to come back and tell my people they must be good and love one another, and not fight, or steal, or lie. He gave me this dance to give to my people. (Mooney, 1892/1953, p. 412)

The Ghost Dance, accompanied by specific songs, was to be performed 5 nights in a row every 6 weeks. Other tribes adapted Wovoka's teachings, and the movement spread across the Plains. The Indians came to believe that the white ghost shirts they wore during the dance would make them impervious to gunfire. Performed in a frenzied trance, the dance spread from reservation to reservation. White authorities became concerned. In December of 1890, Sioux adherents of the movement, with their leader Sitting Bull, were massacred at Wounded Knee, South Dakota. This massacre effectively halted Indian resistance for almost a century, but it has served as a rallying point for Indian activism in the 1970s.

Further discussion of the role of individual leadership in social movements will be discussed in the chapter on politics and leadership. The point we want to stress here is that individuals can change the direction of social life, and prophetic leaders often do so through use of dreams and other forms of altered states of consciousness.

As we stated at the beginning of the chapter, no individual can experience the total designs for living found in a culture. Furthermore, an individual can recognize expressions of these designs by observing the experiences of others, even though he or she may not experience them directly. (The designs themselves, however, are held largely at an unconscious level.) As we have seen, though, the individual can have an influence on the construction of new designs or the reformulation of old ones. It is the individual that anthropologists deal with most frequently in the field. And it is individual behaviors that provide the basic raw material for the initial inferences that lead to statements about a given cultural system.

Summary

1. Every individual is born into a culture whose preexisting designs for living are communicated from one generation to another. No individual operates with every one of a culture's designs, but most individuals understand their own cultural system sufficiently to function within it. The relationship between individuals and the larger social groups of which they form a part is the concern of psychological anthropology, known traditionally as the study of culture and personality.

2. *Personality* may be thought of as the organized response patterns within every human being. These patterns determine the behaviors of the individual in various life situations, and within each individual are more or less consistent with each other throughout life.

3. Culture is a major factor in the forma-

tion of personality, but it is not by any means the only one. Among other influences are human physical factors; the environment; and personal experiences unique to each individual.

4. The *conflict theory* of personality formation, formulated by Freud, states that personality is formed as a result of constant conflict between the desires of the individual and the constraints imposed by society. *Fulfillment theory* holds that all beings strive for optimal self-realization and that culture provides the framework within which potential can be attained. *Consistency theory* sees personality formation as a lifelong process in which new information must be integrated into the world view accumulated through prior experience. *Cognitive dissonance* refers to the situation in which an individual's outlook comes up against an inconsistent set of experiences. The inability to integrate such experiences into one's life may result in *culture shock.* The approach of consistency theory is most useful in anthropological contexts, although the other two have validity also.

5. *Socialization* and *enculturation* are terms that, with slight shadings of meaning, describe the processes whereby an individual becomes a functioning member of a specific society.

6. *Role theory,* which came out of the work of George Herbert Mead, showed that children's concepts of self develop concurrently with their growing understanding of society. The child is first influenced by *significant others,* those people who interact most intimately with the child. The child soon learns that the larger society, which becomes a *generalized other,* expects much the same things as did the intimate agents originally. Children learn the social roles of their society by observing *role models* in areas of age, sex, and occupation.

7. The earliest years of life are generally considered to be crucial for personality formation; this belief is known as *childhood determinism.* Studies by Margaret Mead, Cora Du Bois, and others have contributed to our understanding of the interactions of culture and the growing child. Mead, for example, found that culture was more influential than biology in the development of sex role behavior.

8. *Basic personality structure* was postulated by Kardiner as the shared personality tendencies common to members of a given culture. Basic personality is shaped by *primary institutions* and is expressed in *secondary institutions.* Du Bois's concept of *modal personality* derived from the frequency with which specific traits appeared in individuals of a given culture, as determined by projective psychological tests in addition to ethnographic research.

9. National character studies during World War II were primarily concerned with modern nations. They developed techniques using interviews and cultural materials such as history, art, films, and literature for analyzing "culture at a distance." Benedict's classic study of Japan, derived from this methodology, approaches national character as cultural character and notes the association of culture patterns or configurations with patterns of individual personality traits.

10. The Six Cultures Project was a culture and personality study using standardized and detailed methodology for observation of various cultures. Anthropologists engaged in the study looked for cross-cultural correlations among child-rearing practices, childhood experiences, and cultural institutions. They found, among other things, relationships between subsistence method and child behavior and between family type and child behavior.

11. Altered states of consciousness, such as dreams, trance, hallucination, and spirit possession are highly individual experiences regarded differently in different cultures, and may be accorded great significance. Analysis

of dreams indicates that actual dream content appears to be culturally patterned.

12. The behavior that in one cultural context is interpreted as conferring leadership ability may be seen elsewhere as abnormal. One can become an agent of social change, sometimes as a result of an altered state of consciousness, often through some degree of deviance. Often looked at as "prophets without honor," deviants may still rise to positions of leadership through personal charisma, the force of events, or both.

PART TWO

Cultural Variation

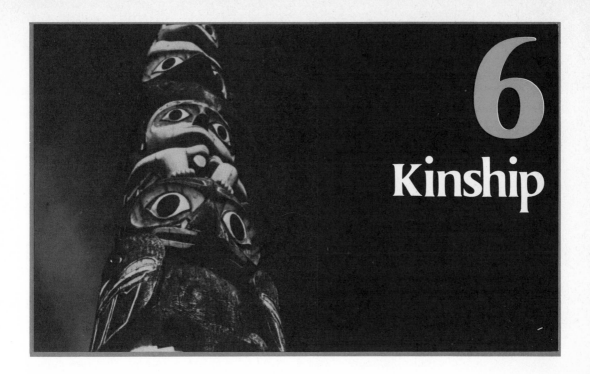

6 Kinship

THE preceding chapter was concerned with the relationships between the individual and culture. In this chapter our focus shifts to social activities and the formation of social groups. In societies usually studied by anthropologists, kinship is often the major organizing principle for social grouping. *Kinship* refers solely to the relationships based on descent and marriage. Kin, or relatives, are of two types: *consanguineous* kin, individuals who are thought to be biologically related by "blood," and *affinal* kin, individuals who are related legally through marriage. The study of kinship identifies and describes the relationships that individuals have with consanguineal and affinal kin and the social systems that are built around these relationships.

Kinship, marriage, and *family*—terms that we will be using in this chapter and the next—are part of everyone's daily experience.

Therefore, we might think that we know exactly what the terms mean and that the issues involved are quite simple. This is not the case, however. Some of the most complex and most debated issues in anthropology lie in the realm of kinship. Careful analysis of a variety of kinship systems, including our own, reveals that kinship is a remarkably intricate invention with widely different solutions to common biological givens.

Kinship has two essential implications for all individuals. First, it is one of several basic attachments that all people have, a fundamental tie. As Geertz (1963) puts it: "One is bound to one's kinsmen . . . as the result not merely of personal affection, practical necessity, common interest, or incurred obligation, but at least in great part by virtue of some unaccountable absolute import attributed to the very tie itself" (p. 109). Second, kinship permeates the social life of most peoples in a number of ways. In any society, individuals assume a variety of social roles. A man, for example, may be son, husband, father, landowner, provider, religious observer, and political supporter. Although he may not act in all these roles at any one moment, he may assume a number of them in the course of a single day. Kinship is the idiom by which many people, particularly in small-scale, traditional societies, comprehend these roles and activities. Gluckman (1962) refers to this overlapping of roles as "muliplex" relationships. He points out that when individuals interact intensively in a variety of roles, each of their actions takes on a larger moral significance. That is, the moral judgment that is applied to a man who is negligent in his work as cultivator may be applied not only to his roles as husband and father, sibling and son, but to his political role in the social group as well. On the other hand, if he quarrels with his immediate kin, they may fail to cooperate with him economically and politically. Thus,

every activity is charged with complex moral evaluations, and defaults strike not at isolated roles but at the integral relations which contain many roles. (Gluckman 1962, pp. 28–29)

Kinship is, of course, a construct, a cultural artifact created in every human society. But because kinship touches upon many areas of social life, it is an artifact that primarily shapes people, rather than one that is shaped *by* them. Although kinship relations and even the rules on which they are based may be consciously challenged by an individual or group, these relations generally involve understandings and ideals that act on the life of the individual rather than vice versa. Kinship relations are, as we have said, some of the most basic attachments an individual has in any society, traditional or otherwise. For this reason, kinship relations are generally unquestioned and unquestionable.

The Atom of Kinship

Any discussion of kinship naturally considers the family. Contrary to what we might think, the type of family with which we are most familiar—the *conjugal* (or *nuclear*) *family,* consisting of two mates of opposite sex and their offspring—is not a universal arrangement.

Until early in the twentieth century, it was widely held that the conjugal family structure was a "higher" form of family, since it was (and still is) characteristic of our civilization. It was believed that "simpler" peoples had family forms that were holdovers from an earlier stage in human evolution. Forms different from the conjugal family were pointed to as remnants of an earlier type of social organization. As anthropologists have accumulated more information on kinship, they have found that the conjugal family also exists among such technologically and economically simple groups as the Bushmen of South Africa and the peoples of the Andaman Islands (southwest of Burma), and of Tierra del Fuego (off the southern tip of South America). All of these groups are seminomadic bands, having minimal technology and little or no political organization. Thus, the conjugal family appears at various levels of civilization, in the most primitive hunting-and-gathering bands as well as in the most modern industrial states.

In most societies of intermediate complexity, family arrangements of other types are common. Among the Nayar of the Malabar Coast of India, for example, adult males at one time comprised a warrior caste living for the most part at a distance from their native community. Adult women, belonging to a different caste, were married in a symbolic ceremony to these men. Once married, a woman would leave the village of her husband and return to the home of her mother, where numerous lovers could freely visit her. Any resulting children belonged to the mother and her family line. This arrangement permitted adult males to perform their military functions without interruption. Authority over the family, including land tenure, was exercised by the woman's brothers.

This family arrangement of the Nayar was highly specialized and adapted to a peculiar situation, but it represents an extreme example of arrangements that are more common than might be expected. In the United States at present there are a number of situations in which nonconjugal family arrangements occur: single parenthood; divorced parents; parents separated for professional purposes. But in all of these cases there usually is at least an occasional affiliation of a "father" with the mother-child unit. The Nayar, in establishing a situation in which the father was consistently absent, represent a rare and extreme instance. Nevertheless, male authority figures were present in the form of the woman's brothers.

A very different nonconjugal family arrangement was found among the Toda of Tibet and Nepal. Among the Toda, polyandry (the marriage of a woman to more than one husband at one time) was a common practice. Several men, usually brothers, shared one wife. Within this system, the legal father of the children was considered to be the man who participated in a special ceremony with the woman upon her first pregnancy. Although he might not have been the biological father of any of her children, he continued as their legal father until one of her other husbands replaced him by participating in the same ceremony with her.

Toda polyandry required a greater number of males than females, a situation which was maintained by means of female infanticide. After the British colonial administration interfered with this practice by making it illegal, the Toda experienced a female population boom. To maintain their polyandrous family

organization, a group of brothers, instead of sharing one wife between them, married a group of sisters—an apparently genuine case of group marriage, but one that has followed rather than preceded other marriage forms.

One must also consider those family arrangements at the other extreme, in which men have a high degree of involvement by playing continuous and significant roles in the formation of family groups. Throughout most of Western Europe of a century or two ago, for instance, the major social unit was a family in which land ownership and all economic and parental authority was exercised by the oldest male or set of males. This grouping consisted of the oldest male (or set of brothers from the senior generation) and his wife (or their wives), the married sons with their wives, all the unmarried daughters, and the young

The minimum social unit is the mother-child relationship, to which various combinations of individuals may be added to form families.
(Picatti, Jeroboam)

dependent children of all the married pairs. This form is often called the *extended* (or *joint*) *family*. It would be misleading to think of these larger groups merely as a series of conjugal families. To do so would ignore the very reasons for the formation of such an extended group.

Thus, it is increasingly clear that the irreducible minimum social unit, or atom of kinship as Lévi-Strauss (1963) calls it, is the mother-child relationship. Everywhere, this primary bond forms the basis of kinship. To the mother-child unit, as we have seen, a number of individuals may be added in a variety of combinations to make a family. Sometimes these additions are extended to include three or more generations within a single household. Such combinations have led anthropologists to conclude that, beyond the mother-child bond, kinship has little to do with the facts of biology and that it is, first and foremost, a cultural construct.

Thus the study of kinship is concerned with the familial *relations* that cultures add to the primary mother-child unit, and not with the *kinds* of families per se.

Forms of Kinship Extension

Although the mother-child relationship is the atom of kinship, nowhere and at no time has it stood alone. In every society other kin relationships are grafted onto it. Recruitment of additional kin is necessary in order for the basic unit to function effectively as a domestic unit. Ways must also be devised to transmit property and other functionally valuable rights (such as names and occupations) from one generation to the next. This is done by *descent* —the principle which links one generation to another in a systematized manner. In various descent systems, certain links are stressed whereas other links are ignored.

Kinship relationships are commonly illustrated by means of diagrams such as that shown in Figure 1. Ego is the person who serves as the point of reference for the diagram; the square representing Ego means that Ego's gender is unspecified. Where gender is specified, triangles designate males and circles represent females. A generally accepted notation of kinship terminology consists of the following abbreviations:

Ego: the person who is the point of reference for the diagram
Fa: father
Mo: mother
Br: brother
Si: sister
Hu: husband
Wi: wife
So: son
Da: daughter

A group of kin related by common descent —by certain specified rights and obligations across generations—is called a *descent group*. A descent group may share a name, jointly own property, and participate together in economic and other social activities. In terms of defining who is and who is not a member of a descent group, one must consider the rules of membership as they are defined within the society. These rules include or exclude people on the basis of genealogical distance, gender, and whether the relationship occurs through marriage or through parentage.

Unilineal Descent

The most common rule of descent— *unilineal descent*—traces relations through one line of parentage, either the father's or the mother's line. Unilineal descent is termed *patrilineal* (or *agnatic*) when links through males are recognized; it is called *matrilineal* (or *uterine*) when links through females are counted. In theory, unilineal descent is a

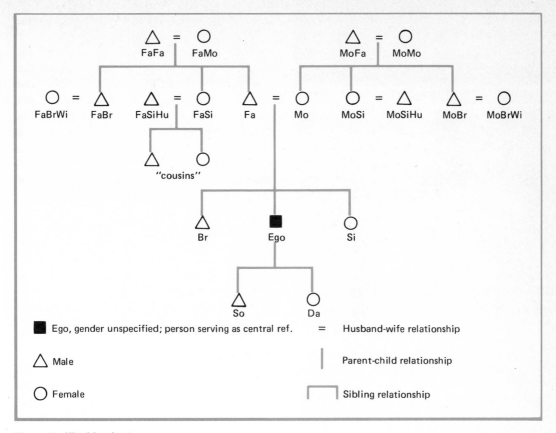

Ego, gender unspecified; person serving as central ref.   =   Husband-wife relationship

△ Male | Parent-child relationship

○ Female   ⌐⌐   Sibling relationship

Figure 1 Kinship chart

"neat" concept. It is easy to determine who is and who is not a member of one's descent group, since the individuals concerned are clearly specified, generally by common names. Anthropologists recognize various sorts of unilineal descent groups.

Lineage and Clan. The criterion for membership in a descent group may be known and demonstrable relationships between individuals; such a group is called a *lineage*. When the relationships between the members of a descent group cannot be demonstrated and are simply assumed, the group is called a *clan*. The members of lineages generally trace their descent to a common ancestor who is known to have lived a number of generations back. The members of clans, on the other hand, frequently trace their descent to an ancestor who is thought to have lived at some time in the distant past and thus lies at a much greater genealogical distance. Clans sometimes claim a symbolic association with a plant or animal. This symbol or emblem—called a *totem*—is considered a sacred object to the group. It cannot be killed or eaten except under special circumstances. Further, the totem identifies who is and who is not a member of the clan. If the totem of your group were Fox, you would know right away that individuals whose totems were Eagle, Horse, and Snake were not members of your clan. The totem also identifies whom one may or may not marry, as well as serves as a symbol and focus for the group. Because both lineages and clans trace descent to a common ancestor, they are termed *ancestor-focused* groups. Anthropologists point out, in examining these groups, that they exist independently of their individual members and that they therefore continue in perpetuity, since they do not depend on the life spans of individuals.

Phratry. Sometimes a clan subdivides over a period of time, with each segment still claiming descent from the original common ancestor. The several clans that make the claim of common descent are together known as a *phratry.*

Moieties. Sometimes a society as a whole is subdivided into two groups for purposes of exchanging women through marriage. Each of these groups consists of a number of other large groups, either clans or phratries. These dual groups are called *moieties.* Among the Miwok Indians of Central California, for example, every lineage belongs to one of the two moieties, Land or Water (Gifford, 1926). See Figure 2 for an illustration of a society divided into lineages, clans, phratries, and moieties.

Patrilineal Descent. *Patrilineal descent* traces ancestry through the male line. A patrilineage, then, consists of a man (the founder); his sons and daughters; his sons' sons and daughters; his grandsons' sons and daughters; his great-grandsons' sons and daughters; and so on. Women such as the founder's daughters and the founder's sons' daughters, and so on are part of the patrilineage. But these women cannot pass on their rights and duties within their lineage to their offspring. These rights and duties can only be transmitted through males in the line. A simplified example of patrilineal descent is illustrated in Figure 3.

In patrilineal descent systems, relations of

Figure 2 Subdivision of a society into various unilineal descent groups

Figure 3 Patrilineal descent. The solid color indicates those members of the patrilineage through whom descent passes. The stripe of color indicates individuals who are members of the patrilineage but who cannot pass on the descent affiliation.

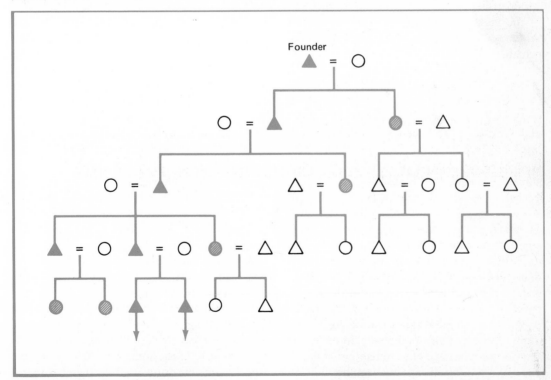

descent, authority, and residence reinforce one another. Among the Yoruba of Western Nigeria, for example, social order depends on the integration of political, economic, and religious activities through the system of patrilineages, known as *idiles*. The oldest male member of an *idile* is its acknowledged head. He exercises religious and political authority over his lineage mates. Female members of the lineage must marry men from *idiles* other than their own, and invariably they move to the communities of their husbands. Most of the male members of an *idile* reside in a single community with their wives. Members of other lineages may reside in that community as well, although in lesser numbers. But for all practical purposes—political, economic, and religious—a community is identified with its predominant *idile* (Schwab, 1955). The pattern of residence in which a married couple lives near or with the husband's family is called *patrilocal*. It usually goes hand in hand with patrilineal descent, ensuring that the men of the lineage will be a physically close-knit group so as to maintain their control over valuable resources.

In patrilineal systems, marriage is of considerable importance. In matrilineages, as we shall see, marriage is less significant, and a casual male attachment may accomplish the biological purpose. The women who marry into a patrilineage are important to the system, since they produce the heirs that allow the lineage to perpetuate itself. A patrilineage is exogamous, that is, the men choose as wives women born into other lineages. They may not impregnate the females in their own lineage to provide heirs. But the women from other lineages bring with them more than their capacity to bear children. They bring rights and privileges held in their own patrilineages; the claims they are able to make on the basis of these rights can be significant in a number of fields of activity. In many instances, the marriage of a woman into a man's lineage creates an alliance between her lineage

and that of her husband. Often, too, the woman's children will, by virtue of the link with their mother's lineage, have access to its resources and other assets.

Segmentation of the Patrilineage. As generations pass, the patrilineage expands. It may acquire so many members that it outgrows the resources available to it. When this happens, some of the members must seek other resources and move to another location, sometimes traveling long distances. The patrilineage then subdivides. One group splits off from the original lineage and moves elsewhere. Or, after the death of the father, who served as a unifying factor, the sons sometimes separate from the group or from each other to head subgroups of their own. The subdivision of a clan or lineage into subgroups is known as *segmentation.* Large descent groups, whether lineages or clans, are candidates for segmentation.

Segmentation can be compared to the branching of a tree. The original lineage or clan is the main stem or trunk. Sublineages, created as segmentation is repeated over a period of time, form the branches, twigs, and even leaves (Fox, 1967, p. 12). In a later chapter we will review the political implications of segmentation; here we examine the various mechanisms by which it takes place.

To return to the Yoruba, a male may leave his *idile* to become the founder of a new segment. Likewise, any of his male descendants may create yet other groups once the demands and claims of its members cannot be met. But the members of all these segments continue to recognize their descent from a common male ancestor and can trace their genealogy back to the original lineage. Due to segmentation, an *idile* can consist of as few as 15 members or more than 500 (Schwab, 1955).

If segmentation results in a permanent break between two or more lineage segments, the process is known as *fission.* Fission would occur if each of the sons, with their wives and descendants, went off on their own to begin a

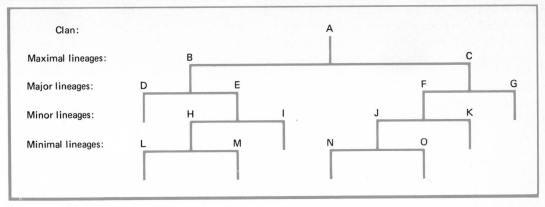

Figure 4 Clan segmentation. Adapted from E. E. Evans-Pritchard, The Nuer of the Southern Sudan, p. 285, in M. Fortes and E. E. Evans-Pritchard, *African Political Systems.* Oxford University Press, 1970.

new sublineage. Among the Nuer of the southern Sudan, for instance, the primary political structure centers on the clan. Each clan consists of an interrelated network of lineage segments and subsegments. Evans-Pritchard (1970) describes clans segmenting into maximal lineages which, in turn, segment into major lineages, each of which may subdivide further, forming minor lineages and each of these in turn into minimal lineages. Figure 4 illustrates such segmentation of a clan. Members of each group are loyal to their group against the members of other equivalent groups. Thus there may be competition among the maximal lineages of a single clan. Or hostility may erupt among members of the major lineages that segmented from a maximal line.

The process of recombination of segments also takes place at times. This recombination, called *fusion,* is usually temporary and occurs as a response to a specific need. For certain purposes, such as seeking vengeance for a homocide, several minimal lineages may find it necessary to consider themselves as one minor lineage. Or two minor lineages may combine and regard themselves as the major lineage from which they sprung. In certain circumstances, this process may repeat back up

again to the level of the clan (Evans-Pritchard, 1970).

Among the Nuer, the fission of larger kin-groups into lesser segments occurs constantly. But, in practical terms, the fusion of all groups into larger groupings from which they sprung may also operate. Both fission and fusion operate most markedly in groupings where there is a high degree of correspondence between authority, residence, and descent relationships. As we shall now see, they therefore occur more often in patrilineal than in matrilineal systems.

Matrilineal Descent. *Matrilineal descent* traces ancestry through the female line. A matrilineage consists of a woman (the foundress); her sons and daughters; her daughters' sons and daughters; her granddaughters' sons and daughters; her great-granddaughters' sons and daughters; and so on. It is only through the foundress's female offspring that the rights and duties of the matrilineage can be passed on to the next generation. Figure 5 illustrates matrilineal descent.

In matrilineal systems, women must mate with men from other groups. Although inheritance rights are transferred through females, authority is vested in the males in many in-

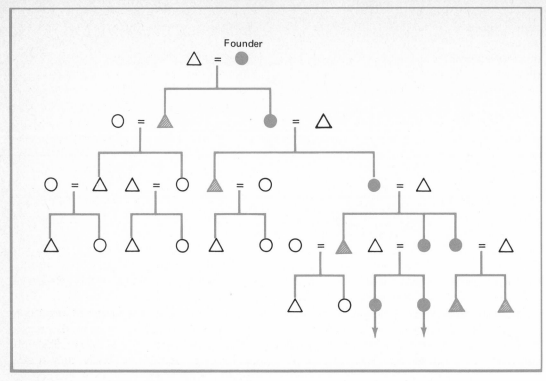

Figure 5 Matrilineal descent. The solid color indicates those members of the matrilineage through whom descent passes. The stripe of color indicates individuals who are members of the matrilineage but who cannot pass on the descent affiliation.

stances, giving brothers control over their sisters' children. They provide competition to any relationship she may have with a husband, who is an outsider in her family group (when he is in it at all). The crucial relationships in a matrilineal system are between mother and daughter, brother and sister, and mother's brother and sister's son. Consequently, the conjugal relationship is relatively unimportant, and the matrilineage has little need for the social roles of husband or father. Thus the biologically necessary male role may be fulfilled as casually as is socially possible.

Matrilineal and patrilineal descent are not simply opposites. Whereas patrilineal descent generally combines residence and authority with the descent group, this patterning of relations is seldom effected in a matrilineal system. Authority relations usually pose a problem. Matrilineal organization does not necessarily mean high status for women within the matrilineage. Although primary rights and duties are transferred through the female line, authority is often vested in the males of the matrilineage. Problems arise as a result of the discrepancy between relations of residence and descent, on the one hand, and authority relations on the other.

Matrilineages, which are exogamous, must establish relationships with men from outside in order to reproduce. But the rule of descent keeps rights and duties out of the hands of the males marrying into the group. In matrilineal systems, then, men generally retain power and control within the lineage of their mothers and sisters, but inheritance passes to their sisters' sons. Consequently, it is the relationship between a man and his sisters' sons on which we must focus. There are three possible solutions to the problem of male control in a matrilineal system (Fox, 1967). The first and most complete solution is represented by the Nayar.

The Nayar Solution. Among the Nayar, as we have already seen, there were at one time no significant marital alliances, nor did significant father-child interaction take place. Hence, the men of the matrilineage had no divided loyalties. The family home (or *taravad*) was the center of the matrilineage. Nayar brothers returned to it after their military service. The women remained there, except for the brief duration of their symbolic marriages to men of another caste and village, and their children lived there with them. This residence pattern is called *natolocal;* that is, members reside in the houses in which they were born. Within the *taravad,* the eldest brother was the authority figure. He directed the other male members of the group in working the land and tending the livestock which were the lineage's property. On occasion, population pressure within the *taravad* led to segmentation. However, the sublineages maintained close relationships and shared in religious ceremonies.

The Navaho Solution. The second solution is represented by the Navaho. In Navaho society, a man went to live with his wife and her matrilineal relatives after marriage. This pattern of residence is called *matrilocal.* The man's own property and powers remained in the matrilineage of his mother and sisters and sisters' children. The senior brother was the male head of the matrilineage, and the children of his sisters were his heirs. In such an arrangement, marriage tends to be a weak institution, and a woman is easily able to divorce a husband who is no longer wanted. In the case of Navaho divorce, the man simply returned to his matrilineal home (the home of his mother or his sisters). Here the relationship between brothers and sisters was crucial, and it was likely to come into conflict with the relationship between the sisters and their husbands.

The matrilocal solution of the Navaho maintains the unity of the females of the lineage. But it does not solve the problem of male control, because the men of the matrilineage are scattered. Most matrilineal descent groups are in fact matrilocal, and this arrangement can work fairly well, with two provisos. First, the matrilocal units should be close geographically so that the men can commute readily between their homes and wives and the homes of their sisters and maternal nephews. Second, the lineage should be relatively weak, with few specific functions to perform and with the ownership of property vested in its women, while men engage in hunting and warfare (Fox, 1967, pp. 103–104). If the property and political rights of the matrilineage become significant, the men of the matrilineage need a more structured connection to the source of the family's power. This leads to the third solution, as exemplified by the Trobriand Islanders.

The Trobriand Solution. In the Trobriand Islands in the Pacific, upon marriage a woman goes to live with her husband, whose home is in the village of his own matrilineage. A village centers around the men of the matrilineage—the mother's brothers and sisters' sons —since the mothers, sisters, and daughters of the matrilineage live in the villages of their husbands' families. When a son reaches puberty, he goes back to the village of his mother's brother. This combination of residence with the husband's family (*virilocal residence*) and residence with the uncle (*avunculocal residence*) results in a community that consists of all males who are matrilineally related along with their wives and dependent children.

The Trobrianders believe that a woman's husband is not an equal procreative partner but is simply the "opener of the way" for the child, whom the woman conceives in a "spiritual" manner (Malinowski, 1929). Whereas the Nayar eliminate the father altogether, the Trobrianders retain him but minimize his biological role. Both explanations, however, serve to reinforce the matrilineal descent ideology in the respective societies.

An avunculocal solution, or the viriavunculocal combination of the Trobrianders, keeps the men of the matrilineage together in order to exercise authority and to control property. But at the same time the solution creates a situation in which a man loses his sisters and his own children as well. Malinowski (1929) reported that as a result there was frequent hostility between a man and his wife's brother. The matrilineal problem is not completely solved by the avunculocal solution. There is inevitable conflict between the role of a man in the matrilineage and the role of a man with his wife and children. As Fox puts it,

On the one hand [the man] is a husband and father and wants to have his wife around, while on the other hand he is a maternal uncle with lineage responsibilities to his maternal nephews and hence needs to keep some control over them and their mother, his sister. (1967, p. 108)

To summarize, matrilineal systems can take one of several possible forms. In one form, emphasis is placed on the relationships between blood-related kin in the lineage —mother-daughter, brother-sister, mother's brother-sister's son. The men (sons and brothers) maintain their control over the group's affairs and retain authority. In another form the mother-daughter-sister relationships are emphasized by means of matrilocal residence. The women of the lineage are the property holders, and they provide lineage continuity, as their brothers commute between the home of their lineage and that of their wives. In still another form, the brother-sister-sister's son relationships are central. Avunculocal residence or some other mechanism provides the sister's brother with

control over his nephews. Male authority is a very real factor in all three of the solutions, although it is minimized in the second (the Navaho) form. In an avunculocal society, such as that of the Trobriand Islanders, female status is lowest.

Advantages of Unilineal Descent. In most societies, political and economic control is vested primarily, if not totally, in males. We have examined the problem that this creates in matrilineal systems, in which various arrangements are worked out to deal with the conflict between male authority and female line-of-inheritance. This problem does not exist in patrilineal systems in which relations of authority, residence, and descent are conveniently combined.

The members of a patrilineage have a different problem: they must secure females from outside the group in order to produce heirs. Consequently, the patrilineage must lose its own women—sisters and daughters— to other groups. It appears that as a compensation for the loss of their female kin, the men of the patrilineage have more complete rights over their children. In a patrilineal system, the father-son and brother-brother relationships are of prime importance, but a man's relationship to his wife cannot be ignored. In patrilineal systems, marriage is highly significant since only the acquisition of a wife or wives from outside the group makes possible the male heirs on which the system depends. As already indicated, marriage also serves to establish alliances between groups that exchange women. These alliances can prove useful during warfare or other times of difficulty.

The various complications of patrilineal and matrilineal systems are relatively minor in view of the overall efficiency of the unilineal descent principle. Where group membership is assigned to individuals through a single line, it is clear who is and who is not a member of the group. Where individuals belong to more than one group, problems such as divided

"I told you you'd regret getting all involved with this 'roots' business." (Bill Maul)

loyalties and conflicts of interest, or competitive claims on property or nonmaterial rights, are likely to crop up. As a way of transmitting rights from one generation to the next, both matrilineal and patrilineal systems provide for inheritance in as clear a manner as possible. Inheritance is restricted to specific categories of kin. Rights transmitted through kinship are attached not only to land and other forms of property, but also to other things such as game and fish, political and ritual offices, craft or other occupations, and cult membership.

Unilineal systems specify which rights are to be acquired through males and which through females. Although a system may be defined as either matrilineal or patrilineal, it does not mean that relationships through the other kinship line are ignored or unimportant. On the contrary, people seldom, if ever, follow one pattern exclusively in all aspects of their social life. They may follow varying modes of inheritance for such different aspects as group name, property, ritual rights, residence, and so on. One can tell whether a descent system is matrilineal or patrilineal by determining in which line the most important rights and duties are transmitted.

In virtually every unilineal descent system, however, certain secondary rights and duties, complementing the primary ones, pertain to kin in the other line of filiation. In a patrilineal system, then, one might be able to obtain access to a variety of resources and/or services from the relatives on one's mother's side (one's *matrilateral* relatives). Such access might determine survival during a period of drought, for instance. Then, one's matrilateral relatives, whose area of residence has not been affected to the same degree, could be a dependable source of sustenance. Or, in a matrilineal system, one's *patrilateral* kin (the relatives on one's father side) might provide assistance in time of emotional or political conflict.

In unilineal systems, then, one has affiliations to one's father's group *and* to one's mother's group.* Relationships through the parent who does not determine descent is called *complementary filiation.* In a patrilineal system, for example, one's complementary affiliation is to the mother's group. In unilineal systems, there are variations in what particular rights and duties are defined as being of primary importance for each group. The fact that one has affiliations with both father's and mother's kin introduces flexibility into any social system based on unilineal descent.

There is another way in which an individual might obtain access to resources and services not his or hers by right of descent, and that is through the claims of marriage, or *affinity.* Affinal relations usually set up exchanges of resources and services between the groups involved. These exchanges occur usually at the time the marriage is proposed, when it takes place, or when a child or children are born. Frequently, one can, through one's spouse, make additional claims in various areas of activity. It is generally assumed that what one may receive during one season will be returned in another if and when one's affinal kin are in need.

Double Descent. There is still another type of descent, called *double descent,* that uses a variation on the unilineal principle. Double descent differs from matrilineal and patrilineal descent by recognizing lines of descent

*Possible exceptions are the Nayar and any similar groups where there is, to all intents and purposes, no father.

through *both* males and females. The operation of double descent can best be understood in terms of the affiliation of an individual with his or her grandparents. In a unilineal system, an individual traces descent through only one of the four grandparents. In a matrilineal system, descent is traced through the mother's mother. In a patrilineal system, descent is traced through the father's father. In a system of double descent, the individual traces descent through both the mother's mother and the father's father (Murdock, 1940).

In a double descent system, each line of kin usually serves specifically different functions. Among the Ashanti of West Africa, for example, property and authority are inherited in the female line. The relationship between the mother's brother and her son is crucial, because it is the line of inheritance of crucial resources. The matrilineal group, generally the more important one in Ashanti life, also participates in an ancestor cult and performs various funerary and other rituals. At the same time, "spirit" is the primary inheritance through the male line. Residence among the Ashanti is patrilocal. Upon being married, a woman goes to live in the household of her husband's patrilineal extended family (Rattray, 1923). Thus both lines of descent are recognized culturally and are used for distinct purposes.

Elsewhere in Africa, the Herero, a southern Bantu people, have matrilineal kin groups that have primarily economic functions, alongside patrilineal groups that have primarily religious functions. Real property is inherited matrilineally, but access to sacred knowledge and resources is transmitted in the male line. Still another African example is provided by the Venda, who define descent, succession, and property inheritance patrilineally. The matrilineage is important in social and religious aspects of life, involving participation in an ancestor cult (Murdock, 1940).

Double descent has been described in other parts of the world as well. The Toda of southern India, the Aranda and other Central Australian tribes, and the Manus of Oceania all have both matrilineal and patrilineal desent groupings. With few exceptions, wherever double descent has been described, both patrilineal and matrilineal kin groups are exogamous. Property inheritance and succession are usually patrilineal, and residence is usually patrilocal (Murdock, 1940).

Parallel Descent. There is yet another possible form of unilineal descent—*parallel descent,* which is extremely rare. In parallel descent systems, males trace ancestry through males and females through females. Many anthropologists have considered this variation to be possible but, not having found a verified instance of it, they usually conclude that it does not exist. However, Jane Safer (1975) has recently described a parallel descent system as she observed it among the Saha, who live in the Santa Marta mountains near the Caribbean coast of Colombia, close to the Venezuelan border. Here, boys belong to the descent groups of their fathers, and girls to those of their mothers. These descent groups, called *sana* and named for certain animals, have both male and female members. The *sana* itself owns certain ritual property, such as songs and dances, and has an alleged place of origin to which members go to give offerings. Among the Saha both women and men may own property, which includes livestock, houses, and land. But the property of a wife is not merged with that of her husband. Males inherit from males, and females from females. All property is inherited within the *sana* except that, before death, a man with no sons or a woman with no daughters may elect to leave his or her property to a child of the opposite sex—and therefore of a different *sana*—rather than to his or her own same-sex sibling.

Cognatic Descent

Not to be confused with double descent is *cognatic descent,* a system in which the individual reckons his or her ancestry through lineal relatives of both sexes with little or no formal distinctions among them. This is the descent system used in our society. In this system, all four of Ego's grandparents count, as well as all eight great-grandparents, and so on as far back as one can go. In a cognatic system, all the descendants of the same ancestors are considered relatives as well, regardless of their sex. That is, the individual acknowledges a relationship to all of the descendants of his or her grandparents, great-grandparents, and so on—the uncles and aunts, great-uncles and great-aunts.

This nonexclusive mode of tracing descent seldom provides the clearcut access to rights, duties, and resources that a unilineal system can, due to the fact that any given individual belongs at the same time to a number of descent categories. The problem in cognatic descent is to find a means to include some individuals for purposes of mutual cooperation and benefit, while at the same time excluding others who are eligible. Rights to inheritable positions and property can be maintained and responsibilities can be assigned according to the cognatic principle of descent without the necessary formation of formal corporate groupings. Circumstances of life history (such as living closer to some kin than to others), as well as economic considerations or simple affection and attraction, may operate to include some eligible members in such transactions and to exclude others. At the same time, though, if the local situation demands it, formal groups as tightly organized and as efficient as any found in a unilineal system, can also be formed according to the cognatic principle.

The Kindred. The most commonly recognized form of kin grouping found in cognatic descent systems is that of the *kindred.* A kindred is composed of any group of consanguineal relatives without reference to either maternal or paternal line of descent. In our society, a kindred tends to be the group of relatives we

KINSHIP

might see with some frequency at family reunions, weddings, funerals, holiday celebrations, and so forth. The kindred consists of people closely related to oneself, rather than to an ancestor. Thus, a kindred is considered an *ego-focused group,* in that it begins with oneself and works outward. Membership in a kindred group is based on one's degree of relationship to a given individual. Some people, for example, belong to "cousins' clubs." These clubs may consist of first and second cousins of the founding individual, along with their spouses and children. The members of ego-focused kindred are linked to each other by relationship to the central member, but (except for full siblings) they are not necessarily related to each other.

There is a potential kindred centering on every person in a society, and every individual is also a possible member of a number of kindred centered around other relatives. One may receive birthday and holiday cards or gifts from members of one's kindred and will owe cards or gifts in the other kindreds of which he or she is a member. Since the kindred is an ego-focused group, it exists only for the life span of the individual at its center. It is not generally a corporate group in that it does not hold property or exclusive rights to be passed on from one generation to the next. Groups mobilized according to kindreds tend to be temporary and come together for specific ritual or ceremonial occasions such as weddings, funerals, christenings, and the like.

Much of the literature on cognatic descent groups has been generated from materials collected in the Pacific where examples of corporate cognatic groups seem to be clearly found. Fox (1967, p. 156) defines three kinds of cognatic descent groups: unrestricted, restricted, and pragmatically restricted. A group is *unrestricted* when all descendants, both male and female, of an acknowledged ancestor are included. Every individual will be a member of as many unrestricted groups as he or she has ancestors (Goodenough, 1957, p. 197). In a *restricted* descent group, all of the founder's descendants have a *right* to membership, but some limitation is placed on the ways in which they may claim this right. For example, they may be obliged to reside in the founder's territory or on his property in order to exercise their rights to membership in his descent group. Individuals thus are obligated to choose with which of several possible groups to reside. Once the individual has made a choice, his or her rights to other lands are surrendered. In a *pragmatically restricted* cognatic system, individuals retain rights of membership in all groups to which they are entitled to belong, even though they are affiliated for practical reasons with only one such group.

Kindreds are loosely organized groups of persons related to a central individual. They come together for ritual or ceremonial functions such as weddings, as has this group of Spanish gypsies. (Josef Koudelka, Magnum)

We must not lose sight of the fact that although cultural features are studied by anthropologists independently of one another, they *are* highly interrelated. Thus, the distinctions between different kinship patterns are not abstract or arbitrary. Rather, they have to do with property ownership and the economic-productive organization of the community, along with other factors. A lineage or other group will live on land it owns or is economically bound to in some way. Kinship and residence determine not only which individuals see each other daily but also who works alongside of whom and to what purpose.

One of the most complex kinship systems is found on Gilbert Island in the Pacific. There, five different types of kinship groupings, including three separate cognatic groups, may be found. All three of these groups are connected in some way to land. The multiple cognatic system of the Gilbert Islanders illustrates an adaptational advantage of such groups: flexibility in coping with inevitable demographic fluctuations. Where a unilineal descent group must inhabit a prescribed and limited territory, the population of the lineage may become too great to be supported by its land, or a lineage's membership may decrease. A run of female children would result in substantial loss of membership to a patrilineal group, for example. Or through good management or good fortune a lineage may acquire more land than its members can work efficiently. In a cognatic system, on the other hand, an individual will be a member of several groups and can claim rights elsewhere in response to land or population pressures. Under demographic pressures, a unilineal descent group that is also property-owning may be helpless because of its rigidly prescribed membership qualifications. A cognatic group can redistribute both land and population in a relatively rapid response to demographic pressure (Goodenough, 1957).

Many anthropologists believe that the need for a redistribution of property can lead to a restructuring of descent groups. In particular, patrilineal systems tend to become cognatic. Cognatic groupings frequently have, in fact, some patrilineal elements. There is a fairly universal tendency toward keeping the males of a family—the fathers, sons, and brothers—together for work, property ownership, defense, or other purposes. Thus, residence is frequently patrilocal even in a cognatic system.

Kinship Terminology

Thus far our discussion of kinship systems has focused on the ways in which people organize their relationships with kin and some of the social uses that kin groups can serve. We now turn our attention to kinship terminology, the terms that people use to classify or categorize their relatives.

At the outset, it must be understood that the set of kin terms provided by our culture is neither exhaustive nor universal. As we shall see, many other categories of relatives—and ways of establishing such categories—exist. The system of kin groupings with which we are familiar is in a minority position in the ethnographic world.

Kin everywhere are given names designating certain categories of relationship. A people specify the kinds of relatives it is possible to have in their society by classifying them into categories. By designating the categories of kin in a given society, the kinship terminology system maps the social universe of a people.

Kin terminologies seem to constitute a precise and self-contained set of data with which to work. As such, kinship terminology has for over a century provided anthropologists with a domain in which to apply their various theoretical points of view. Over the years, perhaps more controversies have raged over the analysis of kin terms than over any other aspect of the study of kinship.

As a topic for anthropological analysis, the significance of kinship terminology was recognized more than a century ago by the American ethnologist Lewis Henry Morgan. In the course of his pioneering fieldwork among the Iroquois of New York State, Morgan noticed the same word, *hanih,* was used for father and father's brother but not for mother's brother. He also noted that the word for mother and mother's sister was the same, but different from that for father's sister. This terminology was strikingly different from his own father-uncle, mother-aunt terminology, which does not distinguish between the brothers of father or mother, or between the sisters of father or mother. Morgan became more intrigued when he found a similar usage among the Ojibwa Indians. To learn about the kin terms used elsewhere, he devised a questionnaire which he sent out to hundreds of travelers, missionaries, and colonial administrators in all parts of the world. His analysis of the terminologies that were collected in this way was published in 1871 as *Systems of Consanguinity and Affinity in the Human Family*.

Approaches to Kinship Terminology

Over the years, different approaches have been taken in the analysis of kinship terminology. One approach is historical. It sees kin terms as a set of clues to relationships that have existed in the past, and then compares cultures in a given region in terms of the linguistic similarities in their terms. This historical approach is based on the premise that language is more resistant to change than are social institutions. Therefore, the words used to define kinship would be older than the customs of the period in which the terms are collected, and can thus tell something of past cultures.

The second approach is that of the functionalists. It is concerned with the ways in which kin terms relate to actual behaviors of individuals, and with the correlation of terminology with such social institutions as marriage, descent groups, and residence patterns.

A third approach is that of the cognitivists. This approach investigates kin terms as a set of classificatory categories organized on the basis of a limited number of distinctive features or components, such as age, gender, and generation. The cognitive anthropologist analyzes these components in an attempt to discover the underlying set of principles that a society uses to place individuals into particular categories. Analysis of distinctive features thus becomes a means of investigating cognitive processes by seeking to explain cultural categories.

Some anthropologists have questioned whether one should view kin terms as referring primarily to biological relationships or to social roles. For example, the Trobriand term *tama* refers to the father, father's brother, father's sister's son, and all male members of the father's matrilineage in the same generation as the father and in succeeding generations (Keesing, 1976). Does this mean that the individual cannot distinguish between his or her mother's husband and other male kin? Some early investigators believed so and built whole theories around the fact that some peoples seemed unable to distinguish among their fathers, uncles, and cousins. When we examine the *social* role of the individuals designated by the single word *tama,* though, it becomes clear that this word is used to distinguish a specific category of individual. Keesing (1967) suggests that it should really be translated as "domiciled man of my father's subclan hamlet" (p. 268). Similarly, the term *tabu* refers to all males and females of the grandparent or preceding generations; it also

CULTURAL VARIATION

refers to all females of the father's, the father's father's, or the mother's father's clans. *Tabu* is a reciprocal term like our word "cousin"; someone whom I describe with this term also uses it to describe me. Keesing suggests that, in the context of Trobriand life, those classified by the term *"tabu* are in fact classed together not because of some positive feature they share in common, but because . . . they are distant and marginal to [the individual]" (pp. 268–269). The term has a functional purpose as well: it indicates the category of persons from which a man may find a wife. In the matrilineal system of the Trobrianders, the term *tabu* identifies women who are outside the matrilineage and who, by the rules of exogamy, are therefore possible marriage partners.

The meaning of a society's kin terms must be understood in conjunction with an analysis of the society's social structure and institutional frameworks. It is one thing to call your mother, your mother's sisters, and your mother's brothers' daughters by the same term (which is done in the Omaha system, as we shall see below), but it is quite another thing to treat them similarly. The view of culture that we have been expressing in this book fits better with this emphasis upon group interactions and alliances than with a biological-genealogical orientation toward kinship terms. Emphasis on the social significance of kinship terminology is a relatively new development in anthropological studies. From the beginning, Morgan's breakdown of the data he had gathered focused on terminology as it described biological relationships.

Kinship Terminology Systems

Morgan divided the terminologies he collected into two categories, descriptive and classificatory. In a *descriptive* terminology system, only primary terms referring to what Morgan took to be direct biological relationships are used: terms such as father, mother, son, daughter, grandmother, grandfather, brother, and sister. Those people related in other ways are called by combinations of the primary terms: mother's brother, sister's son, and so on. A *classificatory* system uses one term to refer to a class of relatives in both ascending and descending generations. Thus, *lineal relatives* (those in a direct biological line, such as father or mother) may be included in the same term as *collateral relatives* (relatives such as father's brother or mother's sister who are not related in a direct biological line). The Iroquois use of one name for both father and father's brother is an example of a classificatory system.

The distinction between descriptive and classificatory is now seen as only one of a variety of kinship factors. Other factors that are considered in classifying kin terminology were identified by Kroeber in 1909. These include:

- *generation*—the difference between Ego's generation and that of the relative in question;
- *gender*—whether the person is male or female;
- *affinity*—whether the relationship is affinal (through marriage) or consanguineal (through direct biological lines);
- *bifurcation*—the incorporation of lineal and collateral relatives in one line but not the other (for instance, FaBr and Fa comprise one term that is distinct from MoBr);
- *polarity*—reciprocity, or whether the same terms are applied by the relative or group of relatives to the speaker, and vice versa.

Three subsidiary factors noted by Kroeber include relative age, speaker's gender, and decedence (whether the person through whom the relationship occurs is living or dead (Kroeber, 1909).

Working from the Human Relations Area Files at Yale University, Murdock classified the relationship terms used by 250 societies. He identified six distinct types of kinship terminology systems. They focus particularly on the ways in which cousins are distinguished. There are four possible kinds of cousins: the father's brother's child; the father's sister's child; the mother's brother's child; and the mother's sister's child. *Parallel cousins* are children of the same-sex siblings of one's parents. Thus the children of one's father's brother and one's mother's sister are parallel cousins. *Cross cousins* are children of the opposite-sex siblings of one's parents. Thus one's cross cousins are the children of one's father's sister and one's mother's brother.

The six kinship terminology systems identified are Eskimo, Hawaiian, Crow, Omaha, Iroquois, and Sudanese. They are named after societies that exhibit the systems most clearly.

Eskimo System. The Eskimo system of terminology is the one used in our own culture. (See Figure 6.) It centers on the nuclear family—father, mother, brothers, sisters. Unlike the other systems we will look at, no other relatives are referred to by the terms used for these family members. Descent in cultures that use Eskimo terminology is based on the cognatic principle. Since both sides of Ego's family are of equal importance, the terms used for sisters and brothers of mother and father are the same (aunt, uncle). Similarly, no distinction is made between cross cousins and parallel cousins; a single term is used to identify all cousins.

Hawaiian System. Of the six systems we will look at, the Hawaiian system of kinship terminology uses the fewest number of terms. (See Figure 7.) Relatives of the same sex in the same generation are referred to by the same term. Thus, father, father's brothers, and mother's brothers are grouped together, as are mother, mother's sisters, and father's sisters. Brothers and male cousins are denoted by a single term. Likewise, sisters and female cousins are called by one term.

Crow System. Crow kinship terminology is usually associated with matrilineal descent systems. Because the line of matrilineal descent is emphasized, matrilineal relatives are differentiated across generations. (See Figure 8.) In a matrilineal system, mother's brothers are likely to be Ego's most important relatives (other than mother and father) because they control the rights and privileges associated

Figure 6 Eskimo kinship terminology

Figure 7 Hawaiian kinship terminology

Figure 8 Crow kinship terminology

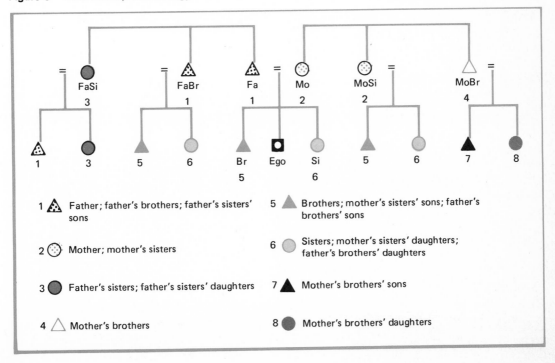

with the matrilineage. And because of the close connection with mother's brother, there is also likely to be a close connection between Ego and mother's brothers' children. Thus, there are unique terms for mother's brothers and for matrilineal cross cousins (mother's brothers' sons and daughters). Because they are of less importance, patrilineal relatives in the Crow system are grouped together across generations. That is, father, father's brothers, and father's sisters' sons are denoted by the same term. A single term also identifies father's sisters and father's sisters' daughters. Finally, notice that in the Crow system, mother's sisters are called by the same term as mother, and father's brothers are called by the same term as father. Consequently, the children of mother's sisters and of father's brothers (Ego's parallel cousins) are called by the same terms—"brother" and "sister"—as are used for the children of Ego's mother and father. In other words, parallel cousins are re-

ferred to in the same way as Ego's brothers and sisters.

Omaha System. The Omaha system of terminology is usually found in patrilineal descent systems. It is, therefore, the mirror image of the Crow system. (See Figure 9.) Patrilineal relatives are distinguished across generations. Separate terms identify father's sisters and father's sisters' sons and daughters. In the less important matrilineal group, mother, mother's sisters, and mother's brothers' daughters are grouped together under the same term. Likewise, mother's brothers and mother's brothers' sons are referred to by a single term. Again, parallel cousins are called by the same terms as those for Ego's brothers and sisters.

Iroquois System. The Iroquois system of kinship terminology is similar to the Crow and Omaha systems at the level of Ego's own generation. (See Figure 10.) As in the Crow and

Figure 9 Omaha kinship terminology

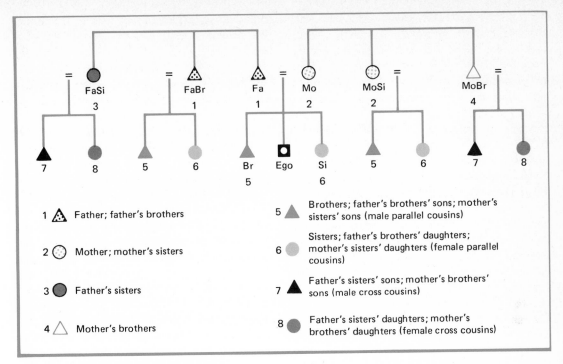

Figure 10 Iroquois kinship terminology

Omaha systems, mother and mother's sisters are denoted by the same term. Similarly, one term is used to identify father and father's brothers. The opposite-sex siblings of Ego's parents—that is, mother's brothers and father's sisters—are called by separate terms.

In both the Crow and Omaha systems, though, one set of cross cousins was grouped with the generation above. The difference in the Iroquois kinship terminology is that there are separate terms for female and for male parallel cousins. Usually the term for brother is applied to male parallel cousins. The term for sister usually is used to refer to female parallel cousins. Sometimes, though, separate terms exist for brothers, male parallel cousins, sisters, and female parallel cousins, as well as for male cross cousins and for female cross cousins.

Sudanese System. The Sudanese is the ultimate descriptive terminology. It differs from the other five systems we have looked at in that it has a different term for each of the 16 relatives on the chart. (See Figure 11.) No relatives are grouped with any others in their own or in a different generation. Societies with Sudanese terminology tend to have patrilineal descent systems, with a great deal of class stratification or political complexity, which the kinship terminology reflects.

These categories are useful pigeonholes in which to tuck away certain types of data. But they represent merely one attempt to organize the available information on kinship terminological systems, which is admittedly unwieldy. The categories should not be seen as a rigid typology into which all kinship systems can be placed. Indeed, the data do not always fit the categories neatly. Nevertheless, much of the literature on kinship refers to these systems, and for this reason they are presented here.

Murdock's typology represents a genealog-

Figure 11 Sudanese kinship terminology. (1-16: separate terms for each of the 16 relatives)

ical approach to kin terms. That is, the relationships and terminologies as he views them refer to kinds of genealogical connections rather than kinds of people. But what kinship is all about is the interactions among people. Kinship terminologies are of significance in cultural studies because they ultimately concern the relationships between individuals. As Bohannan reminds us, "kinship terms refer not merely (and often not even primarily) to the facts of biological relationship but also to the cultural image of them—that is, to the social facts of role expectations" (Bohannan, 1963, p. 67). All societies place kin into categories that are recognized and given names. Behind the categories and the terms for them, there is always a set of relationships which must be investigated.

The Significance of Kinship

It is not always easy to determine which type of descent category—matrilineal, patrilineal, or cognatic—describes the actual situation in a given culture. Under some circumstances, a patrilineal system can seem more similar to some cognatic systems than to other patrilineal systems. The way in which one classifies a kinship system depends not only on an analysis of the rights and obligations people have toward one another, but also on how the people understand the workings of their own system (Bender, 1970). We have spoken in previous chapters of the importance of considering the native's understanding of his or her society. With this in mind, we must not overlook the natives' consciousness of kinship and how it operates for them.

"Matrilineal" and "patrilineal" are categories devised by anthropologists to describe certain observed similarities in the patterning of kinship in various societies. Such categories exist for *our* convenience; we should not make the mistake of assuming that these categories necessarily have reality for the people whose groupings we so describe. A Navaho man, for instance, does not go around saying "I belong to a matrilineal, matrilocal society which creates certain problems for men." The typologies we have been discussing allow *us* to describe and compare kinship patterns. But peoples everywhere—with the exception of anthropologists and their students—simply *live* their kinship arrangements and do not try to categorize them for comparison with other kinship systems.

When it comes to kinship, people can be surprisingly pragmatic. For example, it is not unusual for people to misstate or try to alter their biological connections in order to take better advantage of a given situation. In our own society, numerous people have made claims about biological relationships in order to profit from someone's will. The economic and political demands of a particular time and place frequently lie behind such manipulations. Also important is the significance that people give to descent and kinship in their conversation and daily activities. Bender (1970), for instance, points out that the Ondo are not usually very conscious of their relationships with kin. The subject of kinship only comes up for them on occasions when people may derive some practical benefit from it. When this is the case, the reckoning of relationships is geared to the specific situation and may be ambiguous to some extent. A wider range of claims can be made on kin when the rights and duties defining their relationships are not well-defined. This lack of definition of kinship roles or of one's rights and duties can be beneficial in allowing for flexibility, both in making claims and in responding to them once they are made.

When it comes to determining how kinship fits into a people's scheme of things, anthropologists look, first, to what extent descent groups dominate their social structure. Second, they observe whether there is a correspondence between relations of descent and the patterning of residence and to what extent the membership of a descent group lives in a particular area. It usually takes quite a bit of probing to determine the functions of any particular kinship arrangement in the social organization of a people.

Summary

1. In the societies traditionally studied by anthropologists, kinship is often the major organizing principle for social grouping. *Kinship* refers to relationships based on marriage and descent. Kin acquired through marriage are *affinal* kin; biological or "blood" relatives are *consanguineal* kin.

2. The irreducible "atom of kinship" is the mother-child unit. To this unit, a number of individuals may be added in a variety of combinations. Our society typically adds a father, to form the *conjugal* (or *nuclear*) *family*. Some societies minimize the role of the father, even to the point of eliminating him altogether, as do the Nayar. Elsewhere, as with the Toda, sociological fatherhood may have absolutely no relationship to biological fatherhood. At the other extreme from the mother-child minimal family unit is the *extended* (or *joint*) *family*. The variety of observed family forms leads to the conclusion that beyond the mother-child bond, kinship is a cultural construct.

3. Recruitment to the basic mother-child unit is necessary in order for the kin group to perpetuate itself and to pass on rights and property. *Descent* rules recognize links between generations. In various descent systems, certain links are stressed whereas other links are ignored. A group of kin related by common descent is called a *descent group*.

4. *Unilineal descent* traces ancestry through either the male or the female line. Descent is *patrilineal* when men are the linked relatives and *matrilineal* when women are. Unilineal descent groups are exogamous —that is, their members must marry members of another group. There are several types of unilineal descent groups. *Lineages* are groups in which descent may be traced to known and demonstrable relationships between individuals. *Clans* are descent groups in which descent cannot be demonstrated and is simply assumed. Clans frequently trace descent to a mythological figure and often claim symbolic association with a *totem*. A *phratry* consists of the several descent groups that claim common descent from a particular clan or lineage. *Moieties* are the two groups into

which a society may divide, each consisting of a number of kin groupings.

5. Patrilineal descent is relatively uncomplicated; it provides a tidy package of descent, authority, and residence for male members of the patrilineage. As a patrilineage expands, it may outgrow its resources and thus have to segment into smaller groups. *Fission* refers to a permanent break between lineage segments. *Fusion* describes the temporary recombination of segments in reaction to a specific need.

6. Matrilineal descent creates a problem regarding the relationship of men to the lineage. Although inheritance takes place through the female line, authority in a matrilineage tends to rest with a woman's brothers. The Nayar, the Navaho, and the Trobriand Islanders each have separate solutions to the problems of male control in a matrilineal system.

7. All unilineal systems specify which rights are to be acquired through the father and which through the mother. The basis for defining a system as matrilineal or patrilineal is the line through which primary rights and duties are transmitted. Everywhere, though, certain secondary rights and duties are received through one's *complementary affiliation,* the parent who does not determine descent.

8. *Double descent* is a type of unilineal descent that recognizes lines of descent through *both* the mother and the father. In double descent systems, specific properties or rights are transmitted by each lineage to which an individual belongs.

9. Another possible form of unilineal descent is *parallel descent,* in which males trace ancestry and inheritance through male lines and females through female lines. Recorded cases of parallel descent are extremely rare.

10. *Cognatic descent* is the system used in our own society. It traces ancestry through lineal relatives of both sexes. Any group of close blood relatives, without reference to either the paternal or maternal line of descent, constitutes a *kindred,* an *ego-focused group* that is unique to a given individual.

11. Kinship terminology refers to the names that people use to identify their relatives. There are many ways of grouping kin. Kin terms specify the kinds of relatives recognized in a given society. There are a number of ways of looking at kinship terms, and many typologies have been worked out. More than a century ago, Morgan divided terminology systems into *descriptive,* in which only primary terms referring to direct biological relationships are used, and *classificatory,* which combine *lineal* and *collateral* kin under one term. Murdock's six-part typology—Eskimo, Hawaiian, Crow, Omaha, Iroquois, and Sudanese—focuses on terms for parents' siblings and on different categories for cousins.

12. The true importance of kinship terminology is as a guide to cultural behavior. All human beings are born into a kinship structure of one kind or another, and the social ways in which a given society utilizes kinship have consequences for the ways in which individuals live.

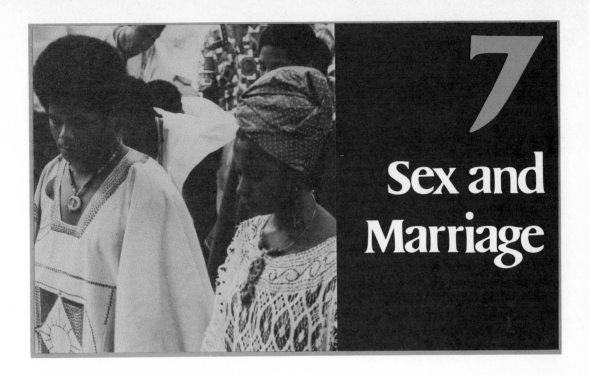

7

Sex and Marriage

As we pointed out in the preceding chapter, in all human societies kinship bonds and networks are based on two types of relationship: consanguineal and affinal. Different societies use these relationships in a wide vareity of ways. In the previous chapter, we examined the bonds and groupings, including those of descent, that develop through consanguineal ties. Here we will complete the study of kinship by examining relationships based on affinity.

The central concern in any study of affinal relationships is, of course, marriage. In the course of our discussion, it will become apparent that the understanding of marriage by most Europeans and Americans is not universal. Many characteristics of our marital arrangements are, in fact, rare among the cultures of the world.

Males and females are the single universal components of the relationship we call marriage. Every society makes some provision for this relationship between the sexes. But, as we shall see, monogamous marriage in the form we know it is neither universal nor predominant in human societies. What is necessary is some sort of socially approved relationship between adult males and females. Such a relationship serves a number of functions. It provides for the fulfillment of human sexual needs; furnishes domestic and economic services; gives children a legitimate standing in society; specifies property rights and lines of inheritance; and may establish group interdependencies and rights. However, the particular functions served by marriage vary from one society to another, although sexual union and legitimate parenthood seem to be nearly universal characteristics. Marriage is, though, only one form of relationship between men and women. The universal fact of human sexuality provides the starting point for an examination of the relationships between

132 males and females that are found in any given society.

Human Sexuality

Human sexuality and marriage are closely related in virtually all human societies on which we have information. Nevertheless, the cultural norms governing sexual relationships are different from those governing marriage. This was as true for the Victorian English as it is for the Nayar of India, as valid for the ancient Greeks as for the modern Japanese. Everywhere, a description of marriage involves inquiry about sexual relations, and everywhere, sexual arrangements exist that do not involve marriage. Before we discuss marriage itself, then, it will be useful to consider human sexuality in order to comprehend how it is channeled by means of culture.

In any discussion of human sexuality, there are at least two categories of comparisons to

Differences in ideas of beauty and attractiveness vary from culture to culture, as can be seen from the body painting of an Asurini girl of Brazil (note her rubber thongs) and scarification of the face of a Makonde woman from Tanzania. (Jacques Jangoux, Peter Arnold Photo Archives; Lynn McLaren, Rapho/Photo Researchers)

be made. The comparative perspective is one from which we may judge the forms and uses of human sexuality. But we also compare human sexuality with that of other animals, so that we can appreciate the extent to which we participate in the basic mammalian sexual heritage and can note ways in which we differ.

For most mammals, sexual activity is restricted to the periods during which fertilization is possible. Sex is thus linked directly to species reproduction. Generally, lower mammalian females offer themselves to males only when they are "in heat"—that is, during the limited periods, perhaps only at one time during the course of a year, when increased production of hormones stimulates the female. Among all but the simpler primates, however, female sexuality is less specifically tied to hormonal activity. Female chimpanzees, for example, have been observed during infertile periods making advances to, and receiving the attentions of, males.

Obviously, human sexuality is not controlled solely by hormones. This is not to say that humans are not influenced sexually by biological factors, including hormones, although the extent to which this is true is not clear. There is assuredly a high level both of individual variation among humans as a species and of variation for a given individual over time. However, most postadolescent individuals have direct experience of the fact that being aroused is usually a case of mind over matter. Human sexuality may have more to do with mental set and social environment than with any biologically measurable factors.

There are a number of other aspects of sexuality shared by humans and other mammals. Self-stimulation or masturbation is general in mammalian species. Juvenile sex play is found in many species; its frequency and variety tend to increase from the lower mammals to the higher. The specifics of the sex act— male erection and ejaculation, genital stimulation by means of rhythmic pelvic thrusting— are reflexes found in all mammals. Mutual

grooming, a characteristic of precoital behavior in a number of human societies, is common to all subhuman primates that have been studied (Ford & Beach, 1951).

Thus, human beings bring to sexual behavior a heritage shared with other mammals, and especially with the higher primates. Certain basic sexual behaviors appear to be universal to human beings as a consequence of biological evolution. But, for *Homo sapiens,* the forms with which these behaviors are expressed are shaped largely by learning and through the cultural experience.

Sexuality and Culture

Not even the necessity for sexual learning, however, is unique to humans. Behavioral studies have shown that "at least some, and perhaps all, male chimpanzees have to learn how to copulate" (Ford & Beach, 1951). There are indications that sexual learning is required by other primates as well.

There is a surprisingly large range in which sexual behavior can be learned. At an early age, Marquesan males (of Polynesia) learn to maintain erections and delay ejaculation for prolonged periods. It is not clear to what extent males are capable of achieving this in our society, but there is much evidence to show that such practices are not universal. The influence of culture on sexual behavior is particularly evident in the topics of childhood sexuality, precoital stimulation, extramarital sexual activity, and homosexuality.

Childhood Sexuality. The degree of freedom that children and young people have to explore their bodies and experiment with their developing sexual capabilities varies enormously. Among the Toba Indians of northern Argentina, for instance, children touch their genitals and play love-making games with dolls and other play objects, showing intercourse between the objects of play with no objection from adults. The play is ignored rather than reprimanded or laughed at. Similar adult indifference is found among the Trobriand Islanders, where children listen to ribald conversations and observe adults engaged in intercourse. Early childhood sex play, including mutual stimulation of genital organs, is casual and frequent. Older Trobriand youths and girls are encouraged to form sexual attachments. By midadolescence they have graduated from a series of frequent but casual liaisons to a more permanent relationship that may culminate in marriage.

Precoital Stimulation. In virtually all societies, some form of precoital stimulation is practiced. However, its extent and nature may be quite different from one society to the next. The kind of mutual grooming practiced by most primates and some human societies may be stimulating in some groups, but in our own society it would most likely be counterproductive. Among the Sirionó, the Truk, and Trobriand Islanders, both men and women learn early to interpret certain hair pulling, or being scratched or bitten, as a signal of sexual arousal. These sensations, elsewhere considered painful and unpleasant, here become erotic stimuli, a form of grooming (Ford & Beach, 1951). A minority of Americans and Europeans, however, have learned to associate the infliction and/or reception of pain with sexual pleasure. Sadomasochistic practices are more generally considered "sick" or "kinky" and have been the subject of numerous psychiatric studies.

The human ability to respond to symbolic stimulation may reduce the amount of direct physical stimulation preliminary to intercourse. But the nature of the symbols that may have the desired effect is highly variable, perhaps even within a given culture. This is certainly true within our own culture, where the sight of the naked body of the sex partner may be sexually stimulating, or where the sight of the clothed or partially clothed body may be equally so. What causes physical arousal in some individuals may be offensive or distracting to others. The degree to which symbolic stimulation substitutes for actual physical stimulation may be uniquely human.

Extramarital Sexual Activity. Similarly, wide variation is found in the extent to which extramarital sexual activity is permitted, condoned, or prohibited. In one study of 139 cultures, 39 percent approved of some form of sexual liaison outside of marriage (Ford & Beach, 1951, p. 113). The Toda allow a woman to have not only more than one husband but a number of lovers as well. This pattern should be seen as a convenience for males rather than as a license for females since the Toda have a disproportionately low number of adult females, due to female infanticide. At the other extreme was the culture of early New England, where adulterers were physically punished or exiled. Hester Prynne, with her scarlet letter "A" in Hawthorne's novel, constitutes a mild example. In other societies certain liaisons are approved. The Sirionó permit a man to have a sexual relationship with his wife's sisters and his brothers' wives and their sisters. Sirionó women are not discriminated against in this regard and are permitted sexual activity with their husbands' brothers and their sisters' husbands. The Marquesans similarly permit men and women to have extramarital intercourse with siblings-in-law.

A particular form of extramarital relationship is wife-exchange or wife-lending, practiced by the Eskimo and related cultures. Since the Siberian Chuckchee reindeer herders must travel widely, a man will arrange for the services of his host's spouse in each village on his route and will permit the same exchange when these men visit his community (Ford & Beach, 1951). A total range of wifely services, including but not primarily sexual ones, is provided in this way. A wife is valued as an economic asset and literal helpmate. No northern man can deal with the environment without such absolutely essential wifely services as boot-chewing and clothing repair (LaBarre, 1954).

Homosexuality. There is no society in which homosexuality is the sexual preference of the majority of adults, but the extent to which it may be encouraged, tolerated, or tabooed varies widely. Homosexuality does occur among a minority of people in every society, and wherever it is found, it is more prevalent among males than it is among females. Homosexual relationships were accepted among all males in ancient Greece and Rome. Among the Keraki of New Guinea all men are expected to have homosexual experience before marriage and are considered abnormal if they do not (Ford & Beach, 1951).

In some societies, specific provision is made for individuals who have a homosexual preference. For example, among the Chuckchee of Siberia, certain shamans "marry" a spouse of the same sex. These shamans are called upon in their early youth by various tribal spirits to undergo a change of sex, a call that is "much dreaded" but heeded nonetheless (Bogoras, 1953). The transformation takes place in stages, beginning simply with the adoption of a female hair style. But in the third and final stage, the young man

leaves off all pursuits and manners of his sex, and takes up those of a woman, [which he learns to use] quickly because the "spirits" are helping him all the time . . . . Generally speaking, he becomes a woman with the appearance of a man. . . . The "soft man" begins to feel like a woman. He seeks to win the good graces of men, and succeeds easily with the aid of "spirits." Thus he has all the young men he could wish for striving to obtain his favor. From these he chooses his lover, and after a time takes a husband. The marriage is performed with the usual rites, and it forms a quite solid union, which often lasts until death. . . of one of the parties. The couple live much in the same way as do other people. . . . (Bogoras, 1953, p. 108)

This custom of homosexual marriage, called *berdache,* is found also in some American Indian groups. The Nuer have a similar but reverse practice, in which women become the "wife-husbands" of other women (Evans-Pritchard, 1940). Our own culture seems to be in a state of transition from total aversion to moderate tolerance of homosexuality.

In our own culture in general, the range of socially acceptable sexual behavior has changed vastly in the twentieth century alone. Between the "spooning" of the turn of the century and the "living together" arrangements of the 1970s lies a multigenerational chasm.

Incest

No matter how permissive a society may be in sexual matters, there is always some rule limiting the category of appropriate sexual partners. Prohibitions usually apply to varying categories of relatives, and almost universally to all members of the conjugal family (except, of course, the husband and wife). The term *incest taboo* is applied to the prohibition of sexual access to certain categories of kin.

The relationships that are tabooed vary widely. In our own culture, incest taboos extend from members of the nuclear family to include aunts, uncles, and usually first cousins (the laws on this vary from state to state). In previous chapters, we mentioned a number of societies in which marriages between those relatives we call first cousins are in some cases preferred and in some abhorred. In many cases it is considered desirable for cross cousins (the children of one's mother's brothers and father's sisters) to marry; in such cases parallel cousins (children of one's mother's sister and father's brother) come under the same incest prohibition as siblings. However, we also have mentioned the Bedouin Arab preference for marriage between patrilateral parallel cousins. The ancient Egyptian practice of mating between brothers and sisters in royal families, found also among the Inca of Peru, is a classic example of the extent of incest variation.

An example of a preferred marriage between relatives who in most cultures would be forbidden access to each other occurs among the Saha of Colombia, South America. Here, every person is expected to have at least two marriages in a lifetime. The preferred second wife for a man is the daughter, by an earlier husband, of his first wife. Such a marriage is termed a mother-daughter marriage. In general, the Saha prefer marriages between close kin, who must be members of different but linked clans. Therefore, marriages occur between individuals already having a number of relationships to each other.

The topic of incest has attracted considerable interest in anthropology, and numerous theories have been proposed to account for the presumed universality of incest prohibitions. One theory assumes strong sexual attraction among family members and postulates, therefore, that equally strong societal controls are necessary. Thus, it has been suggested that the control of sexual impulses at an early age is essential for the socialization of the child. Other anthropologists, taking a complementary view, have argued that mating outside of the family is required for broad-based cooperation and group survival. According to still another theory, sexual access would be appropriate within the family except for the fact that when one family member reaches sexual maturity there would not likely be available an individual of the opposite sex and appropriate age.

Psychoanalytic Theory. A different explanation of the incest taboo was offered by Freud. According to his theory, a strong sexual attraction exists between mother and son and between father and daughter. In the course of socialization, the child learns to repress his or her feelings out of fear of punishment or injury from the parent of the same sex. Although repressed, the sexual attraction continues to exist in the unconscious mind of the child. The incest taboo is, therefore, another line of defense against the forbidden impulse.

Childhood Familiarity Theory. Even though Freud's theory can account for some observable situations, many anthropologists find it an inadequate explanation for both the origin of the taboo and its many cultural expressions. In the 1920s, Edward Westermarck proposed an alternative explanation that has come to be known as the childhood familiarity theory. Westermarck held that the intimacy existing among family members resulted in sexual aversion among them. This theory was vulnerable on two points. First, cases could be found in which family members *were* sexually attracted to each other. Second, if familiarity caused lack of interest, why was an incest taboo needed in the first place?

Recently, Arthur Wolf set out to test Westermarck's hypotheses. He considered various data, including verifiable gossip, for several hundred marriages in two Chinese villages in Taiwan. Two types of marriage—major and minor—occur there. "Major" marriages are contracted between partners whose relationship was initiated in adulthood. "Minor" marriages take place between a man and a woman who was adopted into his family at an early age to be raised as his potential marriage partner. The partners of a minor marriage are, therefore, "a couple whose experience of one another is as intimate as brother and sister" (Wolf, 1970, p. 504). Wolf hypothesized that if sexual aversion results from childhood association, that aversion should show up in a minor marriage and mar the relationship between husband and wife. In fact, the minor marriages did consistently result in fewer children than did major marriages. The lower fertility rate also correlated with higher rates of infidelity, separation, and divorce. Wolf believes that "there is some aspect of childhood association sufficient to preclude or inhibit sexual desire" (p. 515). The incest taboo, he concludes, is a formal statement on the general sexual aversion among close kin.

Inbreeding Theory. David Aberle and colleagues (1963) examined inbreeding in animals in an effort to determine the sociobiological roots of the human incest taboo. They found behavior ranging from no matings among family members (except the parents) to intensive family matings. In the Canadian goose and a few other species of birds, individuals raised in the same brood appear to instinctively avoid mating with each other. Among mammals that avoid inbreeding, the reason may be connected with competition between a parent and a child of the same sex. The parent usually is sufficiently strong to force the child to leave the family—and find another pool of mates—as it nears sexual maturity.

Aberle and his colleagues theorize that the incest taboo originated in the time lag between sexual maturity and self-sufficiency of offspring. Human parents do not generally force children to leave home upon reaching sexual maturity. They therefore need to solve the problem of sexual competition among family members and still maintain an organized family life. The incest taboo serves this purpose. However, in the long run, the taboo proves to be a selective advantage to the species in avoiding the genetic ill-effects of repeated inbreeding (Aberle et al., 1963).

A variety of studies have been undertaken to explore the alleged ill-effects of inbreeding. Reid, for example, interviewed several hundred married couples in Sri Lanka, Ceylon, where there is a high percentage of marriages between first cousins and other close relatives. He found that the closer the consanguineal relationship of the conjugal pair, the fewer the pregnancies, live births, and living offspring. However, the consanguinity of married couples does not seem to affect the rates of spontaneous abortion, stillbirth, or later death of offspring. Reid concluded that consan-guineous couples had significantly lower fertility levels and that "this result remains consistent with the belief that inbreeding reduces Darwinian fitness" (Reid, 1976, p. 144).

The foregoing theories are only a few of the approaches taken by anthropologists in the study of incest. As in the story of the blind men and the elephant, no one has grasped this subject in its totality, but each has contributed something toward an understanding of the sizable whole. Taken together, all the points of view represent useful keys to improve our knowledge of this phenomenon—or these phenomena, as Needham (1971) would perhaps urge. He holds that because incest prohibitions differ from one society to another, no general theory can apply to them all. The cultural meanings of incest taboos differ for every society although incest regulations have in common the prohibition of sexual access. However, with the exception of the mother-son relationship, there is no truly universal proscription. From the perspective of a study of marriage, the significance of incest taboos lies in their opposites. Since they list categories of persons not available as sexual partners, they make implicit statements about acceptable sexual and marital unions.

Defining Marriage

But what is marriage? In the previous chapter, we examined a variety of marriage arrangements:

- A situation in which several men obtain both sexual and domestic services from one woman, but only one man legitimizes her offspring (the Toda)
- Situations in which one man may have all of these rights and obligations toward several women (the Yoruba and others)

An African wedding rite, performed by a couple in New York City. (Katrina Thomas, Photo Researchers)

- Situations in which a man may have all these rights and obligations to one woman but virtually none of her children even though they be recognized as his (the Navajo)

Since there is a wide variety of marriage arrangements, a definition of marriage has to be broad enough to accommodate them all. One key point is recognition of sexual relations between the sexes. Since we have come across cases in which a man takes the role of a wife and a woman the role of a husband, we shall use male and female to refer to sex *roles* rather than to biological differences. Marriage gives primary sexual rights to the partners in the marriage, in that it is accepted that a sexual relationship of some sort will exist between them. As we have seen, the sexual rights that

accompany marriage are not everywhere necessarily considered exclusive, as they are for the most part in our own society. A second important consideration is that, although formalized by different means in various societies, marriage is publicly recognized and socially sanctioned. It is entered into with some expectation on the partners' parts that it will endure for some period of time, if not forever. Third, marriage brings with it certain other rights and obligations between the husband and wife. These may be domestic cooperation or exchange between groups, practices and understandings of the society in question.

To sum up these factors, we will use the following definition: *marriage* is a socially recognized and relatively stable union providing sexual access, legitimating offspring, and establishing other rights and obligations between the marriage partners and other units of society.

The Nayar Case

Although the above definition of marriage has almost universal application, there is one major exception—the Nayar from the Central Kerala of India. The marriage customs of this group differ markedly from those of any other group known and studied to date.

The only marriage ceremonies among the Nayar are group affairs held every few years for all the girls who have not yet attained puberty. These prepuberty marriage rites for girls, aged 7 to 12, are essential for establishing the girl's place in the community.

Preceding the marriage ceremony, the neighborhood assembly meets and, on the advice of the village astrologer, selects the ritual bridegrooms for all the girls. For 3 days prior to the ceremony itself, the girls are secluded in an inner room of a nearby house. On the appointed day, the ritual bridegrooms arrive in a procession at the house where, after various ceremonies, each ties a gold ornament (*tāli*) around the neck of his ritual bride.

Then, each couple is secluded in private for 3 days, during which time sexual relations may take place but often do not. At the end of the 3 days of seclusion, each couple is purified from the pollution of cohabitation by a ritual bath. Following this, the ritual husbands depart.

After the 4 days of ceremonies, the ritual husbands have no further obligations to their brides. The brides have only one further obligation to their ritual husbands: they and all their children by whatever father have to observe rites upon the death of their ritual husbands.

Although the *tāli* rite does not establish husband and wife as an institutionalized, legal, residential, or economic unit, it is absolutely essential for establishing the woman's place in the community. The ritual bride's life actually depends on the ceremonial marriage because, if she is not ritually married before puberty, she faces excommunication and even death. The *tāli* rite endows a girl ceremonially with sexual and procreative functions and confers upon her the status of a woman. After the rite, when she reaches puberty, a girl can receive visiting husbands. A woman usually has a small number of visiting husbands at one time. Among them could be her ritual husband, if both are willing, but he has no special priority over other men.

A husband visits his wife after supper at night and leaves before breakfast in the morning. He places his weapons at the door of his wife's room, and if others arrive while he is there, they are welcome to sleep on the veranda of the woman's house. At the beginning of the relationship, the visiting husband usually gives the woman a cloth of the type worn as a skirt, although it is not essential. Later he is expected to make small personal gifts to her at the three main festivals of the year. Failure to do so is a sign that he has ended the relationship. A passing visiting husband, a man who does not live in the same or nearby community, gives the woman a small gift at each visit. Both husband and wife are free to terminate the relationship at any time with no formalities.

When a woman becomes pregnant, it is necessary for one or more men to acknowledge fatherhood. This is done at the time of the birth of the child. At that time, the "father" pays the midwife, which is considered an open acknowledgment that the child has a father who is a man of the required rank. If no man comes forth to pay the midwife, it is assumed that the woman has had relations with a man from the wrong caste, and she can be banished or killed. Once the birth fees are paid, the father has no economic, legal, or ritual rights or obligations to his children. Women and their children are maintained by the matrilineal group.

All of a woman's children call all her current husbands by the same word, a term meaning "lord," and no particular ties distinguish a direct father-child relationship. A woman's ritual husband is the only one who has any rights in her children: they are expected to mourn his death even if he has not fathered any of them. Although the Nayar marriage ceremony does not create an institutionalized family unit, it does provide ritual and legal recognition of both the woman's and her children's status in the society (Gough, 1959; Leach, 1955).

Marriage Rules

All societies have restrictions on whom one may or may not marry. Through incest taboos, as we have seen, societies prohibit sexual access between certain categories of kin. While incest taboos provide negative regulations regarding choice of marriage partners, certain other positive regulations specify which categories of females are to be considered marital preferences (or even prescriptions) by the males in a society, and vice versa. These regulations constitute the other half of the marriage coin.

Whom May One Choose as a Mate?

As we have said, in every society the choice of potential marriage partners is in some way restricted. Some societies go further and specify which persons one *will* have as a mate. Two forms of restriction are endogamy and exogamy.

Endogamy and Exogamy. *Endogamy* refers to the expectation that a marriage partner will be chosen from within the social group of which one is a member. *Exogamy* refers to the expectation that the choice of a marriage partner will be from a social group of which one is not a member. In every society there are both endogamous and exogamous groupings. The Toda of India, for instance, are divided into two endogamous groups (or moieties), each of which has separate economic and ritual functions. Each moiety is subdivided into a number of exogamous clans. Marriage is exogamous—that is, a woman must marry a man from another clan of her own moiety (Murdock, 1934). In our own culture, although the nuclear family and close kin are exogamous, ethnic, racial, religious, and/or economic class considerations may be (explicitly or implicitly) endogamous. In every society, individuals come of age knowing pretty well what is expected of them in the choice of a spouse.

It has often been theorized that exogamy developed as an extension of the incest taboo covering various categories of relatives. But exogamy is more than merely the extension of incest prohibitions. Marrying outside one's group has the functional advantage of bringing to one's group certain benefits. Exogamous groups are often well aware of this advantage.

In European royal marriages over the centuries, the importance of contracting political alliances appeared to take precedence over personal considerations. Americans are also aware of marriages that unite families that are socially prominent. The possible benefits to all concerned are matters of public speculation. Apparently anthropologists are not the only persons who are aware of the benefits of exogamy.

Another reason for the practice of exogamy may be group survival. The notion of marrying outside of one's group or dying out has been pervasive ever since the earliest anthropological writings on marriage. Exchange of marriage partners between groups establishes alliances between them. This is not to say that marital exchange necessarily brings peace. But the rule of exogamy forces two groups to depend on each other for continued reproduction, and the knowledge of this fact helps to regulate relations between the groups.

We should keep in mind when discussing exogamy that there may be differences between the requirements of incest taboos and of exogamy. That is, incest taboos restrict sexual relations—whether outside of or within marriage. Exogamy regulates only the choice of potential marital partners. In terms of this distinction, two individuals might be prevented by rules of exogamy from marrying each other. Yet they might be allowed a sexual relationship if there were no incest prohibition operative between them. The Toda demonstrate this difference: marriage between individuals of different moieties or within the same clan is not permitted. However, sexual relations between members of the two moieties, and also between members of the same clan, are tolerated (Murdock, 1934, p. 122).

Cousin Marriages. In some societies, restrictions on marital partners are also accompanied

Potential bilateral cross-cousin marriage partners (father's sisters' daughters or mother's brothers' daughters)

* Potential matrilateral cross-cousin marriage partners (mother's brothers' daughters)

* Potential patrilateral cross-cousin marriage partners (father's sisters' daughters)

Figure 1   Possible cross-cousin marriages for Ego who is male

by a preference for marriage with certain other relatives. The most usual preference is for marriage between cross-cousins. *Cross cousins* are children of the opposite-sex siblings of one's mother or father. Specifically, one's cross cousins are the children of one's mother's brothers and one's father's sisters. In some cases, the obligation involves more than a preference—it is required. Societies in which such obligations apply are said to have *prescriptive marriage rules.*

Theoretically, there are three possible kinds of cross-cousin marriages: bilateral, matrilateral, and patrilateral. Figure 1 shows the possible cross-cousin marriage for Ego who is male. In bilateral cross-cousin marriage, a man marries from among either his mother's brothers' daughters or his father's sisters' daughters. In matrilateral cross-cousin marriage, he marries one of his mother's brothers' daughters only; and in the patrilateral cross-cousin marriage he finds his wife from among the daughters of his father's sisters.

Figure 2 shows the cross-cousin marriages allowed Ego who is female. Bilateral cross-cousin marriage is an exchange arrangement that requires only two reciprocating kin groups, although more may be involved. Matrilateral and patrilateral cross-cousin marriage (both of which are relatively rare) require at least three intermarrying groups, and may involve many more.

Rare also is a preference for parallel-cousin marriage. *Parallel cousins* are children of the same-sex siblings of one's mother or father. That is, one's parallel cousins are the children of one's mother's sisters and those of one's father's brothers. As we have mentioned in previous chapters, this is considered one of the ideal arrangements among the Middle Eastern Bedouin. In their case, parallel-cousin marriage serves the practical, and stated, purpose of keeping property within the landholding group.

Clearly, if prescriptive marriage rules are followed generation after generation, rela-

Figure 2   Possible cross-cousin marriages for Ego who is female

tionships among family members will operate on several levels at the same time. For a male Bedouin (Ego) about to marry his patrilateral parallel cousin, his father's brother (already his "uncle") will become his "father-in-law." Such relationships become more complicated over several generations.

The Kareira are among the several indigenous Australian groups practicing bilateral cross-cousin marriage. Here, Ego's father's sister, who is one of his potential mothers-in-law, is probably married to his mother's brother. And so while it might seem that Ego could at least choose between his father's sister's daughter and his mother's brother's daughter, these females might be one and the same person, as well as the sister of his own sister's husband.

Kin groups that regularly exchange spouses are likely to interact in a number of other areas as well, each of which reinforces the others. Marital reciprocity is only one of a number of relationships—in the economic, ritual, and political spheres—that exist be-

tween descent groups in a society with prescriptive marriage rules.

Levirate and Sororate. The levirate and sororate involve special cases of marriage regulation. They go into effect following the death of one member of a married couple. *Levirate* is the practice of requiring or permitting a man to marry the wife of his deceased brother. A good example is found in the Old Testament:

If brethren dwell together, and one of them die and have no son, the wife of the dead shall not be married to a stranger; her husband's brother shall go in unto her, and take her to him to wife and perform the duty of a husband's brother unto her. And it shall be that the first-born that she beareth shall succeed in the name of his dead brother that his name be not blotted out of Israel (Deuteronomy 25:5–6).

The wording of this command indicates that the need for a legal heir for the deceased is a prime concern. Elsewhere, the Old Testament indicates the property and other rights that might be involved. In early Biblical times, women had little say in the matter; all members of a household were subject to the authority of its oldest male head. But later, when the Israelites were a settled agricultural people with some degree of political organization, women had the right both to complain about and publicly humiliate a brother-in-law who refused to comply with the levirate (Patai, 1959, pp. 92–96).

The levirate often coincides with polygyny (the marriage of one man to two or more women), patrilineal descent, and patrilocal residence. These conditions result in an extended patriarchal family, as they did in the early Old Testament days. The levirate is still permitted throughout the Middle East to this day, though it is now found only rarely. Patai (1959) has shown that a man's exercise of his levirate duties establishes his claim as his brother's heir in property and other rights. In the past, such claims also applied to a father's property. In this case, the heir of a deceased man might inherit his father's wife or wives (exclusive, of course, of his own mother) together with the father's other property.

In the Old Testament version of the levirate, any children born are considered to be the heirs of the deceased husband. A variation is found in the so-called "ghost marriages" of the Nuer. The brother of a man who had died without children could marry a woman "to the name of" the deceased. The offspring of this union would be regarded as children of the dead man and, thus, as his heirs (Evans-Pritchard, 1940).

Another variation on the levirate is found among the Kadara of northern Nigeria. There, a man may be required to marry the widow of his elder brother or the widow of his father's father (Smith, 1968). Marriage to one's elder brother's widow is the most frequent type. In reality, the second situation would occur only when the father's father left no surviving junior siblings and, therefore, no one else to provide for his widow. Again, the importance of the levirate for the raising of heirs is em-

phasized. A man's lineage mates would usually object to a marriage with his *maternal* grandfather's widow, since the offspring of such a union could be claimed by the lineage of the maternal grandfather. But if a man married either his brother's or his *paternal* grandfather's widow, children would belong to his patrilineage, and the patrilineage would lose neither members nor property as a result of the marriage (Smith, 1968).

The *sororate* is a complementary practice to the levirate, in which a man marries the sister of his deceased wife. The term also sometimes applies to the situation in which the husband of a childless woman is given her sister also in marriage, in which case some of the children born to the sister are counted as those of the childless wife. The same principle applies to each: the services agreed upon at marriage remain an obligation between the groups. As with the levirate, the sororate occurs with patrilineal descent, patrilocal residence, and polygyny, since an important alliance has been established between the wife-giving and the wife-receiving groups. Sometimes, it is the natural extension of *sororal polygyny,* the marriage of a man to two or more sisters at the same time. Marriage to one woman may give a man the right to marry her unwed sisters as well. If a woman dies, her family may be expected to provide a replacement, especially if the man and his kin provided a sizable bridewealth at the time of the original marriage.

Among the Arapaho and other Plains Indian groups, levirate and sororate both provide a widower and widow with a new spouse. These practices maintain the alliances set up by the original marriage between two exogamous kin groups. This differs somewhat from the emphasis in the Middle Eastern version of levirate, where the original marriage may well have been endogamous. Endogamy introduces differentiation within the lineage and serves to segment groups within it. In this case, provision for a second marriage is clearly tied to providing an heir for the dead as well as to ensuring the continuity of the descent group for the purpose of property inheritance.

Both levirate and sororate are widespread in one form or another. Well over half of the societies in Murdock's (1949) study practiced levirate marriage to a significant extent (127 out of 185 groups for which there was data on this point). Nearly as many practiced the sororate.

How Many Mates Does One Choose?

One of the areas that consistently interests anthropologists is the question of how many persons one may marry at a time in various societies. Our society is so decidedly monogamous—pairing one man and one woman at a time—that different patterns are a matter of some curiosity. Once again, the possible patterns are these:

1. *Monogamy:* the marriage of one man to one woman at a time
2. *Polygyny:* the marriage of one man to two or more women at a time
3. *Polyandry:* the marriage of one woman to two or more men at a time
4. *Group marriage:* the marriage of two or more women to two or more men at the same time.

Polygyny, polyandry, and group marriage are all forms of *polygamy,* or plural marriage. We will look at each of these marriage patterns in turn.

Monogamy. Anthropologists who took an evolutionary approach to the study of culture once believed monogamy, like monotheism and industrialism, to be a sign of progress and civilization. Most anthropologists now view social and cultural differences simply as differences and not as lags, evolutionary or otherwise. Whether a society permits one marriage partner or a number of partners at a time is no way related to that society's level of civilization.

Monogamy occurs worldwide with less frequency than many Westerners expect. In their sample of 185 societies, Ford and Beach (1951) found that 29 of them (or less than 16 percent) were monogamous. Of those, fewer than a third approved of extra- and premarital sexual liaisons. Recent analysis of a much larger cross-cultural sample had much the same result: of 854 societies, 16 percent were exclusively monogamous (Bourguignon & Greenbaum, HRAF, 1973). However, an additional 39 percent of the societies sampled practiced monogamy with occasional polygyny. Polygyny is permitted (or even preferred) in these societies, but in practice monogamy is more frequent there. Economic and population factors tend to limit the number of polygynous marriages. In some cases, only the most powerful or wealthy men can afford to have more than one wife. In other cases, there simply are not enough women to allow for two or more wives to every man.

The form of monogamy that characterizes Western society has been referred to as *serial monogamy.* This consists of a pattern of marriage, divorce, and remarriage. Thus, although the individual is married to only one person at a time, over a number of years he or she may have had a number of spouses.

Polygyny. Worldwide, polygyny is certainly the most popular form of marriage. Of the societies analyzed by Bourguignon and Greenbaum, 44 percent (or 379) were predominantly polygynous. As we have noted, nearly as many—39 percent (or 335)—were monogamous with occasional polygyny (1973, Table 27, p. 51). The incidence of occasional polygyny was broadly scattered, but occurred in half or more of the societies of east Eurasia, the Insular Pacific, North America, and South America. By comparison, polygyny is the predominant form of marriage among 85 percent of the groups studied in sub-Saharan Africa; in over a third of the groups in the

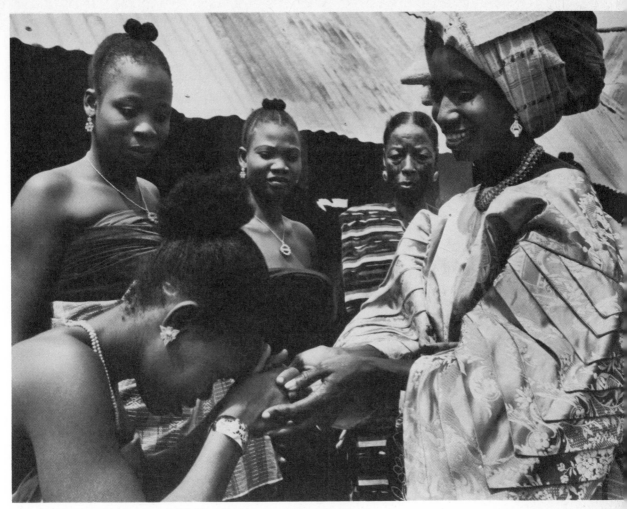

The number one wife of the deji (king) of the Yoruba of West Nigeria is being greeted by other wives of the king. (Marc and Evelyne Bernheim, Woodfin Camp)

circum-Mediterranean region; about a quarter of the societies of the Insular Pacific and South America; and in only 13 percent of the groups of east Eurasia. Almost everywhere, however, monogamous unions are more numerous than polygynous ones, even where polygyny is preferred.

Typically, a husband in a polygynous marriage has the same rights and obligations to each of his wives, and will be the legitimate father of all children born to them (even though the wives may sometimes be permitted to have sexual relations with other men). In some instances, a first or a last or a favorite wife may have rights in addition to those of the other wives. She may serve as an economic or labor supervisor over the secondary wives, or have social and/or ritual obligations and recognition that subsequent wives lack. In such cases, this may form the basis for segmentation in the lineage at a later time. Usually, "each wife considers herself the guardian of her children's rights within the family created by the polygynous marriage" (Marshall, 1977). This can also create conflict and cleavages within the lineage.

A common form of polygyny is *sororal polygyny*. In marrying one woman, a man may acquire the right to claim her sisters in marriage as well, with or without additional payments or ceremonies. People in polygynous societies frequently verbalize approval of sororal polygyny. They believe that sisters get along well together as wives of the same man, since they are used to cooperating and being together in the same household. A well-known Biblical instance of this practice was the marriage of Jacob to Leah, the older sister, and then to her younger sister Rachel, the woman he had chosen originally (Genesis 29). (Both women were, incidentally, his mother's brother's daughters—his matrilateral cross cousins.) In this case, however, there was a good deal of envy between the sisters: Leah envying Rachel, who was preferred by Jacob, and Rachel envying Leah, who was able to bear children (Genesis 30). Despite expectations to the contrary, sisters in sororal polygynous marriage do not necessarily cooperate as co-wives. Marriage creates new interpersonal relations that may interfere with cooperation, as it did for Leah and Rachel.

The Baganda of Uganda represent a good case of the preference for polygyny so widespread in sub-Saharan Africa. Sororal polygyny is preferred, but unrelated women may be married to the same man as well. A man must accumulate a substantial amount of property—several goats or a cow and thousands of cowrie shells—to give to the family of his prospective bride. A Baganda king can afford to have hundreds of wives; chiefs may have dozens; even a commoner may have two or three. A wife is an economic asset, since the fruits of her labors go to her husband. Because a wife has a very heavy work load, she may gladly welcome additional

spouses for her husband, especially if she is the first or second wife, since the first two wives have higher status than succeeding ones. Women not married to the head of the household, such as unmarried female relatives and slaves, may also be attached to it. After a man dies, the first wife must tend his grave. Other wives may be claimed by relatives, and those remaining go, along with the rest of his property, to an heir designated by the clan of the deceased. (Sons do not inherit directly from their fathers.) The first wife may remarry also, but her brother will have to refund to her deceased husband's relatives the payment made by the groom when the couple were married. A widower may take a new wife from the clan of his former wife, but must, again, reciprocate the appropriate goods (Queen & Habenstein, 1974, pp. 72 ff).

Polyandry. Polyandry is a rare form of marriage. Only four instances were found in the Bourguignon and Greenbaum (1973) sample of 854 societies. Murdock (1949), citing two cases in his sample of 238 societies, regarded polyandry as "an ethnological curiosity." The Toda of India, who practice *fraternal polyandry*—marriage of a woman to two or more brothers—are considered the classic example. Fraternal polyandry is the counterpart of sororal polygyny in that an arrangement is made for a category of males rather than females. A similar instance is the Sinhalese of Sri Lanka (Ceylon), where two brothers may live in a household with one wife, although there are also households where two or more brothers each live with a separate wife. Polygyny is also permitted among the Sinhalese (D'Oyly, 1929, p. 129). In Sinhalese polyandry, unlike the Toda version, the first husband must consent to his wife's successive husbands and to her sexual activities with them. And unlike the Toda case, each Sinhalese husband legitimizes the children he has fathered. Inheritance is bilateral, in that all of a woman's children have an equal claim on her property in addition to the right to inherit from their respective fathers.

Among the Toda on the other hand, inheritance is patrilineal, and there is a preference for cross-cousin marriage. So no matter which husband legitimizes the children, the property stays in the family; the several husbands of a Toda woman are likely to be brothers, and therefore her child would belong to the same patrilineage as all of them (Murdock, 1934, pp. 114–122). One would therefore expect less conflict over rights and less fissioning among the Toda.

Nonfraternal polyandry is found among the Marquesans of Polynesia, who are the only people outside of the Indian subcontinent known to practice this form of marriage. There, a number of unrelated men join the household of a woman of high status and participate jointly in economic responsibilities and sexual privileges (Murdock, 1949, p. 26).

The "visiting husband" of the Nayar women may be seen as a variant of nonfraternal polyandry. It should be emphasized that these relationships are not casual liaisons. Rather, they are mateships, since they are on-going and of some durability. The woman is free to receive casual visitors, as long as they belong to the appropriate subcaste. Furthermore, when she becomes pregnant, one of a woman's visiting husbands must acknowledge paternity by providing a fee of cloth and vegetables for the midwife who delivers the baby (Gough, 1959).

Group Marriage. Group marriage appears very seldom, even as a minority practice, although early ethnologists believed that it was characteristic of an early stage in social evolution. Murdock (1949) found group marriage occuring more frequently among the Kaingang of Brazil than in any other culture. Yet, in a statistical analysis of that group's genealogies for over 100 years, he found that only 8 percent of all Kaingang marriages were group marriages. Of the remaining marriages, 14 percent were polyandrous, 18 percent polygynous, and 60 percent monogamous. Murdock concluded that group marriage does not exist anywhere as the prevalent marriage form. However, as we noted in the preceding chapter, fraternal-sororal group marriage was succeeding or supplementing polyandry among the Toda of southern India, as the prohibition of female infanticide altered the demographic imbalance of the sexes.

Where Does One Live after Marriage?

When a marriage occurs, either or both parties must change residence. As Murdock puts it, "the possible alternatives are few in number, and all societies have come to adopt one or another of them, or some combination thereof, as the culturally preferred rule of residence" (Murdock, 1960, p. 16). The possibilities are

1. *Neolocal residence:* the newly married couple establishes its residence without regard to the residence of either partner's family of origin.
2. *Patrilocal residence:* the bride goes to live with the groom in the household headed by his father. (This pattern is sometimes called *virilocal residence,* to indicate that the bride goes to live with the groom in the vicinity of his kin group or family of origin, rather than in the father's household per se.)
3. *Matrilocal residence:* the groom goes to live with the bride in the household headed by her mother. (This pattern is called *uxorilocal residence,* to indicate that the groom goes to live with the bride in the vicinity of her kin group or family of origin, rather than in the mother's household per se.

4. *Bilocal residence:* the couple has a choice of living with or near the parents or kin group of either bride or groom.
5. *Ambilocal residence:* the couple is expected to live for a period of time with or near the bride's parents and for another period of time with or near the groom's parents.
6. *Avunculocal residence:* the couple lives with or near the groom's mother's brother.

In some cultures, the pattern includes change from one type of residence to another after a specified period of time. Thus, there may be an initial period of matrilocal residence, followed by patrilocality, or there may be a shift from patri- to avunculocality (Bourguignon & Greenbaum, 1973, p. 53; Goodenough, 1956, p. 25). Among the Toba, for example,

the couple traditionally lived with the wife's family until the first child was born, after which they were free to join the husband's group, a form of ambilocal residence.

Worldwide, an overwhelming majority of societies favor patrilocal or virilocal residence. In the Bourguignon and Greenbaum study (1973), these patterns together characterized nearly 70 percent of all societies. Matrilocal or uxorilocal and avunculocal societies combined accounted for only 17 percent of the 854 societies in the sample.

The location of postmarital residence is neither an isolated nor an idle choice. It is deeply bound to other facets of the social and economic system with far-reaching political and psychological consequences for the individuals and families involved. Leach argues

A Bedouin bride in Libya rides hidden from sight on the way to her husband's village, where the couple will live. (Dr. Georg Gerster, Rapho/Photo Researchers)

that one can draw correspondences between the nature of the marriage institution and the principles of descent and rules of residence in a given society. For instance, patrilocality correlates with patrilineal descent. Among patrilocal societies with patrilineal descent, Leach finds that concern with legal fatherhood "is far and away the most important element." Among the Trobriand Islanders, on the other hand, where virilocality is associated with matrilineal descent, giving a husband the property rights of his wife is more important than legal paternity (Leach, 1955).

One might expect that residence choices would be a simple and clear-cut issue, but this is not the case. The interpretation of residence rules, as you may recall from an earlier chapter, was the subject of some disagreement between Goodenough and Fischer. In 1947, Goodenough found a predominantly matrilocal pattern in his study of residence patterns on the northern Pacific island of Truk. Three years earlier, Fischer had concluded that residence on Truk was bilocal.

Comparing their findings, Goodenough determined that the difference between their interpretations was the result of each ethnographer having utilized somewhat different concepts of residence. As an example of the ways in which data can be misinterpreted, Goodenough cites a family unit consisting of an elderly man with his second wife, his three sons by his first marriage, and the wife of his eldest son. On the surface, this appears to be a typical patrilocal extended family. However, on closer examination, it turned out that the family was residing in a house and on land belonging to the matrilineage of the older man's first wife, to which his sons also belonged. Thus the real situation was that of an initial uxorilocal residence by the father and avunculocal residence by the son (Goodenough, 1956).

Goodenough proposes that anthropologists investigate the conditions and considerations that influence the decisions concerning residence after marriage. He states that it is necessary to examine a sufficiently large number of cases before a statement can be made about the residence rules of society. Census data alone are insufficient to discover the rules, and what may be relevant information for one society may be irrelevant for another.

Some studies have attempted to correlate residence patterns with other cultural patterns. Perhaps because data in various studies are not always comparable, the correlations are not clear-cut. Ember and Ember (1971) found, for example, that female dominance in subsistence activities was associated with matrilocal residence in North America but not anywhere else. They have also attempted to correlate viri- or patrilocal residence (male localization) with a number of factors that Murdock believed to be associated with high status for males, but their findings are inconclusive. Only herding and intercommunity political organization "turned out to predict more than half of the cases in which males are localized after marriage. . . .Two other conditions— polygyny and slavery—predict male localization weakly. And the last two conditions— warfare and division of labor—do not predict male localization at all" (1971, p. 593). However, the Embers did find some evidence that warfare is distinctive when one contrasts matrilocal with patrilocal residence. The presence of warfare *within* a society tends to be accompanied by patrilocal residence. Matrilocal residence tends to characterize societies that are engaged in warfare only with *other* societies. In this case, while the men are engaged in warfare, the labor needed to maintain subsistence is performed by women. Thus, residence tends to center around women where cooperation and family arrangements make for the smooth operation of the domestic unit. (1971, p. 593). The nature of various other social conditions that might affect residence patterns is an open question and one that calls for further research and discussion.

Marriage Transactions

In nearly all societies, as we have seen, anthropologists find certain correspondences between the character of marriage institutions and such other features as rules of descent and residence. These features focus on the intergroup relationships that marriage brings with it. In most places, the importance of marriage is tied to its implications for the social group as a whole, and marriage can be viewed as a contract between two groups rather than simply between two individuals. Here, we will look at the variety of transactions and exchanges that accompany marriage, especially with regard to property distribution and group alliances.

Marriage arrangements can best be interpreted in terms of the theories of alliance and exchange proposed by Lévi-Strauss. Rules of exogamy and endogamy set up social boundaries, thus clearly defining and limiting the types and intensity of exchange between social groups. Within the appropriate boundaries, exogamy sets up the exchanges that tie social groups together. Marriage exchanges focus on women and the ways in which a given society circulates women in marriage. This exchange corresponds to other types of exchange among the groups concerned.

Elementary systems of marriage specify the categories or groups from which spouses must be chosen; complex systems (such as our own) only specify those ineligible to be spouses. Elementary systems circulate women in two

A groom in Israel signs the marriage contract just before the wedding ceremony, while his future father-in-law, *right,* **looks on.** (Dan Porges, Peter Arnold Photo Archives)

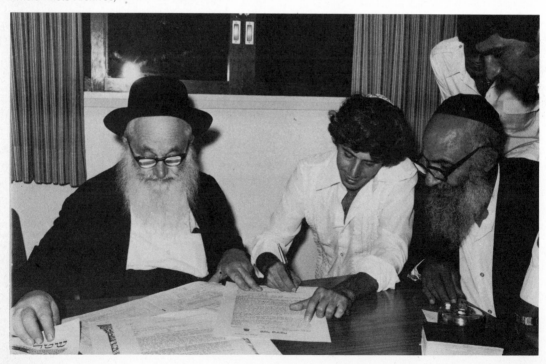

ways: by direct (or symmetric) exchange, in which two groups simply take wives from one another. Thus, men of group A take wives from group B, and men of group B take wives from group A. In indirect (or asymmetric) exchange, women circulate in one direction only. Women from group A marry men of group B; women of group B marry men of group C; and women of group C marry men of group A. As Figure 3 illustrates, direct exchange requires only two exogamous intermarrying groups, whereas indirect exchange requires at least three (and theoretically could involve an infinite number of) exogamous groups.

In elementary systems, marriage links kin groups together. The groups involved in an elementary system may be as minimal as small family bands. Usually the groups are on the order of lineages, clans, or moieties. Repeated marriages between two groups over several generations perpetuate alliances. Thus, the groups with which one's own group has such long-term marital exchanges becomes recog-

nized and identified. This relationship may be acknowledged verbally or ceremonially, or may have more far-reaching implications for political alliance and economic cooperation.

Even where the forms of marriage are somewhat atypical, these intergroup relationships are recognized. The Saha of Colombia have descent groups, *sana,* that customarily follow certain intermarriage patterns. Each *sana* is associated with an animal, believed to be ancestral to its members. Thus, the Saha say that "jaguars must marry armadillos" (Safer, 1974). Among the Nayar, there are linked lineages with specified ceremonial responsibilities to each other. A woman's ritual husband must come from an appropriately linked lineage. Even though, in this instance, the husband's role is minimal, the linkage between lineages is highly significant (Gough, 1959, p. 173).

Property and Service Transactions

Gifts and exchanges of property and other related transactions serve as public recognition of the transfer of rights that takes place at marriage. In elementary systems of marriage, alliances between linked exogamous groups are solidified by such formal transactions. In complex systems, which do not set up such alliances, marriage exchanges symbolize the temporary associations between two groups.

The most frequently found property and service transactions are

1. *Bridewealth:* goods given to the bride's kin group by the groom or his kin group.*
2. *Dowry:* goods given to the bride or the newly married couple by the bride's kin group.

*The terms *bride-price* and *bride-service* used to be used to refer to *bridewealth.* They are no longer preferred because they carry the implication of payment made for the acquisition of a woman at marriage.

Figure 3   Circulation of women in elementary systems of marriage

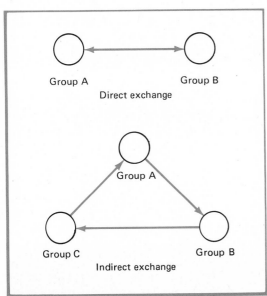

Group A   Group B
Direct exchange

Group A

Group C   Group B
Indirect exchange

3. *Gift exchange:* exchange of gifts or goods by each of the two kin groups being linked to each other by a marriage.
4. *Suitor service:* a period during which a groom lives with and works for the kin group of the bride.

In only a few societies is there an absence of any property or service transaction at or around the time of marriage.

To view these transactions as payments by a male or his kin group for the person or services of the female is not merely an oversimplification but also a distortion of the facts. Fortes (1962) points out that the exchanges of goods and services made during the course of marriage arrangements are a "means of winning and preserving the goodwill of those with the power to transfer marital rights" (p. 10). These are not one-sided transactions but, rather, exchanges in which valuable goods are passed both ways. Marital rights may simply be given in exchange for cattle, cowrie shells, coins, or whatever. But there may also be an exchange of material goods in *both* directions. In this case, the goods given by the kin group of the woman usually are of no more than

Figure 4 **Marriage transactions.** (Goody, 1973)

token value; in surrendering the woman herself, this group is parting with its most valuable commodity. Figure 4 illustrates the usual movement of goods and services in various marriage transactions.

Bridewealth and Dowry. Bridewealth and dowry, although given by the kin groups of groom and bride respectively, are not opposites. Bridewealth is given by the bridegroom and his kin group to the kin group of the bride in return for certain rights to the bride. The bridewealth is not given to the newly married couple but is kept by the bride's kin group. It is sometimes seen as compensation for the loss of her productive services or of a potential heir, since in patrilineal systems where bridewealth is most often given, a woman's child will become a member of her husband's kin group. In most cases, the bridewealth becomes a sort of circulating capital investment. It is used, in turn, to make the bridewealth payment when a brother of today's bride takes his own wife tomorrow (Tambiah, 1973, p. 61).

Dowry, on the other hand, is not a payment to a man or to his kin group. Nor is it to be understood as an exchange for his services in marriage. Rather, a dowry is the woman's share of her inheritance, which she takes with her at the time of marriage. As a sort of early inheritance, the dowry is available to the newly married couple for their own use (Tambiah, 1973, p. 64).

Bridewealth is a custom particularly widespread throughout Africa, where the amount of goods exchanged can be quite elaborate. Generally, the higher the amount, the higher the social status of the bride, and the higher the economic worth of the groom. Among the Baganda, the bridewealth may consist of several goats or a cow, and thousands of cowrie shells. If a man can accumulate enough property, he will invest it in bridewealth payments in order to secure additional wives and, thereby, raise his status even higher.

An Arab woman, wearing part of her dowry.
(Thomas Hopker, Woodfin Camp)

will reimburse him for these gifts and services, and the arrangement is terminated. If the marriage is to take place, however, the suitor gives the bride's father a further gift. This gift "includes as its essential element the precise sum in cowries that was paid to the midwife who brought her into the world, [signifying] that the bride has belonged to the groom's family, as it were, from birth" (Murdock, 1934, p. 580). The gift reinforces the alliance between the groups. After a third gift of livestock, palm oil, vegetables, and liquor, which is sacrificed to the bride's ancestors, the marriage is finalized. In poorer families, sister exchange replaces the midwife fee and fulfills the requirements of intergroup alliance.

In a second type of Dahomey marriage, which takes place when the "girl's clan is depleted in numbers," the payment of the midwife's fee is omitted. The bride then remains at her ancestral home, and her children are considered to belong to her clan (Murdock, 1934, p. 581).

When bridewealth is given, women and property move in opposite directions; when dowry is paid, both women and property move together in the same direction (Tambiah, 1973). Although bridewealth and dowry are different, they need not be mutually exclusive. In India and Ceylon, for example, both are given. In these societies, where property is transmitted through both males and females, these two different kinds of transactions coexist within a complex network of marriage transactions (Tambiah, 1973).

Bridewealth may also be considered a guarantee on the part of the groom and his kin group that the wife will be well treated in her new home. If she is not well treated, she may return to the home of her parents, and the husband will lose his investment in her (Murdock, 1960, p. 21). An important difference between bridewealth and dowry shows up in the case of divorce. In theory, when a divorce occurs, either all or part of the bridewealth that has been transacted must be returned by

Among the Dahomey of West Africa, there are various bridewealth exchanges, each indicating a different form of marriage. Usually the prospective suitor gives a betrothal present of cowrie shells, cloth, and grain to the father of the bride-to-be. This gift, which may be arranged while the two are still infants, commits the male to participation in funeral rites and performance of certain services for the female's kin group. If, when the female is older, she refuses to marry him, her family the wife's kin group to the kin group of her husband. But if the wife has received a dowry, she will be able to take the remaining portion of it away with her when the marriage ends, since it has always been legally her property (Tambiah, 1973).

Gift Exchange. Gift exchanges may range from a competitive attempt to outgive the new kin group to a token exchange of customary

"Pin money"—actually pinned to the bride and groom—is given by friends as gifts at this wedding on Cyprus. (Paul Conklin, Monkmeyer)

presents. Gift exchange accompanies marriage in our own society. Usually both kin groups and friends of the bride and groom give gifts to the bridal couple. In some instances, there may also be gift exchanges between the two nuclear families. Frequently, there is an attempt on the part of relatives to outdo the other group. The emphasis is on helping the newlyweds off to a comfortable start, but often there is also concern about giving gifts commensurate with those received on previous occasions. And, like many other peoples, we also offer gifts that are primarily symbolic in nature. The double ring ceremony popular in the United States symbolizes the vows taken by each new spouse; it also serves to symbolize the equality with which, at least theoretically, a man and woman enter into marriage in our society.

Suitor Service. In a number of societies, the groom must live with the bride's kin group for a particular period of time, which may range from a token few days to several years. During this time, he works with or for the bride's kin group. Sometimes he must produce a definite quantity of food supplies or give specified gifts. In some cases, his kin group must also supply gifts during this period. After the required period of service has been completed, the couple either returns to the husband's kin group or sets up housekeeping on their own.

A combination of suitor service and bridewealth was found among the Hupa and Yurok Indians of California. Postmarital residence was usually patrilocal, but a man who could afford only half the customary bridewealth would reside with and work for his father-in-law for a special period of time in lieu of the remaining bridewealth (Murdock, 1960, p. 21).

Among the matrilineal Hopi, there was a token form of marriage service, but in this case the bride lived with her husband's family for 3 days immediately preceding the wedding. She carried to her prospective mother-in-law a gift of cornmeal that she had ground. In the course of her 3 days' stay, she had to work industriously to grind additional cornmeal as well. During this time, her future mother-in-law had to defend her from mock attack for "laziness" by the paternal aunts of the groom. After the wedding, the couple continued to live with the husband's kin group for a few weeks, until he had finished weaving the special wedding clothes for his bride; she could not return to her home without them. When she did return home, both kin groups exchanged gifts and the marriage was consumated. Thereafter, the couple lived with the bride's kin group, and the husband worked for them (Queen & Habenstein, 1974, pp. 57–58).

All of these marital transactions may be spread out over a substantial period of time. Certain gifts or payments may be offered at the time the marriage is first considered. Sometimes additional payments must be made when a child of the couple is born or, later, when a child reaches puberty. The different payments or stages in property transactions usually represent stages in the process of allocating different rights. Among the Zulu, a particular payment (the *mfuko*) gave a husband exclusive sexual rights to his wife. If the *mfuko* had been paid, a wronged husband could claim compensation for adultery. Claims against an adulterer were not valid, though, if the payment had not been made. Other payments (in the form of cattle) transferred the rights to the couple's children to the father's kin group. Until this payment was made, rights to the children still belonged to the mother's kin group (Mitchell, 1962).

The types of property transaction accompanying marriage in any given society depend on several factors, among which are the nature of the prevailing economic system and the way in which descent and inheritance are determined. Leach contrasts situations in which property rights are vested solely in men, and situations in which property rights are vested

in women as well. In the latter case, marriage establishes a unique bundle of property rights; the children of any one marriage have a different total inheritance potential from the children of any other marriage.

In many societies, even where women may hold property, there exists the ideal that landed property should remain intact in the hands of male heirs. This creates a dilemma: on the one hand there is the notion that full brothers and full sons of full brothers *ought* to remain together in their ancestral home and work the ancestral land. On the other hand, when the wives of these men join the household, they bring with them property that will be inherited by their own children but not by their husband's nephews and nieces. Thus, each new marriage creates a new block of property interests, vested in its offspring, which is in conflict with the ideal of maintaining the social solidarity of male siblings.

There are several ways of resolving the dilemma. Leach mentions endogamy and fraternal polyandry as two different ways to keep property in the man's kin group. Fraternal polyandry seems to be particularly effective, for as Leach states:

If two brothers share one wife so that the only heirs of the brothers are the children born of that wife, then, from an economic point of view, the marriage will tend to cement the solidarity of the sibling pair rather than tear it apart, whereas, if the two brothers have separate wives, their children will have separate economic interests, and maintenance of the patrimonial inheritance in one piece is likely to prove impossible. If the ethnographical evidence is to be believed, polyandrous institutions, where they occur, are deemed highly virtuous and tend to eliminate rather than heighten sexual jealousies. (Leach, 1968, p. 79)

In the case of nonfraternal polyandry, as sometimes occurs among the Sinhalese, children inherit from their mothers and from the appropriate genitor/husband. The matrilineal Nayar avoid the predicament altogether by keeping children and property in the woman's kin group, where her brothers are in control.

Divorce

Now that we have considered marriage in some detail, we will look briefly at attitudes and practices that surround the dissolution of marriage—divorce. Discussions of divorce in other social sciences tend to regard its occurrence as a kind of breakdown of or deviance from socially acceptable norms. The comparative perspective of anthropology provides a useful corrective to such culture-bound views. In most of the world's societies, marriage is not considered to be the sacred once-and-for-always bond that our Judeo-Christian culture makes it out to be. Rather, marriage is usually recognized as being a fragile relationship that individuals may attempt a number of times before settling into a permanent arrangement. Riviere comments, "permanency in marriage. . . is certainly not a necessary characteristic of the union," and cites the *expectation* among the Irigwe of Nigeria "that a woman will move from husband to husband" (Riviere, 1971, p. 70), perhaps never achieving a permanent relationship, or perhaps achieving it only late in life.

Similarly, among the Toba of Argentina, it is expected that several trials will be necessary before the right combination is found to work. The right combination involves not only compatibility between husband and wife but also agreement of the wife's kin in particular. According to traditional sources (and confirmed by contemporary accounts), the customary rule of residence among the Toba has been matrilocal, particularly until the birth of the first child. After that, the couple might reside with the husband's kin. There is still a marked tendency to reside with or near the wife's family. This kin group often will bring pressure to bear on a relationship, ultimately deciding whether a man should stay or leave. A Toba woman with one or more children is a highly desirable commodity, and she can readily remarry if her husband should leave. No formal arrangement is necessary to dissolve a marriage union; the man simply leaves the residence and indicates that he has no intention of returning. He might return to his own kin group or take up residence with a new woman. This latter form of "trial" marriage has occurred frequently, but it is not necessarily considered desirable or preferable. Although those cases in which a couple's first marriage has lasted a long time have been relatively few, the husbands report proudly to a researcher that they are living with their first and only wife. Today Toba marriages appear to be in the process of becoming both less readily formed and less easily dissolved. Legal marriage documents are now required by Argentine law. These documents have an influence on marriage stability, but more importantly, residence changes due to land tenure problems and job opportunities seem to be playing an important role in the change.

But what exactly is marital stability? Many of us know of couples in our own society who stay together "for the sake of the children" or who, for some other reason, are never counted in the divorce statistics, even though their lack of compatibility or extramarital activities are common knowledge. We will consider *divorce* as the lawful dissolution of the legal ties established at marriage. Thus, separation and other breaks in marital relations, although they may occur with fair frequency, will not here be considered as divorce. Our society, which traditionally provided relatively greater accessibility of extramarital sexual relationships than of divorce, is not alone. Among the Nuer, for example, divorce, which is signified by the return of bridewealth, is rare, but conjugal separation is relatively frequent (Evans-Pritchard, 1940).

It is not unusual for the initiation of divorce proceedings to be a male prerogative. Among the Aranda of Australia, "a man may easily dispose of his wife. A woman, however, cannot secure a divorce; she can only run away" (Murdock, 1934, p. 39). Among the Baganda of Uganda, "a man can divorce his wife whenever he wishes." The primary reason for divorce here, as in many places, is a wife's barrenness. However, instead of divorcing an unwanted wife, a man will usually simply neglect her. Women are not without resources in this situation; a neglected or otherwise ill-treated wife will run away to her relatives. Her husband must then

explain his conduct to the men of her clan, give them a goat and a pot of beans, and, if proved in the wrong, make his wife a present and promise to reform. If she runs away repeatedly, he usually lets her stay and demands the return of the bride-price from her clansmen, thereby leaving her free to marry again. (Murdock, 1934, p. 541)

Among the Toda of India, "a man may divorce his wife on the grounds that she is lazy or a fool, not, however, for barrenness or adultery. He pays her family a fine of one water buffalo and receives in return any buffaloes he has given as funeral contributions" (Murdock, 1934, p. 121).

In Samoa, on the other hand, divorce is easy for both parties. Either of them may decide at any time to end their marriage, and do so by dividing up their property, including their children. Younger children go with the woman; older children go with the man (Murdock, 1934, p. 75). And among the Semang of the Malay Peninsula, partners can be changed with great frequency, especially when a couple has no children:

The husband simply leaves or is told to leave the shelter, which is the woman's property. If the wife terminates the union, her father must restore the bridal gifts or their equivalent to the husband, but if a man leaves his wife he forfeits the bride-price. The children normally remain with their mother. Either party may remarry, except that marriage between a man and the divorced wife of his younger brother is forbidden. (Murdock, 1934, pp. 99–100)

Divorce among the Hopi is similarly simple. A man may simply leave and return to his mother's house. A wife who wants to end her marriage announces this by placing her husband's belongings outside the door of their home (Queen & Habenstein, 1974, p. 68). Because of the strengths of the extended matrilineal household, the conjugal family can break up without disrupting the household very much. Nearly one out of three Hopi marriages ends in divorce, a rate that is, as Queen and Habenstein point out, roughly the rate in American society today.

In some societies, the position of women is far from being weak or vulnerable. For example, in a Dahomey marriage in which the full bridewealth has been paid,

the wife can obtain a divorce if the husband fails to perform his ceremonial duties toward her ancestors, or neglects his annual services to her father, or commits adultery with the wife of one of her near relatives. The husband, however, has no right to initiate a divorce. If he wishes to terminate the union, he can only neglect his spouse, insult her relatives, and resort to petty annoyances in order to force her to take action. A council of her kinsmen then assembles, reviews the evidence, and announces the divorce, which usually involves the return of the bride-price and other presents. (Murdock, 1934, pp. 582–583)

Full-bridewealth marriages among the Dahomey are less likely to be terminated than those in which the midwifery payment has not been paid and the wife continues to live with her kin group. Either party to the marriage can end this type of union, probably in recognition of the additional pressures that living with the woman's clan and kin in a predominantly patrilocal society can create (Murdock, 1934, pp. 582–583).

The role of extramarital sexual relationships in contributing to divorce is variable. It depends, naturally, on whether marriage in a particular society also confers exclusive sexual rights. It may depend somewhat on the kinship system of the society as well. Among the Haida of British Columbia, for instance,

either party may have relations with a clansman of the other, and the injured spouse, though he may object, can take no action. But adultery—a liaison with anyone else—gives adequate grounds for divorce. A husband can take personal vengeance against neither his adulterous wife nor her lover. The latter, nevertheless, must pay damages—not, however, to the husband, but to the wife's mother. (Murdock, 1934, p. 252)

Among the Yao of Nyasaland, women can sue for divorce only on the grounds that their husbands are impotent; most divorces are granted at the suit of men who take action following a wife's adultery. The adulterer is considered to be a thief who has stolen the husband's rights, and compensation is paid to the husband for loss of these rights (Lloyd, 1968).

Within a given society, the degree of marital stability is influenced by a variety of factors. Gibbs (1963) identifies characteristics of the social system that tend to contribute to marital stability:

1. Clear marital norms. The social system spells out clearly just what is expected of a husband and wife, assigning specific rights to each and formalizing the marriage in some more or less official manner.
2. Rewarding of conformity to marriage norms. The personal rights accorded to married individuals are considered highly desirable and are not available outside of marriage. Sexual or reproductive rights, for instance, may be limited only to married people. Or, in some societies, where women are an important source of labor, a wife may significantly add to her husband's economic and social status.
3. Punishment of deviance from marriage norms. Through various sanctions, especially the removal of personal rights or by subjecting the spouses to group controls, or both, individuals are strongly discouraged from nonconforming behavior.

Gibbs predicts that relative marital stability is also connected to kinship organization and descent. The relationships between marital stability and type of descent system and kinship organization are, however, far from clear. Matrilineal systems usually give women ready access to means of dissolving undesirable marriages, and matrilocality certainly makes the procedure easier. But, at the same time, these conditions place exceptional pressures on the marriage by surrounding the husband with his wife's kin at every step. And Gluckman (1950) has hypothesized that marital stability would be extremely high in strongly patrilineal societies where women were completely transferred into their husbands' lineages. These and other possibly relevant factors still remain as questions for further study and research.

Summary

1. Marriage as we know it is neither universal nor predominant in human societies. But some sort of socially approved relationship between adult males and females, providing for the fulfillment of sexual needs and the legitimacy of children, *is* necessary and universal.

2. Human sexuality and marriage are related in virtually all known human societies. Sexuality provides the biological basis of

human reproduction and the preservation of the species. Many characteristics of sexuality are shared by *Homo sapiens* and other mammals, but for humans the forms in which these behaviors are expressed are shaped largely by learning and cultural experience. The influence of culture on sexual behavior is particularly evident in the areas of childhood sexuality, precoital stimulation, extramarital sexual activity, and homosexuality, all of which are expressed in a wide range of forms in different societies.

3. No matter how permissive a society may be in sexual matters, there is always some rule limiting the category of appropriate sexual partners. The term *incest taboo* is applied to the prohibition of sexual access to certain categories of kin. The existence of incest prohibitions in some form is almost universal for all members of the nuclear family (except the husband and wife). But the tabooed relationships vary widely. Many theories have been proposed to account for the universality of the incest taboo—among them Freud's psychoanalytic theory, Westermarck's childhood familiarity theory, and the inbreeding theory.

4. *Marriage* is a socially recognized and relatively stable union providing sexual access, legitimating offspring, and establishing other rights and obligations between the marriage partners and other units of society. This definition has almost universal application— except for the case of the Nayar of India.

5. All societies have restrictions on whom one may or may not marry. *Endogamy* is the expectation that a marriage partner will be chosen from within one's own social group. *Exogamy* is the expectation that the choice of a marriage partner will be from a social group of which one is not a member. In every society both endogamous and exogamous groups exist. Anthropologists recognize that marrying outside one's group brings certain benefits to one's group. It also may be related to the necessity for group survival.

6. In some societies, restrictions on marital partners are also accompanied by a preference for marriage with certain other relatives. The most usual preference is for marriage between *cross cousins.* Societies in which such preferences are considered to be obligations are said to have *prescriptive marriage rules.* If such rules are followed generation after generation, close ties between the intermarrying groups will develop. The levirate and the sororate are special cases of prescriptive marriage rules. The *levirate* prescribes that a man marry his brother's widow. The *sororate* prescribes that a man marry the sister of his dead wife.

7. The possible patterns regarding how many persons one may marry at a time are *monogamy,* the marriage of one man to one woman; *polygyny,* the marriage of one man to two or more women; *polyandry,* the marriage of one woman to two or more men; and *group marriage.* Polygyny, polyandy, and group marriage are all forms of *polygamy,* plural marriage.

8. When a marriage occurs, either or both parties must change residence. Possible residence patterns are *neolocal,* in which the couple establishes residence without regard to the residence of the kin group of either partner; *virilocal,* in which the couple lives with or near the groom's family; *uxorilocal,* in which the couple lives with or near the bride's family; *bilocal,* in which the couple may live with or near the parents of either the bride or the groom; *ambilocal,* in which the couple is expected to spend time with the relatives of both the bride and the groom; and *avunculocal,* in which the couple lives with or near the groom's mother's brother. The location of postmarital residence is deeply bound to facets of a society's social and economic system, and it has far-reaching political and psychological consequences.

9. Various exchanges and transactions accompany marriage. Exchanges of women among social groups serve to tie the groups together in economic and political matters.

The property and service transactions that may accompany marriage are *bridewealth,* goods given to the bride's kin group by the groom or his kin group; *dowry,* goods given to the bride by her own kin group; *gift exchange* between the two kin groups; *suitor service,* in which the groom lives with and works for the family of the bride for a period of time. All of these marital transactions may be spread out over a period of time.

10. From the comparative perspective of anthropology, *divorce* is the lawful dissolution of the legal ties established at marriage. In many societies, marriage is recognized as a trial-and-error period, and series of marriages are not unusual. Grounds for divorce, economic transactions that accompany divorce, disposition of children, and rules regarding remarriage vary significantly from group to group.

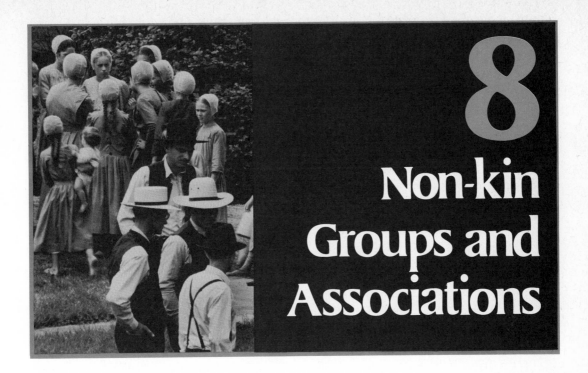

8

Non-kin Groups and Associations

I N the preceding chapters, we discussed some of the social implications of kinship and marriage in small-scale, traditional societies. Although the organization of these societies is dependent more upon the structuring of kinship and marriage, perhaps, than upon any other pattern of social relations, the principles governing kinship, residence, and marriage constitute fundamental building blocks for the formation and maintenance of social institutions in virtually every human society.

We now will turn our attention to other patterns that also contribute to ordered social life. These patterns include ritual kinship ties, the criteria of age and sex in forming groups, secret societies, voluntary associations, and ethnicity. In this chapter, we shall investigate the ways in which all of these are organized, the place each of these plays in ordering social life, and their contributions to social integration and/or conflict. In a later chapter, we will

consider caste and social class as other patterns of social organization.

The Nature of Social Groups

First, we must understand the nature of social groups generally before we look at specific instances. *Social groups* are composed of individuals who interact over a period of time in relatively consistent and predictable ways. A group comes into existence for the purpose of achieving certain common aims or goals, and individual members are expected to act in ways that best serve the interests of the group. Even though many social groups form purely for some temporary purpose—such as providing relief for a group of disaster victims—they are distinguishable from crowds, gatherings, and other collectivities that arise spontaneously and dissolve just as quickly after brief, unpredictable interaction. Thus, the members of a religious congregation who gather to worship together every week may be considered a social group, but those individuals who fill a football stadium to urge the home team to a play-off berth are merely members of a crowd.

A social group whose membership is based on face-to-face interactions is called a primary group. Naturally, primary groups are usually relatively small—for example, the members of a conjugal family or the religious congregation mentioned above. *Secondary groups,* on the other hand, are generally large—for example, a clan or all the members of a college's alumni association—although size alone is not a reliable indicator of the nature of a given group. The employees of a small factory, some working days and others nights, would be a secondary group because not all of its members interact on a firsthand basis.

Some of the descent groups discussed in the chapter on kinship are primary groups. Others have become secondary groups, because they are geographically scattered and have been segmented for so long that their members do not always know one another and often will never meet. A social group, then, is defined by its internal organization, that is, according to the ways in which its members are related to one another.

Recruitment to Social Groups

The key to the formation and persistence of any social group is recruitment. If membership in the group is voluntary, there must be ways to encourage prospective members to join. Even if membership is involuntary, there must be some means to compel members to act in the group's best interests. Culture plays a crucial role in encouraging recruitment to social groups.

The rules and procedures of recruitment rarely are so clearly defined or so potent that the individuals involved have no choice over whether they will participate or, conversely, that those nominally excluded may never arrange to become members. Instead, recruitment designates who is *eligible* to join a specific social group. It is often left up to the individual to decide whether to participate in the affairs of the group and, if so, to what degree. There are cases, of course, of groups whose membership is predefined and automatic, such as societies which organize their members into age sets or age grades where no choice is possible to the individual. In a society organized into special age categories, an individual enters the youngest age grade upon reaching a certain age and passes successively to more senior grades as he or she grows older.

Anthropologists who take a structural-functional approach believe that every social group serves an adaptive function in that it enhances the chances of survival for the larger community. For example, among the Masai of East Africa, the age-grade system provides for community defense and protection of herds, communication with neighbors, and maintenance of public order. But the functions of societal institutions and arrangements may change as social needs change. If the Masai were to cease to be herdsmen and turn to agriculture, the economic function of their age grades would either shift to the agricultural sphere or, if this proved impossible, would significantly decline. Similarly, in nineteenth-century America, when horses supplied the chief means of transportation and agricultural power, blacksmithing was a thriving trade, and blacksmiths' associations were numerous and economically powerful. When automobiles and tractors replaced horses and mules, the blacksmith became economically marginal, and his associations vanished because they no longer served a significant function. Thus, technological change as well as function influences the formation and persistence of social groups.

Ritual Kinship

Ritual (or fictive) kinship serves as a bridge between the kin group and the larger society. *Ritual kinship* describes the formalized relationship modeled on kin relations that one may have with a nonkin individual. A common form of ritual kinship is *compadrazgo,* or godparenthood, which itself shares many features both with kinship and with other kinds of social relations. By examining several of the forms ritual kinship may take, we shall be able to see how and why this kind of relationship has come to play an important role in some societies.

Godparenthood is the example of ritual kinship par excellence. Individuals become godparents by agreeing to "sponsor" a child, usually when he or she is baptized. Although the apparent focus of this relationship is on the godparents and the child, the primary focus is on the relationship between the parents and the godparents. The godparents agree to become coparents with the child's actual parents. In other cases of fictive kinship, "brotherhood" is entered into by means of a ritual performed by the individuals themselves. This ritual may involve the mixing, exchange, or ingestion of some ritual substance—blood, saliva, semen, food, alcohol. A weakened form of such ritual may be detected in the sealing of a bargain between two parties with a drink, the drinking of toasts, and the division

Godparents in Mexico participate in the baptism of their godchild. (Herb Taylor, Editorial Photocolor Archives)

of a large cake for the celebrants at a birthday, wedding, or holiday feast. In some cultures, no direct or formal exchange is necessary. Among the Eskimo, delivery by the same midwife establishes a bond of brotherhood. In fact, children delivered by the same midwife are subject to an incest taboo, perhaps because the Eskimo stress roles (as brother and sister) rather than position in such matters.

From the point of view of the community, there are advantages of *compadrazgo* and other forms of ritual kinship. The system of obligations and prestige placed upon the parties to such a relationship makes "the immediate social environment more stable, the participants more interdependent and more secure" (Mintz & Wolf, 1950, p. 344). It does this by linking in a relationship of mutual obligation and trust members of society who would not otherwise be related. In some cases, it serves as a social leveling device by which the poor have access to more wealthy members of the community. In other cases, ritual kinship may serve to unite individuals for other purposes. For instance, two men may establish a *fictive kin* relationship in order to avert a possible adultery (and the jealousy and hostility that might ensue) between the wife of one and a close male friend of the family. In small societies, such jealousy is not only disruptive but can lead to fission of groups into population levels that may make subsistence difficult. By establishing a ritual kinship that entails sacred privileges and obligations, possible trouble is nipped in the bud (Pitt-Rivers, 1973). Ritual kinship serves as an addition to actual kinship in most cases. An adopted kinsman does not give up the association with his or her real kin. Because ritual kinship may serve functions and needs that actual kinship does not, the two relationships may coexist.

The most striking contrast between ritual and actual kinship involves the matter of choice, already noted. Parents are free, at least in theory, to ask any other members of the community to serve as godparents to their children. Sometimes godparents are chosen from a social group that has higher prestige and/or wealth than the social group of the infants' parents. This ensures access to—and the possibility of help from—the social group represented by the godparents. Mintz and Wolf (1950) point out that parents choose godparents from outside their own social group only when there is cultural or economic reason to do so. For example, a local peasant who has no hope of achieving upward mobility either for himself or his children is unlikely to seek godparents outside the peasantry. Instead he would seek, by his choice of *compadres,* to solidify his position within his own group or community. Mintz and Wolf (1950) provide several other examples that serve to illustrate this point.

The Maya Indians of Tusik, in the Yucatan Peninsula, comprise an agricultural society, raising maize, which they consume, and chicle, the only cash crop. No member of the society enjoys inherently higher economic status than the others, although some may accumulate more wealth by extracting more chicle than their neighbors. They carry on their trade with traveling merchants, with whom they enjoy good relations. But they make no effort to bind the merchants to the community by choosing them as *compadres,* preferring instead to employ the child's grandparents or tribal chiefs for this purpose. The reasons for this seem to lie in the fact that there are no social means of mobility between the Tusik Maya community and the broader society. Since the Tusik Maya apparently lack any effective mechanism for improving economic relations with the merchants or an acceptable means for attaining prestige with members of an outside group, they are content to confer *compadrazgo* upon their own folk.

The sugar cane fields around Barrio Poyal, a rural community on Puerto Rico's southern coast, were formerly owned by local plantation owners. Residents of the barrio who make up the labor force once chose compadres for their children from among these wealthy landholders, but now that the land is owned by large corporations, the workers pick as *compadres* their neighbors and fellow workers. Members of the managerial and entrepreneurial class—foremen, administrators, public officials, shopkeepers—are shunned because they no longer interact with the workers. Furthermore, many workers migrate to the United States and no longer provide a stable working-class community. Today, if a worker seeks a wealthy *compadre,* he is criticized by his compatriots. In this case, the lesson seems clear: unless there are social and economic advantages to *compadre* relationships, these will disintegrate and disappear.

A contrasting example is provided by the practice of *compadrazgo* in Moche, a community on the coast of Peru. The Mocheros, who are native to Peru, are rapidly assimilating a Spanish way of life, owning land individually, taking jobs outside the community, and entering the professions. But although many native customs have died out, *compadrazgo* has grown stronger than ever before. Godparents are sought not only among the Mocheros but from outside the community as well. According to Gillin (1945), parents aspire to secure godparents who are well-off, influential, and socially well-connected and who will help both child and parents to achieve social and economic advancement. Thus, ritual kinship serves to support social mobility when it is already present, but it cannot establish social mobility in and of itself.

The case of Moche reveals the attempts of a community to reduce as much as possible the friction between itself and the larger society with which it seeks to merge. By this means, the process of assimilation is facilitated. Other examples provided by Mintz and Wolf, such as San José, a coffee and farming community in Puerto Rico, reveal how *compadrazgo* may stabilize relations between landholders and agricultural workers or between large and small landholders in an area where little or no social mobility is possible. Large landholders serve as *compadres* for small landlords, and small landholders for landless workers. In this manner, important social links are provided in a society where inequality of wealth could produce friction and potential conflict.

Social Categories Recruited by Age

Age Grades

All known societies differentiate members according to age. Our English terms infant, child, youth, teen-ager, adult, and elder, among others, all indicate age categories, however imprecisely defined. They differ from the age terms found in other societies by lacking clearly defined boundaries. Except for teen-ager, we would be unable to set with certainty the chronological limits of any of these terms. If we were to try, we would discover a good deal of overlapping adjacent terms. For example, youth and teen-ager appear to refer to similar age periods, but for many they are probably not identical. We might think of some preteens as youths and some teen-agers as adults. In fact, we would be unable to agree on the age at which a member of our society becomes an adult, although a number of possibilities suggest themselves, such as the minimum age for voting or entering military service, marrying without parents' permission, or even viewing an X-rated film.

So much imprecision and variance in our classification of age categories may lead us to suspect that our society lacks *age grades*—categories of persons arranged according to age only. This suspicion is correct, for, in fact, our society does lack a specific, uniform set of terms designating age grades, and we do not designate age grades at all. Of the terms we examined earlier, some have fairly precise definition, but others do not. For example, how should we refer to the newborn: infant, baby, or child? The law, whose terms best approach the technical precision of age grades in our language, uses only the term infant for anyone who is not an adult. This state of affairs may be contrasted with the Masai, for example, who divide their males into uninitiated youths, young men or warriors, elders, and ancient elders (Gulliver, 1965). Every male in the community belongs to one of these grades—and over the course of his life, he may belong to all of them. The roles and behaviors of each grade are so specific that every male knows what is expected of him both in public and private life as a member of the age grade.

These boys of the Namba tribe have been initiated into puberty by a rite of passage, which consists of circumcision, a period of segregation, a washing ceremony, and a feast, after which they return to the community. (Kal Muller, Woodfin Camp)

A system of age grades is characterized by orderly sequence of membership from one grade to another and specific behavior required of members of a given age grade toward members of one's own and of other grades. Entry into the lowest grade occurs at a specified age. Members of younger grades pass into progressively older ones at certain times, usually either when they, as individuals, reach a particular age or when an entire age grade is initiated into the next grade in the sequence. Whether shifts of grade are done on an individual or on a group basis, they are usually accompanied by some rite of passage or some other ceremony such as a feast.

The Jie of Uganda appear to have a rather straightforward age-grade system. Generations are established at approximately 25-year intervals, when members of the junior generation begin to be initiated. There are, in theory, only two generations, senior and junior, though in fact there are generally a number of young men and boys too young to go through the initiation ceremony with the current junior generation. They will be held over to form part of the next junior generation. Each generation adopts a name, usually of some animal—buffalo, jackal, snake, leopard—and small groups form within generations, also according to age. The age-grade system of the Jie serves to perpetuate traditional ritual activity and to establish ranking and leadership according to seniority. Seniority is precisely established and carefully maintained. Within a group, any member of a senior group is senior to all members of junior groups.

However, the actual operation of the Jie age-grade system is not as straightforward as it sounds. Seniority may not be determined simply by chronological age. For example, A may be senior to B because his father was senior to B's father, though A himself may be younger than B. This determination of seniority is a common feature of age-grade systems. It is also common for entry into one's age grade to be postponed for a number of reasons. If the initiation period is long, a prospective initiate may be held back by his family if his labor is needed at home. If initiation is expensive, it may be postponed because a family cannot afford the fees. In other cases, initiation into age grades may be accelerated. A man may marry young, thus graduating from the bachelor grade to the grade of married men. Or a young man may be suddenly promoted to the status of head of family because his father has died, although his coequals continue to be members of the "boys" grade. There are thus many cases where the age grade of an individual may be at odds with the chronological age (Gulliver, 1965).

Many age-grade systems are organized around specific biological or developmental events rather than other features of age. The age-grade systems of the Kayapó of Brazil are an example of this sort of developmental classification. Unlike the Jie, the Kayapó rank both males and females according to age in a number of grades ranging from infancy to old age. The stage representing infancy lasts up to approximately the age of 4. A single term is used to refer to both boys and girls in this grade. From about 4 to 8 years old, children are referred to as "little boys" and "little girls"; and from then until they are approximately 12 years of age as "boys" and "girls."

The next stage, the initiation into manhood or womanhood, shows clearly the developmental properties of Kayapó age grades. Initiation into adulthood takes place when the youth becomes capable of producing children, sometime between his or her twelfth and sixteenth years, and is a true puberty rite. The initiation period of young women is quite brief, but that of young men consists of a 4-month isolation in the forest. This difference between the sexes is typical of age grades in many societies. Initiation into manhood involves a number of other individuals of the same age, whereas initiation into womanhood tends to occur without so much public recognition. Thus, initiation into adulthood tends to be a more public and social occasion for young men than for young women.

By the time they are 18, most Kayapó young men and women have already married, thereby passing into the adult age grade. At this point, terminological distinctions between male and female vanish (as they were absent in infancy). The Kayapó use different terms for childless adults, adults with one child, and those with two or more children. Another term designates grandparents or people old enough to be grandparents.

At his initiation to manhood, a young man joins the men's society to which his nonkin guardian, or "substitute father," belongs. However, he does not become an active member of the men's house until he marries and his wife has borne a child. He is therefore excluded from participating in the important political activity of the society and village. But he may engage in sporting events such as wrestling and field hockey with senior members and participate in village rituals, singing, and dancing. Thus, the men's houses allow for

the expression and resolution of hostility among members, especially between younger and older members, by creating certain traditional modes of rivalry (Bamberger, 1976). By the time the young man joins the adult age grade in his society and begins to participate in village affairs, he will have successfully integrated his own interests with those of the community.

Age Sets

As we have seen, the term *age grade* refers to a category of people ordered according to age. An *age set,* on the other hand, identifies the group of members of a given age grade who pass together through various life stages. Age sets are usually given names and take on a group identity. The name may be a traditional one, used on a rotating basis with a number of others. Or it may be used once, then retired and never repeated. To illustrate, although we do not specify age grades and age sets in our society, we might roughly consider the cate-

Masai warriors of Kenya, with heads freshly shaved, assemble inside the circle of huts built especially for the ceremony in which they move into the junior elder age set. (Jen and Des Bartlett, Photo Researchers)

Figure 1 Nandi age-set system. (Adapted from Huntingford, 1953)

Initiates

Warriors in power

Small boys

Juma

Sawe

Maina

Oldest men

Kipkoiimet

Nyongi

Youngest of the old men

Kaplelach

Kimnyike

Old men

Old men

Elders

☐ Nandi age grades

☐ Names of the age sets occupying each age grade in 1938, at time of research study

gory "college freshman" as an age grade, while a particular freshman class—(say, class of 1984)—would be somewhat equivalent to an age set.

Members of a single age set enjoy certain privileges and have certain duties in relation to other members. They may be expected to offer one another support in arguments or fights, to lend money or offer other economic help as necessary, and in general to be generous and helpful to one another. Toward members of older age sets they must usually be respectful and obedient, but at the same time they often have the right to expect indulgence and favors from their seniors. One age set may exert some control over younger

age sets, but its members must usually present an example of proper behavior.

An example of an age-set system of some complexity is provided by the Nandi of Kenya. The influence of the age-set system upon military and political life is profound, and it plays an important role in regulating social and kinship behavior as well. Every Nandi male is a member of one of seven age sets; each set consists of the males born during a period of approximately 15 years. Each set, identified by a name that is kept throughout the lifetime of its members, passes through the following age grades: small boys (uncircumcised), young men (circumcised), warriors in power, and four sets of elders. (See Figure

1.) The changeover of each set from one grade to the next is marked by ceremonies, the most important of which is the circumcision ceremony. Each set moves through the various age grades; finally, the name of the age set of the oldest men passes around to the bottom of the cycle to the next set of small boys. In addition, each age set is subdivided into four *mats,* or associating groups, which remain constant as the members pass through the various grades. Huntingford explains these groups as follows: "The word *mat* . . . means 'fire,' and the term is derived from 'the fire that roars in the seclusion huts . . . of those who are being circumcised, and those who share such a hut are of the same mat.'" Members of the set of young men (initiates) gradually assume the duties of the warriors in power, thus allowing for gradual retirement of older members and continuity of power (Huntingford, 1953). Thus, age may serve as an important criterion for incorporating members of society into significant groups that share common identity and purpose.

Social Categories Recruited by Gender

Just as all societies establish social categories according to age, so gender is universally employed as a means of sorting people in one form or another. Mothers are distinguished from fathers in all societies purely on the basis of the biological differences between them, although the role of a mother in relation to her child and husband is not identical in every case. Here we will focus on the ways in which gender serves to recruit individuals into groups and categories of various sorts all over the world.

Groups consisting solely of men are more common the world over than those with entirely female membership. The men's houses of tropical South America, various parts of Africa, and Oceania are common examples of groups recruited according to gender. In many cases, the men's houses or societies have important ritual functions. But these practices often seem to do little more than mask the groups' role as the principal economic, political, and social force in the community.

In most societies in which it appears, the men's house serves as a meeting place and the area for preparation and storage of ritual paraphernalia. It may also serve as a dormitory for village men who must avoid becoming impure or polluted by living with women during their menstrual periods, for visitors, or for young bachelors. The chief purpose of the men's house, however, is to provide a place where men may discuss trade and hunting expeditions, warfare and politics, and everyday affairs. Affiliation with a men's house confers considerable prestige upon a male.

In a typical village containing them, the men's houses stand in the center of the community, surrounded at the periphery by the family dwellings and any other village buildings, such as the chapel or school. Distinguished by its position and size—the men's house is invariably the largest building in the village—it is a physical reminder of the significance of the social, economic, and political activities conducted there. Women are generally forbidden to enter the men's house and are confined to the domestic dwellings on the periphery of the village.

It might be expected that the men's houses and the societies that conduct their business within them would reduce the factionalism in the social group at large that often results from kinship loyalties and interests and thus produce social harmony. However, this is not necessarily the case. The Ge of Brazil, for example, promote aggressiveness, rather than harmony, as a virtue (Maybury-Lewis, 1974). Women in particular seem to be the targets of

Men's houses are familiar features of communities in South America, Africa, and Oceania. Here, Kamayara men of Brazil sit in front of their men's house. (Loren McIntyre, Woodfin Camp)

aggression in many men's societies among the Ge, but the aggression is not by any means confined to them. Aggressive relations are the rule between men of different factions within the same group, as well as in relations with outsiders. Maybury-Lewis attributes this antagonism to the strong sense of difference between a member's feelings about his own group and all other groups. Even in societies like that of the Sherente of Brazil, which are not organized around men's houses and associations, each village reveals a two-faction system and a strong sense of opposition

between factions. Those societies that stress aggression between age sets or genders express this aggression in open hostility.

Although men's groups are more common than are groups composed solely of women, some societies—the Plains Indians, for example—organize both men's and women's social groups. The Cheyenne had men's societies devoted to the making of shields and women's groups specializing in weaving. Membership in each was similarly restricted, and each group's work was equally guarded by secrecy and ceremony (Grinnell, 1962).

Virtually every society recruits members to social groups according to gender, and this preference is variously explained by each society. The important point to note here, however, is that gender constitutes a means whereby some members are included and others are excluded from a given social group.

Secret Societies

Another type of nonkin social grouping—secret societies—exists in one form or other all over the world. Much of what we know about their organization and function derives from studies of the secret societies of West and Central Africa. In these areas, secret societies have flourished, serving ends accomplished elsewhere by age grades and other nonkin groups. In West Africa, for example, secret societies superintend training in social conduct, teach local crafts and traditional lore, determine and enforce sexual and marriage codes, play key roles in tribal trade and politics, perform medical services, serve as local judiciary, conduct religious affairs, and provide entertainment and recreation. They also establish a social bond among members who may otherwise be loyal to different tribes, families, or territories and thus integrate a much larger population.

One of the key activities of any secret society involves the initiation and indoctrination of new members. The activities of the initiated group may vary slightly from those of other social groups in societies without secret organizations. But the fact that here it is accompanied by secrecy serves to strengthen new members' obedience to the authority of the group.

The initiation rites of the Poro society of the West African Mende show the breadth of the education received by initiates as well as the emphasis that is placed upon the group's social and spiritual nature.

The Poro

The initiation period of the Poro commences with a ceremony of feasting and ritual during which the young boys are marked or scarred on their backs in a manner symbolizing that they have been "swallowed" by the snake spirit, the marks having been made by the spirit's teeth. After a period of training in the bush, the boys emerge as if reborn and are granted full adult status in the community.

The training period consists of lessons in lore, crafts, politics, and law. The boys are expected to endure hardship in the bush, to cooperate with their companions in providing for the group, to participate in tribal ritual on cue, and to learn various points of lore and crafts from local specialists who instruct them. In Mende society these specialties include native law and practices, agriculture, building, weaving, fishing and trapping, drumming, singing, and acrobatics.

One important effect of the initiation practice and a source of its value to the community—as well as a key to the survival of the secret societies themselves—is the attachment that it engenders among members of the initiation group. Torn from their families at a rather early age and subjected to an experience that is exciting, strange, and somewhat terrifying, the initiates rapidly develop a sense of loyalty to their cohorts—a "corporate sense," as Little (1949) expresses it—that transcends local feelings arising from family, village, tribe, and even religion. A different secret society among the Mende regulates marriage and mating in the community. This society, called the Humoi, is headed by a woman. It determines to whom marriage is permissible, what constitutes forbidden and incestuous intercourse, rules of sexual hygiene, and punishment and compensation for infraction of its rules. If a trial or hearing were necessary in the event of a sexual transgression, however, it would be conducted by the Poro, which is the judicial body of the Mende. The courts of the Poro are composed of senior members of the society, who are usually also political leaders and whose authority and influence, especially when they sit in judgment masked as *jamu* (Great Masked Figure), is considerable.

Although the importance of secret societies such as the Poro has waned because of persecution from colonial governments, their influence continues to be strong. Initiation continues to be practiced, although it is briefer than it once was. Political leaders among the Mende invariably belong to one of the secret societies. The Poro determines the seasons for fishing, planting, and harvesting; sets rates for labor; regulates trade in certain areas; and even issues its own currency. It is no wonder that there is some tension and conflict between formal colonial governments and the powerful secret societies that serve many of the functions that governments seek to control.

Secret societies serve ritual and entertainment functions as well. Important events in the community are often marked by celebrations featuring the spirits of the secret societies, one of whose purposes is to amuse and entertain. Each spirit is impersonated in these celebrations by a member of the group who is hidden entirely behind a wooden mask. The "spirit" dances through the town accompanied by attendants, pausing to perform in front of the houses of prominent villagers. On occasion it dances to the beating of a drummer or, if the event is unusually important, to the singing of a group of women and the percussion of rattles and drums. Members of the community eager to achieve or maintain prominence throw money at the dancers (Little, 1949).

Secret societies are not confined to tribal cultures but may be found in every type of social organization. In our own society, secret societies may develop when other legal and educational institutions fail to accomplish what a number of individuals desire. They operate in secret, sometimes because their activities are outside the law, at other times because secrecy permits the members to carry out their objectives more easily, especially if those objectives could not gain approval from the larger society. In every society, whether or not formal secret societies exist, some forms of knowledge or skill are kept secret and remain the special province of a single group. Although secrecy is universally held to be advantageous, some societies do not form secret organizations to achieve their goals. Rather, they form age grades, associations of other sorts, or even informal groupings.

Voluntary Associations

In the United States in 1968 there were close to 11,000 national associations devoted to everything from sports, religion, and education to science and business. The diversity of these groups reflects the range of interests in our society. From the American Society of Golf Course Architects to the American Vegetarian Union and the Society of Descendants of Colonial Clergy, people join social groups whose interests and needs in some way match their own. Such groups are called voluntary associations.

A *voluntary associaton* is any group that one joins by choice in order to accomplish a common purpose. It contrasts with kinship and age groups to which one belongs by virtue of birth and maturation and with other groups in which membership is compulsory. In general, the more developed and urbanized the society, the greater the number and importance of voluntary associations. For example, in small, technologically simple societies, voluntary as-

Voluntary associations to help and protect migrant farm workers have grown in power as they have changed into modern trade unions. (Mimi Forsyth, Monkmeyer)

sociations often provide only recreation and may indicate distinctions in social rank. In larger, more complex societies such as our own, they also tend to serve political, economic, and even military functions.

One example that provides an excellent contrast between the organization of a small group on the basis of kinship and the more complex organization made possible through the formation of voluntary associations is offered by the Blackfoot Indians, who roamed the Great Plains in the nineteenth century and subsisted mainly by hunting buffalo. From autumn through early spring, grazing was poor and the buffalo divided into small herds. The Blackfoot correspondingly banded in small kin groups to hunt. In late spring and summer, however, the buffalo formed huge herds because grazing was abundant. The Blackfoot then organized on a larger basis by forming associations that migrated, hunted, and cele-

brated together. The choice of association was, within limits, up to the individual, so these large communities were voluntary in nature, even though every Blackfoot joined one or another of them (Banton, 1968).

Such voluntary associations were more closely connected to matters of survival than are voluntary organizations in technological societies. Yet, voluntary associations may fulfill similar functions today. The Blackfoot availed themselves of voluntary groups in order to solve problems that arose cyclically or periodically. Nowadays, an association may be formed to deal with a problem that arises rather suddenly as the result of rapid technological change or the migration of people from villages and towns to large cities. Industrialization in many societies has presented workers with unprecedented problems with which they deal by forming workers' associations that, in many cases, evolve into modern trade unions. But the problems of the worker who comes to the city from the countryside may not be confined to the work place. In some instances, workers' associations have become involved in matters of health, death, legal aid, unemployment, and savings. We recognize in these the health plans, burial insurance, legal aid groups, funds for workers who have been laid off, and credit unions that are frequent adjuncts of trade union organization. In small-scale societies, functions similar to these are served by kinship.

Similar organizations, in this country and elsewhere, are based upon the geographic or ethnic identity of their members rather than upon common occupation. In Sierra Leone, these groups are known as dancing *compins* (Creole for companies) and serve as mutual aid and protection societies as well as means to bridge the gap between small-town and urban life. Membership is sometimes open, but most members of a single association come from the same region or social group. Equivalent groups also exist in Ghana and Nigeria (Little, 1967).

Among the functions served by such voluntary associations are the following: financial assistance to members, especially those who must make the transition to an economy based chiefly on money; orientation to an environment consisting of diverse cultural and racial groups; teaching members how to dress and act in their unfamiliar surroundings; and protection of members, especially women, while they adjust to new social and sexual customs. These associations often have rules protecting the female members against seduction; they may fine members who are found guilty of adultery or other behavior detrimental to the good reputation of the society. On the other hand, members who run afoul of the law are assisted by the association, and members are encouraged to settle their differences through the association.

In general, voluntary associations such as these in Africa try to foster the feeling of an extended family among their members; to encourage the intimacy and generosity that is more characteristic of families than the formal, legal relations of the city; and to offer comfort and sociability. These practices foster feelings of solidarity among members and provide protection from other groups who are not sympathetic to them. They also help to form a base of self-interest from which political power may often be pursued by members of the association.

The common thread that runs through organizations of migrants to West African towns and cities extends also to associations of migrant laborers and squatters in the United States and elsewhere. In several parts of Latin America, and in North Africa, Turkey, and Iraq, residents of migrant settlements have organized committees aimed at providing electricity, running water, and other amenities of urban life. Many of the features of traditional "neighborhoods"—visiting, mutual aid, and benevolent relations—are in evidence despite the relative deprivation of individual residents and the absence of similar relations with people outside the immediate vicinity. Studies have suggested that life in the migrant settlements is usually less desperate and predatory than slum life in the same city or town.

As we have just seen, voluntary associations are often organized for the purpose of achieving specific, often temporary, goals. They thus reveal a flexibility that other social groups may lack and may be formed and disbanded when it is convenient to do so. Task forces formed to attack a single social or political problem, tenants' groups organized to force a landlord to make needed repairs, volunteers who collect food and clothing for people left homeless after a flood, or concerned citizens who respond to the mayor's call for volunteers to clean up a local park—all are examples of the kinds of voluntary associations that form briefly in our own society, accomplish their goals, and then pass just as quickly into oblivion.

"Ethnicity" and Ethnic Groups

Ethnicity is one of those terms that has come to mean all things to all people and is consequently impossible to define with any precision. Nevertheless, it is used here because it does call attention to group identity that cannot be distinguished on any other clear basis. Although it includes kinship, ethnicity is wider and larger in its reach than any arrangement of kinship. It is generally agreed among anthropologists that an *ethnic group* is a population with the following traits: it is biologically self-perpetuating; shares fundamental cultural values which are expressed in unified cultural forms; is charac-terized by internal communication and inter-action; and is considered by itself and others to have particular identity (Barth, 1969). The features of this particular identity are cultural similarities and differences that the members of the ethnic group itself consider significant. These are not necessarily features that indi-viduals outside the group would regard as identifying characteristics. Barth finds such identifiers to be of two types: (1) overt or ob-vious signs that people everywhere use to show identity, such as language, dress, or housing; and (2) basic values, the standards by which performance and activity are judged. Again, it is the individual members of the group—and not people outside the group— to whom these features are meaningful. Mem-bership in an ethnic group, then, results from the individual's self-identification as part of the group. By emphasizing their similarities to

The Amish are a still-recognizable ethnic group within American society. (David Strickler, Monkmeyer)

the overt features and basic values shared by others in the group, individuals declare "allegiance" to the ethnic group (Barth, 1969, pp. 14–15).

The Amish are an example of a recognizable ethnic group within the larger American society. They retain a distinctive appearance, pursue a life style that is at odds with increasingly technological habits, and insist upon their own educational system in order to teach their young people Amish values rather than those of the society at large. Thus, the Amish have managed "to maintain cultural continuity and cultural integrity, to remain a discrete minority, steadfast to their own vision of the good life" (Hostetler & Huntington, 1971, p. 116).

In addition to those communitarian societies like the Amish which maintain their identity by living in relative isolation from the larger community, there are ethnic groups which are not geographically isolated. Some degree of concentration and communication must be maintained, however, in order for ethnicity to persist. Identifying another person as a member of one's own ethnic group allows for further expansion of the social relationship between the two, especially in communities (such as large cities) where ethnic groups are not geographically isolated. Two such people recognize that they are, as Barth puts it, "playing the same game" (1969, p. 15). Thus, they are more likely to share understandings, judgments, and interests than they would be if they were not of the same group.

Likewise, one of the functions of ethnicity is that it structures interactions between groups. Specifically, ethnicity may facilitate successful commerce, especially for a group that is itself reluctant to engage in trade. In Thailand, for example, where the belief that commerce is "crooked" persists, the native population is ill-disposed to involvement in trade. "Crookedness" has been exemplified by villagers as "selling for more than the purchase price" (that is, making a profit) as well as giving short weight and offering goods of poor quality. Much of the commerce in Thai society is, therefore, conducted by foreigners and particularly by the Mon, a prominent minority group that began to emigrate from Burma in the sixteenth century.

In many respects, the Thai and Mon are culturally and racially similar, but the Mon practice elements of Buddhism borrowed from India and retain their own language as well. They engage extensively in Thai trade, especially in the manufacture and sale of bricks and pottery, the selling of thatch and firewood, and the hauling of these and other goods on boats and barges. They are able to engage in commerce because their ethnic differences permit them to minimize the friction inherent in trade, by ignoring the cultural discouragements from trading found among the Thai (Foster, 1974).

Ethnic groups often do not share the goals and objectives either of the larger community or the other ethnic groups who are their neighbors. As a result, multiethnic communities often experience conflicts and tensions among groups. The nature of these conflicts and the importance of resolving or controlling them will be discussed in the next chapter. Non-kin groups and associations, then, serve common purposes within the broader social system of which they form a part. They provide group identity and give a means for expression of common values.

Summary

1. A *social group* is distinguished from a casual gathering by its organization, duration, and predictability. Although kinship is the basis for organizing social relations in small-scale traditional societies, other groups are re-

cruited on the basis of age and gender. Still others are formed on the basis of voluntary association. Every social group, if it is to persist, must serve a useful function in society, and thus may change or disappear as social needs change. In industrialized, large-scale societies, an increasing number of social functions are served by voluntary associations.

2. *Ritual kinship,* of which *compadrazgo* is a classic example, serves to unite unequal elements of a larger social unit when other mechanisms in the society do not do so. It may function among members of the same group, as well as different groups, to increase interdependence and mutual security. Social or economic gain may be intended as well. Ritual kinship provides person-to-person relationships in an increasingly impersonal social structure and is a transition from kin-based to urban, industrial-based societies.

3. All societies categorize their members by means of age, but some more than others. An *age grade* refers to a category of people grouped according to age, through which members of a society pass at some stage of life. An *age set* is the specific group of people occupying a given age grade at a single time. A strict age-grade system entails orderly sequence and a code of rules governing relations between grades. Age grades participate in the conduct of important affairs including economic, political, military, and ritual activities.

4. Categorization according to gender is also common to all societies. Gender often serves to promote male control of the community. Men's societies are often identified with a men's house placed at the center of the village, from which women are excluded and where political, economic, and military discus-sions are held. Men's societies frequently serve ritual functions as well; their rituals commonly express hostility toward women and outsiders. Although men's groups are more commonly found than women's groups, many societies contain both.

5. Secret societies often develop to accomplish some objective not served by the broader society. These objectives may include education, the settling of disputes and legal questions, determination of political and economic policy, ritual expression, and entertainment. Secret societies almost always require lengthy, arduous initiation of new members, which serves to instill respect for authority and ensure their continuance in power. Initiation also binds those initiated together. Even cultures lacking secret societies usually reserve some knowledge or skill for a select few.

6. *Voluntary associations,* including many nonkin groups, are those which members join freely. In general, voluntary associations are more numerous in more complex societies, as they are better suited to promoting the political and economic goals of those societies. They often provide assistance to immigrants who are unfamiliar with the new environment and who join associations, often consisting of members from their native region, which assist their adjustment to their new experiences. In many instances, trade unions were originally workers' associations that served health, financial, legal, social, and educational needs of members. Migrants and squatters often form similar organizations.

7. *Ethnic groups* are biologically self-perpetuating, share and express common cultural values, demonstrate internal interaction, and are considered by themselves and others to be a distinct group.

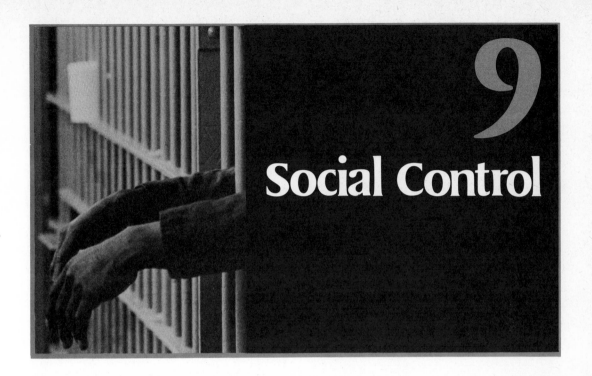

9

Social Control

IN the preceding chapter, we focused on the various rules that govern the formation of social groups in small-scale, traditional societies, as well as on some of the functions that these groups perform. In this chapter, our emphasis shifts to the topic of how social order is maintained. That is, we will look at the question of what makes people in a society act in the ways they are expected to act. How does any given society get its members to conform to its expectations and requirements? These questions were touched on in an earlier chapter where we discussed the relationship between the individual and culture. It will become apparent, also, that many of the non-kin groups that we discussed in the preceding chapter play a significant role in maintaining social order, and that many of their functions will also be pertinent here. Politics touches on the topic of social control as well. We will look at politics in a separate chapter later in the book; here we will focus on the kinds of control mechanisms that operate independent of political processes per se.

Conformity, Deviance, and Social Order

The problem of social order is basic in all of the social sciences. All consider principles of integration—that is, explanations of why and how humans interact with one another in meaningful and practical ways. The most basic integrating principles in a society are its rules, which govern such minor matters as table manners, and important ones such as trade and litigation. Many of these rules operate at an unconscious level. Individual members of a group are often unable to express in specific

Imprisonment is a formal means of social control that occurs most frequently in large nation states; small-scale societies tend to use other kinds of sanctions. (Paul Conklin, Monkmeyer)

customary, or they may be formally expressed as law.

Every society not only defines what it considers to be deviant or unacceptable behavior but also provides means for dealing with individuals who behave in deviant or unacceptable ways. The means of dealing with such behavior are known as *sanctions*. If, for instance, you take off all your clothes on a public beach and go swimming in the nude, you may be arrested, or at least get strange looks from the other bathers, depending on the beach. But sanctions take many forms besides strange looks or a night in jail. They are, in fact, some of the most diverse institutions studied in anthropology, as we shall see in this chapter.

Why Do People Conform?

Freud argued that social standards or rules are often at odds with individual drives and desires. The result is that people must block and sometimes suppress some of their basic drives. In recent years, this point of view has been modified somewhat. Society is increasingly regarded as channeling rather than blocking individual urges. But whether basic drives are blocked or channeled, the question that remains is, why do individuals conform to the rules of a society? Why don't they simply ignore what is expected of them and act totally in accord with their own desires and interests? What makes a person wear a bathing suit on a deserted beach when he or she could probably get away with swimming in the nude? Why does the driver of an automobile stop and wait through a red light at 3 A.M., when there are no other cars in sight? These are the kinds of questions that interest anthropologists and others involved in the control of human behavior.

terms the nature of the rules they are following. When rules *are* known and individuals are able to comment on them, anthropologists have frequently found that the rules are not always clear or unambiguous. Whether they operate at conscious or unconscious levels or both, rules embody a society's norms, its notions of acceptable and unacceptable behavior. As we shall see, rules may be unwritten and

Consensus Versus Coercion

In a discussion on social conflict, Ralf Dahrendorf (1959) presents two models that social scientists have used to account for the order and coherence of society: consensus and coercion. The *consensus model* is based on the idea that social order results from the general agreement of the members of a society on a set of values that are more important to them than any differences of opinion they may have. In short, it focuses on social commonalities. This model assumes that

1. every society is relatively stable;
2. every society is a system of interrelated or integrated position and roles;
3. each element in the system has a function (that is, it contributes something to the continuation of the system); and
4. the system is based on agreement among its members as to fundamental values and goals.

This model, as exemplified by the theories of Talcott Parsons and Radcliffe-Brown, dominated sociological and anthropological thought in the mid-twentieth century. As we discussed in an earlier chapter, one way by which individuals reach general agreement as to values and goals is through socialization. This is the process by which an individual internalizes the rules of his or her society. It provides the person with a recognizable identity as a group member. Internalization leads individuals to act the way they are expected to act without being fully aware that they are doing so. If, for example, you are convinced that it is wrong to steal, you will not steal even when it is clear to you that you would not get caught. Socialization is an important element in social order.

The *coercion model* presents a sharp contrast to the consensus model. It focuses on differences among members of society. The model is based on the belief that social order is a product of force and constraint. Its central idea is that there must always be some people who dominate and some others who are dominated. The assumptions of this model are that

1. every society is continually undergoing change;
2. every society displays disagreement and conflict;
3. each element in the structure of a society contributes to its disintegration; and
4. every society is based on coercion of some members by others.

Karl Marx, among others, held a conflict model of history.

These two models of social order are basic to all social thought, and both are widely used. They have generally been considered to be mutually exclusive. That is, if a society is stable, it cannot be continually changing; if every element in the society is contributing to the continuity of the whole, it cannot at the same time be contributing to its disintegration; and so on. Dahrendorf suggests, however, that it is not necessary to adhere to one model and reject the other entirely. There are some questions that fit the framework of the consensus model while others can be explained only in terms of the coercion model. Still others can be analyzed using either model. In short, the two models may be seen as complementary rather than alternative. As we have seen, some models may apply more to particular problems than do others.

How can these apparently contradictory models be viewed as complementary? According to Dahrendorf, every society is characterized by all the factors we have mentioned: stability coexists with change, integration with conflict, consensus with coercion. In fact, none of these factors can exist in the absence of its opposite. There can be no conflict if there is no integrated system within which conflict may occur. For example, conflict is unlikely between American hockey players and Tibetan monks because they do not share a common frame of reference. When conflicts do occur, as they often do in hockey matches, the source of the conflict is the differing interests of those involved.

Formal Versus Informal Control

Yehudi A. Cohen (1971) uses both the consensus model and the coercion model in accounting for the maintenance of social order. In his view, consensus is more prevalent in societies operating under informal control mechanisms such as customs. Coercion is found more frequently in societies that have specialized legal institutions and roles. Since this distinction between formal and informal mechanisms will serve as the framework for the rest of this chapter, it is worth discussing it in some detail here. Before we continue, however, we should mention the problem of relativity encountered in any comparison of social control mechanisms in different societies. As we have seen, not all societies hold people liable for the same acts. Even when they are held liable for the same acts, they may not be punished in the same way or to the same degree. Killing, for instance, is not always considered criminal in all societies. When killing *is* considered a criminal act, in some societies the guilt must be shared by the kinsmen of the murderer, whereas in other societies only the murderer is subject to punishment.

With this warning about relativity in mind, we will turn to the definitions of informal (or customary) control and formal control. *Informal control* consists of traditional or customary rules, beliefs, and procedures that are not arranged systematically. In some cases, as we mentioned earlier, some of these customary rules operate at an unconscious level. Cohen points out that resolution of disputes by informal control occurs in face-to-face, interpersonal contacts. *Formal control,* on the other hand, is characterized by a systematized set of rules and procedures—laws—for managing disputes. In systems of formal control, institutions and individuals emerge to interpret and enforce the law. This distinction between formal and informal systems of control is largely artificial. It does not mean that informal techniques are no longer in use in complex societies, nor does it mean that fairly formal control cannot be achieved without formal institutions. The distinction is useful, however, in that it helps us to identify the legal forms used in any given society. The distinction is purely analytic made for the purpose of understanding the differences and similarities among the ways in which social order is maintained in various societies.

Types of Informal Control Mechanisms

There are many informal means by which a society can get its members to act in expected ways so that the social system will function smoothly. Informal mechanisms are many and varied, as the following examples show.

The Reference Group. The concept of *reference group* has been developed most fully in social psychology and sociology. It refers to groups with which individuals either identify themselves as members or aspire to be identified. By adopting the values and interests of the group, individuals not only increase their chances of becoming a member of that group but also make it easier for themselves to adjust to the group once membership has been achieved. The reward for conformity—group membership—is so desirable to the individuals that it controls their behavior.

The role of the reference group can be seen clearly in many societies. The age grades and age sets studied in the previous chapter all act as reference groups. In such groups, the individual's sense of relatedness to the group is stronger than any sense of loyalty to abstract laws. If a person commits a serious crime—particularly theft or adultery—the group takes punitive action. The guilty person may be fined, ostracized, or perhaps banished from the group. The group's moral code may be reinforced by religious beliefs. It may be held that a person who commits a crime, and possibly other members of the group as well, may suffer bad luck, sickness, or some other misfortune.

When a member of a reference group commits a crime outside the group, the group remains important, though it usually acts differently than it would if the crime were committed within the group. This is because to outsiders, the criminal represents not himself or herself but the group as a whole. The group will usually try to defend and aid the offender. If a crime is committed by an outsider against a member of the group, the group often makes sure that proper compensation is made to the wronged member.

The Ndembu of Zambia, in particular, illustrate the role of the reference group as a form of social control. Victor Turner (1957) has shown that the ties that bind the Ndembu together as a group are not based soley on kinship or on politics but also on ritual system. Two kinds of rituals take place in Ndembu society: life-crisis rituals and cults of affliction.

Life-crisis rituals recognize significant points of biological and social development in Ndembu culture. The most important of these rituals signal puberty in girls, circumcision of boys, and death. Performance of rituals upon these occasions serves to reaffirm ties among various groups within the society. The rituals also recognize and deal with the changes in the social structure that will occur as a result of the life crises—the death of the head of a family, for instance.

Cults of affliction are performed to rid individuals of sufferings supposedly caused by various infractions of socially acceptable behavior. These afflicted persons are said to have been "caught" by spirits that have been made angry. An individual may be "caught" for forgetting to honor ancestors with small gifts or prayers at village shrines or for quarreling with his or her kinspeople. A man who is "caught" may be afflicted by bad luck in hunting (the Ndembu's primary mode of food getting). A woman who is "caught" may suffer from reproductive disorders, or, she may simply become ill.

The spirit that does the afflicting is a deceased relative, known and named, of the afflicted person. The treatment is carried out by a number of people—called "doctors"—who have been involved in performance of this ritual in the past. The status of the participant within the cult becomes higher the more he or she participates in the rituals.

An important function of the rituals connected with the cults of affliction is to revive the memory of dead relatives and thus remind the living of their kinship connections. During the ritual, the "doctor" with the highest status of those present frequently speaks to the afflicting spirit, mentioning its kinship connections with the participants. The "doctor" also discusses the unacceptable behavior that is believed to have caused the spirit's anger. In this way, the society as a whole (represented by the participants, of whom there may be a great many from various villages in the community) is involved in the resolution of the conflict. Thus, the group simultaneously reinforces its feelings of kinship and social unity and deals with behavior that violates the group's norms.

184   **Social Pressure and Gossip.** Another informal mechanism of control is social pressure. An example is found among American teenagers, who often experience heavy pressure to conform to group norms. Those who do not or cannot conform often are ridiculed and made to feel like outcasts. Social pressure can

Gossip can be an effective form of social control in small-scale communities, as in this small village in Spain. (Mathias T. Oppersdorff, Photo Researchers)

be a major tool of control everywhere; it is especially so in Far Eastern societies such as Japan. The Japanese make extensive use of shame as a way of punishing individuals who do not live up to expectations. Attempts to shame are so effective that they sometimes drive people to suicide.

Gossip is a common form of social pressure. Particularly in small-scale, face-to-face social groups, it can effectively shape social behavior. Gilmore (1978) found that in a rural Spanish community, for example, no woman could resist joining the group of gossipers in her street, for fear that she herself would become the subject of the gossip. Nor did any woman spend less than an hour making a purchase in the local shops "because of the polite necessity to chat with the salesgirls" (p. 91). The same fear of being gossiped about also applies to the men, who hang out in the bars and barbershops. The fear of gossip has a tremendous impact on the everyday lives of the members of this community. Most women in the community do not allow neighbors into their houses for fear of the gossip that might follow the visit. Even the most private decisions are based on "what people will say." Thus, most newly married couples have their first child right away so that the husband's virility will not be open to question. Gossip can clearly be a powerful technique for controlling social activity.

Ostracism. Another informal control mechanism is *ostracism*—the rejection or exclusion of an individual by the general consent of the group of which he or she is a member. Many groups use ostracism to some extent. In a recent case, an Old Order Mennonite was involved in a dispute with his wife's brother, who was also the minister of the church, the center of the social life of the community. As a consequence of the dispute, the man's wife and family, as well as the other members of the community, ostracised him. Their refusal to communicate with him in any way ranged from not eating with him to not engaging in everyday economic transactions involving him ("Mennonite Dissident Shunned by Church and Wife," 1973). In this case, the informal mechanism of ostracism was joined by the formal mechanism of the church supporting the ostracism. The threat of ostracism and its uncomfortable effects on the individual may in some societies serve to control behavior along socially acceptable lines. Ostracism is more likely to be an effective control mechanism in a small community than in a large one. A large community offers alternatives to the ostracized individual that do not exist in smaller communities. Such alternatives make ostracism seem less powerful a force.

Song Duels. The song duel is a rare form of social control found both among the Eskimos and in central Nigeria. Among the Tiv of Nigeria, it takes the following form: a person who feels that he has been wronged hires a song maker and brews a large quantity of beer. When both the beer and the songs are ready, he has a party at which the song maker teaches the songs to all the guests. The songs, which attack the character of the supposed wrongdoer, are then sung loudly and with gusto. Because the community is so small, the wrongdoer cannot avoid hearing them. The only honorable thing for the subject of the songs to do is to hire his own song maker, brew some beer, and have a competing party. This situation continues until the elders of the community invite the competing groups to submit both the songs and the original dispute to them for a decision on the merits of both. The person who wins the case may not necessarily be the person who wins the song duel.

Economic Adaptation and Social Control

Why do some societies tend to use customary control while others tend toward formal control? Cohen believes that the answer to this question depends on the way a given society has adapted to its environment. As we shall see, the control systems of hunting-and-gathering societies, horticultural societies, and modern nation-states differ according to the way each society distributes its resources and goods and the hierarchical organization that forms on the basis of this distribution. In other words, every society has rules governing the relationships between people and things. Anthropologists have observed that when these relationships change, legal institutions and codes also change.

Hunting-and-Gathering Societies. Hunting-and-gathering societies hunt game, fish, and gather wild plant foods as their primary means of subsistence. In hunting-and-gathering societies, no single member has exclusive control over the group's resources. Every member of the group has an equal right to hunt and gather within a given territory. As a result, there are no individuals with the power to enforce decisions by denying others access to resources. Therefore, coercion is less apparent, and formal law does not develop in these societies.

A hunting-and-gathering group generally is small. Relationships within the group are close and personal; in fact, the members of the group are highly interdependent. Almost all of their activities take place in the open. Such conditions are conducive to customary rather than formal techniques for settling disputes since customary techniques are based on face-to-face interactions. Examples of such informal techniques are the mechanisms of witchcraft accusations, sorcery, joking, and teasing.

If these methods fail, there is another possible solution: one or both of the disputants may leave and join another camp. Since the members of a hunting-and-gathering society have few possessions and do not own any particular territory, this is relatively easy to do.

Besides, intermarriage with other groups is so widespread that any individual can usually find kin in another camp and use affinity as a basis for joining these camps. This technique for settling disputes shows adaptive behavior in that it is necessary for hunting-and-gathering groups to divide periodically in any case in order not to put excessive pressure on available resources.

In hunting-and-gathering societies, every person frequently is expected to settle his or her own disputes. A person must serve as his or her own lawyer and judge, using the customary standards of the group as the basis for the ultimate decision. Thus, in these societies there is no particular specialization of roles—legal or otherwise—nor is there any differentiation of institutions—such as courts—for settling disputes.

Horticultural Societies. Horticultural societies are those that use plant cultivation, usually with rather simple tools, as their primary means of subsistence. In a horticultural society, individuals are tied to the land and depend on it for their sustenance. As a result, particular groups acquire exclusive rights to particular territories, and individuals within the groups are given the right to use portions of that territory. Membership in the group and the right to use its land are both inherited.

It follows that a horticultural society will develop rules of property—techniques to protect the cultivator's right to continuous use of the land. In addition, the fact that land suitable for cultivation is usually in limited supply means that the group—not the individual—must control the distribution of land. Since the group is usually a kin group (such as a lineage or clan), it is likely that the head of the group will become a headman or chieftain who may resolve disputes among the members.

The system of social control in horticultural societies is more impersonal than that in hunting-and-gathering societies. Although individuals no longer solve all of their disputes on their own and some submit to the chief for arbitration, informal techniques continue to be used in most cases.

The Nation-State. According to Cohen, the replacement of customary control with formal control is an outcome of the establishment of a nation-state. State formation occurs as the result of a mixture of political, economic, and historical circumstances. Simply put, a state is formed when one group gains centralized political control over all the other groups within the society, usually by means of coercion. The ruling group is then faced with the problem of maintaining that control, and for this a formal legal system is essential.

The shift to formal law does not occur all at once, however. In newly formed state societies, informal techniques continue to be used in personal and village relationships, between neighbors and among kinspeople. Formal law is used in matters relating to the central government, in taxation, military service, and the like. The two types of control can exist side by side because informal control involves continuous face-to-face interaction while formal control does not.

Centralized authority is almost always achieved at the expense of local autonomy. The rulers are continually attempting to gain more power while local authorities try to retain as much autonomy as they can. A successful state is one that has managed to persuade or coerce local leaders to transfer their loyalties from the local community to the ruling group. The state continues to be divided into local areas, but this is primarily for administrative purposes. The benefits of such a system are efficiency and equality of treatment. But it results in a highly impersonal and often complex relationship between the individual and the state.

Law and Legal Processes

Whatever the specific definition of law, it is generally agreed that it involves some form of social control—some way of responding to deviations from the society's norms. In our society, social control through law takes the form of a complex system of police, lawyers, judges, and juries. In other societies, there may be no courts or policing, but there is law, nonetheless. Consider the following example:

A Florida Seminole kills one of his fellows and, according to Seminole law, the oldest member of the victim's family is supposed to take revenge by killing the murderer. In one case, an old Seminole of more than ninety years had to be propped up with a gun and told to pull the trigger. The state of Florida, of course, has its own law and in accordance with this law the old man was arrested and brought to trial. The point is that by acting in accordance with his own law, the Seminole violated the law of the white man. (Dundes, 1968, p. 253)

When does customary law, such as that of the Seminole, become formal law? When there are courts and judges? When the laws are written down? What happens when dif-

Legal proceedings may be more or less formal depending on the size and character of the society in question. Here, a woman of the Kpelle tribe in Liberia is being tried in a village court; the "town chief," at right, presides. (Jacques Jangoux, Peter Arnold Photo Archives)

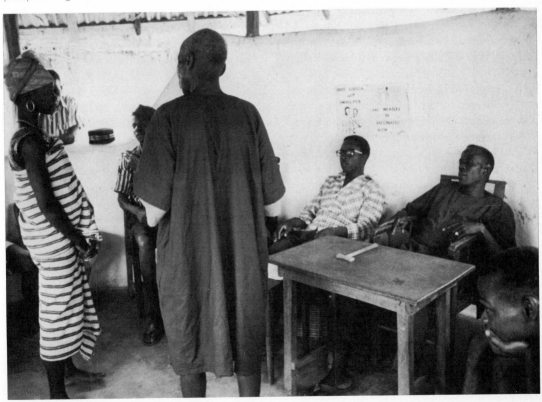

ferent legal systems come into contact with one another, as they do increasingly in the modern world? There are almost as many ways of looking at law as there are students of law. In this section, we will discuss some of the approaches to law and present an illustration of a society that is in the process of substituting formal law for customary law.

Approaches to the Definition of Law

The "Reasonable Man." Max Gluckman (1963) sees legal systems as being based on what the "reasonable man" would consider fair. He illustrates this principle with a discussion of a case involving a marital dispute that was decided by a Barotse court (the Barotse are a Bantu people who live in Rhodesia).

In Barotseland, men can divorce their wives simply by sending them home. But in order for a woman to divorce her husband, she has to prove in court that he has not behaved as a reasonable husband. Thus, Barotse judges have to decide what is involved in being a "reasonable" husband. This is not easy under any circumstances, but in Barotseland it is complicated by the fact that in order to provide material goods for his wife, the man must go away to European settlements to earn wages. However, if he does so, he is unable to sleep with his wife or be a companion to her. The Barotse have therefore passed a law stating that a husband cannot be away for longer than a fixed period. If he is absent for a longer time, his wife is entitled to a divorce.

In the case in question, a woman brought suit for divorce, stating that her husband had been away longer than the period fixed by law; the court granted the divorce. It turned out that her husband had been on his way home when the divorce was granted. The woman wanted to go back to her husband, but her father claimed that this would be a new marriage and that he should therefore receive a new marriage payment. The court ruled that it would not have granted the divorce if it had known that the husband was on his way home. It interpreted the law's phrase "return home" to mean "leave place of employment," because the purpose of the law is to maintain marriages, not to encourage divorce.

The point here is that the Barotse judge has to interpret what is reasonable in each case that arises. Basically, the definition of reasonableness is derived from the standards of the community as a whole, from its opinions and customs. When these standards change (as they have been in Barotseland since the advent of European influence), the judge's interpretations change. Thus, a reasonable Barotse husband has always been expected to provide both material goods and companionship. When it became necessary for the husband to be absent for long periods in order to continue providing material goods, a law was passed to put reasonable limits on such absences. When the letter of the law was violated, the court made a decision on the basis of what was now reasonable under the new circumstances. Most members of Barotse society would agree with the court's interpretation.

Submission to Authority. In the preceding chapter, we discussed the Poro of the West African Mende as an example of a secret society. Such secret societies are instruments of social control in that they function to maintain the status quo and to enforce adherence to traditional norms. James Gibbs (1962) points out that the Poro of the Kpelle also requires unquestioning acceptance of authority. This respect for authority carries over into Kpelle political life, in which authority is exercised by elders and chiefs.

In Kpelle society, disputes are settled in a court presided over by the chief. The settlements reached are usually satisfactory, particularly in cases dealing with assault, theft, or possession of illegal charms. When it comes to marital disputes, however, the decisions of the court are less effective and often seem arbitrary. The coercive nature of the court's rulings often add to the tension among the parties rather than restore harmony. Thus, according to Gibbs, the respect for authority learned in the Poro leads the Kpelle to accept arbitrary decision making in the courts. This makes it possible for the courts to serve as a powerful force in sanctioning deviant actions, but it also limits the courts' effectiveness in certain matters.

From the Personal to the Impersonal. We have just described a legal system that appears to be based on consensus (the Barotse) and

Formal law tends to be impersonal and to involve specialists—judges and lawyers such as these in an Algerian courtroom—whose relationship with the disputants of a case extends only to interpreting the legal code of the society. (Coster, Monkmeyer)

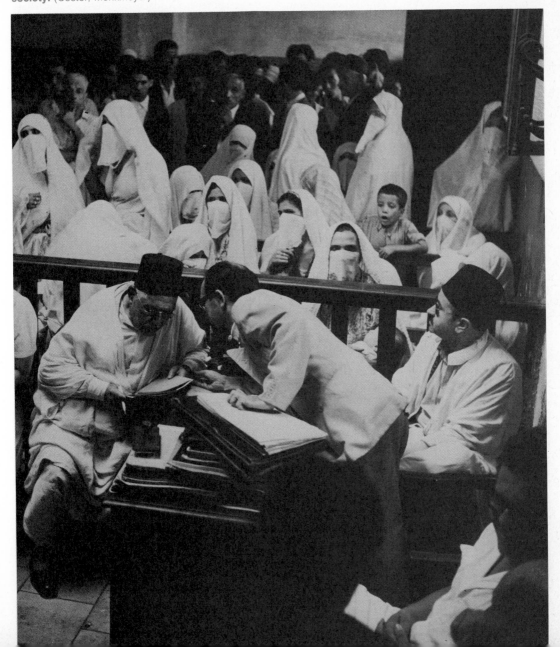

one in which coercion seems to dominate (the Kpelle). In both systems, we find courts and judges, but neither is entirely "formal." Customary law continues to play an important role in both Barotse and Kpelle life. Clearly we need a different standard than the presence or absence of law courts for determining whether a legal system is formal or informal.

In their discussion of social control and law in African societies, the Ottenbergs (1960) point out that the legal system in many African societies is concerned at least as much with reconciling the disputants as with arriving at a settlement. Since the members of these small-scale societies tend to be in frequent contact with each other, it is as important to restore social harmony as to exercise social control. Reconciliation between the parties can be even more important than determining blame or guilt. The speed with which a matter is settled is not as important, though, as thorough presentation and discussion of the information. Verbal recall of similar cases by the elders is highly valued: "In many parts of Africa there is great admiration for the well-tried case, for the speaker who summarizes a dispute or gives the judgment with clarity, for the elder who is able to cite past cases of significance or quote proverbs to make a legal point" (Ottenberg & Ottenberg, 1960, pp. 59–60).

The Ottenbergs' discussion illustrates an important point: informal law is personal, whereas formal law is impersonal. The legal process itself is specialized and specific. The disputant's relationship with a lawyer or a judge is to the case at hand and carries with it no other commitments or obligations. The relationships involved are simple in nature; the individuals' various roles do not overlap and are not juxtaposed. Where control mechanisms are more informal, as in the societies described by the Ottenbergs, this is not the case. The disputants and the elders have dealings with each other every day on a wide variety of matters. Their relationship is not limited to the settlement of a particular case in a specified field of activity. In other words, the relationship is multiplex.

The Sebei in Transition

When economic shifts occur in societies, laws and legal systems must change as well if they are to be useful in dealing with the new circumstances. Goldschmidt (1967) describes such an adaptation in the legal system of the Sebei of western Kenya. The Sebei were originally a pastoral, herding people. Their legal system was based on the fact that in pastoral societies land and water must be freely available to all the members of the group. Over time, though they did not give up pastoralism entirely, they became a horticultural people. In a horticultural society, as we have seen, the legal system is based on the relationship of people to the land—land ownership—since people depend on having the right to use the land continuously and to exclude others from its use.

But legal systems do not change all at once. The history and attitudes of the members of a group have a significant effect on the new situation. They place limits on the changes that may be made and the speed at which those changes may take place. Thus, the legal system of the Sebei shows a mixture of the more customary law of pastoralism with the more formal law of horticulture.

The Sebei approach to land ownership is adapted from their notions of livestock ownership. The men own the land, even though it is cultivated by the women. The men are obligated to supply their wives and their sons with land; they allocate land to their wives, just as they used to allocate cattle. However, the meaning that cattle had for the Sebei has not been transferred to land. Land is not used in paying a bride-price, for example. Yet the

Sebei value land: they have boundary markers, they argue over land rights, sometimes they build up large personal landholdings.

Along with the formalization of land ownership have come more or less formal ways of dealing with disputes over boundaries and the sale and purchase of land, as well as various contractual arrangements for its utilization. At the same time, however, the Sebei have developed an unusual technique of controlling individual behavior, a ritual called *ntarastit*. It consists of an oath that tribesmen take, indicating one's intention to behave lawfully and one's acceptance of punishment for unlawful behavior. Walter Goldschmidt (1967) describes this ritual as follows:

All circumcized men gather naked at the specified location, and before an altar of implanted branches of certain specified plants of ceremonial significance, swear as follows: "Anybody who kills anybody passing by (or who takes things belonging to others, etc.), may the earth eat him." They thrust their spears at the altar in unison each time they recite this formula, naming a different kind of offense. (p. 125)

Ntarastit thus consists of calling upon supernatural authority to punish individual offenses and thereby maintain peace in the community. It has several interesting features. *Ntarastit precedes* the deviant act and is thus the group's statement of the law. Furthermore, it is backed up by the group's readiness to act. If a member of the group commits one of the offenses named in the oath, he will be punished by the group after an informal hearing. (The punishment, incidentally, takes the form of destruction of the offender's property.)

Ntarastit is clearly a customary or informal method of social control. But it coexists with a more formal legal system having to do with land. In a nation-state, both the offenses covered by *ntarastit* (murder and theft) and matters of property would be settled in the courts—that is, by formal methods of control.

The Impact of the Nation-State on Traditional Means of Control

The development of a nation-state entails, in part, the coming together of a number of different groups under a single political umbrella. This can be a long and complicated process, since the various groups do not always share the same values and interests. The problem of forming a nation is not a simple one, since it involves political, economic, and legal changes in the organization of a society.

The Problem of Identity

One of the most difficult problems facing the leaders of a nation is how to persuade its citizens to identify with the nation as a whole rather than with their particular linguistic, religious, or tribal subgroups. Pandit Nehru, who guided India from 1947 to 1964 while it was becoming a nation after winning independence from Great Britain, was forced to recognize the linguistic variety of his people and to organize the nation along linguistic lines, despite his personal dislike of such an organization. He feared that the "narrow loyalties, petty jealousies, and ignorant prejudices" of the subgroups based on language would threaten the potential for the country's political unity (quoted in Harrison, 1956). Divisive contrasts in various countries throughout the world are based on racial or tribal groupings, language, religion, social customs, and region.

Clifford Geertz (1963) explains the problems of the coming together of old societies and new states as arising from two distinct and often opposed motives: (1) the desire to retain one's identity, which is often defined in terms of race, language, or tradition; and (2) the desire to be part of an efficient, modern state, which implies a rising standard of living, political order, and greater social justice. How can such opposing impulses be reconciled? Sometimes a new regime simply will ride roughshod over the attachments of individuals to their groups. This course of action may have the opposite effect from the one intended: feelings of identity with one's way of life may actually be stimulated or sharpened by the formation of a nation-state. At the same time, people and groups feel vulnerable and unsure of what will result when their old attachments are threatened by new influences in the nation-state.

Legal Pluralism

Apparently, then, the ties of individuals to their own language, religion, and so forth need to be recognized in some way by the leaders of a new state. Such recognition is often expressed in the newly formed legal system. The existence within a society of more than one legal system at the same time, some of which may actually be in conflict with one another, is referred to as *legal pluralism.* In many African nations, for example, there are European groups, Africans who have adopted "modern" European life styles, and many Africans who have begun to abandon their ancient traditions and accept European values but who have not done so entirely. The law for Europeans often is different from the law for Africans, and among Africans the law varies from one tribe to another.

As new states have been formed out of a number of tribal communities, a uniform set of "territorial" laws has been superimposed on the "personal" laws of the various tribes. But in many cases the tribal law is still in use. According to Max Rheinstein (1963), if this legal pluralism is used cautiously and wisely, it can

be a valuable tool for integrating different groups into a new nation. However, it should not be expected to work by itself, for pluralism has educational, economic, and cultural aspects as well. Native courts can handle cases involving matters such as the sale of cattle or payment of bride wealth, or even bodily injury resulting from a fist fight or damage done by stray cattle. Murder and transactions involving large amounts of money or property are increasingly handled by some sort of higher court.

But what happens in cases of intertribal conflicts? Rheinstein lists three possible ways of handling them:

1. simply applying the law of the court in which the case happens to come up;
2. developing a special set of laws for intergroup conflicts;
3. developing a set of rules for deciding which of the several sets of laws already in existence should apply to specific types of intergroup conflicts.

The first approach is unsatisfactory because it is unsystematic and may result in widely different decisions. An example of the second approach was found in the legal system of the Roman Empire. Originally, Roman law was the law of the city of Rome. When the Romans conquered Italy, Greece, and surrounding regions, they did not impose Roman law on their new subjects. Rather, they allowed each city or region to retain its own law. But as commerce and other contacts developed among different parts of the empire, disputes arose that had to be settled by the Roman authorities. The technique used by the Romans was to apply to such cases neither the law of any subject region nor the law of Rome itself but a new law of their own creation, the *ius gentium* "law of nations," as opposed to *ius civile,* or "civil law," of the city of Rome). Over time, the *ius gentium* swallowed up the *ius civile* as well as the laws of the various subject regions and became the universal law of the Roman Empire.

As Rheinstein points out, it would be difficult to develop such a universal legal system in many African nations. This would require law schools, libraries, knowledge of legal language, and long years of study. Even if such a legal system were developed, it would not apply to all kinds of intergroup conflicts. Some would still require the third approach—the development of rules governing which set of tribal laws should apply in any given case. This is also a very difficult task. Thus, there is a strong tendency for national leaders to favor uniformity over pluralism in the legal system of the new state.

Summary

1. Every society has rules governing the interactions of its members. These rules are often unconscious and may be ambiguous, but they are nonetheless effective in maintaining social control. Every society has means of dealing with individuals who deviate from its rules. These means are known as *sanctions,* and they take many forms.

2. Anthropologists are interested in what makes individuals conform to the rules of their society. The *consensus model* assumes that all the members of a society agree on that society's values. The *coercion model* assumes that social order is a result of force and constraint. These models can be seen as complementary rather than contradictory if it is assumed that the members of a society agree on its basic values but often have interests that are in conflict.

3. Techniques of social control may be seen as *informal,* or customary, and as *formal,* categories that are roughly equivalent to the consensus and coercion models. This is an artificial distinction, however; informal techniques can sometimes be highly coercive, and both formal and informal techniques may be used within the same society.

4. The *reference group* is the most important informal technique of social control. Because an individual's ties to the group are stronger than his or her loyalty to abstract laws, this serves to control the individual's behavior. Other informal control techniques include social pressure and gossip, *ostracism,* witchcraft and sorcery, and the song duel.

5. Anthropologists have found relationships between economic adaptation and social control. Hunting-and-gathering societies tend to use customary law because they have no central authority and can split up easily if a conflict cannot be resolved by other means. In horticultural societies, individuals are tied to the land they cultivate, and rules of property become important. In such societies, formal and informal techniques of social control may coexist. A nation-state is formed when one group gains control over all the other groups in the society and develops formal, impersonal means of maintaining that control.

6. It is difficult to draw a line between customary law and formal law. Societies that have courts and judges may have a legal system based on either consensus or coercion and still use relatively informal techniques of control. More formal legal systems are less interested in restoring harmony among the disputants; moreover, they entail impersonal relationships between the disputants and the legal authorities.

7. The leaders of a new state face a major problem in trying to persuade its members to transfer their loyalty from their local groups to the state itself. The desire of the individual to retain an identity that may be defined in terms of race or religion often conflicts with the desire to be a member of a modern state.

8. *Legal pluralism,* a system in which tribal law continues to be used in some cases and territorial law in others, could be a valuable tool for integrating the people of a new nation. However, the resolution of intergroup conflicts presents a problem. Should such cases be settled by the court in which they happen to come up? Should a new set of laws be developed for settling them? Or should a set of rules be developed to determine which of the sets of laws already in existence applies to a given type of case? The first approach is unsatisfactory, but either of the other two is very difficult.

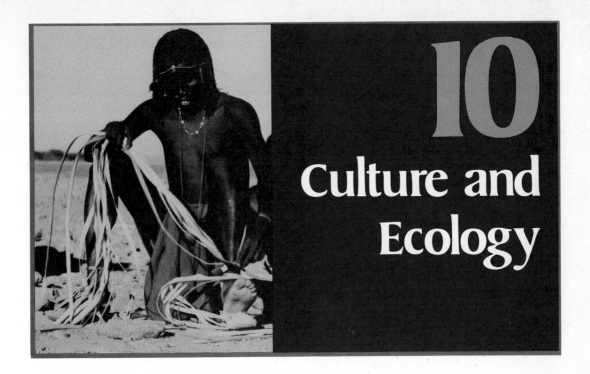

10
Culture and Ecology

WE are all by now as familiar with the word ecology as we are with the problems that first brought it to our attention: lakes and rivers polluted by industrial wastes, cities blanketed by smog from automobile exhausts. By dumping pollutants into the waters or discharging them into the air, people put the ecology of their cities and their regions out of balance. Environmentalists have been trying to correct the damage done by this exploitation or destruction of natural resources. When we look at ecology in this way, humans often appear as selfish, sometimes unconscious, meddlers with environments that would do quite well without them. For example, human communities require energy for heat, light, and other basic needs. A nuclear power station might be built for the purpose of supplying the energy required by a large population. Such a power station requires large quantities of water for its cooling opera-

tion. When the water is returned to its source, it will be considerably hotter than when it was withdrawn. The resulting thermal pollution may seriously affect the capacity of this body of water to support plant and animal life. Thus, in order to provide for human comfort, the ecology of a region may suffer.

Ecologists, however, do not view the human role in the natural scheme as so limited. Humans are part of a larger community that includes plants and animals as well as the physical features of the environment. This community is called an *ecosystem.* A single ecosystem may be quite small—a drop of pond water and the micro-organisms that live in it—or it may be considerably large—the earth and its plant and animal life. Whenever humans are part of a given ecosystem, they are its most dynamic members.

Ecology studies the ways in which all living organisms interact within the environment. The concept of ecology and its relation to culture will be the focus of this chapter. The interaction between culture and environment (or, more precisely, between specific cultural phenomena and environment) has always been a primary concern of anthropologists. The nature of the relationship between human populations and given ecological niches (that is, the totality of the natural habitat within which a population is located) continues to merit discussion and debate. We shall examine some early theories regarding these interactions, and then go on to survey more recent investigations of ecosystems and human populations.

Culture and Environment

Implicit in all ecological studies in anthropology is the notion of adaptation. That is, a human population adapts to its habitat when it is able to survive and perpetuate itself. Culture is the means by which humans make this adaptation. Some populations are better adapted than others; they are, in Darwinian terms, "winners" in the struggle for existence.

Culture and environment studies have generally attempted to deal with two different kinds of problems. First, they seek to explain why particular elements or sets of elements exist at particular times and in particular places. Second, they attempt to interpret how these particular elements function within a given cultural and natural habitat.

Environmental Determinism

The early generations of anthropologists, around the turn of this century, believed that the cultural features of a group were caused by the environmental setting in which the group was located. *Environmental determinism* (or *environmentalism*) held that the reason for the presence of a specific culture feature could be traced to the habitat in which it occurred.

Environmental determinism has a long tradition in Western thought. Some of the earliest histories of ancient Greece, particularly those of Aristotle and of Pliny the Elder, were based on similar notions. In the early eighteenth century, Montesquieu wrote of ancient Greece in a like manner. He believed that "the sterility of the soil of [Athens]" was responsible for the development there of popular government, while "the fertility of [Sparta]" fostered "an aristocratic ruling class" (quoted in Sahlins, 1964, p. 132). Even less convincing today is Montesquieu's notion that weakness and timidity, as well as indulgence in extraordinary sexual practices, were sure to be found among those who inhabit a warm climate (Netting, 1971, p. 2).

Environmental Possibilism

As comparative cultural data accumulated early in this century, the theory called *environmental possibilism* began to displace environmentalism. Possibilism claimed that environmental factors limit the adaptive possibilities for a given culture but do not determine which adaptations or choices a society makes. For example, arable land makes it possible for a society to practice agriculture but does not guarantee that it will. Aided by the growing number of studies of various cultures, anthropologists noted that quite different cultural phenomena frequently arose under identical environmental conditions. In a famous instance, Kroeber (1923) observed that in the same region of the American Southwest lived Pueblo Indians, who farmed and lived in highly concentrated settlements with sizable populations, and the Navaho, who followed a nomadic way of life, dependent largely upon hunting.

Kroeber argued that cultural phenomena are caused only by other cultural phenomena (1939, p. 1). He cited as an example the spread of agriculture through the Americas, carried by cultural contact from its origins in southern Mexico or Guatemala, first to the American southwestern tribes and eventually across the entire continent to Indians of the East Coast:

. . . the Southwestern Indians did not farm because nature induced them to make the invention. They did not make the invention at all. A faraway people made it, and from them it was transmitted to the Southwest through a series of successive tribal contacts. These contacts, which then are the specific cause of Southwestern culture, constitute a human social factor; a cultural or civilizational factor. Climatic or physical environment did not enter into the matter at all, except to render agriculture somewhat difficult in the arid Southwest, though not difficult enough to prevent it. (Kroeber, 1923, pp. 185–186)

Kroeber acknowledged, of course, that the environment did play a limiting role: "Had the Southwest been thoroughly desert, agriculture could not have gotten a foothold there." But within these limits, societies chose freely from a number of possibilities. The Pueblos, as mentioned, farmed while the Navaho hunted. Thus, although the natural environment made agriculture possible, it was the human environment—contact with people from agricultural communities—that made farming a way of life for many tribes of the Southwest and, over the years, for other native populations on the continent.

The possibilists recognized the importance of such environmental features as climate, topography, and available natural resources, but they gave greater stress to historical and cultural factors. Drucker (1963), for example, observed of the Northwest Coast Indians: "In a sense, the natural environment favored the development of the woodworking craft, for the towering trees of the Northwest contained a number of useful and readily workable woods" (p. 61). The most useful of these woods were the red and yellow cedar. Even the northerly Tlingit, though they lived beyond the cedar forests, insisted on importing cedar bark for clothing, containers, and other items of everyday life. This is clearly an example of a cultural choice that goes beyond what the immediate physical environment has to offer. The environmentalist, who expected a society passively to accept the limited available resources, would perhaps be surprised by this early instance of significant trade. The possibilist, who assumed that humans actively select, develop, adapt, and retain elements from the environment, would not.

Possibilism advanced but did not resolve the environment-culture question. By the middle of the twentieth century, anthropological thought was moving toward a more balanced concept of the interplay between the physical environment and cultural systems. This latter approach, which has become known as cultural ecology, concerns itself with the ways in which particular environmental features are interwoven with specific aspects of culture, selecting only those environmental characteristics and those particular cultural arrangements which can be functionally related.

Cultural Ecology

Cultural ecology focuses on the relationship of specific cultural features to a group's adaptation to its total habitat. Julian Steward, the primary advocate of cultural ecology, was interested in the patterns of activity adopted by social groups in order to exploit a particular ecological niche. He was especially concerned with ascertaining whether specific adaptations were associated with particular environments, or whether a society could in effect select from a range of possibilities in its adjustments to and utilization of a given environment.

To illustrate the concept of adjustment, Steward cited the differences between two groups of hunting tribes, each sharing a common technology but living in different environments. One group hunts large herds of migratory animals—bison or caribou—that can be followed efficiently by a large group of people over a great distance. The other hunts smaller game which neither migrates nor gathers in large herds. The roving group of hunters will form a mobile social group that is potentially large, given the nature of the food supply and the technology needed to exploit it. The second will remain rather small in size and range over a limited territory. The type of leadership and the units of production will vary significantly in the two groups.

Kroeber had emphasized that various cultural adaptations were possible within a given environment. Steward argued instead that the role of environment goes beyond merely permitting certain cultural adaptations and that there is a degree of inevitability in such adjustments. Steward believed, for instance, that the Arctic winter virtually required the more or less isolated conjugal family to be the effective social group. This is because herding requires a degree of nomadism and a small-scale social organization, and because wild vegetation necessitates food gathering on an individual or family basis. Cultural diffusion may be of enormous value in enhancing the ability of a people to exploit their environment—as the use of the horse aided the Plains Indians or the nomads of Central Asia. But it can also be of no value at all—a horse would be of little use to an Eskimo. Only specific cultural traits that serve the adaptive strategy of a given population are assimilated.

As set forth by Steward (1955), the study of cultural ecology involves three basic procedures:

1. Analysis of the interaction between the environment and the technology that uses it. Some environmental features may be

Cultural ecologists point out that features of the environment, including available natural resources, affect the tools and techniques used in various societies. Canoe-making in two different cultures illustrates this point. At left, young men of the Abruré tribe of the Ivory Coast carve a dugout canoe out of a large forest tree. At right, two Njemps men of Kenya shred saasevlera into rope-like strips to be used in canoe construction. (*Left:* Marc and Evelyne Bernheim, Woodfin Camp; *right:* Jen and Des Bartlett, Photo Researchers)

more crucial than others in influencing culture and technology. No society (including our own highly technological one) can make use of every aspect of its ecological niche. The features of the environment that are utilized depend upon the culture. Steward held that simpler cultures are more directly affected by the environment than complex ones. Thus, our culture has softened the effects of climate with heating and air-conditioning devices and has overcome the limitations of geography by constructing railroad tunnels, superhighways, aircraft, and space satellites.

2. Analysis of the patterns of activity required by the exploitative technology used in a given area. Does the technology require cooperation? Does cooperation result in more efficient utilization of resources? Through invention and diffusion, new tools and techniques become available, but the social activities these bring about depend upon the adaptive strategy of the group found in a given environment. Cultural ecology must study not only "the habits concerned in the direct production of food and of goods but [also the] facilities for transporting the people to the source or supply of the goods to the people" (Steward, 1955, p. 41).

3. Description of how the behaviors involved in exploiting the environment affect and are affected by other aspects of the culture. The organization of kin groups, sociopolitical organization, population density, architecture, and lore are only a few of the areas of social life that may be involved. These questions have proved to be as valid for modern industrial states as for traditional hunting-and-gathering bands.

Stewards's formulations helped move anthropology away from the preoccupation with issues of origins that was characteristic of the earlier evolutionary outlook. Instead cultural ecology came to focus on how a wide variety of factors work in their specific cultural contexts, without regard to their origins. On the basis of cross-cultural comparisons, Steward observed that certain interrelationships between cultural and environmental variables recurred in cultures that were not in contact with each other. These recurring patterns led him to the tentative conclusion that there are certain "essential features" of particular groups (such as patrilineal bands) that are found universally. Consequently, certain ecological factors may be considered causative. Peoples as diverse as the Bushmen, Congo Negritoes, Australians, Tasmanians, and Fuegians, all of whom inhabit very different environments, have similar cultural inventories and patrilineal band organization. Steward argued that these similarities exist "because the nature of the game and therefore of their subsistence problem is the same in each case" (Steward, 1955, p. 38).

For example, among hunters and gatherers such as the Shoshone Indians, the unpredictable supply of food, the lack of means for harvesting and storing it in quantity, and the fact that cooperative action on the part of large groups could not improve efficiency in collecting wild seeds and roots, all combined to make scattered nuclear families the effective food-producing units (Steward, 1955, pp. 105–107; Vayda & Rappaport, 1968, p. 484). Or again, sparse distribution of game, inefficient transportation, and low population density produce patrilineal, patrilocal bands:

Were individual families to wander at will, hunting the game in neighboring areas, competition would lead to conflict. . . . (But) as the men tend to remain more or less in the territory in which they have been reared and with which they are familiar, patrilineally related families would tend to band together to protect their game resources. The territory would therefore become divided among these patrilineal bands. (Steward, 1955, p. 135)

Since Steward pioneered the concept of cultural ecology, others have used it in their

Irrigation canals and terraces in Bali. (Klaus D. Francke, Peter Arnold Photo Archives)

research, but they have developed it somewhat differently. In Geertz's comparison of irrigation in Bali and Morocco, for example, he shows that each culture is so much part of its ecological niche that it is difficult, if not impossible, to think of the cultures independently of their ecological settings. Although these two societies have many things in common—among them "Islam, poverty, nationalism, authoritarian rule, overpopulation, clean air, spectacular scenery, and a colonial past" (Geertz, 1972, p. 24)—they are very different. The differences are exemplified by the patterns of irrigation in each society. In southeast Bali, irrigation canals, divided and subdivided in measured fashion, form a neat and complex network down every mountainside. These canals are maintained and controlled by a corporate organization known as a *subak*, which allots water equally to all holdings in its territory. So well organized is the system that the times set for each of nine specified stages of rice cultivation are staggered in every area in such a way that the *subak* highest on the mountainside opens its water gates earlier than the one directly below it. "The result is that, at any one point in time, the drainage area as a whole shows a step-by-step progression in the cultivation

sequence as one moves downslope" (Geertz, 1972, pp. 30–31).

In contrast, the workings of the east-central Moroccan irrigation system, rather than being strictly ordered and supervised, are the subject of constant squabbling among individuals over the allocation of so many hours of water rights in each of several canal systems. In Morocco, the canals are diverted frequently —perhaps every 3 hours, or as often as every hour—to water the several fields of different owners. Water in Morocco is only one of several kinds of property held in private ownership, and one's water rights may be loaned or rented out to others.

Geertz shows that the patterns tied in with irrigation and cultivation are repeated in the respective climates of Bali and Morocco. Not only are the climates totally opposite in terms of water availability—Bali receives heavy rainfall and Morocco is semiarid—but the predictability of the Balinese climate and the extreme variability of Morocco's weather seem to be paralleled by the behavioral patterns associated with cultivation. Irrigation in Bali is predictable and regular; in Morocco, it is variable and dependent on individual efforts. For Geertz, then, ecology plays such a central role in the joining of all the elements that constitute a culture, that the separate analysis of ecology and culture as set forth by Steward would be meaningless. As he puts it, nature is not just a stage upon which culture performs:

a society tunes itself to its landscape, mountainside, river fan, or foothill oasis, until it seems to an outside observer that it could not possibly be anywhere else than it is, it could not be otherwise than what it is. (Geertz, 1972, p. 38)

Steward's formulations are fundamental to the ecological approach in anthropology, which strives for descriptions of the functional relations or interplay between specific environmental features and cultural traits. Vayda and Rappaport (1968) rightly criticize Steward, however, for failing to test his model with adequate cross-cultural samples. They point out that Steward was content to select those examples that fit his thesis. Further, they believe he failed to show to what extent similar adaptations may occur without the cultural traits in question, or to note instances where the same traits may be present but not accompanied by the same adaptations. They also point out that even where certain correlations between cultural traits and given adaptations can be shown, the task remains of showing which is cause and which is effect. They suspect that such correlations are more intertwined than directly causal. However, it must be noted that Steward realized that the interactions between culture and ecology are complex; he only suggested that cause-and-effect relationships might have prevailed in those situations where parallel developments were unusually striking in geographically separated cultures with no contact. His classic example was the effects of the adaptation of the horse among the Plains Indians and among Indians of the pampas in Argentina, where parallel developments in tribal organization could be recognized.

The notion of "inevitability" of cultural characteristics is also challenged by Vayda and Rappaport, who point out that functional relationship is not identical with inevitability. They suggest broadening the bases of environmental features to be studied by considering nonhuman interactions as well as human ones. This approach led Rappaport to consider a systems approach to human populations and ecology, which will be considered in more detail below. Nevertheless, Steward's principal contribution has endured. Social activities are now studied not in isolation or in relation to arbitrarily selected environmental factors but as part of an ecosystem, where the internal dynamics of these activities, biological transactions, and physical processes may be recognized most clearly.

Tools, Technology, and the Harnessing of Energy

Technology—the production and use of tools—is the means by which human populations at all times and in all places exploit the environment in order to satisfy their basic needs for food and shelter. In fact, some anthropologists have insisted that the primary defining feature of humanity is the creation and use of tools. Kenneth Oakley (1959) proposed such an argument when he defined culture as "the ability to make tools and communicate ideas" (p. 1). All other physiological distinctions of *Homo sapiens*—upright posture, bipedalism, opposable thumb, conceptualizing brain—are significant, Oakley believed, because of their contribution to the human ability to construct and use tools.

Two anthropologists who have placed great stress on tools and technology in the growth and development of culture are V. Gordon Childe and Leslie White. Childe (1951) argued that tools are the principle means

Through the use of tools—even very simple ones such as that being used here by a cultivator in Spain—humans are able to increase their control over nature. (Rick Windsor, Woodfin Camp)

whereby any society adapts to its natural and social setting. As such, tools are the critical factors in human history. Through the invention and spread of increasingly efficient tools, humans were able to increase their control over nature and to bring about technological achievement. A recent example comes from a developing region on the edge of the Indian desert. One Indian camel can carry a 600-pound load; if it is harnessed to a two-wheel bullock cart, the carrying capacity of one beast increases to more than a ton. But the bullock cart, familiar elsewhere in India, cannot be used on the sandy ground in this area because of its narrow wheels. When discarded heavy aircraft tires are used, however, the two-wheel

cart with camel dramatically increases the transporting facilities of the region (Borders, 1978). However, societies have not always perceived such progress as advantageous. In many instances, opposition and conservatism has had to be overcome before new tool inventions were accepted.

White (1949; 1959), on the other hand, saw technology in even more deterministic terms. He divided culture into three subsystems: a technological system, a sociological one, and an ideological one. He saw the three systems hierarchically layered, so that the technological layer determined the nature of the other two systems, while the reverse was not true.

For White, the technological system includes tools of production, subsistence technology, materials from which shelter is constructed, and the instruments by which people protect themselves and wage war. The sociological system consists of the networks of interpersonal relationships and activities for all facets of social life—kinship, political, religious, occupational, recreational, and so on. The ideological system is the collection of ideas and beliefs expressed through mythology and theology as well as "legend, literature, philosophy, science, folk wisdom, and common sense knowledge" (White, 1949, pp. 364–365).

As White saw it, these three subsystems do not make equal contributions to culture. The technological system—through which humans adjust to the natural environment in terms of food, shelter, and defense—is the primary influence. If technology is the primary determinant of the course of culture, White reasoned, energy is the primary influence on technology. Through technology, energy could be harnessed and used to satisfy human needs. White saw all life as a struggle for effective control of free energy. Some technologies are, naturally, more efficient at harnessing and using energy than are others (White, 1949).

White developed a formula to show the relationship between tool efficiency, energy, and cultural growth and progress: $E \times T \to C$. The three variables in this formula can be found in every cultural system. E represents the amount of energy harnessed per capita per year. T represents the efficiency of tools used to control and direct energy. C stands for the degree of cultural development, as determined by the production of "human need-serving goods and services" (White, 1949, pp.

The harnessing of animal energy is thought by White and other cultural ecologists to contribute to the development of culture. (Marc and Evelyne Bernheim, Woodfin Camp)

368–369). Thus, White held that the development of culture—cultural evolution—takes place in proportion as energy utilization and tool efficiency are both increased and act upon each other.

White's stress upon the capture of energy is useful and applicable to human culture everywhere. However, his confidence in the positive aspects of technology and his evolutionary premises came to be questioned in the 1960s and 1970s, when it became apparent that instead of being life-enhancing, new forms of energy developed by Western technology could destroy human—and other forms—of life.

White's belief in the primacy of technology and energy, the material aspect of cultural systems, was taken up by Marvin Harris. His analysis (1974) of the multiple role of the cow in India uncovers and makes sense of the cultural importance of cattle to the energy and technological needs of that country. Although sacred cows symbolize life to the Hindus, some observers have alleged that cow worship is at the root of India's extreme poverty and hunger. They point to as many as 100 million "useless" beasts competing with humans for available food while contributing little to the economy. Indeed, the sight of cows wandering about and stalling traffic in city and countryside and helping themselves from gardens, marketplaces, and garbage bins is a familiar one throughout the country.

The cows do provide milk, although only a small amount by Western standards. The average Indian cow gives under 500 pounds of whole milk a year, compared to more than 5,000 pounds for an average American dairy cow. Moreover, in any year about half of the Indian cows are dry and give not a drop of milk. Any available beef is eaten only by some members of the untouchable caste, as well as by non-Hindu Indians. However, a beef-raising industry in India is unthinkable, but not alone because of the widespread taboo on the eating of beef. Rather, a shift to beef consumption would be nutritionally counter-productive because it would, as Harris explains, "strain the entire ecosystem." When vegetable products are directly consumed by humans, more calories are available per capita than when vegetation is fed to domesticated animals which are then eaten by humans. In India, the per capita calorie intake is already substandard. Thus, using crop lands to feed animals, in order to feed humans, would result in higher food prices and poorer diets for most families (Harris, 1974).

What critics also fail to realize, Harris points out, is that India's special relationship to the cow is at the core of a complex economy that ultimately makes possible human survival in this low-energy, animal-based, labor-intensive ecosystem. For example, the cattle of India are put to a number of uses—plowing, carting, and supplying milk, meat, leather, fuel, and fertilizer. Some of these uses are apparent, but others require explanation. Milk, meat, and leather are not the only things produced by cattle. The most plentiful product of all is dung—some 700 million tons per year—and little of it is wasted. In Harris's words, "cows and oxen provide low-energy substitutes for tractors and tractor factories . . . [while] carrying out the functions of a petrochemical industry" (Harris, 1974, p. 18). The collection of manure gives employment to many who would otherwise lack cash-earning jobs in the present economy. About half the total dung output is left in place or scattered in the fields, for use as fertilizer. Combined with water, dung forms a paste that converts a dirt floor to a hard, durable surface. Dried in cakes, it is the ideal cooking fuel for Indian cuisine, which requires the clean, slow, long-burning flame dung provides. Annually, dung provides "the thermal equivalent of 27 million tons of kerosene, 35 million tons of coal, or 68 million tons of wood," none of which is avail-

In India, cow dung is collected and dried in cakes, like those on the roof of this dwelling; it is then utilized as a long-burning cooking fuel. (Norman Weiser)

able in India in significant quantity (Harris, 1974, p. 19).

In addition to having all these uses, Harris points out that the Indian cow is a hardy, energy-storing, disease-resistant animal, able to survive with scant water and food over long periods of time. Far from competing with humans for a meager supply of food, the cow is a scavenger, consuming primarily inedible portions of food grains such as rice husks and wheat bran. From a cultural ecology viewpoint, then, a belief in the sacredness of the cow is technologically functional in India. By this example, Harris was able to demonstrate

Energy and Ecosystems

Thus, the role of energy and its control lies at the heart of all ecological studies. One of our concerns here is with the biological energy exchanges that take place within ecosystems. These energy exchanges are illustrated by a model known as the food chain, which consists of links, each of which is a feeding relationship between two organisms. At the base of every food chain are green plants, which provide the ultimate source of energy available to all other organisms in the system. Simplifying somewhat, the next link consists of herbivores (plant-eating organisms). These in turn are consumed by carnivores (meat-eating organisms, including humans). At the other end of the chain are decomposers, bacteria, and other agents that reduce organic remains to nutrient and mineral components. Decomposed material then goes back into the soil, there to nourish the vegetable matter with which the food chain began.

Each link in a food chain, then, is a feeding relationship of energy transfer. But loss of energy occurs with every one of these feeding relationships. Generally, only about 10 percent of the energy available at the start of any one biological energy exchange is carried over for use at the next level. Plants have relatively large chemical energy content, but the herbivores that feed on them contain only about a tenth of that. The simple carnivores whose dietary habits constitute the next step in the food chain possess only about a tenth of the chemical energy of the herbivores. As we have just seen in our examination of the sacred cows of India, there is a loss of calories (heat energy) when an animal eats vegetation, and an even greater loss when one animal eats another.

Human Populations and Ecosystems

Ecosystems contain a number of interconnected food chains. But feeding is only one of the processes of an ecosystem. Many ecosystems are relatively simple, consisting of a limited number of interacting populations and a limited range of inorganic features. Such a simple ecosystem is quite fragile, being vulnerable to the slightest alteration in any one of its few components. But most ecosystems are quite complex. Our own—that of the western world—is almost infinitely so. The more complex and diversified an ecosystem, the more stable it is and less likely to change. Its very diversity provides a cushion against disruption (Little & Morren, 1976). In New York City a few years ago, for example, it was found that trees located under certain newly installed street lights were not developing to their full leafy potential, nor did birds come to rest on the leafless branches. After only one or two growing seasons, many of the trees died. But—except for the aesthetic sensibilities of apartment dwellers who appreciated even the minimal plant life and bird song under their windows—no other parts of the ecosystem were significantly affected. In contrast, any interference in leaf development in an area inhabited by hunter-gatherers would be disastrous, since the foliage provides a cover for hunting activities, nourishment for some game animals, materials for the construction of homes, and many useful artifacts, including cord for trapping, plaited sleeping mats, and other necessities.

The complexity of an ecosystem is determined not by the inclusion within it of a human population but by the number and types of interacting populations. Even within a simple ecosystem, human beings interact with other populations with other ecological features, as the analysis of the Arctic Eskimo shows (Little & Morren, 1976).

The Arctic Eskimo. The Eskimos, a hunting society, inhabit the Arctic tundra along the coasts of Alaska, Canada, and Greenland. This habitat consists of a shallow soil level covering permafrost; relatively few species of plant or animal life; a short, cool, summer growing season lasting only 2 or 3 months; low temperatures year round; little annual precipitation (rain or snow); and low levels of solar radiation. Even in summer the soil is usable only to a depth of less than 1 meter. This not only limits root and plant growth but, because of poor water drainage, also creates a marshy landscape over which travel is difficult. The Arctic winter is long and intensely cold, with nearly complete daytime darkness for months at a time. The surface water, thawed in summer, freezes again beginning in early fall when slush starts to form along the coastline. Then the spread of ice into the sea begins; it continues until late March. At this time traditional Eskimo technology—dog sleds and kayaks—provides the most effective means of transportation (Little & Morren, 1976).

Description of the living components and energy exchanges of the tundra ecosystem might well begin with the spring thaw, which makes available water and soil to nourish the sparse growth of lichens, flowering herbs, shrubs, and grasses. This vegetation is eaten by such herbivores as the brown lemming and the caribou. Lemmings are, in turn, eaten by carnivores such as the fox and snowy owl. The Eskimo population functions as a higher-level carnivore, utilizing foods from the vegetation and herbivore, as well as the carnivore, levels. In addition, Eskimos consume marine resources—fish, seals, beluga whales, and walruses—which also provide fuels.

To exploit this environment, human populations follow available food resources by

An Eskimo woman hangs strips of whale meat on a log to be dried for later consumption. (Paolo Koch, Photo Researchers)

CULTURE AND ECOLOGY

moving to the shore regions in fall and winter, gradually working their way inland during the thaws. In the short summer season, some vegetable products and small terrestrial game such as birds and rabbits are available. Then population reaches its greatest concentration in inland settlements. Population scatters with the onset of fall, when small groups follow the sea ice to hunt marine foods most effectively. The available food resources in the tundra ecosystem result in a high-protein, low-carbohydrate diet that is among the most specialized of any in the world.

Inevitably, contact with other cultures has brought changes to the balanced tundra ecosystem. The rifle, motor-powered boat, and snowmobile are replacing the harpoon, kayak, and dog sled. Store-bought ammunition and petroleum fuels are necessary for this new equipment, and continuous participation in a money economy is essential. Even those Eskimos who remain in their traditional communities participate in craft production, receive money-transfer payments from the United States or Canadian governments, and may also for part of the year be employed in low-level service positions in urban communities. These changes, in turn, have created other alterations in life style. Disruption of closeknit family life has occurred, as some members of the family leave to attend government schools or move to seek work in a nearby town or city. The customary high-protein diet has been replaced by one consisting of purchased high-carbohydrate foods.

The long-range effects of acculturation on the tundra ecosystem may well tip the ecological balance. Expanded snowmobile use is likely to degrade the landscape. Moreover, this greater mobility combined with the use of firearms may result in the killing of a greater quantity of game, perhaps beyond the point at which natural increase will compensate. At the same time, the introduction of improved health care has reduced infant mortality and is already creating population pressure as the birthrate remains high.

In this case study, we see overexploitation of the ecosystem becoming apparent. Everywhere, human intervention produces changes in the environment. Sometimes a new balance is created, but sometimes the environment becomes damaged beyond short-range redemption.

The Eskimo case study demonstrates the varieties of interaction that take place in an ecosystem and is a good illustration of the comprehensive ecological approach as it is practiced today. Such studies—well-rounded considerations of human and cultural interactions with nonhuman and inorganic features of the ecosystem—take Steward's notions of cultural ecology and broaden them in accord with the suggestions of his critics. In the section that follows, we shall examine the twin problems of adaptation and change in an ecological context.

Ecology, Adaptation, and Evolutionary Theory

Adaptation refers to the ability of a living system—organisms, populations, and/or communities, in an ecological context—to maintain or regain stability under conditions of environmental change. Physiological adaptation by genetic means has been the mechanism for biological evolution of all living species. Darwin's "natural selection" and "survival of the fittest" are principles which scholars have used to explain why successful adaptations have survived and nonuseful or inadaptable forms perish. But, from the point of view of anthropological studies, adaptations can be social and cultural as well as physiological and genetic.

The concept of cultural adaptation within an ecosystem provides a framework within which social relations can be viewed. Cohen (1971), for example, has applied the idea of adaptation to marriage and the family. He constructs an evolutionary framework for viewing family arrangements, from those typical of hunting-and-gathering bands to those of modern industrial societies.

Marriage and family arrangements everywhere change in response to changing needs for acquiring a livelihood. We see this in our own society as two-job families adapt their child-care, food preparation, and house-keeping responsibilities to fit the changing demands made on them. Cohen points out that relationships within families have effects on relationships between families; these, in turn, are connected with the adaptive strategy of a society.

In the simplest hunting-gathering societies, marriage alliance for purposes of exchanging women is a particularly characteristic adaptation according to Cohen. These arrangements, including especially the Australian aborigines' elaborate exchanges, have long-term adaptive utility in an ecological niche in which

local groups do not have exclusive rights to particular territories or resources. . . .The abundance of food in their habitats varies from year to year, and flexible organization enables people to move from area to area and to join with other groups in coping with this variability. . . . As a result, there develops a system of mutual and reciprocal access to resources incorporating many groups.
. . . Systems of marital exchange that have developed among hunter-gatherers are a result of their unique territorial relationships. . . . Each hunting-gathering camp becomes dependent on others for a supply of wives and is allied with others through. . . (marriage. [This] contributes to the maintenance of peaceful relations among the groups that move around, camp with each

other, and exploit overlapping territories. (Cohen, 1971, p. 25)

Cohen's argument here is that hunting-and-gathering families tend to follow similar patterns everywhere. Food tends to be distributed along kinship lines, and the relationship between family type and economic adaptation can be fairly easily established.

In horticultural economies (those in which simple plant cultivation provides most of the food), however, the relationship of the human population to its habitat changes. There, Cohen argues, "the notion of exclusive rights to territory claimed by a group [is] probably designed. . .to protect investments of time and effort in particular plots" (p. 26). But the transformation to sedentary horticulture does not take place overnight. Archeology and history demonstrate that this evolution proceeded slowly: "At each step along the way, cultivated foods make up a larger proportion of the diet [and] kin group organization becomes progressively stronger" (Cohen, 1971, p. 26). That is, instead of loose family ties, clans and lineages are formed. According to Cohen, horticulturists are more likely to exchange material payments such as bridewealth than to exchange women directly. Territorial alliances become less important, but economic cooperation among households expands. Cooperative landowning and work-organizing groups, such as clans and lineages, are better adapted to exploitation of the environment in a horticultural economy than are the band and named territorial groups. Postmarital residence patterns as well as marital arrangements themselves take on new and more rigid form. The lineage, a corporate land-allocating group usually also involved in social control is, according to Cohen, never found among hunter-gatherers, whereas it is widespread among horticulturists.

For pastoralists, among whom the welfare of flocks and herds is the basic technological requirement, there are seasonal changes in kinship organization. During rainy seasons, there is more likely to be water and vegetation close to home. Kinfolk are then able to live together in large numbers and still provide for the animals in their herds. But during dry seasons, animals must graze over a wider area, and kin members must disperse in order to care for the herd. These seasonal patterns of kinship organization have important implications for the sorts of social institutions that are formed.

Greater variation occurs in the family organization of industrial societies:

In industrial society, where every person barters or sells his labor individually. . .the household ceases to be a productive unit [and] the cooperative labor of kinsmen is no longer required. . . . Traditional kin groups and ceremonial kinship systems tend to dissolve. . . . (Cohen, 1971, p. 281)

We might take Cohen's sequence one step further, into postindustrial or technological society. Here we see that "strategies of adaptation"—such as long-continued education, mobility for educational or occupational reasons, "retooling" for new occupations as traditional fields become outmoded—tend to isolate the individual from family and other kin groups and to create fragmented work and social units that lack continuity over time. Further, such adaptations tend to remove much of the process of enculturating children from the family. They transfer social controls to a shifting peer group and postpone or lead to the dissolution of marriage. Such changes put increasing strains on family and kin organization.

Too often, the view of culture as consisting primarily of adaptive processes had led to an evolutionary perspective that places social and cultural systems in a hierarchy, with Western civilization generally located at the top. While discussion of adaptation cannot be separated

from the idea of evolution, it must not be confused with progress. An evolutionary perspective is one of several useful ways to organize data about human life. But the linkage of evolution with the notion of progress presents a serious problem, and the concept is used with increasing caution in contemporary studies. Where Steward had seen adaptations as being caused by ecological similarities, Cohen views them as being successful in a kind of Darwinian "cultural selection" process. When presented in terms of survival mechanisms found in human populations, the concept of adaptation is useful. But when too closely tied to evolutionary theory, it becomes an ideological statement about one way of life being superior to another, a notion that is contrary to an anthropological perspective.

For this reason, Rappaport's argument—that modern "civilization" may· represent an aberrant form of adaptation, one that might destroy the ecosystem of which it is a part—becomes important. Whereas White (1949) had considered improved energy-harnessing ability an indication of progress, Rappaport suggests that today's high-energy technology has "accelerated" maladaptations. Consider, for example, the different but equally harmful effects of two recent technological innovations: napalm, which devastates a landscape, preventing growth of vegetation for substantial periods of time, but injures relatively few humans; and the "clean" neutron bomb, which destroys organic life over a wide area but leaves structures and habitat otherwise intact.

It is, of course, impossible to describe a culture and its subsystems without discussing the ecological niche inhabited by the population, or the technology and associated activities involved in its exploitation. Whatever the primary interest of the anthropologist—family and kinship organization, religion or whatever—the study of subsistence activities and their related social organization is relevant. The climate can no less be ignored than the house types, the available flora and fauna no less than the systems of material exchange.

Thus, no serious ethnography can today ignore the ecological setting of the culture under study. Those anthropologists who feel that ecology is a primary focus allow it to inform their research at all levels. Even those who find it limiting, so that it is not central in their analyses, must also refer to the ecological concept at some point in study.

Summary

1. The term *ecology* refers to the interrelationships of all living organisms within a total environment. The concept of interaction between culture and environment has always been a primary concern of anthropologists.

2. Implicit in all ecological studies is the notion of adaptation; human populations adapt to habitats by means of culture. Some studies seek to explain why particular cultural traits or sets of traits have originated and existed in particular times and places. Others focus on how these traits function in a given cultural and natural habitat. Early analysts were *environmental determinists,* holding that cultural characteristics were caused by the environmental setting in which a given society was located. *Possibilism,* as expounded by Kroeber, held that the environment made possible a range of cultural responses, but that cultural traits and development were due to culture contact and transmission.

3. The concept of *cultural ecology* appeared around the middle of the twentieth century, with Julian Steward as its primary advocate.

Steward was concerned with the ways in which particular environmental features interact with specific features of culture, and in the patterns of activity adopted by social groups to exploit a particular ecological niche. All organisms interact with their environment but, in the case of humans, the factor of culture is added to the ecological mix.

Steward has been criticized for not giving adequate consideration to the nonhuman aspects of the ecosystem, for concentrating on a limited number of factors, and for failing to provide sufficient empirical data to support his conclusions. However, his emphasis on the crucial relationship between certain ecological conditions and the form that social relations and culture may take has been a major influence in anthropology.

4. *Technology*—the production and use of tools—is the means by which human populations exploit environments for food and shelter. Leslie White emphasized the importance of energy for technology, since the harnessing of energy makes possible all ecological exploitation and adaptation. He developed the formula $E \times T \to C$ to communicate that culture *(C)* develops as both energy *(E)* and total efficiency *(T)* are increased. Following White, a number of studies, such as those of Harris, have concentrated on the material aspects of culture-technology-ecology interactions.

5. The primary energy exchange in an ecosystem is through the food chain, which represents a series of individual feeding relationships. Human populations, because they are superbly equipped through culture and technology to exploit the resources of an ecosystem, usually dominate the ecosystems of which they are part. The interaction of a human population with its ecosystem is intricate. Any change in human behavior may trigger a chain reaction of consequences spreading throughout the system.

6. Adaptation is the ability of living sys-

tems to maintain or regain stability under conditions of change. Adaptation is a process of evolution. But evolution is not necessarily progress. Recent studies, such as those by Cohen, have argued that different stages of technological adaptations affect social systems. Adaptation implies the possibility of maladaptation, and there is a real question whether "advanced civilization," with its high-energy technology and enormous destructive power, may prove to be maladaptive in the long run.

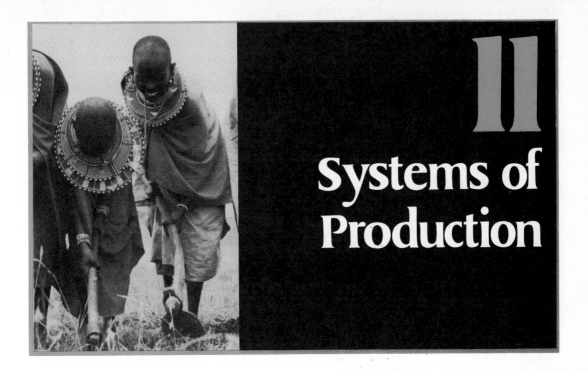

11

Systems of Production

THE study of ecology and the study of economics are closely related. They even have the same Greek root —*oikos,* meaning "house"—which implies that they both have something to do with household management. And indeed both ecology and economics are concerned with the material aspects of survival. One important factor for survival is the availability of material goods necessary to sustain life. Economics is the field of study dealing with human activity in which persons interact with their physical and social environment in order to produce and distribute those necessary materials. Thus, the systems of production and distribution adopted by a society to provide life-supporting materials form an integral part of that society's economy. Economics, therefore, encompasses every aspect of activity that is directed toward provisioning society, including the integration of society with its natural environment. Yet cultural ecologists and economic anthropologists sometimes organize their research and develop their terminologies as if the two fields of study were completely separate. Cultural ecologists, relying heavily on biological ecology, treat humankind as a species and view culture as that species' principal mode of adaptation. Economic anthropologists, recognizing that *Homo sapiens* is the only species that transforms natural materials into life-sustaining products, tend to emphasize social relations at the expense of ecological factors.

Although the sciences of ecology and economics have different goals, they are similar in many ways: they emphasize cyclical processes—or *flows*—of materials, energy, and information. They portray their respective systems as tending toward an optimal state of equilibrium but never actually reaching that state. In short, both ecology and

213

economics are dynamic rather than static in nature.

Economic Anthropology

In this chapter and the following one, we will be concerned with *economic anthropology.* What is the relationship between economics and anthropology? At first it would seem that they have very little in common. Economics is a well-established social science with well-developed conceptual formulations. Cultural anthropology, by contrast, is a younger discipline and less theoretically unified. The data used by economists are largely statistical and usually come from official records and large-scale surveys rather than from individual research. Economists use equations and models to show relationships among the data they collect. Anthropologists use concepts from economics in their attempts to explain aspects of the material conditions of human existence, but their more diversified interests do not always match up well with traditional explanations offered by economics.

Yet each field of study can contribute to the other. Where the economist uses the term *ceteris paribus* ("other things being equal") to cover noneconomic phenomena, anthropologists can fill in the blanks with information not usually considered by economists. And where anthropologists have concentrated on the social framework of economic activity without fully considering the economic process itself, economists can contribute supply-and-demand analyses, techniques for measuring transactions, and general ideas about allocation of resources.

What, then, is the task of economic anthropology? It is, first of all, to describe the variety of economic arrangements developed by humankind in different times and places. Economic anthropologists then sort these diverse arrangements into classes, and attempt to fit them with different types of societies and cultures. As Manning Nash (1966) puts it, economic anthropology must

develop a body of theory which will explain the gift giving of the Plains Indians, the pig exchanges of the New Hebrides, the circulation of valuables in the Solomon archipelago, the persistence of hundreds of separate pottery producers in a single Mayan Indian community, the effects of wage labor and cash cropping in New Guinea, . . . and a host of other real, significant, and puzzling economic and cultural facts. (p. 16)

Anthropologists provide different perspectives on these economic activities than are provided by economists. To the anthropologist, it is the *total* cultural system, the *total* society, that provides the context for investigating and interpreting systems of production and exchange. Take, for example, a simple monetary transaction such as, "I will give you $1.00 for a dozen eggs," or a nonmonetary transaction such as, "I will give you a kilo of rice for a dozen eggs." There is more going on in such transactions than simply an exchange of commodities. Anthropologists are interested in finding out such information as where the commodities come from, who produces them, how they are produced, what is the relationship between the parties involved in their production, who can participate in their exchange, and so on. In comparison to the economist, the economic anthropologist takes a more *holistic* approach.

Formalist Versus Substantivist Approaches

Economic anthropology has been characterized by two fundamental approaches. The *formalist approach* takes traditional economic theory as its point of departure, and stresses the scarcity of resources and the importance of rational decision-making (for example, economizing). The *substantivist approach,* on the other hand, denies that there is any such thing as an "economic sphere" and insists that economic relations can be identified only in the context of each society studied. Substantivists emphasize the ways in which economic activities are intertwined with other social activities in any given society. Their emphasis is on the various ways in which economic relations are embedded in other, broader social relations.

These two approaches present us with a dilemma. According to the substantivist approach, preindustrial social systems have no economic institutions as such, but the social institutions of such societies (such as marriage) have various economic aspects (such as bridewealth). According to the formalist approach, the economy consists of all decisions that have to do with economizing, which means a large portion of all the decisions that are made in any society.

It can be argued that *both* the formalist and the substantivist approaches must be taken into consideration in any empirical study, and that, indeed, what is required is a synthesis of these two approaches. For example, if we wanted to understand how corn is produced and distributed in a society where corn is the staple of the diet, we would want to look at the law of supply and demand (formalist approach) as well as how politics, religion, kinship, and other social patterns and processes (substantive approach) affect the production and distribution of corn. Neither approach on its own would provide all the information we would need, since traditional economic theory alone would not shed any light on the other social factors that influence production and distribution in most societies, and social theory alone would not take into account the formal economic imperatives that exist. We will pursue such a synthesis in this and the following chapters.

The Nature of Economic Relations

In this section, we will examine economic relations in general before turning to a discussion of several specific types of economic systems. Economic activity can be viewed as "activity in which (people) interact with their physical and social environment in the calculated attempt to acquire . . . a living" (Cook, 1973, p. 810). It can be viewed as "a sort of strategy of matching limited means with alternate uses [in order to] get . . . the most out of the available resources" (Nash, 1977, p. 233). It can be viewed as activity concerned with money and prices (a narrow view), or it can be seen as the science of choice (a broad view). But in all of these cases, economic activity is thought of as having to do with the production, distribution, and consumption of material goods. In these processes, people make choices between alternate uses of resources. Thus, for our working definition, we will consider *economic activity* to be the choices people make in determining how available resources are to be used in producing, distributing, and consuming material goods, and the services associated with them.

Two important points need to be made before we continue. One is that it is extremely difficult to isolate economic activities from other activities in most non-Western societies. As Nash puts it, "we have economic activities *and* activities that have an economic aspect. When a temple dancer in Bali dances, that is not economic, but when she gets a gift or payment for the act of dancing, the dancer has an economic aspect" (1977, p. 233). This kind of relationship can be seen in Western societies, too. Consider the artist or writer who seeks self-fulfillment in his or her work, but who also may be paid for painting or writ-

The cultivation being done by these Masai girls in Kenya represents a conscious choice of economic activity. The Masai are traditionally a nomadic tribe who only recently, as part of a community development project, have begun to engage in horticulture. (Marc and Evelyne Bernheim, Woodfin Camp)

ing. Rarely is an activity purely economic, however.

The other point is that economic choices can be both conscious and unconscious. It sometimes has been argued that members of peasant and primitive societies do not make "rational" or "calculated" economic choices; they supposedly have little foresight or sense of value. But even if this were so, it does not mean that their choices are irrational. If those choices "work"—if they achieve the desired results—then they are the proper choices for those people in that society. The !Kung Bushmen, for example, are food-gatherers, and Westerners have assumed that their lives were a constant struggle to find enough food to stay alive. But as anthropologists who lived with them discovered, they spend only between 12 and 19 hours per week hunting and gathering food, and their diet consists of many more calories than nutritionists have estab-

lished as the necessary minimum. Their "decision" to become gatherers rather than cultivators was not likely a conscious one. The question of whether they should turn to what some might consider the higher standard of living of their horticultural neighbors seems to be answered by the fact that they have what they need without the time and effort that horticulture demands. As one of the Bushmen put it, "Why should we plant when there are so many nuts in the world?" (cited in Mair, 1972, p. 163). And in a severe drought in 1965, many of their horticultural neighbors, whose crops had failed, joined the Bushmen in foraging. Even unintentional and unplanned results can be beneficial.

These two points can be illustrated by the *potlatch* ceremony of the Northwest Coast Indians. In this seemingly irrational event (by Western standards), a man would give away or destroy his most valuable possessions. This was an economic activity because it resulted in a redistribution of material goods within the society. It was also a social event in which the person who gave away the most property achieved the highest status. It was "rational" and "calculated" because the redistribution of wealth contributed to the general well-being of all the members of the community, in addition to conferring status on the individual sponsor.

Production

Production is defined as the various modes used by the members of a society to procure their material means of existence. The concept of production encompasses a vast array of activities ranging from food gathering, hunting, horticulture, and craft work to highly organized industrial operations. Productive operations represent a combination of these following primary factors that depend very heavily on one another: the raw materials available, technology and division of labor. Every production process is made up of an ordered series of activities that develop in accordance with the resources of the environment and the social realities of the particular society.

Production is organized on the basis of the relative scarcity of three *factors of production:* land, labor, and capital. Both land and labor are necessary for subsistence. Water (which could be included with land) is also essential. Clearly, one will not find a settled agricultural economy in areas where fertile land is very limited or large herds of livestock where water holes are scarce. Labor may be "scarce" while a family's children are still very young, so that, for example, a herdsman may have to keep his herd with his father's even though the animals are legally his. As for *capital*—the equipment and supplies used in production—there is some debate on the question of what, if anything, can be labeled capital in a subsistence

economy. In modern, industrial economies, capital is the means of production. A system of capitalism is characterized by the relationship—the separation—between those who own the means of production in a society and those who actually do the work of production. The problem in identifying capital in subsistence or other non-capitalist economies is, then, what *is* capital in the absence of the separation of productive roles? In discussing subsistence economies, we shall have to use a definition of capital that does not separate owners of capital from workers, because there is no such separation in these economies. Broadly defined, then, capital in noncapitalist economies is any goods or services—be they livestock, gardens, cultivation tools, factory equipment, or muscle power—used to produce more goods.

A convenient way of viewing small-scale economic systems has been provided by Nash (1977), who divides the topic into four major themes: (1) technology and division of labor, (2) structure of productive units, (3) systems and media of exchange, and (4) the control of wealth and capital. We will give an overview of these four themes here, and then discuss the first two in the remainder of this chapter. The remaining two will be treated in the following chapter.

Technology and Division of Labor. We define *technology* as the tools and processes by means of which material goods can be produced in greater quantity and with less physical effort. The type of technology available to a society plays an important role in its mode of production. Obviously, industrial economies have much more highly developed technologies than subsistence economies.

Tribal and peasant societies are relatively simple in that they have few tools for making tools; they do not have a wide variety of different productive tasks, and do not use or create much energy. The Bemba of Rhodesia, for example, use a mode of cultivation that involves climbing tall trees, cutting a few branches, burning them, and using the ashes for fertilizer. This method requires few tools, few different types of activity, and only human energy. In industrial economies, on the other hand, tractors are used to plow fields, as contrasted with the hand-held hoes used in subsistence economies. Obviously, tractors enable fewer people to cultivate more space than do hoes, thus freeing more people to do work other than food production.

As we have seen, the division of labor in primitive societies is based primarily on sex, age, and sometimes rank. Workers are largely interchangeable. One individual's skill is about as good as that of any other. People in tribal and peasant societies learn socially appropriate skills in the course of growing up, and within age and sex groups, any worker can readily replace any other worker. Children begin to learn farm and household work almost as soon as they can walk. Since men are considered to have greater strength than women and because they are not hampered by carrying children around on their backs, they often do the heavy work, while women take care of the household. The relative simplicity of technology, with little use of machinery, means the lack of a high degree of specialization.

Structure of Productive Units. In small-scale societies, there are no organizations whose only task is production, such as guilds or factories. Nor is any lasting social unit based solely on productive activities. Often family groups are the major productive units, but their reasons for existence and their activities go far beyond economic considerations. Economic life depends on other kinds of social relationships—kinship bonds, political bonds, territorial bonds, and so on.

In subsistence economies, there is little specialization. Each household provides its own food, clothing, and shelter. Along with more advanced technology comes greater *specialization,* or division of labor. Fewer and fewer people are needed to produce food, while the remainder exchange for food the reward they get for whatever other work they do (for example, teaching children, repairing machinery, etc.). In industrial economies, specialization is extreme—rarely does a household produce its own food, clothing, or shelter, though it may produce some small part of each of these.

Stanley H. Udy (1970) divides *production organizations*—groups that are engaged in the production of some type of material goods—in preindustrial societies into four types: familial, custodial, contractual, and voluntary. A *familial* production organization is based on a kinship group, although not necessarily the nuclear family. Production in the pottery-making community of Amatenango in southeastern Mexico, described later, is based on familial relationships. A *custodial* production organization is based on the obligation to participate. Workers are drawn from groups that have political rather than familial ties. There is an institutionalized authority that can compel others, by force if necessary, to participate in production. Plantations worked by slaves, in the pre-Civil War southern United States, are examples of custodial work organizations. A *contractual* production organization is, as the term implies, based on a voluntary contract between two or more parties. No one is forced to enter into such an agreement in the first place, but once a contract has been agreed to, participation is compulsory. Failure to live up to the agreement brings any number of sanctions, depending on the particular group. This is the type of organization that is most familiar to members of Western societies. Finally, a *voluntary* production organization is based on the self-interest of members—anyone who can do the work and is in the vicinity may join, but there are no sanctions for nonparticipation. Contractual and voluntary organizations are closest to the requirements of industrial economies.

Systems and Media of Exchange. Another feature of tribal and peasant economies is that people are seldom obligated to calculate the costs of doing one thing rather than another. Calculating costs is often impossible or unnecessary, since the uses of time, resources, and people occur as a result of the social structure and are not calculated in terms of increasing productivity. For example, in a society where the women are responsible for tending the fields and the men do the hunting, men would not help the women in the fields even if it might enable them to harvest bigger crops, because the division of labor prohibits it. However, under outside pressures, these divisions can break down or be transformed.

An exchange system can be quite complex. For example, among the Tiv of Nigeria, food can be exchanged for food or for brass rods; brass rods can be exchanged for highly valued goods, women, and slaves; but food cannot be exchanged for highly valued goods. We will examine such systems of exchange in some detail in the next chapter.

Control of Wealth and Capital. In small-scale societies, investment takes the form of using resources to expand existing social systems rather than to transform the society. Hence, many such societies have *leveling mechanisms* whereby people are forced to spend accumulated capital in ways (such as loans to relatives, large feasts, and the like) that are not necessarily productive but are conducive to the perpetuation of social traditions. These are ways of "scrambling" wealth so that social relations will remain unchanged. The *potlatch* described earlier is an example of a leveling mechanism.

Amatenango Economics. The pottery industry of the Mexican village Amatenango, as described by Nash (1961), nicely illustrates the themes just presented. The Indians of Amatenango are a horticultural people, but horticulture alone is not enough to enable them to maintain the standard of living they prefer. The making and selling of pottery, a specialty of the community, helps them to achieve the level of living they expect. Of the 280 households in the town center of Amatenango, only two or three are not involved in producing pottery for sale. Girls in Amatenango are taught from childhood how to make pots, and all the women who are born and grow up there are engaged in pottery making. In a neighboring community that has almost the same natural resources as Amatenango, there is not even a single pot produced.

Since the technology of pottery making is simple and inexpensive, even the poorest families in the community have access to it. The skills are passed on from generation to generation, and the materials needed are readily available. The pottery making is done completely by hand. No wheel, no molds, no ovens are used; just a steel blade for scraping, a smooth board for resting pot bases, a burlap bag or skirt under the potter's knees and nets and bags for carrying the finished pots are needed. The total cost of these items is under $3.00—a price that every household can afford.

The quantity of pottery produced is not geared to the prices brought in the market but to the cycle of celebrations, both religious and secular. At festival times, households need cash; at those times there is a high demand for pots so they are made then and sold quickly, which eliminates storage problems.

The units of production in Amatenango are households, which are kinship groups in which membership comes only by being born or marrying into the unit. The household unit limits the number of workers available for pottery making, in that no one hires out to make pottery for wages, and pottery making itself is part of a woman's job as a member of a household. Since pottery making is only one of many things each household engages in, other activities compete with it for the time and energy of the same group of people.

Certain features of assembly-line production are used in the making of pottery in Amatenango. Each woman works on a different part of a pot—base, body, neck, handle—at the same time. As a woman completes a particular operation, the finished parts are partially dried. The division of labor is most efficient if there are four women in the household, because each one can then be working on a different section at the same time, which results in greater efficiency. If there are more than four women, however, efficiency does not increase very much.

The pricing of pottery is a constant topic of conversation in the community. People are highly aware of relative costs and are very sensitive to economic gain, but not for personal aggrandizement. Economically, they operate on a rational level in the sense of bringing means and ends together; but the value system of the community requires that all households remain fairly equivalent in wealth.

Leveling mechanisms are responsible for maintaining this equality. First, Amatenango's low level of technology and its limited land area impose severe restrictions on the amount of wealth that can be attained by the society as a whole. Second, bilateral inheritance requires that all offspring receive an equal share of the parents' estate, which tends to fracture whatever estates may be accumulated. Third, there are a series of communal offices in which men from each household are expected to serve and to contribute financially, which is a drain on both work time and resources. Fourth, forced expenditure in certain ritual festivals is an obligation of the wealthier households. Amatenango is a society in which wealth is not easily turned to technical and economic uses but is drained by social and religious obligations. Several forces acting together combine to keep the fortunes of the various households nearly equivalent and to maintain the shift of family wealth over time.

Thus, Amatenango is a small-scale economy in which the technology and division of labor are relatively simple. The domestic unit, or household, is the center of production; the costs and benefits of production are not calculated separately from those of other activities; and the accumulation of wealth is prevented by various leveling mechanisms. In the remainder of this chapter, we will be concerned with the technology and productive units of small-scale societies. We will deal with systems of exchange and control of wealth in greater detail in the next chapter.

Modes of Food Production

A wide variety of productive systems are known to exist in human societies, and they deal in very different ways with the problem of determining how resources are utilized. These systems may be divided into two major categories: subsistence economies and industrial economies. We will look first at subsistence economies, which make up the vast majority of the societies studied by anthropologists.

Subsistence Economies

In a *subsistence economy,* people use what they themselves produce in order to meet their own needs. Although a degree of trade may be transacted, they do not trade their products for other goods through the medium of money. There are three main types of subsistence economy: those based on hunting (and fishing) and gathering wild fruits and roots; those based on herding domestic animals; and those based on raising crops (often in conjunction with a certain amount of animal husbandry). These three modes of food production were once viewed as successive stages of economic development. Today, however, the mode followed by a given society is generally thought to be determined by the resources available and the level of technical knowledge of the people engaged in it. Let us take a closer look at the three main types of subsistence economies.

Hunting and Gathering.

Peoples who forage for food by hunting and killing animals, by fishing, and by gathering wild fruit, vegetables, and nuts are known as hunters and gatherers. They raise little if any of the food they eat. Hunters and gatherers live in small groups and must move often to find food. Although each hunting-and-gathering group stays within a particular geographic area, it is not a closed social system. There is social communication among groups in the form of visiting, gift-giving, and intermarriage. Thus, hunting-and-gathering societies consist of a set of local *bands*—small groups of families, numbering perhaps 25 to 100 persons, with simple political organization. Hunting-and-gathering bands are part of a larger community whose members speak the same language and enter into various relationships with one another, including marriage.

The organization of food production in such a society has five important features that result directly from the small size and mobility of the hunting-and-gathering band (Lee & DeVore, 1968):

1. Because they move around to get food, hunters and gatherers have little personal property. Since mobility prevents them from acquiring a great many possessions, wealth differences between individuals are kept to a minimum, which, in turn, leads to a generally egalitarian social system. Individuals and families usually own no more than the basic necessities of life, because they cannot transport much more than that when it comes time to move again.
2. The band is kept small by the nature of the food supply, which, because of limited resources, would be quickly exhausted by a large group. Actually, the size of a band tends to change often as people move from one band to another.
3. No single band has exclusive rights to a particular set of resources. Bands have reciprocal access to food supplies. Moreover, visiting patterns create obligations among groups, so that last year's guests become this year's hosts and must share their food supply.
4. Food surpluses are usually small. Everyone knows where the food is and where other bands are. In effect, food is "stored" in the environment, and people work continually to transfer the food from this storehouse to their stomachs.
5. No band becomes permanently attached to any single area, because the livelihood of its people does not depend on a particular area. Frequent visiting of different resource areas also prevents any one band from becoming attached to a particular area. And, because of the limited amount of personal and collective property, bands can change residence without giving up any interests in land or goods.

Hunters and gatherers such as the !Kung Bushmen of South West Africa must move from place to place in search of food. Thus, they live in small bands and have few personal possessions. (Marvin Newman, Woodfin Camp)

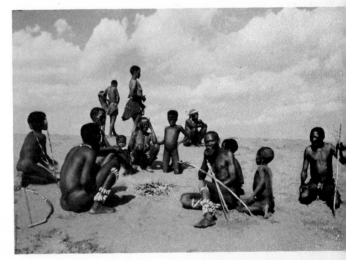

The hunting-and-gathering group, in short, exploits nature directly. This pattern is in sharp contrast to other economic systems, which transform nature for purposes of production.

Economic Implications of Mobility. Marshall Sahlins (1972) notes that mobility is the key to understanding hunters and gatherers. He points out that their economic system is governed by the imminence of diminishing returns. That is, a band will soon use up most of the food resources within a convenient distance from camp. To stay in the same camp is to experience diminishing returns in terms of a reduced supply or a supply of increasingly inferior foods. Anthropologists have also found that when a band does not, for whatever reason, move its encampment, it does so at the cost of searching for food at greater and greater distances from camp. The obvious solution to each of these problems is simply to move to another area.

But the need to move also involves diminishing returns. Tools, clothing, ornaments, and the like become a burden when they have to be moved. The building of large, elaborate houses is out of the question if they will soon have to be abandoned. Thus, small, light objects are better than big objects; one of something usually is better than two of something. Individuals in our society who backpack appreciate the wisdom of such customs.

The fact of diminishing returns, both in productivity and in portability, has social consequences as well. Among these are infanticide and senilicide—the killing of infants and of old people—because they cannot transport themselves. Hunters and gatherers also tend to refrain from sexual relations during the nursing period of an infant (which may be two years or longer) in order to avoid closely spaced births and to control population. Such practices can be seen as resulting from the need to handle people and goods in similarly efficient ways.

Hunting-and-gathering societies have usually been viewed as underproductive and poor. But Sahlins shows that their economic system is actually a creative adaptation to their environment, a way of matching ends and means. Mobility and moderation put hunters and gatherers' ends within range of their technical means. Hunters and gatherers spend an estimated 3 to 5 hours per adult worker per day on food acquisition—a figure many modern workers would envy. In fact, it appears that horticultural economies, which usually have been considered more advanced, actually require more work than the hunting and gathering system. According to Sahlins, the amount of work per capita *increases* with the development of culture, while the amount of leisure *decreases,* since cultivation requires people to work longer and harder in order to produce enough food to survive.

The !Kung Bushmen. Today, societies that depend exclusively upon hunting and gathering are few, but they represent a condition that once characterized all of humanity. In 1966, the population of those who depended exclusively on hunting and gathering was estimated at 30,000—about "enough to fill a medium-sized football stadium," according to Pfeiffer (1972, p. 350), although many more supplement their diets by hunting and gathering. Those few exclusive hunters and gatherers that remain today show great diversity. They are found in every type of region from African deserts, to equatorial forests of Southeast Asia, to Alaskan tundra. These tend to be environments where cultivation would be extremely difficult. Modern hunters and gatherers combine hunting, gathering, and fishing in a variety of ways to obtain sufficient food. Because they are affected by local resources, there is a tendency for particular groups to "specialize" in particular resources, such as caribou or bison, yams or pine nuts, fish or sea mammals.

The !Kung Bushmen of southwest Africa are a classic example of a hunting-and-gathering society (Forde, 1934; Marshall,

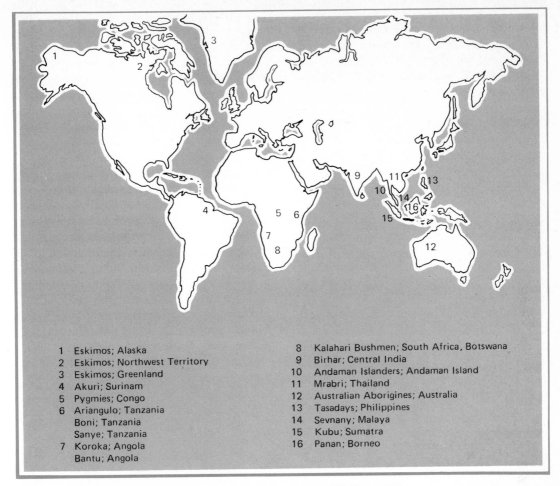

1	Eskimos; Alaska	8	Kalahari Bushmen; South Africa, Botswana
2	Eskimos; Northwest Territory	9	Birhar; Central India
3	Eskimos; Greenland	10	Andaman Islanders; Andaman Island
4	Akuri; Surinam	11	Mrabri; Thailand
5	Pygmies; Congo	12	Australian Aborigines; Australia
6	Ariangulo; Tanzania	13	Tasadays; Philippines
	Boni; Tanzania	14	Sevnany; Malaya
	Sanye; Tanzania	15	Kubu; Sumatra
7	Koroka; Angola	16	Panan; Borneo
	Bantu; Angola		

Figure 1 Known sites of contemporary hunters and gatherers. (Pfeiffer, 1972)

1960). The !Kung are organized into two basic social groups—the family and the band. The family is the primary and most cohesive social unit. At its simplest, a !Kung family is made up of a man and his wife, which may then be augmented by children, dependents such as parents or grandparents, and the daughters' young husbands, who come to give bride-service. !Kung society requires that all men go to live with the family of their brides and give them bride-service, which consists of hunting and providing meat for the bride's family. If the bride's parents are dead, the husband serves whatever relatives she is living with. In a first marriage, bride-service usually lasts until three children are born to the couple. Once his obligations are fulfilled, a man has the right to return to his own family and band, taking his wife and children with him. He may also choose to remain with his wife's family. Since men often marry outside of their bands, the bride-service provides a constant exchange of people among different bands. When the head of an extended family dies, this extended family breaks up, and the nuclear families of the married sons and daughters begin to operate independently of each other. When their offspring marry, these nuclear families become extended families, as the domestic cycle comes full circle.

The band is organized around rights to grassland areas *(veldkos)* and water holes. Individuals have access to water and land only through their band affiliations. Each band has a headman who is the "owner" of the *veldkos* and water and who administers the consumption of these resources by the members of the band. A band is composed of people who are related by birth and by marriage, including the families of parents and their offspring, siblings, aunts, and uncles and cousins. The Bushman band moves several times a year, whenever the food supply becomes scarce. Within the band, each family produces its own food. The women collect roots, berries, and the like, as well as firewood and water. The men go out to hunt almost daily, providing small game such as lizards or rabbits for their immediate families. If any large game is brought into the camp, however, it is usually shared.

The !Kung Bushmen show how closely intertwined economic and social arrangements can be. Bride-service not only provides a framework for deciding who is going to live where and with whom but also ensures that there is a young male hunter in each family. It also acts as a leveling mechanism, since each man has many dependents to support. The primary leveling mechanism, of course, is the fact that a person must be able to carry all of his or her possessions.

Although the different groups of hunters and gatherers that remain today concentrate on different particular resources of the natural environment, their way of life has certain basic characteristics in common: they are highly mobile, constantly moving from place to place; they amass very few personal possessions; they live in small groups, because of the nature of the food supply; food surpluses are usually small; no single group has exclusive rights to a particular set of resources; they have a fantastic knowledge of their natural environment; and no group becomes attached to any single area. All evidence indicates that there is no reason to believe that these fundamental patterns of life observed among present-day hunters and gatherers are substantially different from those followed by past groups.

Pastoralism. *Pastoralism*—raising and herding animals for meat, hides, milk, and the products that can be derived from them—highlights the transition from hunting and gathering to the transformation of nature by cultivation. Pastoralists are found from the equator to the Arctic Circle. Pastoralism, however, has developed as a dominant

Pastoralists may be found from the equator to the Arctic Circle and make their living by raising and herding various sorts of animals. These Finnish Laplanders, for example, raise reindeer. (Dan Budnick, Woodfin Camp)

economy only in the Old World. In the New World, pastoral groups include the Navajo of the North American Southwest and herders in the highlands of South America.

Pastoralists raise a wide variety of animals (camels, donkeys, sheep, horses, cattle, reindeer, llamas, alpacas) and use them for many different purposes. The regions in which they are found include tundra, grassland, desert, and tropical savanna. Pastoralists are not found in forested areas, because their animals usually are not suited to such conditions. Nor are they generally found in well-watered areas—the rewards of cultivation in such areas are higher than the rewards of herding.

There are ways in which pastoralism and cultivation can be combined. One of these is *transhumance,* in which the group winters in permanent villages around lowland pastures, where it engages in some cultivation. It then migrates to the mountains in the summer, taking its livestock along.

Pastoral societies often continue to exist despite the fact that their members are aware of the advantages of cultivation. This may be due in part to a belief on the part of the pastoralists, reinforced by religious sanctions and taboos, that their way of life is superior. The Masai of highland Kenya, for example, have sought to maintain the purity of their particular economy, even using force to drive out cultivators from land that is suited to horticulture. In some places, the pastoralists have subjugated the cultivators and established themselves as an aristocracy. In others, pastoralism is part of a hybrid culture in which the men do the herding and the women do the cultivating. In general, such arrangements are not highly successful.

Pastoralists, like hunters and gatherers, are mobile or "nomadic," but their mobility differs in character from that of hunters and gatherers. Each group has a fairly well-defined territory, and it stays within this area and defends it against invaders (in contrast to the visiting and intermarriage of hunting-and-gathering societies). Within that area are specific sites that are occupied for long periods each year. The life of pastoralists is much less settled than that of cultivators, though; cultivators cannot move quickly—if at all—nor can they take all their food supply with them.

Many, but not all, pastoral societies are characterized by an authoritarian system in which the male head of a household has almost total power over wives, children, and slaves—a pattern that is familiar from Biblical descriptions of the Israelites. It is also common, but not universal, for women to have lower status than men in such societies (but this is often true of horticultural societies as well).

The Ruwala Bedouin. The Ruwala Bedouin are tent-dwelling camel breeders who live in northern Arabia (Forde, 1934). For 9 to 10 months of the year, they occupy well-defined tracts of coarse grassland, rarely entering the sandy desert or rocky country nearby. For part of each year, they must return to settled lands, since the vegetation in their pastures withers during the very hot season.

The Ruwala follow a roughly circular migration pattern. In September, they leave the villages to the west of their territory. They spend the winter moving slowly in scattered groups over the northern pastures. In the spring, they move southward toward the fringes of the desert. Then they follow the pastures and water holes west and north, reaching the villages before the drought strikes. These movements vary in their details from one year to the next, depending on the timing and amount of the rains, though their general form remains the same.

The organization of a Bedouin group is based on the requirements of its animals. The tribal *sheikh* may control a large number of tents, but the tribe does not live as a group. A number of small segments of 50 to 100 people scatter over the pastures seeking grass for their own animals. The camel is the measure

For the Ruwala Bedouin, the camel is the measure of wealth, supplying food and being used as a medium of exchange for other products. (Klaus D. Francke, Peter Arnold Photo Archives)

of wealth. It supplies food and other raw materials, and can be sold to traders or peasants in exchange for weapons, clothing, and grain. A man's wealth depends on the size of his herds, though it may be displayed in the form of slaves, horses, or tent trappings, as well.

Unlike hunters and gatherers, such as the !Kung Bushmen, the Ruwala must store much of their food supply. A well-to-do man starts out from the village with a camel load (about 300 pounds) of grain for each member of his household and an extra load to be used in en-

tertaining guests. The remaining food is obtained from the camel (milk only) or from a few hunters attached to the camp. There is also some gathering of wild foods.

Bedouin tribesmen are related through the male blood line; kin are all descended from the same paternal ancestor and usually remain together. A collection of such groups recognizes the head of the dominant group as its *sheikh*. When families become very large, however, they often must segment into smaller groups, and the ties between them weaken over time. In fact, between different camping groups there may be constant rivalry, as the competition for land and water, in the form of wells, is ongoing. Between different tribes rivalry is intensified, tension is high, and in some cases, a state of war exists between them. Indeed, as Forde (1934) has pointed out, "The life of a [Bedouin] camp is not one of peaceful migration from pasture to pasture. It is punctuated by raiding expeditions small and large against enemy tribes and their herds" (p. 323). This is particularly true during years of severe drought, when pastorage is meager and water is scarce. To the danger of raiding is added that of blood feuds: murder must be either avenged by the kin of the victim by killing the murderer or a relative of the murderer, or a large quantity of wealth must be transferred from the group of the murderer to the group of the person murdered. And yet individual travelers are in little danger. Travelers are welcomed and, by tribal law, given safe conduct through the tribe's territory.

Horticulture and Agriculture. The third main type of subsistence economy is one of plant cultivation. Anthropologists divide cultivation into two types. The first is *horticulture*—plant cultivation using simple tools such as hoes and, mostly, human muscle power. Horticulture is usually done by women on small plots of land. The second type of cultivation is *agriculture*—intensive plant cultivation using plows and other machinery. Agriculture is most often done by men over large tracts of land. Pastoralists and *cultivators*—people who practice some method of raising crops—are often viewed as hostile to one another by nature, and it is true that there have often been conflicts between these groups. Yet it is not pastoralism and horticulture as such that are in opposition but a mobile, relatively unaccumulative life style and a settled, relatively wealthy one. The most prominent characteristics of most cultivating societies is that their members can produce surplus food and thus free others for more specialized tasks.

As mentioned earlier, cultivation can sometimes coexist with hunting and fishing or with herding within a given society, but plough cultivation tends to absorb such a high portion of the community's energy that there is less opportunity or need for other means of food production. Plough cultivators keep animals, but they use them as draught animals, not (usually) for food.

Cultivators vary widely in their economic and social organization as well as in the nature of the crops they grow and the technology they use. Horticulturalists, the most primitive cultivators, use digging sticks with which they make holes for seeds and cuttings and sometimes wooden blades for chopping down weeds. To prepare their gardens, they may use the *slash-and-burn* technique. This involves slashing trees and underbrush, burning off the refuse, and planting in the area thus cleared. This practice is widespread in the Amazon region and has proved to be an effective way of utilizing resources over time, because soil nutrients are replaced by the decaying plant life that covers the earth. New gardens have to be prepared within a few years, since repeated plantings in the same field eventually lead to low yields.

The use of ploughs is characteristic of agriculturalists. In addition to the plough, these cultivators use irrigation devices and fertilizers, as well as techniques such as crop rotation and the planting of crops such as beans that restore the nitrogen content of the soil. There are, however, some advanced cultivating economies that do not depend on the plough. Where rice fields are built in terraces on steep hillsides, as is done by the Ifugao in the Philippines, for example, the plough has no use at all and cultivation is done almost entirely by hand.

The communities of hand cultivators may be smaller and less complex than those of some food gatherers. But, in general, the larger and more stable food supply of cultivators allows them to develop new types of social and political institutions—to organize

The slash-and-burn method of cultivation often involves a considerable amount of work. Notice the scaffold-like structure that was built around the large tree this Yąnomamö man is cutting down as part of the slash-and-burn technique necessary to clear an area for cultivation. (Karl Werdmann, National Audubon Society, Photo Researchers)

in large communities and even into states with formal political institutions. Landholding systems among cultivators range from systems similar to those of hunter-gathers, in which land is held in common, through feudal systems, in which tenants occupy and cultivate plots of land owned by large landowners, as in medieval Europe or in parts of contemporary third-world nations, to private property, as in Western societies today.

Crafts such as weaving, pottery, and metalworking develop further in economies using plough cultivation than in other types of subsistence economies. The reason for this is that, with proper techniques, good land can be used indefinitely and can feed more people than are needed to cultivate it. Thus specialists in other activities can be maintained.

In Western nations, cultivation is closer to an industrial economic system than to a subsistence economy. In fact, it is sometimes called "agribusiness." One farmer, with the help of modern technology and equipment, can manage vast areas and produce huge surpluses of crops.

Although long since out of date, Forde's (1934) description of two cultivating systems illustrates well the types of production systems under consideration here. The Boro and the Cochin systems have subsequently changed, but production systems of this nature are still found in comparable areas.

The Boro of the Western Amazon Forest. The Boro were a group of over 10,000 South American Indians living in about 50 separate settlements in the Western Amazon. They lived in the dense equatorial forest that grows on the rich soil of the region. Their problem was not one of making things grow, but, rather, of clearing the forest in order to plant. To create room for a settlement, they burned down the trees in a relatively open area to make a clearing and then built a single large house 60 to 70 feet long on each side and at least 30 feet high. Each nuclear family had its own fireplace, which is against one of the walls of this house.

Despite all the effort that went into making the clearings and building the communal house, these sites were not occupied for more than a few years. When the gardens lost their fertility and hostile groups learned where the settlement was located, the site was abandoned and a new one found.

The Boro did some hunting but depended mainly on horticulture. The plot owned by the chief of the settlement was usually located in the main clearing. Those of other members of the community were scattered throughout the surrounding jungle, generally within about a mile of the house. To prepare a plot for cultivation, the larger trees were burned down and the smaller growth hacked away with stone axes. At the end of the rainy season, the undergrowth was burned out with a number of small fires. The ground was roughly broken by the men with heavy wooden stakes, and then the women used digging sticks to plant the crops. The men did the heavy work of forest clearing and digging the rough ground and then returned to hunting wild game. The women did the rest of the horticultural work and prepared the food. A plot was exhausted after two or three harvests.

Rice Cultivation in Cochin. Along the Malabar coast of India in the native state of Cochin, an ancient system of plough cultivation was used. Rice was cultivated intensively on thousands of acres of carefully prepared plots. More than half of the population was engaged in rice cultivation and over one-third in various crafts and small-scale industry.

The settlements of Cochin were not compact villages but loose clusters of houses on higher ground that was unsuitable for rice cultivation. The houses of landowners had gardens and groves of fruit trees; those of laborers were scattered among the fields and on the outskirts of the settlements.

Almost all the low-lying land was devoted to rice cultivation. Before the monsoon rains, the plots were tilled with a simple wooden plough pulled by water buffaloes. Women followed the plough and broke up the sods with sticks. Dung and manure were scattered over the plots; after the plots had been soaked by the rains, they were ploughed again. Clods of earth were crushed with a heavy wooden plank, and then a log was dragged over the ground to level it. When the ground had been soaked, the seeds were scattered. Between planting and harvesting, much of the work consisted of maintaining the banks around the fields which controlled the amount of water in them. A second crop of millet, pulses, or oil seeds was grown after the rice had been harvested in order to restore nitrogen to the soil.

Before the British influence became dominant, the political and social organization of Cochin was based mainly on the feudal hereditary rights of landowners and on the Hindu caste system. The royal house was the greatest landowner in the state; large tracts were also controlled by hereditary district chiefs. Some of the land was sublet to tenant farmers, but much of it was worked by agricultural serfs. Subsequently, most of the land was owned by wealthy families and either sublet or worked by laborers.

Industrial Economies

A productive unit in an American automobile plant could consist of a group of machinists who make or assemble specific parts. Consider, for example, the group of workers who make pushrods for the cylinders of an engine. Their activities are limited to producing pushrods and only pushrods. In an industrial economy, interaction among workers is often job specific; that is, it occurs only while they are on the job. The workers have no other rights and obligations to each other. In hunting-and-gathering bands, on the other hand, an extended family not only cooperates in hunting and gathering, but its members also interact socially during the distribution and consumption of the foods collected. They also, of course, share kinship and ritual obligations. Clearly there are important differences between the economy of pushrod makers and the traditional economy of hunters and gatherers. What are those differences?

The Development of Specialization. To begin with, the pushrod makers are engaged in a very small part of the total productive effort. The technology of an industrial economy is highly specialized and job specific, so the work is divided among large numbers of people who specialize in a small part of the total operation. This is not the case among hunters and gatherers, where the only significant division of labor is between the men, who hunt, and the women, who gather. In small-scale societies, the economy is not differentiated from other fields of activity and other domains of thought. It is embedded in a broad web of social relations that serve multiple and diverse functions. How, then, does the extreme specialization characteristic of industrial economies come about?

In small-scale societies, labor is divided on the basis of age and sex. Heavy work is not done by children or old people, but children contribute some work to the household from an early age. Work that has to be done at some distance from the home is usually done by men; men also do work that requires agility, such as climbing trees for fruit. Women cook, gather, and plant, as well as bear children. Some anthropologists have argued that the demands of child rearing, in particular, tend to keep women close to home. Even in subsistence economies, however, there is some specialization. Some members of the society develop skill in weaving, pottery making, or some other craft. But these activities are still centered on the household, and often the items produced are used, exchanged, or given away, not sold.

Greater specialization is stimulated by trade relations with other regions as well as by respect for the skills of the specialist.

Craft specialists do exist even in small-scale, subsistence economies, as exemplified by this weaver in Nepal. (Eugene Gordon, Taurus Photos)

Craftspeople may become organized into guilds, whose members may live close together in a particular village or, as in medieval Europe, a particular quarter of a town or city. The guild is not a kin group but a skill group (although a son may be expected to take up his father's trade).

A specialist may also contribute his or her skills to a cooperative undertaking in which materials and labor are supplied by others. This is a natural outcome of organizing the work through a team—the group that is formed to do a job that requires more labor than can be supplied by a single household (such as harvesting). The "payment" for work of this kind is the right to receive the same kind of help at a later date. In the case of the specialist (for example, the expert who does the carving on a new canoe), the "payment" takes the form of food or some other material good, but the work is done for reasons other than strictly economic ones (for instance, as a political strategy or simply out of neighborliness).

The next step is "entrepreneurship." In the Trobriand Islands, for example, the construction of a sea-going canoe may be organized by a chief who has large quantities of surplus food at his disposal and who sets others to work to enable him to transport the food to another island. But such entrepreneurs do not constitute a class of employers, as they do in an industrial society. It is not until separate classes of employers and employed develop, and the relationship between them is entirely "economic"—that is, one pays the other for labor provided—that the division of labor typical of industrial societies develops.

Other Differences between Industrial and Nonindustrial Societies.

Udy (1970) has noted other differences between industrial and subsistence economies, which include the following:

1. The goals of an industrial enterprise are limited to production; they are *specific.* The goals of a subsistence economy are *diffuse;* its activities have other purposes than production.
2. In an industrial economy, rewards for work depend on the amount of work done; thus, achievement is emphasized. In a subsistence economy, rewards are distributed with little regard for the amount of work done.
3. Recruitment of workers is *territorial* in industrial economies and *social* in subsistence economies, in that participation in production processes depends on prior membership in some other social group.

Udy believes that for an industrial economy to develop, a centralized government is essential. But social scientists have found that the centralization of government tends to encourage custodial rather than contractual forms of production organization. It consolidates control over resources and permits an exercise of power indirectly supported by governmental sanction. And since custodial forms involve social recruitment, reward by ascription, and diffuseness of goals, they hamper industrial development, which is better served by contractual forms of production organization. This may be one reason why industrialization is hard to achieve in many developing nations.

The Colonial Impact. Many of the differences between industrial and nonindustrial economies played a role in the destructive effect of colonialism on the economies of colonized countries. In Africa, for example, where economic and social processes were highly interdependent, European modes of production were meaningless because they required work that was completely separate from social obligations to family, friends, or chiefs. To the Africans, the purpose of work was not only to gain income but also to express and strengthen social relationships. When they were forced to enter the colonial economy as laborers, producers of cash crops, or commercial traders, Africans had to give up many activities that were essential to their traditional social relationships. As a result, the relationships often disintegrated (Dalton, 1967, pp. 76–77).

Many developing nations are organizing themselves in ways that create new and distinctive blends of social and economic institutions—producers' and consumers' cooperatives, for example. This often involves strong central control and "welfare state" policies, in contrast to the relatively uncontrolled market system of the West.

Labor and Leisure

Patterns of Labor

"Primitive" peoples have often been misrepresented by Westerners as lazy. Generally living in climates where nature provides for most of their needs, they supposedly did not have to exert themselves very much—nor did they *want* to work hard enough—to obtain the extra benefits of life. This is a gross misconception. Even the people of the bountiful South Sea islands work hard when hard work is required of them.

Although primitive people may work hard at times and relax whenever they can, this does not mean, as is often implied, that they lack concentration and discipline. The fact is that, like everyone else, they do whatever they need to do to make a living, plus as much more as is necessary to achieve any additional goals that they may have, and that are possible. Primitive people are realists, only their realities differ from ours.

Not only do individuals in small-scale societies perform different amounts of work, but whole families, too, may differ in the amount of work they do. One of the most striking aspects of labor patterns in such societies is the amount of cooperative work performed by groups larger than the conjugal family but smaller than the community—that is, work done through "the voluntary association of a group of men or women whose objective is the completion of a specific, definitely limited task, with which they are simultaneously concerned" (Herskovits, 1965, p. 100). A good example of this type of widespread working group is the *combite* of Haiti.

Essentially, the *combite* is the basis upon which Haitians are able to finish the heavy work of clearing their fields soon enough to get their planting done. When a man needs a field cleared, he puts out the word that he wants a *combite,* or working party, to do the work. As the workers gather, the host prepares food for a feast, either lavish or simple, depending on what he can afford. The work is supervised by a man who makes sure that it progresses quickly enough to finish the work in the available time. The workers, each carrying a hoe, form a line and clear the field to the beat of at least one and sometimes two or three drums, depending on the size of the *combite.* In this way, a field of several acres can be completely cleared in a single afternoon by about 65 workers.

The feast at the end of the day is supervised by the man who supervised the work. He distributes the food, making sure that the best goes to the men who came earliest and worked hardest. Those men who gain the reputation of being shirkers find that when they need help in clearing their own fields, their request is greeted with little enthusiasm.

Thus, it should not be concluded that individual initiative and self-interest are lacking in small-scale societies. It is clear that a person who participates in cooperative work may expect to benefit from the labor of a similar work group in the future. Reciprocity is expressed in diverse fields of activity, including production of goods. Moreover, there is something to be gained—prestige—from being the best worker in the group, and this generates competition that is not always friendly.

Leisure

Anthropologists tend to write very little about leisure, even though it is an important topic. We have noted that people in simple societies work as hard as people in more advanced societies, but we have also mentioned the short working hours of hunters and gatherers. While it appears that they have more leisure than we do, leisure is often seen as a characteristic of more advanced societies.

Every other form of subsistence economy requires more work than hunting and gathering. It is only in the most advanced societies that the invention of "labor-saving" devices becomes necessary. Food gatherers simply refrain from modes of production that require more labor.

The term *leisure preference* has recently been coined by economists to refer to the desire of people in industrial economies to work shorter hours rather than earn more money. But leisure preference may be found in any society anywhere in the world. It prevents some food gatherers from taking up cultivation, and it prevents some cultivators from working to grow more crops. This is not a result of laziness but a purposeful allocation of time to different activities.

"Not By Bread Alone"

It is important to note that "production" in any economic system, even the most simple, is not concerned only with filling nutritional needs. Workers "must produce more than calories if calories are to be produced" (Cook, 1973, p. 850). To produce food, one must first have produced the technology, however simple it might be, that goes into its production. The production of tools and equipment enables humans to provide for their nutritional needs more efficiently. Even hunters and gatherers have weapons, cooking implements, and so on, to make food production easier. And, as was noted earlier, the Bushmen work at food acquisition only a few hours a day, spending the rest of their time otherwise. Many anthropologists have held that humans became "human" when they began making tools and cooperating with one another in food production.

Summary

1. Economic anthropology is concerned with describing the variety of economic systems developed by humankind, classifying them, and relating them to social and cultural arrangements. It takes a holistic approach to economic systems.

2. Economic activity consists of the choices people make in determining how available resources are to be used in producing, distributing, and consuming material goods and services. These activities usually cannot be separated from other activities, and the choices may be either conscious or unconscious.

3. Small-scale economic systems are characterized by simple technology and little division of labor; productive units that serve other functions in addition to economic ones; and the use of leveling mechanisms to prevent the accumulation of wealth.

4. Different modes of production combine with factors of production—land, labor, and capital—in different ways. They also differ in their degree of technological sophistication and division of labor. The nature of the productive unit—familial, custodial, contractual, or voluntary—also varies from one economic system to another.

5. In a subsistence economy, people use what they produce to meet their own needs. Subsistence economies may be divided into three types: hunting and gathering; pastoralism; and horticulture/agriculture.

6. *Hunters and gatherers* live in small groups and move often. They have little personal property, do not produce surpluses, and are not attached to a particular area. Their way of life is not difficult in terms of energy spent, though their standard of living is low, when considered in terms of our own cultural values.

7. *Pastoralism* represents a transition between food collecting and cultivation. Pas-

toralists are nomadic, but somewhat less so than hunters and gatherers. Often they maintain a pastoral way of life even though they are aware of the advantages of cultivation.

8. Horticultural and agricultural societies are settled rather than mobile. Their technologies range from the slash-and-burn technique to plough cultivation. They tend to develop further in social and political terms than societies with other kinds of subsistence economies.

9. The most salient differences between industrial economies and subsistence economies is the extreme specialization characteristic of the former. Others include specific vs. diffuse goals, achievement orientation vs. ascription, and territorial vs. social recruitment.

10. "Primitive" people work as hard as people in industrial societies, but they differ in their leisure preferences. The concept of leisure is culture-bound. Different cultures have different attitudes toward work and time; the attitudes of groups within a given culture may also differ.

12

Distribution and Exchange

IN the preceding chapter, we identified four major features of small-scale economic systems: (1) technology and the division of labor, (2) the organization of productive units, (3) the forms and media of exchange, and (4) the control of wealth and capital. The first two themes served as a framework for our discussion of systems of production; the last two will guide us in this chapter as we study systems of distribution and exchange. *Distribution* refers to the manner in which goods are divided among members of a society. *Exchange* is the process whereby those receiving goods are, in turn, obligated to reciprocate by giving goods in return. What is reciprocated may be other goods or something of equal value, such as money. Although we have separated the four features that characterize small-scale economic systems for easier presentation and discussion, the organization of production in any society is by no means independent of its systems of distribution and exchange.

Any exchange of material goods is just one aspect of an ongoing social relationship—a relationship that shapes and limits the nature of the material transaction. Accordingly, we will focus on the social relationships surrounding the distribution and exchange of goods and services, as well as on the transactions themselves. Not only does the exchange of goods follow the normal patterns of social interaction in a society, but material transactions may underlie or initiate social relationships—"if friends make gifts, gifts make friends."

Systems and Media of Exchange

Systems of exchange of goods and services are necessary to all forms of organized society.

Such systems can be divided into three types: reciprocity, redistribution, and market exchange. This classification system, originally proposed by Karl Polyani (Polyani et al., 1957), is used by most anthropologists in their treatments of the economies of various societies. It is important to note that although every society is organized around at least one of these systems, most are organized around two, and many (both Western and non-Western) around all three.

Reciprocity

Reciprocity is an exchange transaction that involves direct movement of goods or services between two parties: *A* gives something to *B,* and *B* in turn gives something to *A.* This type of transaction is illustrated by the diagram in Figure 1. Reciprocity is sometimes viewed as simply a process of balancing values—a one-for-one exchange. This view, however, is misleading. Various kinds of exchange are included in the term reciprocity. Marshall Sahlins (1972) has pointed out that these can be arranged on a continuum according to the degree of balance involved. At one end of the continuum is *generalized reciprocity*—goods, services, or assistance freely given to kin, friends, and neighbors without any explicit

Figure 1 Reciprocity

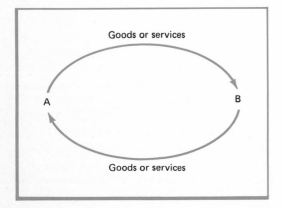

Goods or services

A   B

Goods or services

statement that anything is expected in return. In the middle of the continuum is *balanced reciprocity*—the expectation of goods or services of roughly equal value in return for what one gives. At the other extreme is *negative reciprocity,* in which goods or services are obtained through force or deception. The intervals between the points on the continuum are not only intervals between degrees of balance but also intervals of degrees of social distance, which is important in exchange transactions. The intervals also represent intervals of time within which reciprocal exchange takes place (at some distant time, if ever; at about the same time; never). Sahlins emphasizes that these categories have "moral" as well as "mechanical" implications, as will become clear as we study each in turn.

Generalized Reciprocity. Sahlins labels as generalized reciprocity any transaction that at least appears to be altruistic, such as help, sharing, and hospitality. The obligation to reciprocate, if it exists at all, is vague. In transactions of this type, the material aspects of exchange are much less significant than the social aspects. An extreme example is parents' care of their children—children are not expected to reciprocate in direct ways (though in later years children may wince at the oft-repeated phrase, "After all we've done for you. . ."). In most cases of "free giving," it is understood that the recipient should, at some undefined future time, reciprocate if possible. The value or quantity of the return to the donor is also undefined. Finally, despite the vague obligation to reciprocate, failure to do so does not usually stop the giver from giving again.

Balanced Reciprocity. Balanced reciprocity is direct exchange—one thing is exchanged for another of equal value, without delay. *Perfectly* balanced reciprocity, in which the same types of goods in the same amounts are exchanged, sometimes occurs. You may borrow a cup of sugar or an egg from your neigh-

A direct exchange in which values of goods are calculated fairly precisely takes place in this marketplace in Tego, Lomé. (Bernard Pierre Wolff, Photo Researchers)

bor, which you return in kind. But the term usually applies to transactions in which a return of equal value is made within a definite time, such as buying, selling, trade, and payment. These are known as *generally* balanced transactions.

The social relationship underlying balanced transactions is less personal and more economic than that underlying generalized reciprocity. The two sides in balanced transactions are economically and socially distinct. The material aspects of the transaction are at least as important as its social aspects; and the values of the goods and services are calculated fairly precisely. One-way flows of goods or services are not tolerated.

Negative Reciprocity. Negative reciprocity involves trying to get something for nothing. It includes gambling, theft, and the like. This is the most impersonal form of exchange and

the most "economic" in that the material aspects of the transaction are all-important. The two sides are entirely opposed, and there is not necessarily any interaction between them. The flow of goods is in one direction, but the act is one of taking, not giving.

Factors Influencing Reciprocity. Kinship, as might be expected, has a significant effect on the nature of transactions between individuals. Kin ties tend to create generalized reciprocity. This is related to the multiplex nature of the relationship, that is, the overlapping of multiple and diverse interests. Generalized reciprocity therefore occurs frequently in simple, small-scale societies, in which a large percentage of social life is based on kinship. Among the Bemba, for instance, food is normally shared by close kin; during scarcities it is shared more widely. But there are exceptions, as Richards (1939) reports.

I have often seen women take a pot of beer and conceal it in a friend's granary on the reported arrival of some elderly relative. To refuse hospitality with a pot of beer sitting on the hearth would be an impossible insult, but a bland assertion that "Alas, . . . We have nothing to eat here" is sometimes necessary. This would not be done in the case of a near relative, but only with a more distant kinsman . . . or . . . well-known "cadgers." (p. 202)

Other factors that may affect reciprocal transactions are social rank or prestige; relative wealth; and the type of goods involved. The effect of rank difference is roughly opposite to that of kinship. The reciprocity between the person of high rank and the person of low rank tends to be generalized. Polynesian chiefs, for example, have immense obligations to their people. For a Tikopia chief, generosity is a prerogative of office; he is *expected* to give away the food and other things that he accumulates. If a commoner accumulates goods and then disperses them in chiefly fashion, he is likely to incur severe penalties. In short, "to be noble is to be generous."

Since to be "noble" is often also to be wealthy, differences in economic status influence reciprocity in the same way that differences in social status or rank influence it. In societies in which no clear-cut differences are apparent, such as those of hunters and gatherers, anyone who has food is expected to give to anyone who has none—to such an extent that Eskimo hunters have been known to give all their food to others and have none left for their families (Spencer, 1959).

All of these factors—kinship, rank, and wealth—sometimes influence an exchange transaction. Any one factor cannot be separated from the others, in such cases, except for purposes of discussion.

Functions of Balanced Reciprocity. Balanced reciprocity implies willingness to give in exchange for what is received. It means giving up self-interest or hostility for the sake of mutual benefit. Hence, it serves as a vehicle for many types of social "contracts." This is not to say that the exchange itself is not mutually beneficial; rather, we mean to say that the basic purpose of such transactions is to generate a friendly feeling, a degree of sociability, regardless of the material values involved.

Sahlins (1972) outlines some of the types of contracts that often involve balanced reciprocity, including the following:

1. Formal friendship or kinship—pledges of brotherhood and the like, which may be sealed by an exchange of goods.
2. Group alliances—feasts and similar events in which different clans or villages may affirm their friendship by exchanging goods or entertainment.
3. Peacemaking—exchanges that are part of a settlement bringing an end to a hostile situation (including such exchanges as compensation for adultery or homocide, as well as those that terminate warfare).
4. Marriage transactions—the classic form of social/material exchange. The social effects of exchanging cattle or some other material goods at marriage are comparable to those of the exchanges just listed.

It is important to note that while the basis of reciprocity is the exchange of gifts, any gift carries with it an obligation of return, either expressed or implied. This fact is of primary economic importance, for it stimulates the circulation of goods. Consider the following intertribal relationships, which existed in India before the arrival of Europeans:

[The Kota] were musicians and artists for the three neighboring folk of their area, the pastoral Toda, the jungle-dwelling Kurumba, and the agricultural Badaga. Each tribe had clearly defined and ritually regulated obligations and prerogatives with respect to all the others. The Toda provided the Kota with ghee [liquid butter made from cow's milk] for certain ceremonies and with buffaloes for sacrifices at their funerals. The Kota furnished the Toda with the pots and knives they needed in their everyday life and made the music essential to Toda ceremonies.

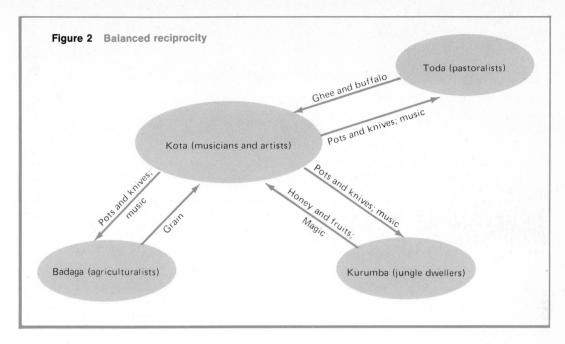

Figure 2 Balanced reciprocity

The Kota provided the Badaga with similar goods and services, receiving grain in return. They stood in the same exchange relationship with the forest Kurumba, but these latter, who could only provide meagre material compensation—honey, canes, and occasionally fruits—were able to afford the Kota supernatural protection, since the Kurumba were dreaded sorcerers, so feared that every Kota family must have their own Kurumba protector against the magic which others of this tribe might work against them. (Herskovits, 1965, p. 157)

These relationships were basically social, involving funerals, feasts, and the like, but they influenced and shaped the economic transactions of the four tribes.

The Kula System. Malinowski's (1920) description of *kula,* the circulating exchange of valuables in eastern New Guinea, is a classic example of reciprocity. The *kula* is a special system of trade, separate from the exchange of items such as pottery, dried fish, or canoes. It consists of the circulation of two items that have high value but no practical usefulness:

shell armbands *(mwali)* and shell-disk neck-laces *(soulava)*. They are intended as ornaments but are rarely used for this purpose. The *kula* system covers an immense area that includes the islands to the east of New Guinea, Woodlark Island, the Trobriand Archipelago, and several other islands and archipelagos (see Figure 3). As the map indicates, actual trade of material goods takes place in addition to the *kula* trade.

Kula is carried on according to definite and complex rules. First, viewing the geographic area covered by the system as a circle, the *soulava* travel only clockwise and the *mwali* travel only counterclockwise. Second, neither item remains for very long in the possession of any individual; both are continually being exchanged. Third, *kula* trade is only one form of interaction between individuals living in different communities who have established a specific, life-long relationship with each other. Chiefs have more such relationships than commoners; older men have more than younger men.

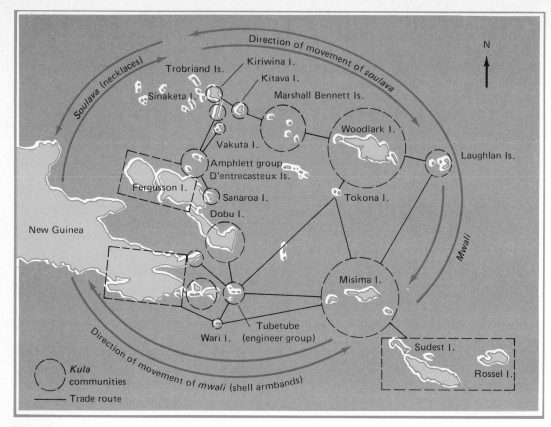

Figure 3 The *kula* system. The dotted circles indicate the *kula* communities; the dotted rectangles indicate the areas indirectly affected by the *kula*. (Malinowski, 1920)

Malinowski described the exchange as follows:

Let us suppose that I, a Sinaketa man, am in possession of a pair of big armshells. An overseas expedition from Dobu in the d'Entrecasteux Archipelago arrives at my village. Blowing a conch shell, I take my armshell pair and I offer it to my overseas partner, with some such words, "This is a *vaga* (initial gift)—in due time, thou returnest to me a big *soulava* (necklace) for it!" Next year, when I visit my partner's village, he either is in possession of an *equivalent* necklace, and this he gives to me as *yotile* (restoration gift), or he has not a necklace good enough to repay my last gift. In this case he will give me a smaller necklace—avowedly not equivalent to my gift—and will give it to me as *basi* (intermediary gift).

This means that the main gift has to be repaid on a future occasion and the *basi* is given in token of good faith—but it, in turn, must be repaid by me in the meantime by a gift of small armshells. The final gift, which will be given to me to clinch the whole transaction, would then be called *kudu* (equivalent gift) in contrast to *basi*. (Malinowski, 1920; in Dalton, 1967, pp. 173–174)

The system is actually more complicated than this. For example, the finest *soulava* and *mwali* have names and histories and are therefore much desired. Those who are especially eager to obtain one of these articles may give its current owner offerings and solicitory gifts. In short, *kula* is an elaborate system of relationships in which both social and economic relationships are governed by the rules of exchange. It is distinctly different from common barter, *gimwali,* since it involves a higher level of trust. The *kula* expresses the value placed on generosity and honor, because the equivalence of the gifts and countergifts cannot be enforced. The temporary possession of a *kula* article brings its owner prestige; but so does the way in which he gives it away.

To put *kula* into perspective, it should be noted that most members of the "ring" are also involved in other forms of material exchange in addition to this form of reciprocity. However, the *kula* transactions form the basis for other kinds of transaction, including trade of consumer products.

Redistribution

Redistribution is a pooling transaction in which goods are collected from the members of a group by a central authority and then divided up among the members of the group. Figure 4 illustrates the process of redistribution. An example of this type of exchange is the Old Testament story in which Joseph interpreted Pharaoh's dream of 7 years of plenty to be followed by 7 years of famine, and Joseph himself was put in charge of collecting and storing food during the years of plenty in

order to redistribute it during the years of famine. One difference between reciprocity and redistribution is implicit in this story, and that is that the social organization of these two types of exchange is quite different. Redistribution is the collective action among several parties, whereas reciprocity is the action and reaction of two parties. Reciprocity requires only two sides; redistribution requires a social center. For this reason, redistribution is associated with groups headed by a central authority, such as a chief. Interestingly, some archaeologists have hypothesized that the building of the pyramids and other monumental architecture in ancient Egypt was also a part of the larger system of redistribution in which both goods and services were "pooled," so that such works were constructed during periods of economic stagnation. Thus, they see them as a kind of huge welfare system.

Redistribution may be a matter of custom, law, or special decision. Sometimes there is actual collection, storage, and redistribution of goods. At other times, the "collection" is not physical but consists of assignment of the right to use the goods in a particular area (that is, group A may have the food grown in this section of field, group B may have the yield from that section). The reason for redistribution can vary too. For example, it may stem

Figure 4 Redistribution

Step 1   Step 2

Sometimes redistribution involves actually collecting, storing, and distributing goods; it can only occur in a social system with a central authority capable of overseeing such activities. (Jason Lauré, Woodfin Camp)

from the fact that different regions of a large country produce things that other regions cannot produce, or that the time at which food is needed and harvest time may be several months apart. Finally, redistribution may apply not only to whole societies but to smaller groups as well. Such was the case in the medieval manor, where a number of serfs

worked for the lord of the manor who then redistributed the goods among them.

The presence of redistribution implies the existence of a hierarchy. That is, redistribution is impossible unless someone is given the authority to carry out the redistribution; hence, the frequent association of redistribution with chieftainship. Indeed, this relation may create the leadership role itself. In most hunting-and-gathering societies, the central authority needed to redistribute goods is lacking, and reciprocity is more likely to occur there. In addition, redistribution is possible only if there is a large enough surplus to make it worthwhile. As a result, redistributive exchange is found in production systems that are somewhat more advanced than that of simple hunting and gathering.

The Potlatch. The word *potlatch* means simply "giving" in Chinook jargon, a widely used trade language of the north Pacific coast. The *potlatch* of the northwest Pacific coast Indians was a ceremony at which one chief and his group gave away goods—usually trade blankets or copper plaques—to another chief or chiefs and their groups. The gifts were distributed according to the ranks of the recipients. Drucker explains the ceremony of the *potlatch* as follows:

The first step after plans and preparations was the dispatching of an invitation party to the village of the guests. This party was ceremoniously treated, and was given a feast where they could deliver the invitation orally to the assembled group, setting the date on which the guests would be expected. . . .

Among many groups, guests of high rank were called in order of precedence, each in turn being escorted by ushers to a place of honor corresponding to his rank. When more than one group of guests had been invited, an elaborate protocol had to be worked out, the chief of the highest-ranking group being seated first, and the chief of the second-highest group next, then that of the third group, and so on. Then those of second rank were seated. . . .

Women from British Columbia with wares to be given away at a *potlatch.*
(American Museum of Natural History)

Men of lower rank and commoners were seated as a group. . . . When large amounts of riches were to be distributed, more guests were individually seated than at small-scale distributions. Speeches of welcome were made and replied to, supplementing those made on the formal arrival. . . .

The next step was usually the display of crests and performance of dances and songs, not just for entertainment but because these referred to the privileges about to be bestowed. . . . The gifts were distributed, the quantity or nature of each gift was announced by the speaker, and the tallymen busily counted bundles of . . . sticks to keep accounts of the presents and the recipients. . . . Thanks were given by the recipient of each gift, and at the conclusion of the distribution the ranking guest or his speaker made a speech of thanks. . . . (Drucker, 1965, pp. 57–58)

While the effect of a *potlatch* was to redistribute goods, it served important social functions as well. It was a declaration by the host himself of his status. Also, it strengthened the bond between the individual and the group on the one hand, as well as the ties between the host group and the guest group on the other. The latter relationship was reciprocal: the guests were expected to "return" the gifts by having *potlatches* to which the hosts would be invited (much as dinner invitations are "returned" in our society).

A variant was the rivalry *potlatch,* in which large quantities of goods were given away in order to shame a rival. These events resulted from competition between two men for a specific status. The first would hold a *potlatch* to announce his claims; the second would offer a rival *potlatch* (to which the same participants or others were invited) at which he denied his rival's claims and emphasized his own. This kind of competition could go on until one of the contestants went bankrupt and lost his bid to status by default (Drucker, 1965).

The potlatch has sometimes been described as irrational behavior because it differs from the acquisitive behavior that Americans consider normal. But it is just as rational as any other way of procuring honor and power, such as committing oneself to heavy mortgage or auto loan payments for the sake of the status that comes with owning a prestigious house or a luxurious car.

The *potlatch* was the fundamental means whereby political influence and social position were established and maintained among the Indians of the Northwest Coast, where social rank was extremely important. The assumption of any new status was validated by a *potlatch* to which the important people in the society were invited. The distribution of food and other material valuables served as an important mechanism for the distribution of goods. But the primary purpose of the *potlatch* was to proclaim and confirm a particular status, which was frequently accompanied by an honorific title. To assume the title was to assert certain rights. These rights had to be reaffirmed at subsequent *potlatches* when the

title or rank came into question. The *potlatch* is a significant example of exchange because it is based on the principle of reciprocity which is fundamental to all systems of exchange. In this case, however, the reciprocal obligation is perhaps more apparent than it is in other systems.

Market Exchange

Market exchange is a price-setting mechanism and is characterized by bargaining behavior. Each party to the exchange wants to arrive at a price that is as favorable to him or her as possible. The important point is that prices can fluctuate; they are not set or predetermined. And since each party is trying to gain an advantage at the expense of the other, the nature of the social relationship involved is basically antagonistic.

The concept of market exchange is inevitably tied to the concept of money. Economists generally define money as a medium of exchange that has no other use and that is taken in exchange for goods and services. The coins, bills, and checks that we use in Western society are, of course, considered money. They are an impersonal, commercial commodity. To people from small-scale societies, however, money may have social, moral, or even emotional connotations. Some anthropologists have included as money the cowrie shells that peoples of Oceania use as mediums of exchange. Others have argued that the shells are not money because their exchange value is limited to obtaining only certain goods or products. The problem of definition stems from using Western money as a model and trying to see whether cowrie shells, cattle, dog teeth, and the like fit the model, rather than trying to find out how the similarities and differences between various types of moneys relate to similarities and differences between various types of economic systems.

The question is, then, what is money? Money may be used for three basic purposes:

1. As a medium of exchange—money enables people to exchange things they want less for things they want more without having to find someone in the opposite situation. Without money, if one needs a specific item, such as a piece of cloth, and has something that he or she is willing to give up, such as an extra chicken, the person may be obliged to hunt high and low before finding someone who wants a chicken and is willing to give a piece of cloth in exchange for it. With money, both individuals can go to a market and buy the cloth and the chicken.
2. As a standard of value—money enables people to compare chickens and cloths, so to speak. Every item that can be exchanged is given a monetary value, and this facilitates its exchange.
3. As a means of payment—money enables people to obtain their choice of a wide variety of products and services. It is unlikely that the bookstore where you bought this book would have appreciated being paid in chickens or pieces of cloth, because it would be difficult for the bookstore manager then to pay bills and salaries with such goods.

In Western societies, money performs all three of these functions. In other societies, however, this is not always the case. Anthropologists therefore distinguish between two types of money—*general-purpose* money and *special-purpose* money (Dalton, 1965).

General-Purpose Money. In a true market economy such as our own, money serves a *general* purpose. It makes it possible to place a value on all goods and services regardless of their type so that they may be readily purchased. It also serves as a general standard of value and is universally used in making pay-

ments. Everything from natural resources to finished goods can be bought in the appropriate market, as can services of all kinds, as well as ceremonial and religious goods. Taxes are paid with money, as are fines. Gifts are bought with money and then given, or the gift itself may take the form of money. In a market economy, even redistribution (taxation) and reciprocity (gift-giving) are transacted by means of money.

Special-Purpose Money. On the other hand, in small-scale economies money may exist, but its purpose is often limited. Such money is termed *special-purpose money*. Different objects may be used in and limited to different types of transactions. Moreover, the objects used may not be "full-time" money, in that they may have other uses as well. Such objects may perform one or two of the functions listed earlier—as a medium of exchange, a standard of value, or a means of payment—but not all three. Special-purpose moneys tend to be used in noncommercial transactions. When tools are exchanged for a bride, the transaction is reciprocal. The tools cannot necessarily be used in other types of transactions but are required for the bridewealth transaction. Similarly, cows, shell armbands, and so forth serve some of the functions that Western moneys serve, but in noncommercial situations. In each case, they are used only for specific transactions. In New Britain, for example, a Tolai man collects strings of shell money to be given out at his funeral; no other form of "money" may be used for this purpose (Matt, 1972, p. 196). In the southwestern part of Zaire, the Lele use raffia aprons as the "price" of initiation into an age set, entry into a cult association, compensation for offenses, and the like. These aprons are rarely used for any other purpose (Douglas, 1958).

Many small-scale societies do not have a single type of money for everything they exchange. Some commodities are used in some kinds of exchange and others in other kinds. That is, various spheres of exchange are sepa-

246

rated from one another and use various types of special-purpose money.

An example of a society with multiple and diverse spheres of exchange is the Siane of highland New Guinea. The first sphere consists of the necessities of life—vegetables, small livestock, household utensils—which the Siane call "nothing things." These are exchanged by kinspeople for "help" (loans or informal gifts). The second sphere consists of precious, but not utilitarian, objects that are exchanged on ceremonial occasions such as forming an alliance; these objects are called "things." The third sphere is made up of "small things" (nuts, oil, tobacco, salt) that are not necessities. They are exchanged for one another and cannot be exchanged for either food or ceremonial objects (Salisbury, 1965). An economy of this sort, using various media of exchange, may be termed *multicentric*. This is in contrast to a *unicentric* economy, which uses general-purpose money.

An old man from Yap explaining stone money to his young listeners. (Jack Fields, Photo Researchers)

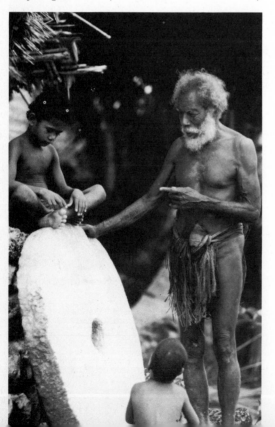

The Impact of Money on the Tiv. When general-purpose money is introduced to a multicentric economy, the effect is to transform it to a unicentric economy. This transformation does not occur all at once, however; the Tiv of central Nigeria had a multicentric economy before the advent of European traders (Bohannan, 1959). There were three spheres of exchange: (1) a subsistence sphere consisting of foodstuffs, household utensils, and raw materials, which were exchanged by barter; (2) a "prestige" sphere consisting of slaves, cattle, large white cloths, and brass rods, which could be exchanged for one another at certain ceremonies (brass rods served as a standard of value within this sphere); and (3) rights in women and children, which could be exchanged only for similar rights, though brass rods could be used to acquire some—but not all—of those rights. On some occasions "conversions," or exchanges between two different spheres, might occur.

Brass rods could not serve as a general-purpose money because they were not divisible (making "change" was impossible) and were worth far more than most subsistence goods. Within the prestige sphere, they served all three functions of general purpose money. Outside of that sphere, they served only as a means of payment for marriage rights, and then only to a limited extent.

When Europeans introduced general-purpose money, the Tiv used it as a standard of value in the subsistence sphere, while continuing to barter goods within this sphere. They also used general-purpose money as a means of payment in the marriage sphere. It also served as a means of exchange within the subsistence and prestige spheres. Thus, the economy of the Tiv gradually became unicentric even though for a long time most Tiv continued to see it as multicentric.

The introduction of money has had a variety of effects on the Tiv, social as well as economic. Trade has increased immensely, not only within the society but with the outside world as well. In fact, so much produce is traded with outside groups that there is occasionally an artificially created internal shortage of some commodities. The degree of differentiation between individuals in terms of wealth has also increased. Finally, the possibility of using money to "buy" marriage rights has led to a form of indebtedness that did not exist before. In the past, "debt" was in the form of similar rights that could be repaid through marriage in the next generation, rather than in the form of money. With the introduction of general-purpose money, differentiation of individuals on the basis of wealth has increased and probably will continue to do so.

Integration of Economic Systems

We have pointed out several times that the economic aspects of a society cannot be separated from its legal, political, and other aspects. This can be illustrated by the role of the marketplace in West Africa. Economic exchanges are not the only ones that occur in the marketplace. Information is also exchanged: announcements are made there, and news and gossip are passed along. The people who gather in the marketplace provide an audience for dancers and entertainers as well as for political leaders. The marketplace serves as a center for legal activities and sometimes for religious activities as well. In short, the marketplace is a meeting place.

The point of this example is that the various aspects of a society are integrated into a cultural system. Moreover, the nature of that integration varies from one society to another. Thus, when an outside influence is brought to bear on a society such as that of the Tiv—and very few societies are so isolated that they are not influenced by the money and goods of Western nations—the way in which that influence is integrated into the culture depends on the *integrating mechanisms* at work in that particular society. In some societies, these may depend largely on religious activities; in

others, on ritual occasions of various sorts, or on political processes. The integrating mechanisms are the means whereby a given society incorporates new elements into its cultural system.

Controlled Wealth and Capital

The task of the anthropologist studying any economic system is to discover not only how goods are produced but also who has access to both resources and goods, who is responsible for their distribution, and finally, how access to goods is legitimated and maintained. In other words, how are production and distribution controlled?

In this section, we will be dealing with two important economic concepts: *capital* and *wealth*. The concept of capital is central to Western economies and can be applied to non-Western societies as well. As for the concept of wealth, at first glance it appears to be a simple one but, as we will see, it is not always easily applied to a particular economic system.

Wealth, Capital, and Interest

If we use the dictionary to define *wealth* as abundance of material possessions or resources that have exchange value, then it is clear that the concept of wealth is foreign to many subsistence economies. In Argentina, a Toba family head who is exceptionally successful in providing for the material well-being of his immediate kin is considered not wealthy but lucky, or perhaps blessed with magical powers. If he is too successful, however, he will be suspected of witchcraft, and he will have to find a way of dispelling those suspicions. This is usually done by means of generosity, which takes the form of a quick distribution of excess goods (usually food or animals). Often this choice is not up to the family head alone; since word travels quickly that a person is well provided for, "relatives" from faraway places who are not as well off may turn up to consume their share. Guests are considered an honor; they are not discouraged from visiting and are not expected to leave until all the goods have been used up and balance has been restored—an effective leveling mechanism. In terms of reciprocity, it is understood that the visiting relatives will reciprocate at some future time, though this does not always happen. If a family does not reciprocate, it may eventually develop a bad reputation and will lack visitors until it can find a means of providing goods that will attract friends and relatives.

The introduction of money and wages to the Toba has had the effect of alienating from the rest of the society a few families that have learned to manage money well and to accumulate wealth. The few Toba who have adopted the notion of wealth have come to identify with the broader Argentine society. The more traditional families still maintain the sharing motif, which contrasts with the concept of wealth. Money management involves controlling equipment, resources, and supplies, and therefore, not distributing excess goods among relatives. Traditional members of the community have responded to this unfamiliar behavior with distrust and suspicion.

Identifying Capital. There is some question as to whether *capital*—equipment and supplies used for purposes of production—exists in nonmonetary economies. Various answers to this question have been proposed. Some anthropologists believe that the capital of such economies consists of crops and livestock. Others suggest that the term capital be applied to resources used in production, such as nets, canoes, adzes, and digging sticks.

According to Richard Salisbury, the capital of nonmonetary economies is "a stock of goods, present before a productive act is performed, used in production and 'immobilized' from direct consumption while the act is in progress" (1962, p. 122). As Mair (1972) points out, this definition includes natural resources such as trees and gardens, manufactured items such as axes and digging sticks, as well as knowledge or skill. These are all goods that are withheld from immediate consumption for the sake of income—an increase in the amount of goods available for future consumption.

In many cases, capital goods are saved in order to be used on some future occasion. This is considered by some to be a form of capital investment. Mair (1972) writes that "when a Tikopia chief lays a taboo on the consumption of particular foodstuffs in order that they shall be plentiful when the time comes for an important ceremony, he is using the unharvested yams or the unpicked coconuts as capital. The same might be said of the stock of blankets that the Kwakiutl chief must accumulate before a *potlatch*" (p. 202). It is true that the activity for which the goods are saved is not primarily economic in nature—it may be a religious ceremony or a social event. There is no direct "return" on the investment of food or goods, but there *are* noneconomic dividends that are of great concern to the participants.

It is somewhat easier to think of livestock as capital, as Mair points out. When a Japanese peasant buys a buffalo with surplus cash in order to sell it later when cash is short, or when a herder sells butter, hides, and wool for cash that can be used to buy land on which to grow grain that would otherwise have to be bought for cash—these examples may be viewed as capital investment.

Lending in Small-Scale Societies. In Orissa, a state in East India, wealthy landowners finance small traders who buy unhusked rice, husk it, and sell it. Loans are made to individuals who have to pay for a funeral or replace a buffalo.

The lender expects return of the loan, with interest. At the same time, the same people may engage in "friendly loans" that will not pay interest—such as the loan of some rice between harvests, or of a tool or a household utensil. Loans of both kinds are common in small-scale societies (Bailey, 1957).

The person who makes such loans may be thought of as making an investment, but they are not true capital investments because they do not increase production. In fact, they may not even be "economic" transactions if the debtor and creditor live in the same village, in which case the repayment of the debt may be governed by social considerations (such as loss of prestige) rather than by economic ones. Here, again, the notion of investment must be expanded to include noneconomic transactions as well.

It is when loans are made by outsiders that purely economic considerations enter the picture. This is a matter of social distance: the more impersonal the transaction, the more "economic" its nature. Borrowing money from a bank where one is unknown, for example, is a transaction based more on one's assets and ability to repay the loan than is borrowing money—even in large amounts—from relatives or friends. Yet the nature of even purely economic transactions is two-sided. Banks *want* to lend money for the interest it brings and thus advertise their lending service. Another example is that of a Chinese shopkeeper in Mauritius who extends credit to his Indian customers. The Indians make small purchases on credit and pay at the end of the month. If the amount outstanding is not paid in full, the shopkeeper might refuse further credit—but at the possible cost of losing the customer. Thus, what happens is that customers never pay all that they owe; a certain amount is left over, an amount that is tacitly agreed upon by both shopkeeper and customer. This transaction has been described as "a kind of capital investment which the shopkeeper makes in his customer," in return for which he keeps the customer's business (B. Benedict, 1964).

As we have seen, the exchange transactions that anthropologists study in societies that depend primarily on money as a medium of exchange as well as in those that do not are diverse and sometimes complicated. In most instances, however, members of the societies concerned can be counted on to make rational choices in order to attain advantages, both material and nonmaterial. They decide to exchange, by whatever method, something they want less for something they want more. Even where material resources are difficult to obtain and are at a premium, the choices available generally are clear to the individual members of a society, and they choose according to what they consider to be their best interest.

Industrialization and Modernization

It remains to explore what happens to a small-scale society as its economy progresses from subsistence modes of production to industrial modes of production, and concepts such as money, wealth, and capital enter the picture. First, however, it is necessary to stress that we are not talking about a one-way process in which non-Western societies become increasingly industrialized and Westernized; this is not always the case. The development of industrialization in the West was a unique process that depended on the presence of certain noneconomic as well as economic factors. We cannot expect that industrialization in Latin America, Africa, and Asia will progress along the same lines and have the same effects as it did in Western nations. Thus, it is impossible to generalize about "industrialization," "modernization," or "West-

This sisal plant in Tanzania illustrates that industrialization in developing countries reflects the individual needs and characteristics of the local communities. (George Gerster, Rapho/Photo Researchers)

ernization," which are actually rather ethnocentric concepts. Instead, we will discuss the process of change or development in non-Western societies within the framework suggested by Neil Smelser (1963).

Smelser lists the types of changes that occur in developing nations as follows:

1. The change from simple, traditional techniques *toward* the application of scientific knowledge to those techniques (the use of improved seeds, for instance, that will result in more disease-resistant crops);
2. The shift from subsistence farming *toward* commercial agriculture (crops that will be sold for cash, and agricultural labor that is paid wages);
3. The transition from the use of human and animal power *toward* industrialization (people operating machines for money wages, which are used to buy the products made with those machines);
4. Population movement from rural areas *toward* urban areas.

These four types of changes often, but not always, occur together. In many countries, for example, agriculture is being commercialized,

but industrialization proper is not occurring. However, these four changes tend to affect the social structure in similar ways. Smelser terms these effects *structural differentiation, integration,* and *social disturbances.*

Structural Differentiation

Structural differentiation entails the establishment of specialized, autonomous social units in the place of multifunctional ones. For example, when factory industry replaces home-centered industry, the economic functions of the family are transferred to the firm. Instead of gaining a livelihood among family members, one leaves them to work in a different setting. Obligations to fellow workers become simply that, with no real obligations outside the work setting. Likewise, family obligations become devoid of their work aspect. Similarly, the educational role of the family is transferred to the school. What is happening is that one social organization—the family—is changing into two or more organizations that are distinct from, though related to, each other.

Other kinds of differentiation may occur as well. The introduction of cash crops usually leads to a differentiation between the contexts in which production and consumption take place. Market exchange may replace reciprocity and redistribution as a determinant of how goods are distributed. At the same time, the family may "specialize" in emotional gratification and socialization. Even value systems can become differentiated: In a new nation, strong feelings of nationalism may motivate people to work hard and make sacrifices; later, values of wealth, power, or prestige may supplant nationalism as guiding principles.

Integration

As differentiation continues, a new social order replaces the old one as the newly established units become integrated with one another. As mentioned earlier, every society has its own integrating mechanisms. In a developing nation, according to Smelser, there is a continual interplay between differentiation (which divides a society) and integration (which unites it on a new basis). We have mentioned that differentiation separates the social setting in which production occurs from that in which consumption occurs. This creates problems of integration—for instance, how will the interests of employers be integrated with those of employees? These problems give rise to a whole new set of organizations: employment agencies, labor unions, welfare arrangements, and the like. While formerly those concerns were handled in the context of kinship or the local community, they are now assigned to union meetings or social agencies of various sorts. Sometimes religious sects arise which provide a basis for mutual interaction and emotional release.

On a larger scale, industrialization not only separates work from the family but may separate the family from its ancestral community. Urbanization gives rise to another set of integrating organizations: churches, schools, and voluntary associations of various sorts. But this process is by no means steady and smooth, and it is here, in the adjustment to new social and cultural settings, that disturbances occur.

Differentiation requires new activities, norms, rewards, and sanctions that may conflict with traditional ones. The notion of working for wages, for instance, may conflict with traditional norms under which work is a kinship obligation. Until integration takes place, threats to traditionally held values may create emotional and social disturbances. For example, when the Toba of Argentina began to work for wages in the cotton fields, both men and women earned money that could be exchanged for consumer goods. Traditional division of labor, in which males provided the protein in the diet and women provided the fiber (vegetables and fruits), was broken down. Furthermore, some individuals considered money a commodity to be shared like food, whereas others did not consider it "soul-linked" and sharable. Thus, internal conflict was introduced where it did not exist before. Moreover, these changes often occur at an uneven rate, so that economic and educational institutions may differentiate rapidly while political institutions remain more conservative. This usually creates disharmony between actual life experiences and social norms.

Responses to the problems of conflict and disequilibrium may take the form of anxiety, hostility, or fantasy. If enough people respond in the same way, the result may be mass hysteria, outbreaks of violence, religious and political movements, and the like. There is some evidence that social movements have their greatest appeal to people whose social ties have been weakened by differentiation but who have not yet been integrated into a new social order (Smelser, 1963).

It is important to realize that "modernization" may not lead to "modernity"—that a people like the Toba or the Tiv may not be markedly different in the future than they are now. Changes in social structure will vary according to the preindustrial characteristics of the society; the conditions that stimulated development in the first place; the path of development followed by that particular society; and the timing of certain events such as wars and migrations. Economic anthropology can play a crucial role in explaining the process of modernization as it occurs in newly-developing areas and point out possible alternatives to the industrial life that is so familiar to us.

Summary

1. Any exchange of goods is part of an ongoing social relationship that shapes and limits the nature of an exchange transaction. The basic types of economic transaction are reciprocity, redistribution, and market exchange. *Reciprocity* involves direct movement of goods between two parties. It may be divided into three types: *generalized, balanced,* and *negative.* Reciprocity is affected by kinship, rank, and relative wealth. Close kinship creates generalized reciprocity, as do large gaps in rank or wealth. Balanced reciprocity serves as a vehicle for a variety of social "contracts" such as peacemaking and marriage. Its economic importance stems from the fact that it stimulates the circulation of goods.

2. *Redistribution* involves pooling goods at a central location and then dividing them up among the members of the group through the work of a central administrator. Redistribution cannot take place unless there is a central authority with the power to redistribute goods; it thus implies a hierarchy.

3. *Market exchange* involves a medium, such as money, on the basis of which goods are assessed at value and exchanged. In a situation of market exchange, each party wants to arrive at the price that is most favorable to himself or herself. The price therefore fluctuates—it is not predetermined.

4. Money may serve as a medium of exchange, a standard of value, and a means of payment. General-purpose money performs all three of these functions; special-purpose money may serve only one or two.

5. Small-scale societies are multicentric —they have several spheres of exchange and use special-purpose moneys. Unicentric economies use general-purpose money.

6. In many societies, wealth—an abundance of material possessions that have exchange value—is an alien concept. In fact, some societies do not allow their members to accumulate wealth.

7. There is some question as to whether capital exists in nonmonetary economies. Occasionally goods and services are withheld from immediate consumption for the sake of an increase in the goods available for later consumption; this may be viewed as capital. Livestock also can be considered capital in this way.

8. Lending at interest takes place in small-scale societies, but such loans do not increase production.

9. *Industrialization, modernization,* and *Westernization* are ethnocentric terms that refer to economic changes occurring in non-Western societies. These changes involve replacing traditional techniques with more modern technology, shifting from subsistence farming to commercial agriculture, replacing human and animal power with machines, and the movement of people from rural to urban areas.

10. The social effects of these changes may involve structural differentiation (which tends to divide a society), integration (which unites it on a new basis), as well as social disturbances (which result from the lag between differentiation and integration).

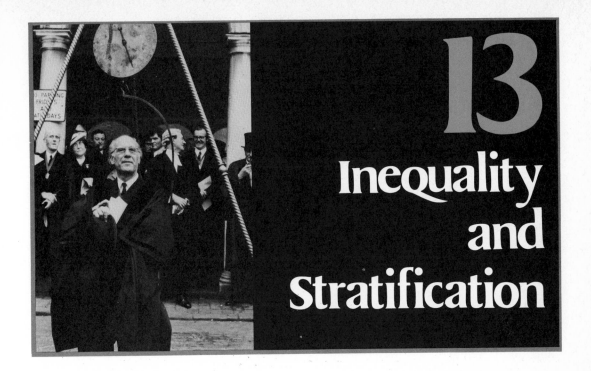

13
Inequality and Stratification

INEQUALITIES are found in all human societies, from simple hunting-and-gathering bands to modern industrial states. In societies such as those of hunters and gatherers, social and economic roles are relatively undifferentiated. Adult males tend to have one type of occupation, and adult females another. In such societies, inequalities are often judgments about individual prowess or the result of some type of supernatural power. As Fallers (1977) points out, every society has its criteria for moral evaluation, an image of the "admirable man." Inequalities exist as a result of comparing how close various individuals come to this ideal.

In complex modern industrial societies, social groups form also on the basis of occupational specialization. Each of these groups possesses a status that is shared by its members. Thus, in complex societies, inequalities often are the result of judgments about rank-ings of one social group versus another. The arrangement of status within a society into a hierarchy of socially superior and inferior ranks is known as *social stratification* (Hunter & Whitten, 1976, p. 359). Stratification is determined by the value system of a particular society and can be based on political, economic, or ceremonial differences. To identify the characteristics of stratification in a society, one must analyze how inequality is institutionalized within the society (Smith, 1966, pp. 147–148).

In this chapter, we will look at egalitarian societies—those that come closest to granting equality for all their members—and at rank societies—those characterized by a hierarchy of socially graduated ranks. We also will examine three major stratification systems—caste, class, and slavery. Finally, we will consider the effects of stratification on modernization in developing societies.

Equality and Inequality in Human Societies

The individual as a participant member of any social group occupies different positions throughout his or her lifetime. As we noted earlier, changes in statuses—social positions—are frequently marked by ritual occasions commonly known as rites of passage. These statuses are not evaluated equally by society; in fact, they are frequently ranked in hierarchical fashion so that individuals in certain ranks or grades have more authority, power, or prestige than individuals in other grades.

Status and Hierarchy

Some anthropological theories seek to account for the existence of status hierarchies in all human societies by referring to the "pecking order" of birds or dominance studies of primates. Although thought-provoking, animal research should not dictate a theory of humankind's "natural" tendency toward hierarchization. Much of the dominance data of primate studies may be invalid because of the conditions under which experiments occurred (laboratory versus natural environment), and due to unprovable assumptions on the part of human observers about what is taking place in the animals' behavior. Thus, the establishment of overall dominance ratings among primates may tell us little about its occurrence in human societies.

In theory, at least, one must allow for the possibility of a human society where all statuses are equal. However, in actuality, all societies assign status, implying hierarchy of one sort or another. Status is based on the relative merit of an individual in comparison to others in a group. Some individuals are judged more highly, and some more lowly than others. A fundamental aspect of human

In unstratified societies, prestige and status result from individual effort and achievement, rather than from judgments made about the ranking of one group over another. (Minoru Aoki, Rapho/Photo Researchers)

psychology, it seems, is the desire to be highly regarded by one's social group. Status is accompanied by prestige—the power to command admiration. In egalitarian societies, status results from one's individual efforts or "gifts"—for example, one's success as a hunter or one's magical or healing powers. In such instances, status is rewarded in terms of prestige and respect (sometimes associated with fear). In stratified societies, status is rewarded with social advantage as well as prestige.

It is important to note that ranking occurs in all societies, whereas stratification occurs only in some (Fried, 1967, p. 110). Egalitarian societies are not stratified in any real sense because no one group of individuals receives social advantage at the expense of another. Rank societies are stratified in the sense that the ranking is highly formalized and based on factors out of one's control, such as heredity. Labor and economic divisions in rank societies are based primarily on age and sex, as in egalitarian societies. Therefore, even though the rank system differentiates, it does so between individuals, not between groups. It awards advantage solely in terms of prestige symbolically represented, as by a title or rank. Both egalitarian and rank societies can be considered basically unstratified.

Egalitarian Society

True egalitarian societies, where all statuses are equal, exist only in theory. Aside from universal differentiation in terms of age, sex, and kinship roles, there are also differences in the degree of excellence with which one performs a role. However, societies in which occupational alternatives are few are referred to as *egalitarian.* If all adult males hunt and fish for a livelihood, for example, there are no occupational choices open to adult males. (There will, of course, be differences in the excellence with which a person carries out the hunting-and-gathering tasks.)

The lack of occupational options obviously has economic and political implications. If there are no occupational options, there are not likely to be economic or political options since there are few resources to control. Furthermore, despite the different status accorded age or kinship roles, each person can expect to go through the same pattern of age and kinship roles as he or she grows older (Fallers, 1977, p. 259). Equality, in these regards, is achieved over a period of time.

All societies require leadership of some sort. The limited occupational options in an egalitarian society may include that of leader, but most often the leader serves only in times of crisis. For the most part, he receives no special privileges. The role of shaman, or medicine man, is another role these societies may provide. The shaman's supernatural power gives him individual advantage over others. But the society may still be considered egalitarian in that political or religious inequality is limited in nature and controlled. In the case of the !Kung Bushmen, the position of shaman is open to anyone who will take it: equal access ensures the society's egalitarianism.

The !Kung Bushmen have only two specialized roles—that of shaman and headman. The headman receives no rewards except first choice of fireplace and campsite after the site for the band has been chosen. He carries his own load. Although he is of higher status than the other tribe members, his role is voluntarily practiced *and* voluntarily recognized (Smith, 1966, p. 152).

In the society of the Argentine Toba, the positions of political leader and shaman traditionally have been combined. Since everyone does the same work, leadership involves additional burdens of responsibility, rather than relief from subsistence tasks.

The Argentine Toba represent a good example of an egalitarian society. Traditionally, they were a hunting, gathering, and fishing group dependent upon undomesticated nature for subsistence. The society consisted of separate social units comprising extended family bands. The bands varied in size in recent years from several dozen to several hundred. The total population in the Toba area of 150 square miles was about 15,000 members. Each band had a name and roamed a recognized territory, using the resources found there. In each band, the adult males hunted and fished; the adult females gathered and prepared food.

Certain family heads became known as shamans because of their ability to contact supernatural powers in order to heal the sick. Though their status as leaders set some individuals off from others in the band, they hunted and fished along with other adult males. They were called upon to lead only in times of crisis. Furthermore, because of their assumed contact with "companion spirits" and their superior knowledge of the environment, shamans were expected to be more successful in hunting and fishing than other adult males.

The position of shamans differentiated them from others in power and responsibility. Thus, they were called upon occasionally to hear arguments and mediate settlements when disputes arose in the group. In this as well as in the role of leading warriors into battle, their leadership was based upon the ability to interpret general consensus, not to act independently. Leadership in Toba society, as in most other egalitarian societies, constituted a position of responsibility rather than one of privilege. Leaders in such societies generally are expected to work harder than the rest of the group members and to share generously with the needy in order to maintain their higher status.

Since no one *class* of individuals in egalitarian societies is awarded exclusive privileges over others, such societies are considered unstratified. The lack of occupational options ensures that all members of the same sex share the same economic status, except where individual achievement varies. Such achieve-

ment is rewarded with prestige, which is transitory and does not enter any other sphere of existence. The best hunter may lead the hunt, but he does not have any more economic or political power than anyone else. As for different statuses applied to different age groups, the transfer of status to different groups at certain intervals—as occurs in rites of passage—ensures that such inequalities are shared by members of the society over time (Smith, 1966, p. 150). Egalitarian societies tend to be found in environments that can support only limited populations with a simple technology. They tend, therefore, to be small.

Societies with Rank and Titles

A *rank society,* as opposed to an egalitarian one, is characterized by its formalized system of graduated social statuses determined by such factors as heredity. An example of a rank society is that of the Northwest Coast Indians who inherited specific names that signified one's distinct rank (Drucker, 1939, p. 63). Among the African Zulus, kinship ties were important traditionally to social status; the closer a prince was to the reigning king, the higher his social status. Likewise, one's rank was higher the closer one was genealogically to an important ancestor (Smith, 1966, p. 153). In small-scale rank societies, rarely do two individuals share the same rank. The results of sharing a rank can be confusing or disastrous as was shown when two separate Northwest Coast rank societies once joined for the winter. The custom of *potlatch,* in which the order of giving gifts is signified by rank, was thrown off by the presence of two individuals for every rank. Feelings rose quite high, until the visiting chief resolved the dispute by deciding that the host should give first (Drucker, 1939, pp. 57–58).

The *potlatch* shows the ceremonial aspect of rank. In addition to its festive nature, it is a necessary part of the procedure by which one assumes rank position. Names in the Northwest coast groups are ranked individually from higher to lower and are inherited. In order to take one's name, one must have a right to it through heredity. In addition, the naming ceremony has to be done publically and formally with the distribution of gifts—that is, a *potlatch*. Not only was one's name considered a form of wealth, but one had to be wealthy in material goods as well to take on the name (Drucker, 1939, pp. 62–63).

Rank societies probably developed out of egalitarian ones with the transition from dependence on nature to domestication of nature. Such domestication, in creating additional food supply, enabled societies to become larger and to amass surplus goods. They also tended to become more permanently settled, as cultivation of plants dictates.

As societies become larger and more permanent and a new redistributive economy develops, a formalized kinship network tends to develop from an egalitarian one in which mythological genealogies serve as the basis for band membership. When a clearly stated descent principle emerges, genealogical proximity to a particular ancestor becomes significant, especially in developing a kin hierarchy. Ranking is the result (Fried, 1967, p. 116).

With a newly concentrated and more certain food supply, an economic process by which surplus food can be divided comes into existence. In egalitarian bands, food is consumed on the spot or reciprocally exchanged. With the existence of a significant surplus, redistribution becomes a viable procedure and goods begin to be pooled for periodic distribution.

The role of redistributor in a rank hierarchy usually falls to the highest ranking member. Such a role carries with it prestige as well as supported political status. In some societies, it is acquired through personal achievement, often evaluated in terms of generalized reciprocity or extreme generosity (Fried, 1967, pp. 117–118).

Another characteristic of the redistributive economy found in rank societies is the supposed ownership of resources by one member, usually the chief, while in fact such resources are owned by the group. In such cases, the chief's role is more of administrator than owner. Although his permission must be requested to use a strip of land, for example, it is not in his power to refuse a member of the group (Drucker, 1939, p. 59). In rank societies in Polynesia, the association of high rank and high religious standing that comes from the ceremonial advantage that rank bestows enables the chief to use "divine" standing to make some areas taboo. In this case, we can see how rank, at one time purely ceremonial, begins to acquire religious and political significance as well (Sahlins, 1958).

In the earlier stages of development from rank societies to egalitarian ones, the two types of societies have certain aspects in common. The division of labor is much the same in that individuals engage in tasks typical for their age and sex. High rank does not generally relieve one of the necessity of performing an occupational role. But, as the rank system becomes more formalized, high-ranking members begin to abstain from menial tasks. In emerging rank societies, the chief is often the hardest working member. His status depends upon his generosity. With the emergence of the redistributive economy, the goods given away belong to the group, not to him alone. He acts as a sort of tribal banker. If he is no longer engaged in the primary occupation, he becomes dependent for his share of the goods upon the generosity of lower ranking members. Often, he will use feasts as a means to bind such members to him (Sahlins, 1958).

In rank societies, authority gradually emerges as a regular force extending into other aspects of social life. In an egalitarian society, leadership occurs as needed; in a rank society, the role of redistributive agent exists at all times. A different feeling, expressed through ritual, begins to surround leadership and, by extension, rank (Fried, 1967, p. 134). In the transition from egalitarian to rank societies, the hierarchical ordering of status positions and prestige becomes more rigid. Ranks, at first of just ceremonial significance, begin to be associated with social advantage (Fried, 1967, p. 183). Yet rank societies are considered unstratified in that differences in status pertain still to individuals. Stratification occurs when social advantage is awarded to one *group* of people over another.

Stratification Systems

In stratification systems, members of various groups, even though they may be of the same age or sex, have unequal access to basic resources. Different socioeconomic classes, with distinct standards of living, emerge as a result (Fried, 1967, p. 225). One theory of how stratification evolves is that occupations become specialized and ranked in terms of prestige and rewards. Kin groups, for instance, often tend to work together at the same tasks, passing skills on from father to son so that an identification between "role occupant" and "occupational role" is made. This is the supposed genesis of the stratified caste system of India. Other stratification systems, such as class, may be achievement-oriented.

In an unstratified society, even a rank society, access to basic resources is not denied even the lowest ranking member. But in a stratified society, access to resources is limited. Different life chances exist for those who own resources than for those who must pay to gain access to them or to acquire products grown on them. In order to maintain such an order of stratification in which some individuals are denied basic resources necessary to sustain life, powerful sanctions become necessary. The state emerges to control the internal pressures that accompany stratifications; its agents maintain socioeconomic divisions by enforcing law and order (Fried, 1967, p. 225).

There are many types of stratification systems. The three we will discuss here are caste, class, and slavery. In reality, there is some overlapping of these systems. Controversy often arises, for instance, over whether a particular system is characterized by class or caste. The systems will be presented as ideal types; as such, they may not coincide exactly with reality in any one society.

Caste

A *caste* is a socially distinct group whose membership is determined by birth. Such a group is assigned a particular position in the social hierarchy. Differentiation in terms of access to prestige and resources exists between castes. Boundaries between castes are clearly maintained, principally by the practice of endogamy. One cannot belong to more than one caste, nor can one change castes. Though interaction between castes is rigidly controlled and enforced by custom and/or law, all are mutually interdependent within a society (Berreman, 1968, pp. 333–335).

Two basic types of caste systems exist. The first is the multiple caste system, which is characterized by the existence of intermediate groups between the uppermost and lowermost castes. Each intermediate group is in a position of both relative inferiority and superiority. This type of caste system is best exemplified by the elaborate system found in India, but it exists throughout Asia and Africa as well. The second type is the dual caste system, in which only two castes exist. Each is greatly separated from the other by the fact that no other castes exist between the two extremes. The lower one is viewed as a pariah caste and, as such, is stigmatized and excluded (Berreman, 1968, p. 337). In the Hindu mul-

In the Indian caste system, one's place in the social hierarchy is determined by one's birth—by the caste of one's family. (Paolo Koch, Rapho/Photo Researchers)

tiple caste system, the pariah caste is the group known as Untouchables; such a caste designation also is found throughout Asia and Africa.

Much of our understanding of the multiple caste system comes from the unique type found in India, so much so that arguments have been made for this being the only true caste system. The Hindu caste society consists of four basic divisions called *varnas,* found across India. The society is divided into hierarchically arranged categories of (1) *Brahmans* (priests); (2) warrior-rulers; (3) merchants; and (4) servants. The individuals outside of these categories comprise the group known as Untouchables, the pariah caste. *Varnas* are not organized groups, but are more like general categories. Membership in a *varna* allows people easily to assess each other's status in their local communities. In addition to these basic divisions, some regions are further divided into permanent caste groups, called *jatis,* which are separated by restrictions on marriage, physical contact, and food. Again, they are hierarchically arranged and occupationally specialized. Hereditary occupations, such as those of potters, barbers, and tanners, are associated with particular *jatis*. These groups tend to be local groups.

The notion of relative purity forms the basis of the caste hierarchy. Members of the top caste are considered the purest. The notion of purity is the reason for the separation between castes and for occupational specialization. Contact with a member of a lower caste is believed to be polluting; restrictions are placed on the higher, purer castes in regard to handling polluting items, usually anything associated with blood, death, and dirt.

The caste system in India is part of a pervasive religious system in which people of all ranks strive for removal of impurities as a necessary step toward personal salvation. The caste system is based on an accepted premise of inequality in the social sphere. In contrast, the social system of the United States is supposedly based on presumed equality of all people and tends to be achievement-oriented; it focuses on an individual's capabilities. The Indian caste system is based on ascription; one's place is fairly firmly predetermined by one's birth. Individual social mobility is allowed for only in the belief in reincarnation. By adhering to one's caste rules and living the caste's definition of a good life, an individual hopes that in the next life, he or she will be placed in a higher caste. Otherwise, one's caste cannot be changed; only rarely can the caste of one's offspring be altered. However, collective social mobility is a possibility. The status of one's entire *jati* may change, and with it will come a change in the status of everyone in the *jati*. But individual social mobility, based on one's personal achievement, is not characteristic of the Hindu caste system (Smelser & Lipset, 1966, p. 12).

Stratification by caste also occurs in parts of Africa. There, caste stratification is often based on conquest and subordination of rival tribes rather than on hereditary ascription. In such a system, the separateness of tribes is preserved, even though they are incorporated into and interact with the larger society. An example is the three-caste system that existed in Rwanda. Each caste there was physically different from the others, and these differences were perpetuated by the practice of endogamy. The groups were hierarchically arranged, with political power held by the king and the Tutsi caste, an aristocracy of pastoralists that comprised about 10 percent of the population. The Hutu, who were agriculturalists, comprised the majority of the society. The lowest ranking caste was the Twa, a small minority who functioned as jesters, potters, and hunters. As in the Hindu system, the caste hierarchy was validated by religion; the three castes were united by their belief in the cult of Ryangombe. Members of the Tutsi, Hutu, and Twa castes were all utilized in this cult but in ways that expressed their distinctions from one another. The caste differentiations were maintained by political hierarchy, but the ritual integration of the society was also firmly maintained (Southall, 1970, p. 242).

Boundaries between groups in a caste system, whether the system is in India or in Africa, are clearly defined and maintained. The idea of distinction is preserved even between two castes with minimal differences and maximal interaction (Berreman, 1968, p. 335). As we have seen, differences are maintained by religious, social, and political regulations and customs. Caste is primarily, however, a hierarchy of prestige. The political and economic aspects implied by caste are secondary. A hierarchy based primarily on political and economic power, and only secondarily on prestige, characterizes class stratification. This is the system most familiar in Western societies.

Class

A *class* is a group that shares the same social or economic status. The fundamental requirement is a sharing of traits by group members that distinguishes them as a separate entity within the society. The common trait or traits also identifies them as a group by the rest of society (Drucker, 1939, p. 55). Since such traits are defined largely in subjective terms, the concept of class is more amorphous and open to debate than that of class.

Class stratification may occur on the basis of some measure of privileges received by a group or simply on the basis of whether those people in similar roles think of themselves and act as a group (Smelser & Lipset, 1966, p. 6). In the latter sense, a class *system* did not exist in Western society until the Industrial Revolution. Although the aristocracy in Europe was a ruling class, the majority of people were unclassed. They were separated from each other by the practice of working in kin groups in the home. With industrialization, work was taken out of such groups and brought to factories. A class consciousness then emerged, due no doubt to many factors —easier communication among members of the working class; the general rise of literacy; increased geographic mobility because of one's labor skills; separation from land ties; deprivation at the hands of owners; and the desire for protective legislation for workers. All of these factors served to aid the workers in acting collectively and thinking of themselves as a class (Bendix, 1970, p. 321).

Once work was removed from the sphere of kinship groups, it was no longer ascription-based. Individuals no longer necessarily performed the jobs their parents had done. Occupation began to be determined by the quality of one's performance. And a job's status became based on the economic rewards and social mobility that the job offered. With individuals freer to choose their own occupations and objectives, an achievement-oriented, competitive class system evolved. It became possible, thereby, to determine an individual's ranking within society by evaluating economic as well as social criteria (Gould, 1971, p. 14).

The criteria for judging class usually in-

In Great Britain, characteristics such as accent, manners, and habits tend to reflect one's class background, which traditionally has been based on family connections. Here, the mayor of High Wycombe is weighed in an annual ceremony. (Homer Sykes, Woodfin Camp)

clude income, occupation, level of achievement within one's occupation, standard of living relative to the rest of the society, kinship connections, education, and relationship to institutions of power such as church, army, or government. The importance of these criteria for defining class varies from society to society. For example, kinship ties may be more important in Great Britain than in the United

States; ethnic characteristics appear to be more important in the United States than in France; education may have greater significance in Germany or Sweden than in the United States; and occupation seems less class-oriented in the United States than in Germany. In the United States, economic factors generally take precedence over all others to a much greater degree than they do anywhere else. Since the criteria are relative, the concept of class cannot by systematized on a cross-cultural basis.

Thus, there is some controversy regarding to what kinds of societies the concept of class can be applied. Some anthropologists insist that class can only be found in market-dominated societies and that it is unique to Western history and culture (Gould, 1970, p. 1; Balandier, p. 91). Although it is true that the manner in which the class system evolved in Western Europe was unique, nontheless class stratification appears to be emerging in other parts of the world, especially in Africa. Occupational prestige, power, income, and education are criteria currently being applied in African societies to produce divisions into class (Southall, 1970, p. 265).

As we have seen, the possibility of social mobility distinguishes class from caste. As the criteria for occupational stratification become achievement oriented, and economic rewards are accompanied by social mobility, a class system of social differentiation may evolve. Class systems are based on the premise that every individual is equal to compete with all others and that the "best" individual will come out the winner in whatever the sphere of competition. However, such a premise describes an ideal state of affairs. In reality, not everyone starts from the same position. Social mobility thereby becomes limited, and inequality tends to gel and become a permanent part of the social system. The stratification system of the United States ideally enables a person to move away from ascribed positions based on hereditary, regional, or ethnic origins. How-

ever, ascribed characteristics—especially racial ones combined with prejudices—tend to hinder the ideal operation of the class system (Smelser & Lipset, 1966, p. 9). The same is true in Great Britain, where ascribed characteristics such as accent, habits, and manners reflect one's background and prevent individual mobility from operating ideally. There, social mobility tends to be collective, involving a family's change of status over a period of some generations (Smelser & Lipset, 1966, p. 10).

Slavery

The term *slave* brings to mind a person without rights who is subject to inhumane treatment and experiences a total loss of freedom. This image comes from what we know of slavery as it was instituted in the Western hemisphere, but this was a unique case. A broader definition of a slave is an individual who has lost control over his or her own labor. Anthropologists define *slavery* as a hierarchical system in which one group of people owns the labor and the products of the labor of another group of people. As such, slavery is found all over the world, even in otherwise egalitarian societies. The highest rate of slavery was found in sub-Saharan Africa (Bourguignon & Greenbaum, 1973, p. 42).

Slaves in Africa were not primarily labor units, as they were in the United States, so much as social and political units. People in African societies were viewed as that society's wealth. They not only belonged *in* a society, they belonged *to* it and could be sold in times of need. Therefore, the more dependents within a society, the wealthier the society. The more "acquired outsiders," the more powerful the chief. The ways to acquire a dependent were to marry, beget, adopt, capture, or buy one (Miers & Kopytoff, 1977, p. 65). In the West, slavery was often characterized by the method in which a person was acquired. Rights-in-a-person were commonly sold in African societies by an individual's family or community during marriage and adoption transactions. To the Westerner, this constituted slavery. To the African, such transactions involving purchasing of rights-in-a-person were indicative of marriage, adoption, *or* slavery (Miers & Kopytoff, 1977, p. 5).

The opposite of slavery to most Westerners was freedom; in an African context, the opposite of slavery was *belonging.* That is, slaves were taken, peacefully or by force, from their communities where they had certain bonds, rights, and a social identity. They were put into a strange environment where they were looked upon as nonpersons. Being a slave, in this context, meant establishing new bonds and beginning to acquire a social identity by having a clear status with formal rights and duties. This was the first step toward integration within the new society. The slave was an acquired outsider on the road to being less of a slave with each tie binding him or her to the new society. Although total integration never occurred for the acquired individual whose background was different from that of others in the society, a slave-to-kinship continuum did exist in most African societies. Slave status was not strictly hereditary, nor was the next generation necessarily free. But one's marginal status was reduced by being born in the community. Thus, offspring could be considered half-slave, and the following generation might be considered free. Initially, the slave might be considered a nonperson but, as marginality was reduced, the continuum led in the direction of quasikinship and finally resulted in kinship (Miers & Kopytoff, 1977, p. 4). This is fundamentally different from the West's conception of slaves as a class apart, never integrated into the society as a whole.

The process of incorporating the slave into the new society began with the acquisition of a master. Having a master indicated formal status, mobility from being mere property to being a person with rights. Emotional ties that developed between slave and his or her new family brought no change in formal status but assured the slave that he or she would not be sold despite the legal possibility of such a sale. Mobility in terms of worldly success also existed for the African slave. A slave could acquire wealth and political power although the legal status would still not be changed. The slave's master still owned him or her, regardless of the power the slave acquired (Miers & Kopytoff, 1977, p. 19).

The use of slaves in Africa as political and social units rather than as labor units is evident in the preference for young women and children to men. Children were easier to integrate into their new society because they were young; women could be married into the society. Men were more difficult to incorporate into the society and were likely to be more difficult to control, especially if they had been taken by force. With the integration of white slave dealers into the African trade, male slaves became of higher value as labor units and greatly changed the structure of traditional African slavery.

Because of this gradual integration of the slave into the new society, it is difficult to determine where slave populations existed. In the West, slave populations made up separate reproductive units whose increase could be easily assessed. But in Africa, the physical reproductive rate diverged widely from the social rate. On the whole, though, the proportion of slaves to free persons was lower in small, relatively undifferentiated societies (Miers & Kopytoff, 1977, p. 60).

In the Northwest Pacific Coast area, slaves were also viewed not so much as labor units but as a measure of status. Therefore, the slave population consisted largely of women and children. An early observer of slavery in this area noted: "As concerns his labor, the slave was no great asset and the principal reason for the "existence of the institution of slavery was that the possession of captives reflected honor and dignity upon their owners" (Curtis, 1913, p. 74)."

According to Drucker, the principal significance of slaves on the Northwest Coast was to "serve as foils for the high and mighty" (1939, p. 56). For this purpose, slaves were sometimes sacrificed ceremonially or killed at the whim of their master, perhaps to show his anger (Fried, 1967, p. 222). Slaves did the same work as everybody else—fishing and paddling canoes. Furthermore, intermarriage between slaves and the free existed. Marriages between free men and slave women were not infrequent. More significantly, slave men and daughters of free men, even daughters of chiefs, married as well. A slave might also become an influential member of society, although his low status as a slave was always remembered and could be used against him (Fried, 1967, p. 223).

Even though slavery is a low-status condition wherever it occurs, nowhere were slaves deprived access to basic resources except in the West. And only in the West was control over one's destiny and the destiny of one's offspring totally lost, to the extent that it continues to temper social relations between blacks and whites today.

Stratification and Modernization

Because modernization first occurred in Western Europe, there is a tendency to assume that the process takes the same form the world over. The process that Europe underwent was peculiar to that area's position as the first to industrialize and assume world power status (Bendix, 1970, p. 327). Nations currently undergoing modernization are in a different position. As "followers," they are able to benefit from Europe's example of what not to do and what to do sooner. But these na-

tions also have feelings of inferiority and domination. Such feelings make it difficult for nationalism to take hold and, in turn, for modernization to develop in the European manner.

The continuity of social change allows for modernization to occur utilizing existing social structure. Eisenstadt (1967) points out that traditional structures in a society shape its modernization process. The example he cites is the initial modernization of India in which the caste system adapted to the new economic and political frameworks. According to Eisenstadt, the fact that modernization was not completed in India had to do with the inability of the new political center to develop common symbols by which to combine the new society with the old traditions, thereby creating a collective identity (1967, pp. 454–456). Eisenstadt's theory of how modernization occurs calls for the existence of independent social, cultural, and political institutions as well as a centralized institutional framework. The centralized institution of government affects traditional structures by redefining individual and group rights and duties as well as maintaining them.

Plural societies consist of people of diverse social, racial, and cultural origin who, during the process of modernization, became more fully incorporated into one social system (Smith, 1970, p. 43). The concept applies to Caribbean, African, Asian, Oceanic, and Latin American nations as well as to the United States. In Polynesia and the Caribbean, pluralism occurred with the intrusion of white settlers who came to trade, proselytize, plant, and administrate (Glick, 1970, p. 95). After this initial intrusion, other immigrant populations followed, either on their own or at the beckoning of planters who needed additional laborers. On the Polynesian island of Vila, for example, after the white immigration came Asians looking for employment, first as laborers, then as shopkeepers and artisans. The next group to come was made up of distant islanders. These groups tended to associate only among themselves, since language was a barrier to interaction between groups and because cultural ties bound group members together. In addition, they often lived separately because of restrictions imposed on housing by the politically dominant white group.

In Africa, plural societies came about again with the intrusion of the white "discoverer." Frontiers between nations were imposed where none had existed before. Within these frontiers were diverse tribes who found themselves amalgamated into one political system without regard to the differences between them (Southall, 1970, p. 257).

These societies, having relatively autonomous social, cultural, and political institutions as well as a centralized government, fill Eisenstadt's modernization requirements. They currently have the task of extending the influence of the centralized institution while also developing a collective identity to incorporate their diverse groups. Jamaica's national slogan, "Out of Many, One People," demonstrates this approach (Smith, 1970, p. 43).

The centralized political institution necessary for modernization also has the effect of giving "official" expression to large-scale stratification. It creates its own hierarchy while imposing the order necessary for modernization. But stratification results from unequal relations. This is true in all societies, from those with minimal government to large-scale, centralized nations (Balandier, 1970, p. 78). It is important to realize that political power and social stratification are linked, so that stratification determines who has power at the same time that those with power influence the social stratification. This is not to say that change will not occur in the system. The aristocracy continued to rule in England during modernization by taking up the middle-class cause. They thereby aided the change in the stratification system to the point where family status and office were separated. It is here that we see the significance of the continuity of social change and the effect of extrinsic factors such as government on existing stratification structure in the cause of the "growth of citizenship" (Bendix, 1970, p. 327).

Hawaii, more than any other state in the United States, represents the incorporation of people of diverse social, racial, and cultural origins into one plural society. (Monroe Pinckard, Rapho/Photo Researchers)

Summary

1. Inequalities exist in all human societies. In egalitarian societies, although lack of job differential ensures that social and economic differences are minimal, inequalities exist on the basis of divisions of labor by age and sex, individual abilities, and the existence of a headman and/or shaman.

2. The division of labor in rank and egalitarian societies is basically the same. However, in rank societies, a formalized system of individual graduated statuses exist, usually for ceremonial purposes. In addition, a redistributive economy develops, which keeps wealth from becoming concentrated in any one family. Societies become larger and more permanent, and a formalized kinship network develops.

3. Egalitarian and rank societies are considered unstratified; neither denies any group basic resources that sustain life.

4. As societies grow more complex, work becomes specialized, and access to basic resources is impaired. True stratification emerges. There are many different types of stratification systems that determine which groups are privileged and which groups are denied privileges.

5. One type of stratification system is the caste system. It is composed of socially distinct groups, hierarchically arranged, whose membership is birth-ascribed and considered unchangeable. Interaction between castes is controlled and endogamy is generally the rule. Two types of caste systems exist—a multiple caste system in which most people are in positions of both relative superiority and inferiority and a dual caste system in which only two groups occur: an elite group and a pariah group.

6. Another type of stratification system is the class system, considered more "open" because social mobility can occur. However, while this is the case ideally, in practice, mobility does not occur with the frequency commonly believed. The notion of class is less clearly defined as it relies on highly subjective criteria for its differentiation.

7. Another type of stratification system is slavery. A *slave* is a person who has lost control over his or her own labor. In Africa, a slavery-to-kinship continuum existed by which the slave was incorporated into the new society over generations. In the Northwest Coast area, slaves could be integrated into the society, often through marriage. Only in the Western hemisphere was slavery a permanent and hereditary classification.

8. The process of modernization is accompanied by three themes, according to Bendix: (1) a continuity of social change, (2) extrinsic factors affecting existing social structures, and (3) a redefinition of individual and group rights and duties.

9. Modernization is furthermore associated with fundamental structural changes determined by traditional social structures, according to Eisenstadt. Autonomous cultural, social, and political spheres as well as a centralized institutional framework are necessary components of a society seeking to modernize. However, their existence does not ensure that modernization will occur but only that the necessary adaptability exists.

10. Many societies currently undergoing modernization are plural societies in which socially and culturally distinct groups are incorporated within a larger societal frame. For modernization to occur, political power must be centralized. Such power is linked with social stratification. Stratification contributes to political power, and political power influences social stratification.

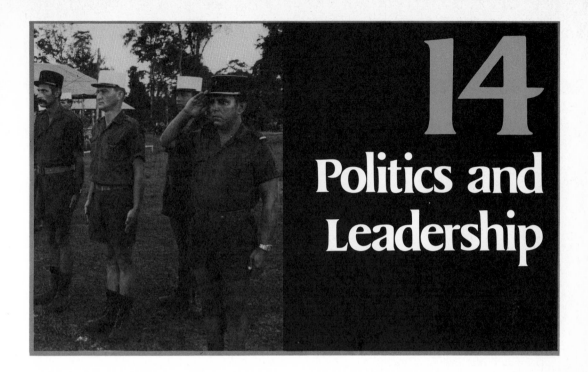

14
Politics and Leadership

POLITICS and leadership are closely linked with the concepts of status and hierarchy because status differences and ranking tend to involve domination and control. And, as we will see shortly, politics is also intimately related to domination and control—in a word, to *power*. A society's leaders exercise power, and they also enjoy high status. Of course, political leaders are not the only people who have power and status, but the connection between the two is most evident in the political arena.

Although political relations are probably as old as human society, political anthropology as a distinct field of study is relatively new. Before the 1940s, anthropologists did not explicitly study the political activities of the members of any given society as a separate field of inquiry, though they did describe political structures and classify political systems according to type. During the past 20 or 30 years, however, there has been increasing emphasis on the competitive aspects of politics—on political factions, the politics of decision making, and political change. Anthropologists now distinguish between the administration of a political system and the struggle for control of that system. Even so, the subject matter of political anthropology is not as clearly defined as that of other branches of the discipline. The study of kinship, for example, is a clearly delimited field of inquiry with a vocabulary of its own. This is not yet true of political anthropology.

In this chapter, we will approach political activities in a manner that is consistent with the view of cultural and social phenomena expressed throughout this book. That is, we will study politics in the context of the total social system, and native ideas about leadership and decision making will be considered in the context of models designed to interpret them. Among the ideas we will consider are the nature of political activity; various types of political systems; the relationship between kinship and politics; conquest and force; and leadership.

The Nature of Political Activity

Political anthropology has been described as "the study of the *processes* involved in determining and implementing public goals and in the differential achievement and use of power by the members of the group concerned with those goals" (Swartz et al., 1966, p. 7).

According to Swartz et al., politics is characterized by three essential qualities:

1. It is *public* rather than private in nature.
2. It always concerns goals or benefits for which there is *competition*.
3. It involves differences in *power*—that is, control—among the members of the group.

The concept of power is at the center of any treatment of politics. Attempts to define power and distinguish it from authority make up a major portion of the study of political anthropology.

Political anthropologists today focus on political *processes*. This emphasis calls attention to the fact that politics is concerned with the arena of political *action* rather than with typologies of political systems. One implication of such an approach is that it entails the study of conflict itself as well as the resolution of conflict. Moreover, it leads us to a focus on the political *activities* of groups ranging from small factions to entire societies, rather than merely on the *structure* of those groups. To use a familiar example: the political system of the United States can be viewed in terms of the three branches of government—executive, legislative, and judicial—and the functions of each. Such a view focuses on structure. The U.S. political system can also be viewed as a continuing struggle among various interest groups for the benefits distributed by the federal government (such as highway funds, tax exemptions, and welfare payments) and the control of valuable resources. This view emphasizes the activities involved in politics.

Power and Authority

The terms *power* and *authority* are often used interchangeably, but to the student of politics they are very different. *Power* is the capacity to take independent action in the face of resistance from persons, groups, or rules (Smith, 1968, p. 193). Thus, power has to do with resistance and confrontation. It is not institutionalized, and it is not always effective. *Authority,* by contrast, is institutionalized and involves the right to take certain actions, including decisions to issue commands. It represents the "set of rules, procedures, traditions, and norms that are regarded as binding when they are applied within a given social unit" (Smith, 1968, p. 193). The leader of a military coup may have power but little authority, whereas an elected official has authority and may often have considerable power as well.

Legitimacy

Political systems combine authority and power; both are needed in the regulation of public affairs. Without power, authority can accomplish little; without authority, power is not institutionalized and thus may lose its effectiveness in the long run. Accordingly, political systems have been defined as being concerned with the maintenance of social order through the use of force. But societies exist in which authority is not backed up by force. Moreover, as Swartz and his associates point out, "force is a crude and expensive technique for the implementation of decisions" (1966, pp. 9–10). Something besides coercion is needed to make a political system work. This additional ingredient is *legitimacy*.

The legitimacy of a political system derives from the values of the members of a society who influence and are affected by the decisions made within that society. Legitimacy is based on the expectation that those who make the decisions will meet certain obligations. Thus, it is not simply a matter of who makes the decisions but also a matter of the content of those decisions. A legitimate court, for example, is expected to arrive at a just verdict.

Compliance with the decisions made in a legitimate system results mainly from the belief that those decisions support the shared values of the members of the society. The degree of compliance within the society will vary, however. For those persons who do not comply with the decisions made by the leaders of a society, coercion may become necessary. This is the link between power and legitimacy: Power is one way of gaining compliance with the decisions made by those who are in positions of authority.

Political Systems and Governments

Anthropologists generally assume that every society has a political system, but those systems are classified in different ways. Some scholars would argue that the term *political system* should be reserved for societies that have governments. Others distinguish between societies that have centralized administrative and judicial institutions—that is, a government—and societies that lack such institutions. In any case, a political system is more than government. It includes both *politics*—the contest to gain power within an authoritative political system—and *administration*—the conducting of public affairs by those who have gained that power. In the following section, we will examine various modes of political organization, emphasizing the way power is achieved and authoritative decisions are made within each one.

Modes of Political Organization

Stateless Systems: Bands and Tribes

Some societies look to a single head, such as a military dictator or a prime minister, as a source of authority; other societies do not. The latter societies are called *acephalous* or "headless." They usually fall somewhere between very small communities (in which a single head is in direct contact with all the members) and very large ones (which can be held together only by a system of authority with a single center). There are some fairly large acephalous communities, however.

An example of an acephalous political system is the Nuer society of the southern Sudan in the early twentieth century. In this society, each kin group was autonomous, and the rights of each individual were enforced by that individual and his or her kin. Homicide, for example, was an injury to the kin group and might be revenged by killing the person who had committed the initial homicide or killing one of the kin. This method of revenge often led to blood feuds, but such a feud could be ended by means of a payment of cattle and a formal reconciliation. Thus, there was a political system of sorts, but no single person was responsible for coordinating the public activities of the tribe.

The Role of the Segmentary Lineage System. As the preceding example suggests, membership in kin groups has a great deal to do with political relations in acephalous societies. Indeed, in such societies, political relations are embedded in kinship relations. This is obvious in societies with segmentary lineage systems.

You will recall from earlier chapters that a segmentary lineage system involves both relations of association and relations of opposition—groups that are associated at one level are in opposition at the next-lower level. In a "segmentary" society such as that of the Nuer, political relations are based on a unilineal system of genealogical relations. The local community is thought of as consisting of a single lineage, but the genealogical system extends beyond the local community.

Relations between local groups—joint or extended families containing three or four generations—are essentially relations between lineages and thus do not change significantly over time, though the groups themselves may vary in size and locality over time. These relations may be competitive, as when rights over land or livestock are in question, but when an outside group threatens these local groups they will merge into a larger group or cluster to oppose the external threat. Thus, the segmentary lineage system serves "the decisive function of unifying 'within' for the purpose of standing 'against'" (Sahlins, 1961, p. 97). It should be noted that the larger entity does not exist under ordinary circumstances. It is called into being when needed and by reference to genealogy; that is, it is genealogically equivalent to groups that merge.

This is, of course, a very general description of how segmentary lineage systems work. There are actually many differences between such systems—in the degree of interdependence among the local groups, for example, and in the degree to which shared religious and social values control relations among them. If the groups are highly independent or very heterogeneous in cultural terms, however, it is unlikely that a true segmentary lineage system exists. Neighboring Dinka tribes, for example, are divided into a number of subtribes with a tendency to fragment into entities that are absolutely independent of one another. But this segmenting tendency is not matched by any tendency toward fusion into temporary larger groupings. The Dinka thus have no way of withstanding external attacks as do the Nuer.

The Tiv of northern Nigeria illustrate the political role of the segmentary lineage system. The Tiv have been expanding their territory in several directions at the expense of other tribes, a movement that Sahlins (1961) describes as "predatory encroachment." Their success appears to be due to the fact that they can put mass pressure on their borders, whereas their opponents cannot call upon large numbers of people to resist the pressure.

Tiv expansion takes two forms. In one, nicknamed "leapfrog migration," a group from within Tivland crosses the border into a new area and is later joined by related groups. In the second form, "steamroller expansion," a border group may be forced by other groups to move into the territory of a neighboring tribe—"the lineage is simply crowded out as the Tiv side of its land is consumed by the appetites of other Tiv" (Sahlins, 1961, p. 111).

To sum up, the segmentary lineage system is "a social means of temporary consolidation of [a] fragmented tribal polity for concerted external action" (Sahlins, 1961, p. 117). It thus substitutes for a permanent political structure, which does not exist in a tribal society. It occurs only in the presence of intertribal competition, since without opposition there is no need to unite.

Decisions in Acephalous Political Systems. In bands and tribes, as in any social grouping, various decisions must be made. These decisions may be divided into three types: (1) reinforcement, or the prevention of deviation from acceptable forms of behavior; (2) administration, or directing the concerted ac-

Among Australian aboriginal tribes, the "old men" of the tribes are the ruling elders and also perform ceremonial and teaching functions. (Monkmeyer)

Yąnomamö men parading during a feast; shows of violence and aggression in rituals carry over into the life style of this people. (Napoleon Chagnon, Anthro-Photo)

POLITICS AND LEADERSHIP

tions of the group; and (3) adjudication, or resolving conflict between people or groups (Service, 1966).

Reinforcement is largely a matter of custom in acephalous societies. If an individual deviates from the society's norms, sanctions such as gossip, ridicule, and withdrawal may be directed at that person. These sanctions do not result from a decision of a person in a position of authority but are based on the general consensus of the members of the group (though the elder males tend to have more authority than other members). In extreme cases, a band may decide to kill a person who consistently harms others. The person chosen to perform the act is a relative of the wrongdoer (in order to prevent a blood feud).

In *administration* areas—decisions that have to do with such matters as moving camp, hunting, and skirmishing with enemies—some leadership is required, but in acephalous systems leadership is not formal. The decision-making authority shifts from one person to another, depending on the type of decision involved. For example, a man who has a great store of ritual knowledge will plan a ceremony, while the most skillful hunter will lead a hunting party. There is no permanently chosen chief or headman. In fact, the word *authority* may be too strong for such situations. *Influence* might be a better word, since the leader is in that position only temporarily, as long as his experience and skill are needed.

Adjudication has to do with how quarrels, feuds, and sometimes wars are settled. This would appear to be a very difficult question in the absence of a formal system for settling disputes. But the fact is that acephalous societies are capable of handling conflict fairly well. When a quarrel occurs, a person—often someone who is related to both parties—will step in to stop the dispute from getting out of hand, as in the following example:

A small crowd had gathered, and, as usual, the family quarrel became a public affair. Several people helped Tu out of the fire, found her barely scorched, but her cousin seized Toma and began to shake him. This enraged Toma so much that he caught the cousin around the waist and threw him into the onlooking crowd. The people said: "We must stop Toma because if he is so angry he may kill someone," and with that they led the cousin out of Toma's sight.

Toma shouted after: "If you do that again, we will get our arrows and fight to the death. Stop here. I am very angry. Do not make me more angry."

One of the men who had helped Tu said to the cousin: "I took his wife from the fire. You, her cousin, almost got killed for the way you went at Toma. If you want to help people, don't get angry with them. Keep calm. Don't increase anger as you did with Toma." With these sage words the incident was over. (Thomas, 1970, p. 308)

If this mediation approach is ineffective, techniques such as the Eskimo song duel or the spear-throwing duel of the Australian aborigines may be used. These contests are decided by public opinion; the loser is considered to have been in the wrong.

Quarrels between people who are members of different bands are more difficult to resolve. One method, mentioned earlier in connection with the Nuer, is retribution. But retribution does not usually restore the original balance between the parties, and feuding may continue for long periods unless some sort of reconciliation takes place.

The Eskimo. The Eskimo provide an example of simple government in bands. They have been described by Lawrence Krader (1968) as follows:

The Eskimos, who live in Alaska in bands of usually no more than 50, have neither chiefs nor advisory councils, nor deliberative assemblies—although they do practice a form of individual economic leadership; in whale hunting, the boat owner has dominance over the crew, and primary right over the catch. Nevertheless, they have no formal government and explicit organs whereby they are ruled; they are without specialized administrators, judges, courts, and written law.

Rather, they have informal means of controlling aggression among people, and righting wrongs. Their primitive legal mechanisms include [for example] the song-duel.

The Eskimos countenance several socially acceptable modes of doing away with people: suicide, senilicide [killing of the old], infanticide, and invalidicide. Homicide is sometimes redressed by blood revenge. . . . The Public or society at large is not involved; it is a private wrong. . . . However, *repeated* murder among the Eskimos is in fact considered to be a matter of public interest; it is a public crime of which the band must take cognizance, and is punishable by death at the hands of a chosen agent of the band. The Eskimos have a simple form of governmental regulation of social behavior: their court is not a permanent institution; it is convened as the occasion warrants, and after the judgment the court is disbanded without fixing a time for reassemblage. (Krader, 1968, pp. 30–31)

Thus, while stateless systems may not have formal government in the way we know it, every society provides means for supporting the rights and obligation necessary for that society to exist. Societies that do not look to a single head for authority are capable of regulating fairly large populations by means of the control mechanisms discussed here and in the chapter on social control.

State Systems: Chiefdoms and Monarchies

Characteristics of State Systems. In a state system, a ruler who is recognized by the society as its head holds supreme authority, which may be delegated to various territorial agents. This is a common form of political system among the societies studied by anthropologists. The state's functions are maintenance of internal peace, defense against external aggression, organization of public works and rituals, and collection of tribute (taxes). Although small societies are sometimes organized in this way, it is more usual among relatively large populations. Naturally, the details of state systems vary greatly. One of the distinguishing features of state systems, though, is that they are run by officials who are free to specialize in the administration of the state. That is, they are not engaged primarily in economic production. This includes both the ruler and subordinate officials.

Subordinates, or agents, are chosen by the ruler or leader. Sometimes the subordinates are kin of the person in authority; sometimes they are nonkin rewarded for loyal service. The subordinate has much to gain from such an appointment—for example, free labor for home and fields and a certain amount of the produce of the community. The duties of the subordinate are to decide disputes, collect tribute, and organize labor for public works. Thus, the positions of both ruler and agent are privileged ones.

It is in the selection of subordinates that politics comes into play. If a central source of authority—that is, a leader—is firmly established, intriguing for one's own or a friend's appointment to an official position consists mainly of pleasing those who are already in positions of authority. If the central authority is weak, political competition may take the form of efforts to gain followers or *clients.* In return for protection, the clients offer service, which can include violent actions such as plundering the possessions of a rival. Those with many followers are more likely to achieve positions of authority in the society. From the client's point of view, the protection involved in the relationship can be highly significant. Mair (1962) describes one such instance of the client relationship:

The client made . . . a token gift—a pot of beer or of the fermented honey which was much prized in Ruanda. . . . The client had the duty of personal service to his lord. He followed him on journeys, to court, or to war. . . . A client who fulfilled his obligations expected to be able to count on his lord's protection in most kinds of trouble. (Mair, 1962, pp. 168–169)

The competition for positions of authority can also extend to competition between princes for succession to a throne. Even when there are specific rules of succession, there is room for such competition. For example, the Zulu rule of succession was that the next chief must be the eldest son of the woman whom his father had married after he himself became chief. But if the heir was a child, a regent would be chosen, perhaps a younger brother of the dead chief. When the heir came of age, the regent, perhaps unwilling to step down, might have built up enough power to prevent the heir from succeeding to the throne. In an effort to avoid problems of this kind, many states have "kingmakers," officials with the authority to choose the successor. Even then, however, competition is not necessarily eliminated. The kingmaker's choice may be challenged, and fighting can continue until one of the rivals is killed.

How States Are Formed. How does an acephalous political system like that of the Eskimos develop into a state system? Some theorists have argued that the state is formed as a result of conquest—one group subjugates another and uses governmental institutions to maintain its domination. Other anthropologists claim that states develop as a result of the unequal distribution of economic goods; those who control more resources can gain control over the rest of the society. But societies have been identified in which neither conquest nor economic control has led to the formation of a state; the Eskimos and the neighboring Chukchi have conquered one another at various times without developing into states.

Krader (1968) believes that statelike institutions—for example, secret religious societies, military or police associations, high councils—play a role in the formation of states. Such institutions tend to counteract the individual's ties to his or her local community and thus link the relationships of local life into a larger whole. They serve the additional functions of providing a wider outlet for tensions generated within small groups and creating a greater variety of choices and more freedom for individuals.

It appears that the crucial factor in the formation of a state is the degree of centralization of authority. Multiple centers of power and authority compete with one another and prevent a state from forming. Several West African peoples, such as the Kpelle, had a king or high chief but also had institutions such as secret societies that had considerable power. Neither the king nor the secret society could achieve ultimate control, and a state did not develop. Similarly, the Plains Indians had well-developed police and military associations as well as chiefs and councils. However, the general pattern of social control was simple and informal, so that no single individual or group could gain enough power to become the dominant force in the society.

As traditional ties are broken down and territorial boundaries become more precise, a state emerges. Eventually, one person or group assumes the central authority in the society, with a monopoly on the legal use of force.

Legitimacy in State Systems. The ruler and subordinates, as we have seen, have a claim to the resources of the country and the labor of its people. Why do the people accept such a system? For one thing, it is often to their advantage to have a relatively formal method of settling disputes. For another, they receive protection against outside attack. And the ritual performed (or financed) by the ruler guarantees the good will of deities or ancestors, something that is considered indispensable in many such societies. The traditional rituals by which a ruler came into office symbolized these obligations: "A Ganda ruler . . . shot arrows towards all four points of the compass to signify that he would conquer his enemies; at the accession of a king of Bunyoro a trial was enacted to remind him of his duty as the source of justice" (Mair, 1972, p. 127).

Counselors and Councils. Even though a state system has a single ruler, it is not necessarily a dictatorship. Decisions are made with the help of counselors. Among the Bantu, for example,

> it was customary for the ruler to have as his chief adviser a man not of his lineage . . . who was expected to be . . . a mouthpiece of popular dissatisfaction. . . . He was expected to listen to people who thought they had been wronged—particularly by unjust punishments—and to remonstrate privately with the ruler and persuade him to make amends without publicly admitting that he was at fault. (Mair, 1972, p. 128)

In most state systems there is also a council of some sort (comprising all the leading subordinate chiefs, for example). This type of arrangement allows for considerable political maneuvering in the decision-making process as well as in the competition for official positions.

An Emergent State System: Ankole. The small kingdom of Ankole in what is now western Uganda provides an example of an emergent state system. It was formerly ruled by the king of the Bahima tribe, to whom other Bahima were clients, following the king in war and receiving in return whatever cattle were seized. (If the king did not share out the booty, the clients might try to overthrow him.) The king was believed to have supernatural powers and was given the titles of Lion, Bull, Land of Ankole, Drum, and Moon. He was required to be virile; if he became ill or senile he was given a fatal poison. Only he had the right to send out raiding parties and make war or peace. He was the highest judicial authority, with the power to sentence clients to death or exile, to torture and curse, and to confiscate property.

Several subordinates were appointed by the king, including the Enganzi, or favorite chief. The Enganzi had to be from another clan and could not himself become king, but he was kingmaker, "prime minister," and war minister. The king ruled through the Enganzi, border chiefs, magicians, and other members of his personal following. The Bahima district chiefs collected tribute from serfs, keeping part and sending the remainder to the king.

The royal succession passed from father to eldest son, but the successor had to be strong enough to withstand potential rivals—younger brothers with greater strength or more followers. During a war of succession, the border chiefs, who could not become king, stood guard against outside invasion. When one of the rivals for the throne had eliminated all the others, the Enganzi enthroned the new king, who then appointed a new Enganzi (Krader, 1968).

Primitive states frequently need to exercise strong control in order to maintain social order.

Colonial Systems

States such as Ankole were radically changed by European colonization in the nineteenth and early twentieth centuries. The goals of the European governments were to gain advantages for their own citizens (in trade, for example) and also to benefit the colonized peoples by teaching them the values of Western civilization. It fact, they believed that it was their moral duty to impose "good" government on primitive peoples. This meant setting up a new hierarchy of officials linking the native officials with the colonial government.

At the interface between the colonial administration and the native peoples was the district commissioner (or some similar official). He did not decide policy but was supposed to see that the central government's policies were put into effect. Among other things, he chose local people to administer those policies—to collect taxes, for example.

Military troops were often part of the colonial apparatus—in this instance, members of the French Foreign Legion in French Guyana. (Y. Jeanmougin/ Viva, Woodfin Camp)

Where possible, he chose individuals who were already in positions of authority. If no such individuals could be found, he would ask the native people to nominate candidates for such positions. This opened up a new arena of competition between native groups in the society. A whole class of people was created, a group that could be considered clients of the colonial government, since they owed their position—and its rewards—to that government. This naturally changed their relationship with the people under their control. They no longer received tribute from the peasants under their authority; instead, they received salaries, which in some cases were substantial. However, under this arrangement, peasants lost the protection and hospitality of the chiefs, while the chiefs became isolated from the people and began to feel like servants of the colonial government.

Max Gluckman (1968) has analyzed the roles of the district commissioner and the native chief under the Dutch administration of Zululand in the mid-1930s. He points out that both commissioner and chief were subject to conflicting pressures because they occupied positions in which two levels of social relations (colonial and native) met and often clashed. The commissioner was at the lowest level of the colonial hierarchy but had some influence over the native people. On the other hand, the chief was at the head of the tribal hierarchy but was at the same time considered a junior official in the colonial hierarchy. The positions of commissioner and chief had little authority.

Both the administrator and the chief were expected to represent the interests of the government at the local level, and both were expected by the local people to represent their interests. This often led to conflict. For example, "a chief who opposed the building of cattle paddocks was praised by his people, but condemned by technical officers; while a chief who asked for cattle paddocks was praised by technical officials and condemned by his people" (Gluckman, 1968, p. 80).

In Zululand, Gluckman found considerable dedication to the native people among the commissioners. They were concerned about producing better breeds of Zulu cattle, for example, or finding ways of helping the Zulu get higher prices for their cattle, or improving their agricultural technology (Gluckman calls this the "development ethic.") The commissioner became involved in "Zulu hopes and fears, aspirations and objections" (p. 75). Many spoke Zulu and knew a great deal about Zulu history and culture.

In general, the policies of colonial governments often failed to take into account the differences in the economics and political organization of the areas under their jurisdiction. Also, the colonial governments were not considered legitimate at the local level and had to depend quite heavily on coercion, despite the dedication of many of their lower-level officials. However, they did make possible the administration of diverse political units, and in this way paved the way for the emergence of modern nation-states.

Political Systems in New Nations

In the new nation-states of Africa, Asia, and Latin America, many diverse groups have had to be united within a brief period. In another chapter, we discussed this process from the standpoint of law. We saw that a basic problem of new nations is that of getting citizens to identify with the nation as a whole rather than with a particular subgroup. As Clifford Geertz (1968) has pointed out, the desire to preserve one's tribal or religious identity can conflict with the desire to be part of an efficient, modern state.

The Need for Integration. As we saw in connection with both social control and with industrialization, the process of development and modernization involves the integration of diverse elements into a new system. This need for integration is especially acute in the political sphere. Somehow, the attachments of citizens to tribe, religion, language, and so forth must be reconciled with the new order. It is not enough simply to deny these attachments, nor can they be wished out of existence.

Political integration occurs in various ways in different states. One tendency that new states have in common, however, is that of lumping together traditional groups into larger, looser units whose frame of reference is not the locality but the nation. In Malaysia these larger groups tend to be ethnic: Malays, Chinese, and Indians. In Indonesia they are commonly regional: the people of Java and those of the Outer Islands. In Nigeria they are based loosely on kinship; in India they have been based somewhat on language. As members of these larger blocks, individuals who never interacted before are doing so now; and in so doing they gradually identify more and more with total society. At the same time, conflicts between the larger blocs are becoming more sharply defined and causing turmoil in the developing states. Such conflicts generate a tendency toward separatism that can disrupt a new state before it has become fully established.

The "Gap." The machinery of government in new states—elections, political parties, civil service—is new, whereas the social structure and culture in these states are traditional. Moreover, the elites created by state formation are concerned about the need for modernization, while the masses—usually peasant majority—tend to be resistant to changes that appear to conflict with traditional values. These factors create a gap between the society as it would like to be and the society as it actually is.

This gap, together with the difficulty of achieving unity in a heterogeneous population, complicates the task of developing the political system of a new state. Traditional beliefs, the existing social structure, and illiteracy tend to hold back modernization. Even when trained people are available to serve in the government, they may feel that they are overqualified for such positions. The public, on the other hand, never having had a voice in political decisions, is likely to be overly submissive. Silence on public matters may cause its members to be either overlooked or ordered around "for their own good."

Government in New States. The task of creating the political system of a new state falls quite naturally on its educated and politically aware members, who constitute its elite. The regime with which these individuals are most familiar is the state's former colonial ruler, often a European nation such as France or England. Thus, the elite tend to favor systems based on a democratic model, but the difficulty of setting up a modern state in an environment in which tradition is more powerful than education often leads to a relatively authoritarian political system.

Still, most new states aim, at least initially, toward *political democracy,* a system in which the central element is an elected legislative body whose laws are carried out by an executive with the help of an organized bureaucracy. Political parties are active and opposition is tolerated; in fact, opposition is necessary in such a system.

For a political democracy to be viable, it must meet certain conditions:

1. It must be recognized as legitimate by most of the society.
2. There must be a corps of political leaders who are reasonably informed, competent, and forthright.
3. The opposition group must be coherent

and responsible (for example, it must not oppose merely for the sake of opposition).
4. There must be a trained, competent civil service (the bureaucracy that administers the laws).
5. There must be respect for the rule of law and a disciplined police force, intelligence system, or military to back up the law.
6. There must be established institutions of public opinion—newspapers, universities, civic associations, and the like—with freedom of expression and association.

It is difficult to meet these conditions even in long-established states. In new states, it is extremely difficult. In many cases, the citizens of the new state are united only by the fact that no other state controls their territory. Not only do the people lack a feeling of solidarity, but the ruling elite itself is often torn by conflict.

When the six conditions just listed do not occur together, a more authoritarian regime is likely to develop. And, indeed, such regimes, called *tutelary democracies,* are commonly found in developing nations. President Sukarno of Indonesia has aptly labeled this form of government "guided democracy." In such a system, the power of the legislature and the political parties is reduced, though these elements are not eliminated, and the press is expected to refrain from criticizing the ruling elite. But although freedom of expression is reduced, the rule of law is retained.

A tutelary democracy requires an elite that is considered legitimate by a significant portion of the population, and that elite must avoid excessive use of coercion. A competent, loyal civil service is also needed, along with an independent judiciary. Of course, such a system presupposes a relatively weak state of public opinion (such as the lack of a communications system that generates creative criticism and enlightened opposition). The citizens must accept the existing regime without much opposition. If they are too apathetic, however—or too rebellious—the regime is likely to become a *modernizing oligarchy.* An oligarchy is a form of government in which ruling power belongs to only a few persons.

The concept of a modernizing oligarchy appeals to members of the elite who are concerned with the rapid achievement of both progress and unity. A more authoritarian regime such as an oligarchy is thought to be the cure for "parochialism, disunity and apathy" (Shils, 1960). It is also encouraged by the presence of a heavy counterweight of traditional beliefs and customs that work against the establishment of a political democracy.

A modernizing oligarchy requires a closed, well-organized elite. If it is a civilian elite, it must have control over the military. No effective legislature is established, and opposition is not tolerated. The will of the rulers is carried out by an elaborate bureaucracy, but there is no independent judiciary. The rule of law gives way to the maintenance of order by the police and the army. Such a regime attempts to reduce local, traditional loyalties to an absolute minimum and to stimulate nationalistic feeling.

Although modernizing oligarchies are not uncommon among new states, none has yet succeeded in winning the support of the entire population. Traditional ties are very resistant to forceful efforts to eliminate them. Thus, while an oligarchical system can make some progress toward modernization in certain areas—such as improved transportation, land reform, and the like, they are less successful in other areas, such as private enterprise.

Politics and Warfare

Throughout this chapter we have mentioned conflict—blood feuds, competition for the throne in a traditional state, intergroup conflict in new states. Frequently, such hostilities lead to minor skirmishes in which few people are killed. Sometimes, however, they build up to the level of warfare.

War is often said to arise out of competition for limited resources. But despite the possibility of economic gain (such as booty, captives, or territory) from warfare, studies of the causes of war have shown that economic motives are much less important than other factors. In fact, any gain that may come from victory is unlikely to make up for the costs of war.

Levels of Violence

Warfare is usually an outgrowth of earlier hostilities rather than a planned undertaking. Among the Yąnomamö of Brazil and Venezuela, for example, two villages that do not have a stable alliance cannot coexist for very long without overt hostility. But the initial conflict will not be a full-scale war. According to Napoleon A. Chagnon (1977), the Yąnomamö have several levels of violence. At the lowest level, accusations of cowardice or malicious gossip may lead to a chest-pounding duel between members of different villages. Such a duel may escalate into a side-slapping contest or, more rarely, a duel with machetes, using the flat side of the blade. The next level is club fights, which may take place either within or between villages and which usually arise out of arguments over women. If such a fight involves many people, it can become quite brutal and may cause a village to split up into two groups.

The next level of violence among the Yąnomamö is the raid, or actual warfare. The goal of a raid is to kill one or more of the enemy without losing any members of the raiding party. If there is a single loss, the raid is considered unsuccessful, no matter how many of the enemy are killed. Such warfare is usually motivated by the desire for revenge and is simply a prolongation of earlier hostilities.

Functions of Warfare

Andrew Vayda (1968) has identified several possible functions of primitive warfare:

1. Regulation of the exercise of authority, that is, limiting abuses of power by those in authority. This function is illustrated by the rebellions that occur when a chief or king fails to divide booty fairly.
2. Regulation of relations with other groups. This applies to fighting for revenge (as in cases of insult, theft, nonpayment of bridewealth, rape, trespass, or wounding) and to whatever fighting is necessary for a group to maintain its integrity and possessions.
3. Regulation of the distribution of goods and resources. Warfare appears to serve certain economic functions. But with the exception of the cattle raids of pastoral peoples, it is not always clear how important warfare is in obtaining material gain. It is often the case that a defeated group is forced to give up its land. Although there are cases in which wars end without displacing a group from its land, over the long run, one group may be weakened to such an extent that it is forced to yield its territory to a stronger group. Most warfare among hunters and gatherers involves disputes over the control of marginal territories and its resources.
4. Regulation of demographic variables. In some instances, the purpose of warfare may be to kill as many of the enemy as possible and thus to reduce the total population. In others, the purpose may be to take captives. It should be noted, however, that wars for the purpose of capturing slaves are rare among hunting-and-gathering groups because food production is not developed enough to support a slave class. In a few cases, wars have been conducted for the purpose of capturing women (or, more rarely, men or children) in order to correct a population imbalance.

Alternatives to Warfare: The Potlatch Revisited

People who have a tradition of warfare have sometimes abandoned war in favor of some other activity that fulfills the same functions. An example of a case in which the substitution of another activity for warfare was unsuccessful is the situation in New Guinea, where the colonial administration forced the native people to take their land disputes to court instead of settling them by fighting. The courts soon became overloaded; moreover, the disputants were never satisfied by their verdicts. This factor, together with increased population pressure, led to renewed warfare.

An example in which warfare may have been successfully replaced by another activity was the case of the North American Pacific Coast Kwakiutl Indians. As the Kwakiutl themselves put it, "wars of property"—potlatches—replaced "wars of blood," and fighting was done with wealth instead of weapons. This shift occurred during the mid-1800s, a time when the population was declining (owing to epidemics introduced by Europeans), and trade goods such as blankets and bracelets were becoming available in quantities that would not have been possible using Kwakiutl handicraft techniques. Since the Indians were usually able to produce what they needed for subsistence, their cash earnings (such as from commercial fishing and lumbering) were a surplus that could be spent on trade goods used in the potlatch.

Another reason that potlatching substituted for warfare was that war was not a central element of Kwakiutl life. Warfare had been an expression of rivalry, of competition for social prestige. And, as we have seen, this function was fulfilled very well by *potlatching,* which itself is a form of rivalry, "ridden with the imagery and drama and meaning of Kwakiutl warfare" (Codere, 1950, p. 128).

Conquest and territorial expansion, then, are only one aspect of warfare, and not necessarily the most fundamental one in primitive society. Modern warfare is ostensibly sparked largely by ideological considerations, although the underlying function of political and economic factors is also crucial. Warfare does not solve problems; it merely reorients them and puts off the need to solve them until a later time.

Leadership

The Yąnomamö say that the headman's privilege is "to walk ahead on the path." It is true that societies need leaders in time of war, but this is not the only function of a leader. In any centralized political system, the leader's role is to serve as the source of authority. A classic analysis of leadership is that of Max Weber (1947). After pointing out that all leadership requires a certain amount of voluntary submission on the part of followers, he divided authoritative leadership into three major types:

1. *Legal* (or bureaucratic), in which authority is based on a belief in the legality of a system of rules, and obedience stems from loyalty to the office, not the person, of the leader.
2. *Traditional,* in which authority is based on belief in the sanctity of tradition and obedience is to the person who occupies a traditional position of authority.
3. *Charismatic,* in which a specific individual, through exceptional "gifts" or strength of character, gains the devotion of a group of followers.

These three forms of authority are, in Weber's terms, "ideal types," meaning that they are not usually found in their pure forms. President Kennedy, for example, is remembered as a charismatic leader, but as president his authority was based primarily on his legal position as president.

The Role of Consent

Claude Lévi-Strauss (1944) argued that *consent* is the psychological basis of leadership and that give-and-take, or reciprocity, between a leader and followers is central to leadership. To illustrate this point, he described leadership among the nomadic Nambikuara of Brazil.

According to Lévi-Strauss, the leadership of a Nambikuara band was not a product of the band's needs, but the reverse. That is, the leader was a stable nucleus around which a band took shape. The leadership role was not hereditary; the headman needed the support of the group. Therefore, leadership was based on personal prestige and the ability to inspire confidence. Moreover, the chief had no coercive power, so that his legitimacy was based entirely on consent. If members of the group felt that the leader was doing a poor job, they could join another band that they believed to be better managed. Thus, Nambikuara bands fluctuated greatly in size and membership and were especially subject to political intrigues and conflicts.

To prevent such difficulties, the headman not only had to do an outstanding job of choosing campsites, directing the group's gardening efforts, and so forth, but also had to be exceptionally generous. It was expected that everything that came into his hands would be given away within a short time. Lévi-Strauss described the consequences as follows.

This collective greediness not seldom drives the chief to an almost desperate position; then the refusal to give plays about the same part, in this primitive democracy, as the threat to resign followed by a vote of confidence in a modern parliament. When a chief reaches the point where he must say: "To give away is over! To be generous is over! Let another be generous in my place!", he must, indeed, be sure of his power and prestige, for his rule is undergoing its severest crisis. (Lévi-Strauss, 1944, pp. 54–55)

Although consent is the basis of leadership, it is expressed in a continual give-and-take between leader and followers. The Nambikuara chief had certain powers but was also expected to be generous. In return for the effort he made on behalf of the group, he was entitled to take several wives. This was no small privilege, since it meant that other Nambikuara men were obliged to do without. Lévi-Strauss added, however, that reciprocity was not the only reason that some people became leaders. "There are chiefs," he wrote, "because there are, in any human group, men who, unlike most of their companions, enjoy prestige for its own sake, feel a strong appeal to responsibility, and to whom the burden of public affairs brings its own reward" (p. 61).

Lévi-Strauss could just as well have been describing leadership in Toba society. In fact, in many small-scale societies—among the Nuer of East Africa, for example—ritual experts and prophets provide the crucial leadership. Although both types of leader (priests and prophets) mediate between the real world and the spirit world, they differ greatly from each other. Priests inherit their position and with it their authority (traditional leadership). Prophets derive their authority from their extraordinary behavior, which is thought to indicate possession of (or by) spirits (charismatic leadership). Yet each may seek to enhance authority by means of techniques often used by the other. For example, priests may try to increase their influence through charisma (for example, leadership in raids), while prophets may seek to convert their charismatic power

into more stable authority by winning public affirmation of their status.

The Big Man Versus the Chief

The role of reciprocity, together with Weber's list of "ideal types" of authority, is illustrated in the contrast between the "big men" of Melanesia and the paramount chiefs of Polynesia. The big man is a traditional type; such a leader is expected to exert strong personal control over local groups. The paramount chief, on the other hand, has more authority vested in his office; his duties are more clearly defined. The power of the big man is personal power, whereas that of the chief is primarily the power of office.

The big man *creates* his position and therefore is very dependent on his followers. He has to win their loyalty and cause them to be obligated to him; he has to reinforce this reciprocal relationship continually. If there is discontent among his followers, the big man may find himself out of power.

The Polynesian chief, by contrast, holds an inherited position of authority over a permanent group. Both the position and the group exist independently of the individual who happens to be chief. The leader's authority comes from his office. Yet the relationship is still reciprocal. The chief has many privileges, but he cannot overload the ability of the people to supply the goods and labor required to maintain those privileges. That is, he cannot "eat the power of the government too much" or rebellion may ensue.

Leadership in New States

The creation of new states out of colonial regimes provides opportunities for charismatic leaders to emerge and to appeal to whatever nationalistic sentiments exist among the people, thereby creating a following who may sweep them into office when the new government is set up. This kind of leadership can be

Charismatic leadership in creating new states out of colonial regimes was perhaps best exemplified by Mahatma Gandhi, who led India's move for freedom from British rule. (Henri Cartier-Bresson, Magnum)

valuable to a new nation. Mahatma Gandhi's role in freeing India from British rule is a prime example. Such larger-than-life individuals may temporarily make up for the lack of political institutions, such as political parties and parliaments, in a new nation. But they do not usually build up such institutions while they are in power. Thus, when they die or are overthrown, the nation may undergo a period of turmoil before a new leader is found or a viable political system is established.

Leadership, then, is clearly associated with political activities and processes. But, in many societies studied by anthropologists, no clear-cut distinction between political and religious leadership is evident. They merge into one, as will be apparent in the following chapter.

Summary

1. Three essential qualities of politics are: (1) It is public rather than private in nature; (2) it concerns goals or benefits for which there is competition; and (3) it involves differences in power among the members of a group.

2. *Power* is the capacity to take independent action in the face of resistance; *authority* is the institutionalized right to take certain actions, including decisions to issue commands.

3. Political systems combine authority and power in regulating public affairs. The members of a political system must believe it is *legitimate* to win compliance with its decisions without undue use of force.

4. Within a political system, a distinction can be made between *politics*—the competition for positions of power—and *administration*—the conducting of public affairs (that is, the carrying out of decisions) by those in power.

5. Stateless or *acephalous* systems—bands and tribes—have no single source of authority. Relations between groups in such societies are sometimes based on a segmentary lineage system.

6. Decisions in stateless systems are largely a matter of custom and public opinion. Tasks that require leadership are coordinated by the person who is most skilled at the task in question.

7. A state system—a chiefdom or mon-

archy—is formed when authority is central-ized in a single source that is recognized as legitimate by the society. The state maintains peace, defends against aggression, organizes public works, and collects taxes.

8. In a state system, the ruler chooses sub-ordinates. Individuals compete for these privileged positions by pleasing those in au-thority or by trying to gain as many clients (followers) as possible.

9. Competition for the throne is not un-common in state societies, even when there are definite rules of succession.

10. Colonial systems superimposed a sec-ond authority structure on the structure al-ready existing in traditional states. This greatly changed political relationships in those societies. Officials that interfaced between the colonial administration and the native peoples were subject to conflicting pressures. They were expected to represent the interests of each group to the other, and those interests often clashed.

11. The main problem facing newly inde-pendent states is that of getting citizens to identify with the nation as a whole rather than with a particular subgroup. An intermediate stage in this process is the formation of larger groups that identify more with the total soci-ety than with a small part of it.

12. New states are at a tremendous disad-vantage in developing their political systems because of conflicting beliefs among disparate members, the lack of an effective communica-tion system, and the absence of enlightened opposition that contributes to the effective implementation of policies.

13. The elite of a new state often tries to set up a *political democracy,* but the difficulty of creating such a system is likely to lead to the establishment of a *tutelary democracy.* Even then, however, the tendency toward au-thoritarianism may cause the regime to be-come a *modernizing oligarchy.*

14. Conflict is frequent in political systems of all descriptions. Sometimes these hostilities build up to the level of warfare, which is usu-ally an outgrowth of earlier hostilities rather than a planned undertaking. There may be several levels of violence before full-scale war-fare occurs.

15. The functions of warfare are regulation of the exercise of authority, regulation of rela-tions with other groups, regulation of the dis-tribution of goods and resources, and regula-tion of demographic variables. Sometimes another activity can substitute for warfare, as occurred when the *potlatch* replaced warfare among the Kwakiutl Indians.

16. Weber divides authoritative leadership into three types: *legal,* in which people are loyal to the office, not the person, of the leader; *traditional,* in which obedience is to the person who occupies a traditional position of authority; and *charismatic,* in which an indi-vidual gains the devotion of followers through exceptional qualities. These types are rarely found in their pure forms, and more than one type may be found in any given society.

17. Lévi-Strauss points out that the psy-chological basis of leadership is consent and that it is expressed in a continual give-and-take between leader and followers.

18. Charismatic leaders often emerge in new states and can substitute for political in-stitutions, but they must eventually organize their folllowers and systematize their author-ity if a viable political system is to emerge.

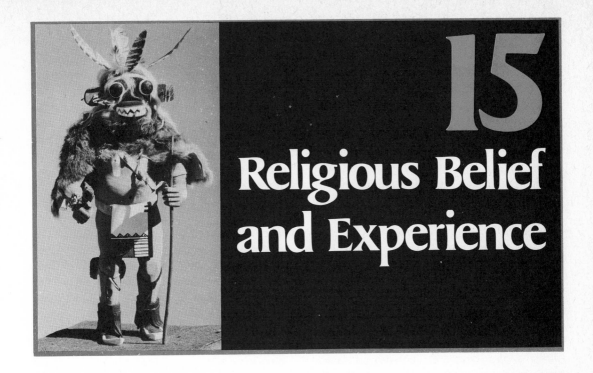

15

Religious Belief and Experience

T HE analysis of the crucial concepts of power and authority in the previous chapter is an excellent background against which to begin our discussion of religion. There is a close relationship between politics and religion, between the concepts of *power* and of the *sacred,* as a number of social analysts have remarked. The interrelationship between politics and religion is particularly apparent to anthropologists because the connection is often articulated by members of the societies in which they carry out research. In these societies, as we mentioned in the discussion of kinship, descent groups are involved with ancestors and places of origin, both mythical and real, and with ceremonial and ritual rights and property. The head of the lineage or clan is the link on earth between the living members of the descent group and the sacred ancestral spirits. Among the Lugbara of Uganda, as among many other peoples, patrilineages serve both ritual/

spiritual and genealogical/temporal functions. Those holding power—lineage elders, for example—seek to validate their position by invoking the ancestral spirits and traditions. But those who seek to attain power resort to manipulation by the techniques of witchcraft to mount sometimes effective challenges to the status quo (Middleton, 1960).

A different kind of example is provided by the Toba of Argentina. Among the Toba, religious and secular leadership reside for all practical purposes in the same individual. Practically speaking, one cannot distinguish between shaman and chief. Here the exercise of spiritual power entails political responsibilities; political leadership without the exercise of spiritual power could not be effective.

It would be a mistake, however, to assume that the sacred and the secular are joined only in hunting and gathering or horticultural societies. This association is characteristic of societies at every technological and political level. In fact, our own society, whose founding documents proclaim the doctrine of the separation of church and state and which is considered to be a secularly-oriented society is considered also to be a God-fearing one. High government officials are sworn into office while holding Bibles, and they often make public demonstration of church attendance; legislative sessions are opened with public prayers; and court proceedings involve the taking of oaths invoking the name of God. Religious adherence continues to play a significant role in legitimizing the social order, as well as in challenging that order.

The study of politics, then, is linked to the study of religion by the concept of power. From an anthropological point of view, every society must be analyzed independently to determine the extent to which a distinction between religious and secular power is meaningful or valid in each case. The anthropological perspective on religion—as on other major sociocultural topics—is fundamentally comparative and concerned with the varying roles of religious beliefs and practices in societies throughout the world and throughout human existence.

Defining Religion

Because of the close association between power and the sacred, it is frequently difficult to establish a boundary between the religious and the political spheres. Sometimes, in fact, it is difficult even to distinguish these realms from social interactions in general. Anthropological definitions of religion have, therefore, ranged widely. For the purposes of this text, let us define *religion* as the system of social interactions consisting of those beliefs and activities that order human life by re-

lating humans to spiritual beings and/or powers.

The study of religion in anthropology parallels generally the history of anthropological theory and has, of course, both reflected and contributed to the intellectual climate of each period of thought. There have been, as Geertz (1968b) notes, four basic approaches to the study of religion. The evolutionist approach, represented by Tylor and Frazer, among others, tended to view all human practices, including those of religion, as stages in a historic continuum. In this view, the practices of so-called "primitive" peoples were considered to be survivals of what our earliest ancestors had believed; our own "advanced" civilization was seen as representing the pinnacle of rationality and development.

In the psychological approach, whose primary spokesman was Freud, in his 1913 book *Totem and Taboo,* "primitive" religious practices and beliefs were seen as expressions of neurotic and even psychotic impulses. Freud believed that well-adjusted individuals were able, through "normal" growth processes, to move beyond such fantasy/obsession stages, while neurotics and "savages" continued to act them out. Both of these early approaches —evolutionist and psychological—focused on such "exotic" practices as magic, faith-healing, and belief in many spirits and gods, and examined them more on an individual case than on a cross-cultural basis.

With the advent of the sociological approach most clearly expressed by Emile Durkheim, the focus shifted to a comparative analysis of the role of religion in human life. Religion was seen both as an expression of the cultural whole and its world view on the one hand, and as a mediator in the individual's relationship to his or her society on the other. This orientation is still very much with us and has influenced much of the research and analysis of religion in the twentieth century. In recent years it has been supplemented by the symbolic approach, best exemplified in the theorizing of Lévi-Strauss, on the one hand, and of Geertz on the other. Religion, one of the sets of symbols used in human societies, provides the conceptual model of reality within which the members of society find meaning.

Over the years, each of these four conceptual orientations—evolutionist, psychological, sociological, and symbolic—has given rise to many contributions as well as to numerous studies that combine and synthesize them. Each orientation has its uses even today, but no one provides a total framework within which to discuss the phenomenon of religion. The discussion that follows will not, therefore, adhere exclusively to any one of these viewpoints, but will provide an overview of anthropological approaches to the religious aspect of human existence.

Belief, Ritual, and Religious Experience

Anthropological studies of religion have tended to focus on one or the other of two major components: belief and ritual. Lewis (1971, p. 11) points out that there is a third significant component—spiritual experience—that has been ignored in most studies, probably because it is more an individualized than a communal/social aspect of religion. These three components or, as Lewis calls them, "cornerstones of religion" are the subject of this section.

Belief

The term *belief* refers to statements that are generally held to be true by the members of a given society. Religious beliefs differ from other types of belief in their assertions about supernatural powers or forces. Two different kinds of supernatural forces have been distinguished by anthropologists: *mana* and *animism. Mana,* a Polynesian term, refers to any power that increases one's natural abilities and thereby allows one to perform otherwise impossible tasks and feats. The Dobuans of Eastern New Guinea, for example, believe that *mana* brought on by various charms and incantations may cause crops to grow, enemies to suffer, and evil spells to be averted.

Animism refers to belief in many spirit beings. These spirits have personalities and, like human beings, desires and purposes of their own. They also are thought to have supernatural powers that enable them to accomplish what they want to do. The people of the Zuñi Pueblo recognize well over a hundred male and female spirit beings who exercise dominion over specific aspects of existence—rain, corn, and so on. Certain spirits, or *kachinas,* have identifying characteristics and are represented among the Pueblo by a carved and adorned wooden figurine and, in various ceremonies, by a human wearing an appropriate headdress and costume.

These two types of supernatural powers—mana and animate spirits—are not incompatible. They may even exist together in the belief system of any given group. Perhaps anthropologists have tended to be attracted to the distinction between the two beliefs because of a Western cultural dichotomy between luck, which can be seen as a kind of manalike view of the supernatural, and divine intervention, which, objectively viewed, is a belief in animism. At any rate, both beliefs rely on supernatural intervention for purposes of assisting human beings, and both can be considered religious beliefs as opposed to nonreligious ones.

A secondary distinction between animism and theism—belief in a god or gods—is frequently made also. *Monotheism* refers to religious systems characterized by belief in one god. However, in several monotheistic systems—including Islam, and Catholicism,

This carved wooden figure represents an "ogre" *kachina,* or spirit being of the Hopi Indians. During ceremonies, a man dressed in this costume, mask, and headdress impersonates this *kachina,* one of many in the Hopi pantheon. (Dr. Georg Gerster, Rapho/Photo Researchers)

among other Christian groups—spiritual beings in addition to an omnipotent god may be included in the belief system (Mohammed in the former instance, and Jesus, Joseph, Mary, and the saints in the latter). Only one deity is conceptualized as the supreme being, however. *Polytheism* refers to religious systems characterized by belief in plural, more or less equally powerful gods. Polytheistic systems also include a number of other spirit powers of lesser potency. Although animism also acknowledges the existence of many spirit powers, unlike polytheism, no single one is considered superior to the others in any but a restricted manner. For example, the Toba of Argentina identify powerful spirit beings who are found on the earth, in the heavens, and in the waters deep below the earth. Each of these may be considered powerful for certain purposes, but no one is inherently supreme or superior over the others.

One might think that the belief gap between monotheism and polytheism would be so vast as to be unbridgeable, but this is not the case. Polytheistic systems have little difficulty in adding yet another deity, including a more powerful one, to their well-populated pantheons. This fact has aided the acceptance of Christianity and Islam when they were introduced to native populations by missionaries. Polytheistic deities and animistic practices may persist in such societies on a folk level alongside of the rituals associated with belief in one supreme being.

An issue that has fascinated anthropologists over the years concerns the extent to which primitive beliefs may be comparable with or inherently different from the beliefs of Western, technologically oriented societies. Is belief in a chemical formula for, let us say, fertilizer, significantly different from belief in a formula of words to make yams grow? Is chemotherapy more efficacious than a medicine bundle, or psychoanalysis than a sweat lodge? Westerners generally assume that the one is based on "scientific" knowledge, whereas the other depends on unproven assumptions about nature. However, the differences may not depend so much on knowledge in a factual sense as on the trust of the society's membership in the authority behind each kind of belief. Like all other beliefs and knowledge, religious beliefs depend for their legitimacy and ultimate value upon the social support accorded them:

In June, when rain is needed for the corn . . . the series of [priestly] retreats begins. . . . All Zuñi awaits the granting of rain during these days, and priests blessed with rain are greeted and thanked by everyone upon the street after their retreat is ended. They have blessed their people with more than rain. (Benedict, 1934/1948, pp. 60–61)

Beliefs that would seem strange in one cultural context are perfectly logical and convincing in another. Non-Zuñi Americans cannot accept that a ceremonial withdrawal by a group of men could bring rain. But the Zuñi would be surprised to learn that a present-day cloud-seeding plane could have an effect on precipitation.

Given the enormous variance of human beliefs, early attempts to order them in an evolutionary hierarchy from the most "primitive" forms of animism to the "highest" forms of monotheism have little value for comparative purposes. Beliefs and doubts probably exist in more or less equal amounts in all cultural systems. Whether the object of belief is a supreme being or a forest spirit makes little difference as far as the belief itself and its role in its cultural context are concerned.

Ritual

Because beliefs are highly subjective, there is a tendency for them to be explained differently even by individuals within the same culture. For this reason, it is somewhat difficult to obtain comparable data from one culture to another. Rather than attempt to compare beliefs per se, anthropologists have turned increasingly to the study of ritual.

Ritual is the demonstration of religious belief through performance of specific acts by members of a society. It is possible to describe and analyze the observable activities that con-

stitute rituals. Leach (1968) points out that rituals are aesthetic and communicative acts, conveying messages about a society's value system to its members. In studying rituals, anthropologists are able to compare standardized activities in related contexts from one culture to another, and to analyze in what ways the messages communicated are similar or different.

There is always some question about how the messages of ritual are to be interpreted. Do they "mean what the actors say they mean?" (Leach, 1968, p. 525). Or must the anthropologist interpret the hidden content of the ritual, meanings that the actors may ignore on a conscious level but may act upon unconsciously? This problem was raised early in this book, and it is particularly relevant here. A thorough study of any given ritual would have to take both its stated and latent meanings into consideration. It would weigh the one against the other and judge in what ways the two meanings are complementary and in what ways divergent, as well as determine how both fit, like pieces of a puzzle, into the cultural context.

Leach (1968) argues that it is the status of the actor that is at stake in ritual. The Zuñi priests whose retreat produces rain not only validate the beliefs of their society but secure their own position within it. But if a ritual is not effective—if it does not serve its designated purpose—the person who has performed the ritual is thought to have "lost his touch." He or she is considered for one reason or another to be lacking in power vis-à-vis the spiritual world, and consequently loses prestige and power in the mundane world as well. Ritual performers who have notable success may also use their power to enhance their prestige. In this way, then, ritual also affects the status of the actor. Successful rituals are successful in two ways: they reinforce the society's beliefs, and they raise the status of their performers (Leach, 1968, pp. 525–526). Rituals may occur for the precise purpose of exalting the status of the performer. In some societies, they may be set up to challenge or demean an individual. And sometimes, as in the *potlatch* of the Indians of the Northwest Coast, rituals accomplish both purposes at the same time. In this situation, the giver of the *potlatch* simultaneously raises his status and publicly shames his rivals.

The different types of rituals described and studied by anthropologists will be the subject of a subsequent section of this chapter.

Religious Experience

As we have already observed, anthropological studies have concentrated on belief and ritual, largely ignoring the individual element of religious experience. But in recent years, a few anthropologists have begun to call attention to actual experiences of the supernatural as data in their own right (Lewis, 1971).

On the individual level, there are a number of different kinds of spiritual experiences. At

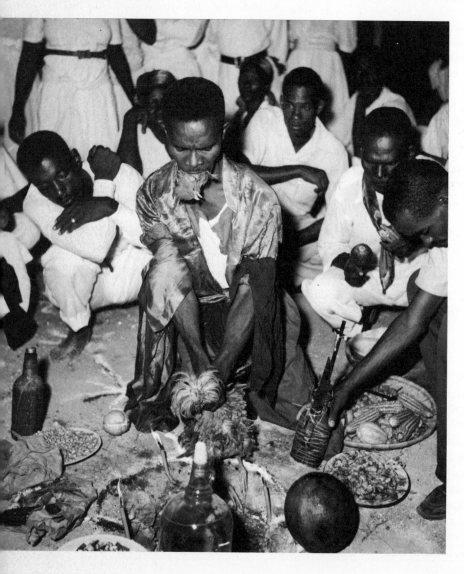

A voodo celebrant in Haiti, possessed by a *loa* or spirit, has bitten off the head of a live chicken. Ceremonial foods are arranged around a central pit, and a participant *(lower right)* holds an aggregation of ritual objects, including knife, fork, and crucifix, secured to a flask. (Odette Mennesson-Rigaud, Photo Researchers)

one extreme are feelings of peace and of being at one with the universe that may come from such activities as participation in a ritual or meditation. At the other extreme are frenzied manifestations, often interpreted as "possession" by some supernatural force. In between lies a whole range of experiences—dreams, trance, speaking in tongues, auditory and visual hallucinations, and so on. The extent to which spiritual experiences may be induced is highly variable. Such experiences have been found to follow activities such as prolonged solitude, meditation, community participation, different kinds of rhythmic and/or other musical stimulation, hypnosis, fasting, self-mutilation, and drug taking. Some of these manifestations and stimuli were mentioned previously in our discussion of altered states of consciousness. It should be noted that whether such experiences are interpreted as being religious or supernatural manifestations, or as something else entirely (as mental illness, for example), is dependent upon the cultural context in which they occur and the individual involved.

Psychological and Sociological Explanations of Religion

Generally, particular religious beliefs and practices have been studied from the point of view of either psychological or sociological theory, or some combination of the two. Freud and Jung provided the theoretical orientations for the psychological approaches to religion, while Durkheim and Radcliffe-Brown contributed the sociological orientations.

Freud, impressed with the ethnographic material accumulating in his day, held that the religious practices of primitive cultures were symbolic reenactments of unconscious psychological drives. In particular, he articulated the idea that *totemism*—the veneration of an animal or animal spirit alleged to be an original group ancestor—was a symbolic vestige of the oedipal drive to do away with the father. Freud later explained religion as an "illusion" that both gives the individual a feeling of control over the forces of nature, and orders interpersonal relationships within the society, thereby holding the society together. The techniques used to influence or placate supernatural forces are of the same order as those learned by children to avoid offending their parents and thus to guarantee their enduring good graces. What Freud did not realize was that, even at the time of his earliest theorizing on the subject of religion, anthropologists had already moved away from the evolutionist approach on which his interpretations largely depended. Nevertheless, his essential notions that religious practices can be seen as expressions of the unconscious mind, and that rituals and beliefs may be wish-fulfillment elements arising from unconscious or hidden desires have contributed useful interpretive concepts.

Jung, who had originally worked with Freud on some of the ethnographic material that led to *Totem and Taboo*, later returned to the subject (Kardiner & Preble, 1961, pp. 232–233). He believed that there were prototypes or themes which appear in all cultures of the world. He saw widespread phenomena such as fertility rites or flood myths as arising from universal realities impressed on the human mind (Geertz, 1968, p. 401). Jung's explanation has certainly not been the last word on the subject of recurrent cultural phenomena, which continues to interest anthropologists. However, emphasis has shifted from the attempt to generalize universal tendencies, to the effort to identify and compare distinctions.

Durkheim's *The Elementary Forms of the Re-*

ligious Life (1912) was written at about the same time as Freud's work and was influenced by much of the same evolutionist anthropological source material. Durkheim felt that religion provided the essential ingredient that allowed society to cohere. He distinguished between the sacred and the profane, the former constituting the essential aspect of religious assertion, which had always to be separated from the nonreligious human attitudes characterized as profane (Geertz, 1968, p. 402; Kardiner & Preble, 1961, p. 127). Durkheim showed that beliefs transform things or activities that would otherwise be profane into objects or acts that are considered sacred.

Radcliffe-Brown, on the other hand, looked at the functions of religion for society as a whole. He held that what was of practical importance to a society became symbolized in ritual or as sacred objects. He focused on the content of sacred symbols and their role for members of a society. In his view, there would be a neat "fit" between the practical imperatives facing a society and its religious practices.

More recently, anthropologists have turned from strictly psychological and sociological arguments to what Geertz (1968) calls the "semantic" study of religion. There is new interest in the many levels of meaning in religious symbolism and in the variety of expressions given to concepts of the supernatural. In this approach, both primitive and modern religions are viewed as "systems of ideas about the ultimate shape and substance of reality" (Geertz, 1968, p. 406).

Whatever else religion does, it relates a view of the ultimate nature of reality to a set of ideas of how man is well advised, even obligated, to live. Religion tunes human actions to a view of the cosmic order and projects images of cosmic order onto the plane of human existence. (Geertz, 1968, p. 406)

Seen this way, the role of religion is to make a society's designs for living congruent with adaptation to reality. Geertz adds that religion becomes "emotionally convincing" and receives its expression through sacred symbols. It is to this consideration of religion—a system of symbols interpreting reality and making it livable for a society—that we now turn.

Sacred Symbols That Order Human Experience

Two lines that intersect, a six-pointed star, a crescent, a many-armed figure of a dancing woman, a circle bisected by a single wavy line—all are familiar symbols of the world's major religions. But only those symbols that pertain to the particular religion to which we ourselves adhere have the power to move us. As for the symbols of someone else's religion, they are usually no more meaningful to us than are any of the secular symbols—letters, numbers, dollar signs—with which we deal every day. We do, nevertheless, have some comprehension of the significance of many of these religious symbols. We understand that on some level they penetrate the experience of their respective believers; we have, through acquaintance with various works of art and literature from their cultures, gained some inkling of the contexts in which they function. Social anthropologists seek to bring equal comprehension to the less known sacred symbols of the world's cultures—a wooden figure bristling with iron nails from the Congo, a wooden antelope head from West Africa, a carved representation of various animals stacked one atop the other from British Columbia, a charcoal drawing of spears hurling toward huge beasts from a cave in Spain, human sacrifice of the Aztecs, or a many-hued feathered cape from Peru.

It should be clear from intimacy with the

symbols of our own religious traditions that symbols everywhere are embued with meaning. A feathered serpent or a wafer, a sacred circle or a sacred cow all contain many meanings. However such symbols are used—acted out or handled in ceremonies, narrated as myth, reproduced as design—they serve as key integrating elements for the cultures in which they occur. Study of sacred symbols often points the way for our understanding of what makes a given culture cohere. For each culture, then, sacred symbols must be analyzed to identify their character, to learn their meanings for members of the society, and to reveal the deeper messages that give coherence and direction to that culture.

Religion attempts to interpret the inexplicable—dreams, suffering, death, human treachery, natural disasters, and so on. It helps adjust peoples' understanding of the-way-things-are to the-way-we-would-like-things-to-be (Geertz, 1970, p. 325). Sacred symbols such as God and the devil acknowledge the existence of good and evil, and the conflict between them. Most usually, Geertz points out, "the reality of evil is accepted and characterized positively, and an attitude toward it—resignation, active opposition, hedonistic escape, self-recrimination and repentance, or a humble plea for mercy—is enjoined as reasonable and proper" (1970, p. 329). The Judeo-Christian tradition certainly offers examples of all of these responses in the face of adversity.

According to Geertz, religious symbols work by inducing responses in the worshipper (1966, p. 4). These responses take form as moods and as what Geertz called *motivation,* the inclination to perform certain acts and experience certain feelings in particular situations (1966, p. 10). Moods and motivations associated with sacred symbols vary from culture to culture. Motivations induced by religious symbols vary widely, too, and may range from charitable giving to self-mutilation.

However, Geertz has also pointed out that sacred symbols not only provide an integrative role in social life but can also produce conflict and disruption. In his classic study, *The Religion of Java* (1960), Geertz isolated three major "religious variants" (based on animism, Islam, and Hinduism), showing that all three are found in one social system, that each variant generates antagonism between its followers and members who adhere to another variant, and that these conflicts tend to be minimized and even turned to positive social uses in the society concerned. Thus, even in their disruption, sacred symbols can be made to serve positive ends. But the disruptive nature of conflicting religious ideas is not always satisfactorily resolved in a social group. Failure to resolve religious differences can cause tension and stress among the members of a society. History offers numerous examples of conflict due to religious differences.

Religious Specialists

If symbols derive their power from the meanings attached to them, their power commingles with the powers of the religious practitioners who manipulate the symbols. Four categories of religious specialist—shamans, priests, prophets, and sorcerers—are usually distinguished by anthropologists. Distinctions among them are based on such factors as the ways in which they acquire authority; the kinds of rituals they perform; the purposes for which rituals are performed; and the nature of the interactions between the religious leader and other members of the society.

Shamans

Shamans are religious specialists whose primary function is healing the sick and pro-

Assurini Indian shamans, in the state of Para, Brazil, perform a healing ceremony over a sick baby cradled in the arms of the mother, who lies in a hammock. A curing ceremony may last for several days and comprise a variety of different rites; shown here is the ritual extraction of the disease-causing substance from the patient's body. (Jacques Jangoux, Peter Arnold Photo Archives)

tecting the community from harm. We class these practitioners as religious because their healing proceeds by supernatural intervention. In our own society at present, the healing function does not usually have supernatural components, except in those religious groups that stress spiritual healing. Shamanism is particularly identified with the circumpolar cultures of Siberia, Alaska, and Canada, but it is a worldwide status, found widely among aboriginal populations in North and South America, in parts of Africa, and in many other locales throughout the world. Societies with a hunting-and-gathering economy are most likely to have shamans as their religious leaders.

Among the Tungus of Siberia, the word *shaman* refers specifically to an individual who has learned healing techniques through direct communication with spirits. In most societies where they are found, shamans generally receive the call to power in dreams and visions, through which they have direct contact with supernatural beings. The skills, perhaps literally the "tricks of the trade," may be revealed in such dreams. But a potential shaman may also be recruited or recognized by an experienced practitioner, often during childhood; the older individual or, on occasion, group of individuals will teach the novice the necessary skills. In Siberia, the call to practice was usually resisted by the individual for as long as possible, and was then heeded only reluctantly. In North America, a vision revealing the gift of healing was usually actively sought, often by solitude and fasting and, in the Plains area, through self-mutilation as well. In Central and South America, such a vision was frequently neither sought after nor avoided, but accepted if it occurred.

Shamans derive power from their ability to communicate directly with the supernatural. Although they may resort to various manipulations and tricks, it is the community's wholehearted belief in and dependence on their spiritual connections that maintain their authority. The rites performed by shamans, while directed toward individual ends, are often public, performed before audiences ranging from a few close relatives and friends of the ill person to an entire village. Shamans conduct ceremonies on an ad hoc basis, whenever someone is ill and requests their services (Lessa & Vogt, 1965, pp. 451–452).

Thus, their work is generally directed toward the satisfaction of individual needs.

Priests

Unlike shamans, *priests* are religious specialists associated with organized churches and are characteristically found in more formally structured societies throughout the world. They receive extensive training, at the conclusion of which they are ordained and legitimated in their offices through formal ceremonies. The members of a priesthood are generally a clearly ranked hierarchy. Priesthood is often hereditary within a family, lineage, or social class. In some cases, however, an individual has a vision or in some other way experiences a "calling" to enter the priesthood. In a number of Catholic communities, a family may select one of its sons at

Novices praying in Bangkok, Thailand. These young boys spend years receiving instruction before becoming Buddhist monks (priests). (Rene Burri, Magnum)

an early age and, in effect, apprentice him to a religious order for his education, with a future career as a priest in view. However recruited, the novice must be taught a substantial body of knowledge concerning traditional beliefs and intricate ceremonials. In religious systems that have a priesthood, these leaders serve as mediators between the people and the supernatural being or beings. Often they are more concerned with the general welfare of the community than with the problems of the individual; in most such societies, there are usually other practitioners of the healing arts who are concerned with the problems of the individual. The other religious leaders discussed in this section characteristically practice as individuals, only rarely participating in group rites and more usually in competition with other practitioners of the same category. Priests, on the other hand, are in constant communication with one another for the good of the community, frequently conducting ceremonies jointly or debating together to resolve difficult issues. The ceremonies presided over by priests frequently take place on a calendric basis, being repeated annually. These ceremonies often reflect the agricultural basis of the society's economy. Our word *ceremony,* in fact, is derived from the name of the ancient Roman goddess of agriculture, Ceres.

Prophets

Like shamans, *prophets* receive visions and communicate directly with supernatural powers on an individual basis. The message contained in the vision is the only preparation required. The Biblical prophetic writings generally, and Isaiah and Jeremiah in particular, are rich in descriptions of prophetic visions. Prophets generally criticize the existing social order and point the way to a better way of life. As prophets gain popularity with their public and develop a following, they sometimes become more priestly than prophetic in function, developing rituals and ceremonies to so-

lidify their authority and to keep followers together in a systematic way. Jesus, for example, was a prophet, not a priest. As the sect based on his teachings expanded, his followers added ceremonial structure to the teachings and eventually founded a priesthood. Especially because the messages of prophets are often conspicuously in opposition to the existing authorities, the tendency to create an alternative power structure becomes quasipolitical in nature. Prophets are therefore prime candidates to lead revitalization movements.

Sorcerers

Sorcerers are religious specialists who can cause harm and kill enemies. Sorcery is often referred to as witchcraft, particularly when evil or harm is the presumed intent or outcome. From the sorcerers' point of view, they also serve community interests since they eliminate the evil that they find therein. They are often required to use their powers against evils brought on by other sorcerers, and are thus in direct competition with one another. Sorcerers are found in societies with varying economic bases. They may receive their calling and skills in a vision; they may also be recognized as powerful individuals by members of their society as a result of a (perhaps inadvertent) demonstration of their power. Lévi-Strauss recounts how one Zuñi found himself both accused and hailed as a sorcerer:

A twelve-year-old girl was stricken with a nervous seizure directly after an adolescent boy had seized her hands. The youth was accused of sorcery [, but although] he denied having any knowledge of occult power [he was not believed. He then] improvised a tale explaining the circumstances by which he had been initiated into sorcery. He said he had received two substances . . . one which drove girls insane and another which cured them. . . . Having been ordered to produce his medicines, he [developed] a complicated ritual [using two roots, simulating] a trance after taking one . . . and after taking the other [pretending] to return to his normal state.

Then he administered the remedy to the sick girl and declared her cured. (Lévi-Strauss, 1963, p. 166)

Despite the girl's apparent recovery, her relatives continued to accuse the lad. In self-defense he created an elaborate story of a family tradition in the magic arts, from which he had inherited the ability to assume the form of a cat and kill his victims. When he claimed that his powers derived from certain magical plumes, he was asked to produce them in evidence. After making up numerous stories about why they could not be located, he finally succeeded in finding an old feather in the plaster of the walls of his home. Then he was required to explain how it was used, which he did with much imaginative invention, concluding his narrative with a lament over the loss of his supernatural powers.

As Lévi-Strauss points out, the significance of this episode lies in the desire of the community to confirm its belief in sorcery as the cause of the girl's illness. The experience itself turned the youth into a sorcerer, at least for the time being. As this episode clearly demonstrates, belief in sorcery is the essential element in the efficacy of sorcery. Belief is, likewise, the key to the effectiveness of all types of religious leaders. Lévi-Strauss distinguishes three areas of belief: the sorcerer's belief in his or her techniques; the victim's belief in the sorcerer's power; the community's belief in the power of sorcery.

The four types of religious leadership just defined are not necessarily vested in separate individuals. These categories are often more descriptive of organization, legitimation, and function than of individuals. There is often an overlap in functions, especially between priests and prophets, priests and shamans, shamans and sorcerers. In a given society, the distinctions between functions may blur so that an individual religious leader may have multiple roles. Among the Toba, for example,

shamans can and frequently do practice sorcery; nor are shamans the only category of healers. These are, then, not so much separate individuals as separate roles or activities that are performed. Religious leaders manipulate key symbols for purposes of gaining advantage, and the control of spiritual power is the essential leadership found in Toba society, however that power may be expressed.

We should note that the manipulation of sacred symbols and of magic can prove dangerous for the practitioner. If harm befalls the community or an individual (as demonstrated in the Zuñi sorcery episode above), the local shaman can be held accountable. If the countermeasures taken do not work, the practitioner may be accused of practicing negative magic on the side, or be thought to have lost power either to supernatural beings or to a more powerful sorcerer.

Some Rituals and Their Uses

Having considered sacred symbols and the practitioners who manipulate them, we turn now to a consideration of the rituals in which those symbols find their uses. The separate acts that, together, comprise a ritual are rites, and so ritual may be considered an aggregation or system of rites. Turner emphasizes that the notion of drama is inherent in ritual: "Both in its plot and its symbolism, a ritual is an epitome of the wider and spontaneous social process in which it is embodied and which ideally it controls" (1968, pp. 273–274).

Most of the anthropological writing about rituals concerns their relation to social structure. We have seen that rituals are, in Leach's view, both aesthetic and communicative acts and that they serve to ratify the values of the society. Vogt (1965), for example, describes the ceremonial meal in Zinacantan in southern Mexico, and shows how it replicates the social structure of the community. Ordinarily, food is served in bowls placed on the floor, but on ritual occasions a special "meal on a table" is served. The table must be a rectangular wooden one oriented on an east-west axis and covered with a pink-and-white striped hand-woven cotton cloth. *Posh,* a native alcoholic beverage, is drunk in a particular way three times during the course of the meal. The bottle containing the drink is placed at the east end of the table, at which the highest ranked male sits. The other participants—as few as four or five in a family ritual meal or more than 60 at the annual community-level Fiesta of San Sebastian—are arranged in descending order of rank from the head to the opposite (or west end) of the table. The prescribed foods are tortillas, chicken in broth, coffee, and special bread. A specific ritual sequence of drinking, toasting, eating, and hand-washing activities must be observed.

The settlement pattern of the Zinacantecos, modern-day descendants of the Mayans, spreads outward from the ceremonial center in a densely populated valley to 11 outlying hamlets. Each individual is in turn a member of a patrilocal extended family occupying a house compound; a *sna* consisting of one or more localized patrilineages; a water hole group composed of two or more *snas;* the hamlet; Zinacantan as a whole. Each unit in the social order, from the patrilineages to the hamlet and community center, has prescribed ceremonies. At the household level there are curing and new house dedication ceremonies. There are various calendar-based land right ceremonies at the *sna* and water hole levels. At the hamlet level there are two annual ceremonies, for the New Year and the End of the Year. Finally, there is the annual San Sebastian celebration held in the community center for all of Zinacantan.

The Zinacantecos have a religious hierarchy of 55 ranked positions grouped into a four-level structure. By living for a year in the ceremonial center of the community and engaging in specific rituals at significant personal expense, a man can rise, one step at a time, to the next higher rank. After a year of service, he returns to his hamlet to farm and accumulate enough wealth to attempt the next higher level until, at the end of the process, he attains the uppermost level. An additional religious hierarchy consists of from 100 to 150 shamans, ranked in order of seniority from the time they received their calling.

Vogt's study showed how the rules that apply to one aspect of religion—in this case, a single ritual meal—relate to structural levels in the society, and it opened up new ways of analyzing selected aspects of ritual.

Ancestor Worship

Ancestor worship is a constellation of religious beliefs and rituals found in horticultural and agricultural societies where a kin group controls land rights and usage. Ancestor worship serves as the focus of social relations among the living and reinforces the corporate kin group structure. The kin group is believed to have perpetual existence. Strong generation-to-generation continuity results from the belief that deceased forbears "are regarded as fully functioning members of their kin groups," constantly interacting with their living descendants. (Cohen, 1971, p. 207). The living members of the society are responsible for maintaining continuity with the traditions of the past. The ancestors have the responsibility to oversee their descendants, punishing neglectful behavior and rewarding proper respect for traditions and obligations. Since living relatives such as fathers and uncles are potential ancestors, they must be accorded a high measure of respect in life as well as being venerated after death.

In a study of ancestor worship among the Tallensi of Ghana (formerly the Gold Coast), Fortes has shown how the practice of deifying the spirits of the deceased validates the social order. Despite great fondness between parents and children, there is an avoidance taboo between a father and his eldest son. The son must not wear his father's clothes, use his weapons, nor even look into his granary. As Fortes explains, "breach of the taboos would be an affront to the father's soul and destiny. For a man's soul is in his granary and his vitality is in his garments and weapons because they are covered with the sweat and dirt of his body" (1971, p. 214). When a man dies, rituals provide for the two transitions that must take place. First, the deceased must be officially "transformed from a living person into an ancestor," and secondly, the eldest son must be formally "invested with his father's status." The first-born son is "responsible for his father's mortuary and funeral rites. . . . If he delays . . . the ancestors will take offense and he will suffer" (1971, p. 216). This son offers a libation at all of the ancestor shrines that had been in his father's care, informing them of his death. Next there is a divination session to determine which ancestor had caused the death, and why; death is never considered "natural." Lastly, the son becomes "the main actor in rites which free him to do those things which were forbidden to him in his father's lifetime. . . . No display of grief is permitted in these rites, but strict silence is enjoined on the actors . . . because the dead is deemed to be participating with them and would strike down anyone who broke the ritual silence" (1971, p. 216).

The son, formerly forbidden to share food or drink with his father, in these silent rites now pantomimes doing so, freeing him from the previous taboo. Various offerings are made to the deceased father during the funeral rites. These are accompanied by a chant calling on the deceased by name to accept the offerings "in order that you may reach and join your father and forefathers and let health, peace, childbearing, fertility of fields and livestock now prevail" (1971, p. 216). Thus,

the close relationship between kinship systems and belief systems is most clearly demonstrated in ancestor worship.

Economic Uses of Ritual

Although Fortes emphasized the sociological implications of ancestor worship in maintaining the continuity of the social order, the actors in the rituals are shown to be concerned not only with their places in life as well as in the afterworld but also with the overall economic welfare of the community. Everywhere, the sustenance of the social group is an enormously important issue, and as such is very often the explicit subject of ritual. Rappaport (1971) discusses the role of religious ritual in economic production, noting its practical application as a component of the adaptive strategies of a society for exploiting and regulating the environment. The Tsembaga Mareng of New Guinea are an egalitarian horticultural people, with no centralized political structure. Their predominantly vegetarian diet comes largely from gardens tended by women, who also care for and feed growing herds of pigs. Pigs keep residential areas clean and, allowed to root about in abandoned gardens, eat shoots and seedlings and keep the soil workable for second plantings. But domestic pigs are slaughtered only on ritual occasions—during warfare, illness, or in cases of injury or death, and during the pig festival—when they are distributed to specific individuals according to the occasion, and are consumed in specified quantities. Consequently, the pig population grows, slowly but steadily, until the care and feeding of the animals becomes a major burden on the Tsembaga women, and pigs invading other people's gardens becomes a major source of friction within the group.

The Tsembaga ritual cycle is noncalendric. A description of the ritual cycle could well start with the outbreak of hostilities between two groups from adjacent territories, an event that can be initiated by any man who puts together an alliance of kin:

Each side performs certain rituals which place the opposing side in the formal category of "enemy." A number of [food] taboos prevail while hostilities continue. . . . Fighting could continue sporadically for weeks. Occasionally it terminated in the rout of one of the antagonistic groups. . . . [With the termination of hostilities a group which has not been driven off its territory performs a ritual called "planting the *rumbim,* a special tree. During this ceremony the ancestors are addressed:] We thank you for helping us. . . . We will kill pigs for you now, but they are few. In the future, when we have many pigs, we shall again give you pork and uproot the *rumbim* and stage a *kaiko* (pig festival). (Rappaport, 1971, pp. 231–232)

At the first postwar ritual, many pigs are slaughtered, cooked, and offered to the ancestors. Most of these pigs are distributed to allies who assisted in the fight, although some are eaten by the local group. Some taboos are removed, but because debts to allies and ancestors still remain, certain taboos persist during the period from the planting to the uprooting of the *rumbim,* a ritual plant, including a useful prohibition against becoming involved in another war. The *rumbim* can be uprooted only when there are enough pigs to hold a pig festival. At the start of the festival, a fifth or more of the total pig herd is slaughtered, much of the meat being distributed to former allies. Periodic dances and food distributions continue for about a year, culminating in a massive pig sacrifice:

The pork yielded by the Tsembaga slaughter was estimated to weigh between 7,000 and 8,500 pounds, of which between 4,500 to 6,000 pounds were distributed to members of other local groups in 163 separate presentations. An estimated 2,000 to 3,000 people in 17 local groups were the beneficiaries of the redistribution. (Rappaport, 1971, p. 234)

When the pig festival is finally over, the pig population has been reduced to only very young individuals and numbers about a third of its previous size. All taboos are removed, and the cycle can begin again. As the Tsembaga move through this ritual cycle, the regulation of meat production and distribution is intertwined with kinship obligations and relationships, including the contracting of both sexual liaisons and marriage arrangements (Cohen, 1971, pp. 226–227). Thus, the functions of ritual are not limited to ideological considerations but also serve an economic purpose, as is mostly clearly evident in this example from New Guinea.

Divination and Rituals of Affliction

Divination, the manipulation of the supernatural to discover concealed information, is a particular category of ritual that functions to maintain the social order. In various cultures, divination techniques may be practiced by sorcerers, shamans, or other individuals. The ultimate goal of the procedures, which vary in their details, is always to discover and remove the cause of an existing social disorder. Divination is often required in cases of individual affliction such as illness, death, and other life crises. It may also be required for "the corroboration of a marriage-choice and in individual or collective moves involving some change in social alignments or, perhaps, economic condition; and in situations of loss, calamity, or unresolved conflict, whether on a personal or a much larger scale" (Park, 1967, p. 234). Wherever divination is resorted to, members of the society know the appropriate occasions of its use. Among the Yoruba, for example, divination is required for the selection of a site for a new house. This method gives community sanction to the decision, which otherwise might be held to reflect the particular interest of one individual in locating closer to or further away from others (Park, 1967).

Park points out that the omission of divina-

Divination is a widespread practice that takes many forms. This pregnant woman in the Usambara Mountains of Tanzania has asked the *magama* whether she will have a girl or a boy. The *magama* examines a hen, which the woman held in her left hand and tapped with her right. He finds a notch in the feathers under the left wing, but not under the right; his client will have a girl. (Tom Pix, Peter Arnold)

tion in a situation that clearly calls for it might well result in difficulties for the person or group who acted without it. Divination gives legitimacy to acts performed following the divination, and relieves anxiety by pinpointing a cause and prescribing counteractive measures. But it is more than a primitive form of group therapy. It is analogous also to our judicial process, in that its outcome may be a determination of guilt and provision for redress to the satisfaction of the injured party. Turner (1968) points out that "divination and redressive ritual are stages in a single process that is peculiarly sensitive to changes, and especially breakages, in the network of existing social relations" (p. 26).

Several distinct stages are involved in divination: the recognition of a problem; the decision to appeal to divination; the divination ritual itself; perhaps an additional ritual to confirm the verdict; and the appropriate redressive ritual. Among the Ndembu of Northern Rhodesia, where social unity is highly

prized, members of a corporate kin group are reluctant to call on a diviner because this would publicly expose the frictions that are a frequent and inevitable consequence of strong social emphasis on male-dominated hunting activities in a matrilineal, matrilocal society. As social pressures build until one individual becomes literally ill, it becomes more important to cure the person than to persist in ignoring or denying friction within the family. At the point where we might call on the psychotherapist or the lawyer (depending on the manifestation), the Ndembu call in the diviner:

Once this first step is taken with full knowledge of what it may entail, Ndembu feel strongly induced to overcome their divisions and reaffirm their unity [despite] the risk, during this ritual sequence, of quarrels so violent that they may not be restrained. . . . Thus, the typical development of a ritual sequence is from the expression of a wish to cure a patient and redress breaches in the social structure, through exposure of hidden animosities, to the renewal of social bonds in the course of a protracted ritual full of symbolism. . . . Diviners give public utterance to what just could not be said under ordinary circumstances. (Turner, 1968, p. 272)

The result of Ndembu divination is the performance of a ritual of affliction to pacify or to remove the ancestor spirits that are believed to have brought the misfortune or illness (Turner, 1962, p. 251). The victim is, of course, the living kin of those ancestor spirits. A particular curative rite is prescribed for each distinctive manifestation of ancestral anger. Once cured, an individual may become a member of the healing cult for that ailment. Thus, the rituals of affliction serve the additional social purpose of providing a means by which individuals can compete for status. The example of Ndembu divination, then, provides an excellent summary for this section, since the ritual sequence involves restoration of the social fabric and ancestral involvement with living descendants, as well as having points of contact with the productive system.

Myth: The Search for Synthesis

Myth is the verbal rationale for religion, differing from other kinds of verbal material in having, in Kluckhohn's words, "the connotation of the sacred" (1942, p. 145). The relationship of myth to belief is clear: beliefs— those meanings held by the society to be true—are expressed through myth. As Turner (1968) explains, "myths relate how one state of affairs became another: how an unpeopled world became populated; how chaos became cosmos; how immortals became mortal; how the seasons came to replace a climate without seasons; how the original unity of mankind became a plurality of tribes or nations. . . ." (p. 576).

But the relationship between ritual and myth is more problematic, and has given rise to a chicken-or-egg type of discussion. Does ritual arise as a dramatization of myth? Or does ritual exist and myth arise, as Boas suggested, "from the desire to account for it?" (quoted in Kluckhohn, 1942). Evidence exists for both positions. Kluckhohn offers the Mohave and the Bushmen as examples of peoples with "many myths and very little ritual," whereas the Central Eskimo and other groups illustrate every aspect of myth through various rites. In some cultures, some myths are never enacted ritually; some rituals illustrate nonmythic content; some myths have real mythic referents, yet others have only vague mythological connections.

Among the Navaho, who had myths without associated rituals, both legends and rituals were alleged to have originated in dreams or visions, and "all ceremonial practice [was] justified by an accompanying myth" (Kluckhohn, 1942). The characteristic ceremony of the Navaho is devoted to healing. It is performed by a chanter who sings a ritual narrative, illustrating it in a drawing made by trickling colored sands through his fingers onto the prepared floor of a hogan. Each practitioner has his own chant or chants, usually learned through apprenticeship and validated through previous cures. The chants are not handed down in letter-perfect form, however. Navaho belief is extremely wary of exactitude and perfection, and every design, every narrative, must be left with an imperfection or gap, however minimal, to serve as a "spirit outlet" (Kluckhohn & Leighton, 1946).

Myth serves the important role of giving coherence and synthesis to a society's world view. The emphasis is not on myth as opposed to empirical truth but rather on myth as idealized construction that gives security in the face of the ambiguities and incongruities of life. As a Navaho informant told Clyde

Sand painting, an essential component of Navaho healing ceremonies, is restaged in significantly modified form for the photographer. In practice, the healing ceremony is performed inside of a hogan, and lasts for several days. Friends and relatives of the sick person may be present, but outside observers are unwelcome. The painting is created as the healer sings the appropriate chant and is destroyed before the ceremony is over. (Josef Muench Pictorial Photography)

Kluckhohn, "knowing a good story will protect your home and children and property. A myth is just like a big stone foundation—it lasts a long time" (1942).

Myth exists in all societies, serving the essential function of easing social interactions by supporting the world view that makes life tolerable. It should come as no surprise that the integration of ritual and social order described above for the people of Zinacantan is also paralleled by a supporting mythology. Inside a nearby extinct volcano, according to the Zinacantecos,

are a series of corrals, one full of jaguars, another full of coyotes, another full of ocelots, and still another full of smaller animals. . . . The total number [of animals] adds up to 7,600, the same as the population, for each Zinacanteco has . . . an animal spirit companion—a kind of wild animal alter ego, so to speak. . . . The ancestral gods [are believed] to live in their houses inside the mountain and take good care of the [animal spirits]. (Vogt, 1965, p. 608)

But if a Zinacanteco does something wrong, then the ancestral gods stop caring for his or her animal spirit. The unprotected animal alter ego may even get out of the corral and wander about in the forest, where it is likely to be injured. No matter what happens to the animal spirit, it is believed that its human counterpart will suffer the same fate.

Lessa (1965) has shown that myth does not always serve as an explanation of social life, since it can lose its synthesizing capability under the impact of culture contact and change. For example, the people of Ulithi occupy several islets in the Carolinian archipelago of Micronesia. A series of traditionally overlapping myths concerning origins of their world and people, and relationships between the islands of the region, supported a long ritual presentation of all turtles found in the atoll to the local king on the isle of Mogmog in a ceremony with both political and religious content. The turtles are clubbed by the king, and then butchered, roasted, eaten, and distributed, with members of certain lineages performing specific rites, and portions being given to certain lineages and people of non-Ulithi islands according to long-standing custom. For many years, however, the turtle ritual was not performed. A king who had taken office without complete ceremonial had "felt unauthorized to partake in the ritual killing of turtles." His successor, who had become nominally Christian, also feared displeasing ancestral gods and was concerned because of the lack of a traditional investiture. Upon his death, two individuals succeeded jointly to the kingship, one assuming the political and the other the ceremonial aspects of the position, and there was popular pressure for the revival of the turtle ritual. Although the myths supporting the ritual had long since lost their force, because Christianity had made significant inroads in Ulithi, the ritual, with some changes, was revived. Lessa concludes that "influences from Christianity have [removed] the fear of punishment should the turtle ritual be performed contrary to traditional religious procedures—specifically, where the man who wields the club has not

been invested as king according to pagan custom. The ritual has had and still retains some political significance reflecting Mogmog's authority" (Lessa, 1965, p. 185). Yet without its myth-derived sanctions, Lessa predicts that the turtle ritual is likely to "disappear under the impact of foreign political administration and changing political ideologies. Myth alone has not and cannot maintain a system in operation unless it is in turn energized by more basic institutions and beliefs" (p. 185). In this instance, then, we see how the original intricate link between ritual, myth, and politics became untangled as a result of changes in a social system due to external causes. Belief and myth went first, and ritual, somewhat changed, remains.

Supernatural Agents of Malevolence

Sorcery and witchcraft are the dark, malevolent side of belief. They do not constitute a religious system; although widespread, they are not found everywhere. But they fall into the study of religion in that their work is accomplished by paranormal, supernatural means. Countermeasures to sorcery and witchcraft, where possible, also involve resort to the supernatural.

Evans-Pritchard's classic study of witchcraft among the Azande of the Congo (1976) is an excellent explanation of supernatural malevolence:

In Zandeland sometimes an old granary collapses. There is nothing remarkable in this. Every Zande knows that termites eat the supports in the course of time and that even the hardest woods decay after years of service. Now a granary is the summerhouse of a Zande homestead and people sit beneath it in the heat of the day. . . . Consequently it may happen that there are people sitting beneath the granary when it collapses and they are injured. . . . Now why should these particular people have been sitting under this particular granary at the particular moment when it collapsed? (1976, p. 22)

The answer in our own society would be simply accident, but apparently there are no accidents among the Azande. There are always reasons why things happen as they do, and the role of witchcraft is to explain the inexplicable; otherwise there would be chaos.

If there had been no witchcraft, people would have been sitting under the granary and it would not have fallen on them, or it would have collapsed but the people would not have been sheltering under it at the time. Witchcraft explains the coincidence of these two happenings. (Evans-Pritchard, 1976, p. 23)

Similarly, among the Argentine Toba unfortunate events are sometimes said to be caused by sorcery. It was claimed, for example, that a certain woman had accidentally killed her son by sorcery. She had intended to kill her brother-in-law, but her son became ill instead and on his deathbed identified his own mother as the source of his illness. When the mother recognized her mistake, it was too late to correct it. She had performed the proper ritual and so death was inevitable, despite the mistaken identity of the intended victim and despite the actual intent of the sorcerer. She did not deny her son's accusation, but no action was taken against her by the immediate family since it was obviously a case of human error. The woman had, in fact, shown hostility toward her brother-in-law, and the accusation that she had killed her son by mistake was comprehensible to all in view of the family conflicts that were known to exist.

Sorcery or witchcraft, if they are to be counteracted at all, usually require using equally strong measures against the original agent. The victim may attempt to return the damage in some way to its initiator. In many cases, this requires divination or some other means to determine the source of the misfortunes.

Sorcery and witchcraft serve to control forces that are potentially disruptive and destructive to social order. In his study of witchcraft in Amatenango, in southern Mexico, Nash (1961b) shows the social process involved. A person or a person's family who has suffered severe illness, death, or other misfortune may suspect witchcraft. If resort to the usual curers does not ameliorate the situation, the person's suspicions may be confirmed. He or she will inquire of a curer to determine who might wish him harm; he might observe his neighbors to determine who might be a suspect. If the person finds a likely candidate and the misfortunes do not abate, he or she determines to kill the suspected witch. The community must then decide whether the killing was justified. This decision depends on whether the community believes the dead person to have been a witch, or whether the killer is believed to have indulged a personal grievance against an innocent member of the community.

The defense of the accused consists, first, of demonstrating that he or she had many misfortunes, undoubtedly the result of witchcraft. He attempts to show that the deceased was a "violator of norms, having acted in various socially inappropriate ways." Finally, the accused tries to convince the community that he is a respected, upstanding individual. The accused, having proved his case, is acquitted by community consensus. Accusations of witchcraft or sorcery that were unacceptable to community moral standards would undoubtedly cause further social disruption, setting off feuds and resulting in deaths held to be unjustifiable. It is more than likely that the alleged witch was someone against whom other members of the community also bore grudges, someone who had given a number of people cause to suspect his or her motives because of antisocial behavior. But lest one imagine that, encouraged by success, the acquitted killer would resort to such action on subsequent occasions, there are social sanctions against such liberties. In a community in which members interact daily, it is difficult to pretend to virtues or status that one does not, in fact, have (Nash, 1961b).

The question is often asked if supernatural malevolence actually occurs or if it is only imagined to occur. The answer seems to be that both may be true, and it is not always possible to determine whether supernaturally caused evils and cures are real or imagined. Belief is the key factor, whether in the efficacy of the sorcerer's malevolence or in the efficacy of the shaman's healing. Lévi-Strauss (1963) identified the combination of three elements, which he called the "shamanistic complex," that apply to shamanistic healing as well as to sorcery. As mentioned earlier, Lévi-Strauss believes that shamanistic healing depends first on the belief of the shaman himself in his calling and his powers. The second element is the belief of the afflicted person. The third source of belief is the community. Kluckhohn showed how these three beliefs interact and are reinforced in the case of a Navaho chanter:

If a Navaho gets a bad case of snow blindness and recovers after being sung over, his disposition to go to a singer in the event of a recurrence will be strongly reinforced. . . . Likewise, the reinforcement will be reciprocal—the singer's confidence in his powers will also be reinforced. Finally there will be some reinforcement for spectators and for all who hear of the recovery. (1942, p. 154)

The cycle of reinforcement among practitioners, patient (or victim), and community constitutes the evidence for the efficacy of the system. Suppose one individual bears ill will toward another and decides to vent unspoken hostilities in some tangible form—sticking pins into a doll representing the victim, or muttering curses while placing twigs on the path that must be taken by the enemy. And suppose, then, that misfortune strikes the intended victim. What evidence does the would-be sorcerer have that the measures taken were not in fact the cause? Is the germ theory of disease any more credible to one who has never peered into a microscope than the notion that a cold is caused by being out in the rain?

Religious Revitalization Movements

The role of a religious conversion experience in changing individual behaviors has been well documented. Our concern here is with the mechanisms by which the conversion experience of an individual becomes the focal point around which a new religion takes shape. Sometimes a cultural system reaches a stage in which its traditional symbols are no longer meaningful and powerful, either because of internal contradiction or through external pressure of some sort (culture contact or natural disaster, for example), or both. At that point, a prophet is likely to come forth. This charismatic individual will lead the group in a movement either to reform an old order or to establish an entirely new one.

Such movements have been known by a variety of terms, including nativistic, messianic, and millennium. Anthony Wallace (1961) proposes that the term *revitalization movements* be used to refer to "conscious, organized efforts by members of a society to construct a more satisfying culture" (1970, p. 372). He argues that religion plays a key role in the revitalization process. According to him, the spiritual experience of conversion is one kind of human response to social and cultural stress. In such situations, there is a perceived need for new codes of behavior and action to deal with the altered situation, since the previous code no longer works. According to Wallace, "new religions are, above all else, movements toward the revitalization of men and society. Periodically, new religions reverse the course of decline and supply the energy and the direction for the upswing toward a new, and often higher, climax of development" (1970, p. 372).

Wallace shows how these elements were involved in the revitalization movement brought by the Seneca Indian chief Handsome Lake to the Iroquois of New York in 1799. The Iroquois had been allied with the British during the American Revolution, in the course of which their warriors were discredited and their villages destroyed. Their traditional land holdings had been confiscated and their people resettled on a scattering of reservations separated from one another by growing communities of white Americans. There they idled, given to drinking and quarreling among themselves.

They faced a moral crisis: they wanted still to be men and women of dignity, but they knew only the old ways, which no longer led to honor but only to poverty and despair; to abandon these old ways meant undertaking customs strange, in some matters repugnant, and in any case uncertain of success. . . .

Into this moral chaos, Handsome Lake's revelations of the word of God sped like a golden arrow, dispelling darkness and gloom. Heavenly messengers, he said, had told him that unless he and his fellows became new men, they [would] be destroyed in an apocalyptic world destruction. They must cease drinking, and quarreling, and making witchcraft, and turn to lead pure and upright lives. He went on, in detailed vision after vision, to describe the sins which afflicted the Iroquois . . . and to prescribe the new way of life. (1970, pp. 373–374)

Only part of Handsome Lake's teaching had specifically religious content; for the most part he dealt with social and economic issues presented by the new situation. He exhorted the Iroquois to accept the agricultural practices of the European settlers, in which men as well as women worked in the fields. He urged that some of them learn to read and write English. And he told them to turn from their emphasis on matrilineal kin group organization and to organize their households around the conjugal family instead. Most of these teachings represented an adaptation to the customs of white Americans of that day, and would have been repugnant to the Iroquois had they not met a clearly felt need in a desperate situation; not been couched in terms of a supernatural vision which was traditionally acceptable; and not been transmitted by a leader with charisma and high credibility among his people.

Another analyst of revitalization movements is Worsley (1957), who offers a somewhat different approach to social and religious movements of this sort. Basing his analysis on studies of such cults as they appeared in Melanesia, he suggests the term *millenarian movements,* which he defines in terms of an expectation of a radical change about to occur in the social order, which leads to activity in preparation for this event on the part of the movements' adherents. These people expect the coming of the millennium—a period of great prosperity, happiness, and peace—and go about preparing for its arrival.

Worsley describes the stages or characteristics of a millenarian movement as found in Melanesia:

A prophet announces the imminence of the millennium. A complete upheaval of the social order is expected: liberators, who may be the spirits of the dead ancestors, American soldiers, or, in one case, the Communist Party of France, will appear, bringing all the material goods the people desire so strongly. Hence the name "Cargo Cult.". . .

In order to prepare for the Day, organizations are set up; new insignia, forms of dress, etc., are adopted; and new codes of morality and of law are drawn up. Often airstrips are cleared in the bush, and huts and stores are built to house the expected goods. (1967, p. 338)

But Worsley further distinguishes between two different types or stages of these movements. In the first, the ideology of the millenarian movement is closely related to the traditional beliefs; there is little attempt to prepare for radical change; preparation activities consist of magical practices intended to secure well-being in daily life. At the other extreme are movements that have clearly political goals and that focus on the construction of a new economic framework; millenarian emphasis in such movements is minimal. Sometimes the political-type movement develops out of the traditional type, but it may also, so to speak, spring fullgrown from the brow of the prophet.

Like Wallace, Worsley sees these movements as heralding a new social order, but he also stresses their political nature in bringing together previously disparate groups. This is where the charismatic leader comes in. In order to become a unifying force, the leader must rise above allegiance to one segment of the community. Worsley points out that this can be most effectively done by projecting his message to the supernatural plane, through a message from a deity or one's ancestors. Appeals to join the movement then rest on allegiance to a common religion that can unite them all.

Both Wallace and Worsley note that there have been many studies of revitalization movements in the Americas, Africa, Asia, and Oceania. All movements seem to share many structural characteristics: a prophet sees a new way; as his followers increase, the message changes to adapt to the new situation. Both Worsley and Wallace agree that these movements represent reorderings of secular and religious life arising out of the emotional atmosphere that accompanies situations of social crisis (Worsley, 1957).

Millenarian doctrines often seem fantastic and illogical to many Westerners. Yet, people who believe in the reality of such cults are unaware of the actual processes by which goods in Western technological society are produced. They are convinced that the Westerners with whom they have contact are concealing from them essential magic techniques that control such goods. The new religious techniques of the cult fill this gap. The Iroquois were fortunate that Handsome Lake's code so accurately responded to the realities of the situation; peoples in Melanesia have been less fortunate in the visions of their millenarian prophets. Worsley shows that these movements tend either to move toward more direct political action or to disappear. If, after a reasonable period of waiting, the ancestors fail to come with the cargo, the cult followers are bound to be disappointed, and will ultimately need a new source of revitalization.

Missionizing Religions

Missionizing religions are those making claims to exclusive insight into "ultimate reality," seeking to spread their beliefs and gain converts by sending representatives to other cultures and peoples. The most expansionist religion is, of course, Christianity. Christian zeal was a major factor in the European explorations and conquests of the sixteenth through the nineteenth centuries. Christian missionaries have circled the globe, frequently arriving at isolated and remote villages before anthropologists. Consequently, the missionary and the anthropologist have had extensive contact with each other, and over the years have developed an ambivalent relationship.

Anthropologists often depend on missionaries for travel facilities, food, and/or lodging until they are able to manage on their own. In turn, missionaries have come to rely on the field knowledge and techniques developed by anthropologists to make contact with native peoples. Morgan inquired of missionaries, among others, for information when he began to study kinship terminology. Numerous other ethnographers have likewise depended on reports prepared by those who were first on the scene. Mutual hostility has sometimes developed over the details of mundane interactions, and even more frequently and basically over the different points of view held by each about the purposes of the other. Many anthropologists charge that missionaries have often made it impossible to

Animal skins and skulls—the wares of the traditional Yoruba "pharmacist"—are symbols that retain their power even as modern medical practice, here exemplified by the physician *(left),* becomes available. (World Health Organization, Monkmeyer)

study a culture in its "pristine," pre-Christian state. They complain also that natives are coerced into adopting new beliefs before missionaries try to understand the value system and world view with which they are interfering. Missionaries, on the other hand, are suspicious of anthropologists who take advantage of their hospitality and knowledge of the language and culture, and then end up criticizing them.

It has been argued that the major impact of Christian missionizing has been secular rather than religious (Miller, 1970). The world view expressed in the day-to-day activities of Christian missionaries is a rational, cause-and-effect response to experience. Missionary attitudes toward and teachings about disease, accidents, natural catastrophes, the learning experience, and even the physical structure of the universe largely reflect naturalistic rather than supernaturalistic beliefs. Events and experiences that were traditionally explained in the context of a supernaturalistic universe are removed from their customary setting. Thus, missionaries often undermine the traditional sacred symbols that provide coherence and meaning to all life, even while attempting to instill new symbols. This process is often concurrent with rapid social, technological, and political changes introduced by nonreligious agents; but missionaries, in effect, support these external pressures.

The acceptance of new symbols is a complex issue, only partially understood. Societies are most likely to adopt those beliefs and practices that make the most sense both in terms of traditional understandings and in their comprehension of the new situation with which they are confronted. The integration of a new symbol or other component is not arbitrary; rather, the utility of the concept for the culture must be demonstrated. For this reason, an external meaning system cannot be imposed on any culture by a single individual. Therefore, anthropologists' concerns about a culture being "ruined" or destroyed by a missionary are largely unfounded.

Christianity is not the only missionizing religion, of course. Islam, although less active today than centuries ago, once spread rapidly throughout the Middle and Near East. Buddhism was exported from its birthplace in India to all corners of Asia (and in our own day is having a significant impact on some members of Western civilization as well). But Christianity has certainly been the most active and persuasive—and at times aggressive—in pursuit of converts. It must be acknowledged that part of the appeal of Christianity and the reason for its success is its close tie to Western ideology and technology. The dominant role played by Western Europe and the United States in world affairs has contributed to missionary success. But because of the relationship between Western political power and Christianity, many third world countries have become suspicious of and inhospitable to all missionaries. Anthropologists too have become unwelcome and for similar reasons, since they are also identified with a social and cultural system that is no longer welcomed by many peoples of the world.

Finally—and especially where the study of religion is concerned—anthropologists unintentionally bring to their research an inevitable taint of culture bias. Most researchers are from Western Europe or North America and are themselves participant members of a Christian culture. Kluckhohn (1942) has stated, for example, that probably because of the emphasis placed by Christianity on belief, which is rare from a cross-cultural perspective, a "cultural screen" existed between anthropologists and their data. Only relatively recently has an objective eye been cast on the function of religion among social subsystems in a given cultural context. The task of the anthropologist is to acknowledge this screen and attempt to arrive at the understandings that lie behind it.

Summary

1. There is a close relationship between politics and religion, between power and the sacred: the leader with authority in the religious arena is often a political leader as well. Even where political and religious authority are separate, however, the trappings of political leadership often become strongly tinged with the aura of the religious.

2. Religion may be defined as the system of social interactions consisting of those beliefs and activities that order human life by relating human beings to spiritual beings and/or powers. Belief, ritual, and individual experience are everywhere components of religious systems.

3. The term *belief* refers to statements that are generally held to be true by the members of a given society. Religious beliefs differ from other types of beliefs in that they make assertions about supernatural powers or forces. *Mana,* the belief that supernatural forces are inherent in animate and inanimate objects alike, and *animism,* a belief in the existence of spirit beings, have been distinguished by anthropologists as two widely held kinds of belief.

4. *Ritual* is the demonstration of religious belief through performance of specific acts. Rituals are communicative and aesthetic acts that reinforce a society's value system by dramatizing and symbolizing its beliefs.

5. Individual experiences in religion may vary from a feeling of "peace with the world" to "possession" by a supernatural force, and include a range of states in between. Some states of supernatural experience may be induced by solitude, fasting, drugs, or even self-mutilation.

6. In all religions, sacred symbols have the power to move the believer. They also serve as key integrating factors in a culture by articulating the "ultimate concerns" experienced by its members.

7. Most societies have one or more kinds of religious leader, whether *priest, shaman, prophet,* or *sorcerer.* The differences between each of these categories depend largely on how the religious specialists are called and trained and how they practice. These terms represent different categories of action rather than individual actors, so that one individual could conceivably practice more than one specialty at the same time. Shamans, prophets, and sorcerers practice as individuals and are most likely to have visions and direct contact with the supernatural. Priests must serve some kind of apprenticeship and learn a large body of belief and ceremonial material. Priests and prophets are largely concerned with the overall welfare of the community. Shamans are predominantly concerned with healing, while sorcerers may cause harm and attempt to ferret out evil influences by destroying the culprits. They may use *divination,* a ritual technique often relied upon to determine the source of misfortune or to solve social problems.

8. *Myth* is the verbal rationale of religion; it is symbolic narrative that has a sacred or supernatural component. Ritual may illustrate myth, but either may exist without reference to the other. Myth provides coherence and synthesis regarding the questions of deeper significance expressed in a culture. It often offers resolutions concerning the ambiguities and contradictions of life.

9. Sorcery or witchcraft reflects the malevolent side of the supernatural. These are explanations of the otherwise inexplicable, resorted to when life and misfortunes become intolerable.

10. Religions change through time—often dramatically, due to the appearance of a charismatic leader who has had a revelation. The appearance of radically new religious

movements at a time of social and economic disintegration has often been observed, and the terms *revitalization* and *millenarian movements* have been given to this phenomenon. The degree of acceptance and persistence of such movements is variable, and depends on individual as well as social factors. Most likely a key determinant is the effectiveness of a movement's teachings in coping with difficult present realities.

11. Missionizing religions make exclusive claims about their grasp of reality. They seek adherents and actively organize their followers in systematic ways. Missionaries and anthropologists often find themselves in conflict, yet depend on one another in various ways.

16
The Arts

THE subject of art is one of the most elusive in anthropology. There is, first, the age-old problem of how to define art. The problem is not merely one of definition, but rather that art is considered something to be enjoyed and appreciated on an emotional-response level as well as something to be analyzed. Western cultural attitudes toward art and those who create it, notions of what is and is not art, and the uses to which art should be put all get in the way of the anthropological study of art. Because no adequate social theory of art has been advanced, anthropologists tend to interpret art from the societies they study in terms of the attitudes associated with art in their own society. As pointed out earlier, culture bias is a major problem for anthropology in general, but it is perhaps even more true with art than with other topics. The antiestablishment stance of the artist, an aesthetic based on relationships of forms, art as status symbol and

object, and the mystique of the creative impulse are only a few of the preconceptions that most Westerners hold that prevent their meeting non-Western arts with open-minded as well as wide-eyed interest.

Toward an Anthropology of Art

The Relationship of Art and Culture

The primary issue facing anthropologists concerns, of course, the nature of the relationship between art and culture. Do all cultures have art? To what extent is art involved in the lifestyles of a given culture? How does the role played by art differ from one culture to another? How is it similar? In order to respond to these questions, anthropologists must arrive at some understanding about what is included in the topic "art."

Even a superficial acquaintance with cultures other than our own demonstrates the enormous variability in the place accorded to art and artists, and the role of the appreciators or audience, in different human societies. Geertz (1976) has pointed out that "the capacity, variable among peoples as it is among individuals, to perceive meaning in pictures [or poems, melodies, buildings, pots, dramas, statues] is, like all other fully human capacities, a product of collective experience." He explains further that "participation in the particular we call art" can develop only "out of participation in the general system of symbolic forms we call culture" (p. 1488). Thus, our cultural conditioning determines the sensibility we bring, as appreciators, to our experiences of any art. Furthermore, a particular view of culture obviously influences the direction from which the study of art will be undertaken. However, in order to determine what is considered art in any given society, it is essential to analyze the cultural system from a broader perspective.

Art is, then, inseparable from culture. But paradoxically, the outcome of artistic activity is often an object that can be (and most often has been) removed from and studied without reference to its cultural context (Merriam, 1964, p. 97). Art, existing in some form at a given time, is by its very nature concrete. But the aesthetic appreciation of art is highly individual and subjective. Precisely because art can be separated from its cultural context, it is attractive as a subject for anthropological study.

One difficulty in discussing art is that it is necessary to translate experiences expressed in visual (or auditory) form into language, using words that are not always compatible with the original expression. Goldwater (1973) sees the arts as being "primary documents" rather than secondary expressions of more fundamental ideas. In other words, art, as an essential part of culture, reflects the cultural whole and is not merely a support for some aspect of it.

The problem of meaning, of course, is central to any discussion of culture and art. All humans are the product of their time and place of creation. The anthropologist must, although this is most difficult, guard against interpreting unfamiliar arts in the terms made familiar by art historians in Western culture (Forge, 1973). We must always pause to realize that our use of categories such as sculpture, masks, and paintings, derives from the history and role of the arts in our own society. Although these are useful categorizations for us, they do remove us from the cultural context at which we are ultimately trying to get. At the same time, we must also recognize that art in other cultures may fall into categories, such as body painting or cuisine, that we have never acknowledged in quite that light. Further, as Forge points out, "some cultures devoid of art in the sculpture and painting sense possess rich visual systems of great aesthetic powers," which focus on other, perhaps natural "art" products.

But there is no question that Westerners have over the years been drawn to the creative products of foreign cultures. Marveled at when displayed by returning explorers in the sixteenth and seventeenth centuries, later collected as curiosities, the so-called "primitive arts" have long appealed to the Western appetite for the exotic. Possession of "primitive" art objects has been a status symbol of sorts for centuries. Displayed by the wealthy, these objects were, along with curiosities of biology and geology, the foundations of collections that would become great museums in the eighteenth and nineteenth centuries. Certainly, in that time, the appreciation accorded such works depended more on their exotic value than their aesthetic worth. But at the end of the nineteenth century and the beginning of the twentieth, painters and sculptors in France became aware of the visual impact

Wood carvings from Africa, such as this head for a reliquary *(left)* used by the Fang of Gabon excited European collectors and artists. (Charles Uht, Courtesy of the Museum of Primitive Art). **Amedeo Modigliani was one Parisian artist whose paintings were influenced by African sculpture. Note the similarities between this *(right)* and the Fang mask *(left)* in overall facial contours, the curvature of the sides of the nose, and the high forehead and arch of the eyebrows.** (The Metropolitan Museum of Art, gift of Charles F. Ikle, 1960)

of masks especially and carved figures from Africa.

But no matter how great the visual power of such objects, no matter how deep our aesthetic appreciation of them, the symbolic content of individual design elements contained within the object is not comprehensible by us in the same terms as those in which they are comprehended by a member of their culture of origin. Beyond the universality of "the human body, its parts, and its functions [as] a source of many powerful symbols in ritual as well as art in most human societies," Forge has noted, "there seems little evidence of genuine universal symbols in the plastic arts or indeed in any other medium of communication" (1973, p. xiv). Even where the same design element appears in the products of vastly different cultures, vastly different meanings are attached to it. The swastika, for example, is a design element whose use is widespread—it was one of the body marks of Buddha in India, it was used in Crete and ancient Rome, it has been an American Indian design to indicate the four directions, it appeared in China as a symbol of benevolence, and of course it was the notorious symbol of the Nazis in Germany. Its use in each context obviously evoked different emotions and held different connotations.

This brings us back to the object itself or, as d'Azevedo puts it, a created "product or effect of a particular kind" (1973, p. 7). Merriam points out that objects or effects that can be considered art are produced in all cultures, although there are many cultures that do not have a concept of art as a distinct category of endeavor (1964). The study of so-called primitive art has increasingly attracted art historians, but dance, music, folklore, drama, painting, and a vast variety of other possible media for artistic activity have attracted the interest of few modern anthropologists or other social scientists. However, such fields as ethnomusicology, ethnodance, and folklore studies are beginning to fill the gap, and art historians are becoming aware of the extraordinarily rich resources to be found in the non-Western arts. In relatively recent years, too, the created works of nonprimitive, non-Western societies have been subjected to cross-cultural analysis and interpretation. This field is potentially an enormously rich one, and must include such outstanding products as the poetry of Islamic cultures; the dance and sculpture of India; graphic, dramatic, literary, culinary, and textile arts of China and Japan; the verbal and occult heritage of Judaism; and architecture as a category in itself.

The Problem of Aesthetics

Aesthetics refers to the study of beauty and of psychological responses to it. The problem of aesthetics is really twofold. First, as we have mentioned in passing in the preceding pages, there is the problem of setting *our* aesthetic standards to one side when confronting the art works produced in an unfamiliar cultural context. Second, there is the question of determining the aesthetic principles on which art of another culture is based. This last point further subdivides into analysis of the problem of aesthetics from the two points of view of creator and appreciator. In some cultures, the same word is used to mean "good" and to describe an aesthetically attractive object. Thus, "good" and "beautiful" become one concept, but the vocabulary for aesthetic appreciation is not further defined, although the

These four sculptures, from different times, different lands, and different cultures share many aesthetic qualities, such as clarity of line and form, a fine surface, erectness, serenity, and balance. *Above left*—an *ibeji* (twin figure) made by the Yoruba of Nigeria (Eliot Elisofon, Museum of African Art, Eliot Elisofon Archives); *above right*—marble caryatids (draped female figures supporting an entablature) from the Erechtheum (porch of the Maidens) on the Acropolis in Athens, fifth century, B.C. (George Holton, Photo Researchers, Inc.); *bottom left*—bronze statuette of a young ballet dancer by Degas (The Metropolitan Museum of Art, bequest of Mrs. H. O. Havemeyer, 1929, the H. O. Havemeyer Collection); *bottom right*—gilded wooden sculpture of Buddha (The Metropolitan Museum of Art, Rogers Fund, 1943)

elements that make one object "good/beautiful" and another not may be explained in detail. An observer in Igala, Nigeria, reports Sieber (1971), had only two words of critique for a mask shown to him: "one identified the mask type, the other indicated that it was well done" (p. 130). But, as Thompson (1971) reports, among the Yoruba, also of Nigeria, several thoroughly understood critical standards are regularly applied to their human figures sculptured in wood. These standards include concepts of clarity of line and form, high polish of the surface, symmetry, appropriate position of various elements, erectness, technical skill, and a term Thompson translates to refer approximately to a suitable balance between representation and abstraction. Most of these qualities can be found also in a Degas bronze figure of a dancer; a marble column in the form of a female figure upholding a pillar of the Parthenon; or a gilded representation of the Buddha. With what words, one wonders, did viewers of turn-of-the-century France, Golden Age Greece, or eleventh-century China appraise these works?

The existence of similarities in the formal qualities of these four objects does not result in similarity of form. Yet all have the power to move us, and they likely held that power in their time and place of creation as well. Is

there, then, a universal aesthetic response? Although no one has actually demonstrated the existence of a universal aesthetic response some hold that there is one. Goldwater, for example, claims that "the aesthetic is concerned with power, with the heightened impact of a perfect object whether it be beautiful, ugly, or frightening" (Forge, 1973, p. xxi).

Stout (1971) emphasizes that understanding of aesthetics from an anthropological perspective will only be achieved through collecting statements from primitive artists about their work and that of their colleagues and through actually studying and being apprenticed to native craftsmen. He suggests, too, the necessity of conducting cross-cultural experiments in which objects from one society are presented to members of another for their aesthetic judgments. This was precisely the

BaKwele mask. (The Metropolitan Museum of Art, The Michael C. Rockefeller Memorial Collection of Primitive Art)

approach taken in an experiment a few years ago in which 39 photographs of BaKwele masks were shown to both a number of art students at Yale University and to BaKwele mask carvers and users themselves. There was a surprising amount of agreement on the order in which the masks were ranked. However, there was also strong evidence that the BaKwele were evaluating in terms of standards different from those of the Yale students. Child and Siroto (1965) suggest that these objects can be appreciated by anyone who enjoys visual art, and that both sets of judges could be sensitive to variations in excellence, despite differences in stated evaluative criteria.

On this evidence one might tentatively conclude that, although aesthetic principles are highly variable from one culture to another, there does exist some widespread human capacity to transcend cultural boundaries in the appreciation of some types of art products. But much more attention to this topic will have to be paid by anthropologists before we can approach any degree of understanding about the universals and the particulars of human aesthetic sensibilities.

Some Conceptual Approaches

Interest in primitive art developed largely in terms of the sculptural arts, these being the most readily separated from their cultural contexts and brought into Western collections. While anthropologists were emphasizing fieldwork as a way to get at cultural meanings, the study of the arts came to be considered an area of interest for museums. Museums set up their own departments of ethnology, and university departments of anthropology established their own museums, as at the University of Pennsylvania, UCLA, and elsewhere. For years, emphasis was placed on "collecting," as opposed to studying the art objects *in situ* (in their original place). Expeditions went into the field to gather as many objects as possible, often at the same time as ethnographers, but with different goals. The long period of collecting, and the consequent study of objects as objects, out of their cultural context, has had several implications. There was, first, a focus on the portable graphic or sculptural arts, and to a lesser extent on the oral traditions; there was comparative neglect of music, dance, drama, body decoration, architecture, and other less collectible products of the creative enterprise. Second, the spotlighted, isolated objects were interpreted in terms of accepted approaches of art analysis—forms, isolated motifs, and comparisons from one object to the next. With this frame of reference, art historians entered the picture as analysts of primitive art, spurred by the discovery of these works by prominent artists. Picasso, Modigliani, and Lipchitz, for example, all incorporated design elements from African sculpture in their work. Third, and as a consequence of the first two considerations, comparisons focused on similarities and differences in the works, and led naturally to speculations about presumed diffusion of elements from one culture to another in the past. Such studies implied that lack of change was inherent in the creative products of non-Western peoples, although familiarity with the history of the products of their own civilization should have informed scholars otherwise.

The study of art in anthropology generally follows the course of the conceptual views of culture outlined in the chapter The Culture Concept. Those committed to an evolutionary view attempt to locate the evolution of art forms; those interested in diffusion (principally Boas himself) attempt to trace the spread of artistic elements from one culture to another as a means of investigating the diffusion of culture. Diffusion is only one kind of interaction in which elements of design or other separable components of the arts move

The similarities of form and design between these two pottery vessels cannot be accounted for by diffusion or culture contact. The polychrome *olla* (bowl) *(above)* was made in Acoma Pueblo, New Mexico around 1900. (Photograph courtesy of the Museum of the American Indian, Heye Foundation). **The large jar *(below)* was made in Iran around 3700 B.C.** (The Metropolitan Museum of Art, Joseph Pulitzer Bequest, 1959)

across cultural boundaries. Mutual borrowing of elements, trading of objects between neighboring cultures, and the commissioning of works by artists of other tribal backgrounds are some other ways that art elements cross cultural boundaries. Beyond these factors, there is the simple fact that artists everywhere can use only the materials at their disposal. We mentioned in an earlier chapter the relationship between the materials available for art and the ecological niche within which a society is located. The available natural materials are similar thoughout a wide region, and so the peoples of that region have similar media at hand. Thus, the peoples of Africa below the Sahara work largely in wood; in desert areas and north of the Sahara, however, sun-baked mud is the more readily available material. American Indians throughout the eastern woodlands laboriously prepared porcupine quills and tinted them with natural dyes to make designs and add color to articles made of deerskin. When more colorful European glass beads were introduced, they were eagerly accepted as an art material, being much easier to work with and capable of producing a more dramatic effect. Eventually, entire new art products were developed, based on new ways of using the new material.

The combination of intercultural diffusion of art ideas and the regional availability of art materials means that art products within a culture area are readily identifiable. Within each culture area, such as West Africa or the American Plains, the distinctive cultural or tribal differences of style stand out. Thus, one cannot talk of African art but must distinguish its different areas and subareas; and then move further to distinguish between Yoruba, Ibo, Ibibio, Ekoi, and dozens more within even such a geographically limited area as present-day Nigeria.

Those anthropologists strongly influenced by the functionalist school tend to emphasize the manner in which art serves to integrate and bolster other aspects of culture. We have discussed above the complex interrelationships between arts and cultures, interrelationships that will become increasingly apparent in the latter part of this chapter as we look at different categories of the arts.

Art as Communication

Without communication, the artist has failed. Picasso's comment on the communicative function of art is well known: "Art is a lie," he said, "that makes us see the truth." Art communicates in the realms of politics and religion, economics and social life—indeed, in every aspect of human existence.

The intention to communicate need not be clearly stated or even intended to accomplish this end. An art product communicates not only what the artist intends but also what the spectator reads into it. Where there is a shared cultural frame of reference, the two kinds of content may merge and become a total or nearly total whole. But where the cross-cultural gap yawns wide, there may be a chasm of meaning. Yale art students and BaKwele mask users may have shared some standards of visual appreciation for masks, but the *meanings* conveyed to members of the two groups were very different indeed. The Americans tended to respond to such qualities as symmetry, idealization of form, and technical skill; they may have envisioned the masks on walls in galleries or homes as objects to be appreciated. They could not have looked at them in terms of how well certain ritual or spiritual functions would be enhanced through their use. Nor could they have envisioned the masks as part of a kinetic experience, as when the masks are worn by costumed individuals moving against the natural backdrop of BaKwele dwellings and scenery to a musical accompaniment. And the Americans could not have imagined the cultural familiarity or the accumulation of experience with such objects that went into the BaKwele appreciation.

Even where directly representational elements appear in art, they carry symbolic content, meanings beyond the forms immediately depicted. The form may itself be a symbol, a unit in a kind of "cultural code" (Munn, 1971, p. 336). Munn shows how, for example, among the Walbiri of central Australia, a simple circle can represent a circular path, a water hole, certain fruits, the base of a tree, or fire. Designs based on the circle, such as concentric circles or spirals, can be totem centers, a totemic animal or plant, buttocks, female genitals, or breasts (Munn, 1973, pp. 194ff), among others. Similar catalogues could be made of meanings attached to other design elements—the oval, arc, straight line. Munn (1971) concludes that, for "any system of culturally standardized representations . . . where one can identify discrete, recurrent units through which visual contrasts are made," it should be possible to define the meanings attached to each symbol (p. 336).

Where Walbiri designs may have secular or religious content according to their context, the design elements of the Tiv of Nigeria have no particular religious symbolism but are instead representations of natural elements such as lizards, swallows, and drinking gourds (Bohannon, 1971, p. 179). In such cases, meanings can be readily determined; according to Bohannon, there is no point in looking further for deeper meaning. At the other extreme, art elements can be intentional representations designed to convey a specific message. The arrangement of purple and white beads in a string of wampum or the design woven into a wampum belt had immediate or historic content for its Iroquois audience; meetings of the chiefs opened with someone literally "reading" the wampum.

The meanings of art can be even more specific than this. It is not necessary to delve into symbolic content of specific design elements to understand the meanings of art objects in terms of the situations that call for their use. A mask worn by a tribal judge in Liberia clearly conveys the power of the judgments rendered by its wearer. When the "mask" speaks, the Dan or Guere people are certain to heed the decision. Similarly, when a Crow warrior carries a painted buffalo-hide shield covered with attached objects, everyone knows that the supernatural spirits have favored him. Art appears at initiation ceremonies as ratification of a belief system, part of the trappings that enhance the prestige of royalty. Art may be purely secular as well, adorning everyday utility objects—a design painted on a jar; animal or human figures carved on the wooden door of a granary; colorful stripes woven into cloth strips; or beaded flowers appliquéd onto moccasins.

Graburn (1976) has shown that one of the most important communications of art is to identify members of an in-group within a society and to distinguish one society from another: "All people surround themselves with material objects that express their individual identity and their identity within a social category" (pp. 23–24). This is as true of our complex civilization as it is of small societies. Thorstein Veblen, the American economist, called attention to the trappings of conspicuous consumption that delineated the nouveau riche from the bourgeoisie out of which they arose; the "old rich" had no difficulty in distinguishing their own set of privileges from those "put on" by upstarts. Similarly, Graburn notes that "threatened identities often lead to a revival of archaic traditions" (p. 25). He cites a number of American Indian examples, such as the renaissance of Hopi kachina figures to counter missionizing attempts of the Catholic Church. More recently we have seen "the new ethnicity" emphasizing traditional national costumes, songs, and so forth. As black Americans find cultural roots in resurrecting aspects

These two examples of utilitarian objects enriched by art are from North America. The baby carrier *(left),* made and used by the Kiowa of Oklahoma, is decorated with colorful bead embroidery and trim. The steel knife *(right)* has a bone handle carved to represent the head of a raven; pieces of shell are inlaid for eyes. It was made and used by the Tlingit of British Columbia. (Photographs courtesy of the Museum of the American Indian, Heye Foundation)

Among the Ashanti of Ghana, men are weavers of kente cloth strips, which are sewn together to form wide lengths of fabric worn as robes *(left).* The carved wooden figure *(right)* is a heddle pulley, made and used by the Baule of the Ivory Coast; it is part of weaving equipment, used to separate warp threads. Two heddle pulleys can be seen in use in the loom pictured at *left.* The Ashanti and the Baule are culturally-related peoples. (Photographs by Eliot Elisofon, Museum of African Art, Eliot Elisofon Archives)

of their distant African heritage (discovering the verbal and sculptural arts of the lands of their forebears in the process), a new Afro-American identity and art are being created.

The Artist and Society

If there are, cross-culturally speaking, few valid generalizations that can be made about art objects, there are even fewer generalizations applicable to artists. In some societies, artists are specialists, individuals known far and wide for their skill (or whose products are known far and wide for their efficacy). The Kilenge of western New Britain, Melanesia,

distinguish between artists and master artists, certain of whom are recognized as possessing particular competence (Dark, 1967, p. 142). The artist, who is an individualist par excellence in our own society, is not always in a similar position in preindustrial societies. Among the Basongye of the Congo, for example, the role of musician—but not that of composer—is one of the few permissible routes to individual accomplishment. Because of the cultural opposition to individualization, musicians deny also being composers and attribute their musical innovations to other nearby cultures (Merriam, 1964, p. 78). The Tiv of central Nigeria are interested more in the art than in the artist and are more concerned with the ideas conveyed by a piece of art than with the way it was created (Bohannon, 1971, p. 175). Among the Tiv, carving

An Eskimo prepares the ivory tusk of a bull walrus before carving. (Georg Gerster, Rapho/Photo Researchers, Inc.)

may even be a communal enterprise, with someone picking up and working on a piece that another has put down. However, carvings of figures, as opposed to utilitarian objects such as bowls, are usually the work of a single individual. Yet the only acclaim such a master carver receives is to have it said that his work always (as opposed to sometimes) comes out well.

Unlike the Tiv, the Eskimos are more interested in the artistic process than in its product: "When you feel a song within you, you sing it; when you sense a form emerging from ivory, you release it" (Carpenter, 1971, p. 165). Carpenter vividly shows us the Eskimo artist at work:

As the carver holds the unworked ivory lightly in his hand, turning it this way and that, he whispers, "Who are you? Who hides there?" And then: "Ah, Seal!" He rarely sets out, at least consciously, to carve, say, a seal, but picks up the ivory, examines it to find its hidden form and, if that is not immediately apparent, carves aimlessly until he sees it, humming or chanting as he works. (Carpenter, 1971, p. 163)

Sometimes artists are self-taught; sometimes they must serve an apprenticeship or pay a fee for instruction and admission to a guild; sometimes they inherit the artistic function in their families. In Japan, a particularly promising apprentice may be adopted into a family of artists to continue a dynasty of creativity. This is especially so in dance and the dramatic arts but also holds true in traditional crafts and graphic arts. Himmelheber (1967) describes the casts of wood carvers and brass casters of the Senufo of West Africa:

These craftsmen do not cultivate fields. They live from what the farmer caste brings them in exchange for their work. They then practice their craft from morning till night, producing an enormous number of woodworks, both artistic and of everyday use (mortars, pestles, handles for axes). They form separate quarters in the villages, even entire villages of their own. Visiting such a quarter one finds a great number of carvers in each compound, sometimes 30 or 40, busily at work. (pp. 195–196)

At the opposite end of the spectrum, there are some societies in which every member is expected to produce works of art. Among the Tiwi of Oceania, all males have a number of opportunities to carve funeral poles, as well as to practice singing, dancing, body painting, ceremonial basket making, and the carving and painting of ceremonial spears (Goodale & Koss, 1971, p. 198). Artistic proficiency brings prestige. Thus, the inexperienced welcome the call to be in the group that will carve funeral poles, which gives them the opportunity to observe more experienced master carvers at close hand.

Much of the recent attention in the anthropological study of art has focused on the artist. In fact, d'Azevedo, who titled his 1973 book *The Traditional Artist in African Society,* considers the role and function of the artist the most important area of research. As he says, the problem is not one of biography but rather of identifying the kind of individual behavior and social action that coincide with artistry. We must not lose sight of the fact that artists are members of their social systems who are influenced by the response to their products as much as by their own creativity. The aspiring Tiwi carver receives a great deal of feedback from his audience:

The workers are commissioned as a group and . . . are given general directions as to how many poles should be cut and how big they should be, directions which indicate the employer's [the family of the dead] wishes and abilities to pay for the work done. . . . Finally . . . the employers judge each pole individually and lay out their payment (in goods) according to their evaluation. (Goodale & Koss, 1971, pp. 188–189)

Meanwhile, there has been much discussion of all the poles by members of the community. Works accorded high payment will be remembered by those who have seen them

Arts intersect each other in many ways. This painting on the bark of the sago palm decorates the front of a spirit house in New Guinea. (George Holton, Photo Researchers, Inc.)

when it is their turn to carve, and those carvers whose works were evaluated highly will be encouraged to continue along the same lines. Thus criticism has a very practical impact.

By itself, studying an individual artist cannot explain art in any type of society. The study can, however, enlarge our understanding and appreciation of the created product. It is to those products that we now turn our attention.

Visual Arts

Under the heading of visual arts are included the best-known categories of the so-called primitive arts—the graphic and sculptural expressions created in numerous cultures of our own day, the recent past, and also of the previous vast period known to us through archaeology. The visual arts also include many less familiar categories: textile (weaving) and other fiber arts, including basketry; body decorating, including makeup, "jewelry," and costume; and architecture.

The term *graphic art* generally refers to such two-dimensional products as paintings and drawings on canvas, cave walls, stones, fabric, bark, and so on. The *sculptural* or *plastic arts* are three-dimensional products, including sculpture and utilitarian items such as furniture, tools, and containers. There is an area in which the graphic and plastic arts overlap, since many three-dimensional objects are adorned with two-dimensional designs applied over or incised into the surface. This is true, for example, of body painting, of the painted funerary carved poles of the Tiwi, and of pottery. It also applies to the *molas* of the Cuna of San Blas Island off the coast of Panama, made by a "negative appliqué" technique in which strips of cloth are cut out to let an underlayer of fabric show through.

As a three-dimensional constructed form, architecture, too, is considered among the plastic arts, although it surely deserves to be in a category by itself. Paradoxically, although dwellings and other structure types are carefully described and their construction detailed in ethnographic reports, the cross-cultural analysis of building styles and materials, and

This Yirrhala (Australia) man is applying a white earth paint to bark cloth. (Georg Gerster, Rapho/ Photo Researchers, Inc.)

their influence on people's lives, has been virtually nonexistent. Potentially fascinating questions for exploration include the relationship of house size and style to social organization, child-rearing practices and socialization of the young, marital and intrafamily relations, cooperation, and division of labor.

Within any one category of the visual arts there are numerous variations. The fiber arts include braiding, knotting, and twining, techniques that produce hammocks, carrying bags, baskets, and ropes. They also include weaving. Even the simplest of looms, such as the plain frame loom of the Navaho, can be used to produce elaborate objects. A backstrap type of loom is found in many parts of South America and Africa. The Senufo and Baule peoples of West Africa carve weaving accessories with as much care as they use for their ritual masks. Fibers and cloth are colored with brilliantly hued earth dyes. The Navaho produce their own wool and dye it. In many African cultures, dried corn kernels or pebbles are tied with string or sewn in a design onto a large stretch of cloth that is then dyed. The wax-resistant batik dying of Indonesia is well known. Other fabric-decorating techniques of note include the block printing of India and the mud painting (using dark clays or mineral powders) of West Africa.

The category of body decorating comprises simple painting with colored earths; scarification; jewelry inserted into openings made in nose, ears, lips, or permanently secured about the neck; other kinds of jewelry; dress, costume, or ornamentation; hairdressing and hair styling. The "mudheads" of New Guinea literally build masks onto their own heads, then paint the masks and the exposed portions of their faces and bodies with light-colored clay for certain ritual occasions. Studies of body decoration identify styles and symbolic content of specific decorative elements. Scarification may indicate the rank of an individual's family, for example, and a hairdo may distinguish married from unmarried women. Such studies also investigate the occasions calling for special dress or appearances, as well as those for which special costume is not required. It would be interesting to analyze, for example, the reasons why a society pays a great deal or no particular attention to clothing and body decoration on such occasions as weddings, funerals, and agricultural or puberty ceremonies.

The technical abilities and skills called for are often outstanding. The ikat dyers and weavers of India and Indonesia, for example, are able to dye fibers so that the design will appear in the weaving. The large bronze heads and plaques of Benin, and the small brass figures of animals and humans of the Ashanti, are created by a process used in our society by jewelry designers and sculptors.

Intimate knowledge of materials and technology is essential. Clay must be selected, processed to remove impurities, tempered with sand or with finely ground pottery so it will fire evenly, shaped with walls of even thinness for even firing, and dried carefully before firing. A small damp patch can cause an explosion in the kiln and ruin a week's output. Fires must be built and tended, paints and other kinds of finishes must be prepared, and perhaps supernaturals must be called on for assistance to ensure the quality of the results.

Today's artists and artisans in our society can buy most of their supplies ready for use, or nearly so. In all other times and places, preparation of equipment has been an essential and time-consuming preliminary to the main event of creating. Cro-Magnon artists, for example, made brushes from animal hair or the ends of twigs, fraying them either by chewing or pounding them with a stone. Paint was daubed on rock walls with pads of animal fur or with the flat side of bones or stone. Powdered pigment could be blown onto a wall through a hollow bone. Flat stones with dried patches of color on them—Ice Age palettes—have been found in caves. And shells stained with pigment—the equivalent of paint jars—have also been found. There have even been flat stones covered with superimposed scratchings—a version of sketchpads (Rensberger, 1978, p. 40). Some of these same materials are used by non-Western artists today. The pigments used in cave painting were made by pulverizing colored minerals and mixing them with binders made from animal fat, egg white, blood, vegetable juices, and fish glue (a gelatinlike substance made by cooking fish scraps in water). Apparently, different binders were used for different types of rock, the selection being made on the basis of a variety of technical problems, such as the texture and porosity of the rock and whether the surface was damp or dry. Because Ice Age artists used such techniques, many of their frescoes have withstood the ravages of time better than have some of the masterpieces of the Renaissance (Rensberger, 1978).

In dealing with prehistoric arts such as cave paintings and some other most expressive three-dimensional products as well, we are truly faced with the concept of art as primary document. Few artifacts of any culture are more expressive than the dramatic and sensitive forms traced in soft-colored earths on the walls and ceilings of Altamira in Spain, Lascaux in France, and numerous other Cro-Magnon cave sites.

The distinction is often made between artist and craftsperson, as though the former produces a finer, more rarified product intended for aesthetic appreciation only, whereas the latter produces only utilitarian objects. This distinction, however, is barely valid for the products of our own culture, and not at all valid for those of most non-Western societies.

In any culture, an artisan/craftsperson may also be an artist, whereas many artists, alas, are found on close acquaintance to be artisans instead. The product—and its impact on its audience—is what counts. All arts, from the anthropological point of view, are practical, in

Arts meet in costume for dances that are part of ritual. *Above*—basket spirit masks are worn by Asmat witch doctors in a ceremony in West Irian, **West New Guinea** (George Holton, Photo Researchers, Inc.); *below*—carved wooden headdress masks are part of the costume worn by the Sande women's society of the Mende of Liberia. The mask represents one of the spirits from which the society derives its authority and function—training girls for adulthood (Clardun, Monkmeyer)

the sense that they serve a cultural function. An easel painting has as specific a role to play in Pennsylvania as does a sheet of bark cloth in Polynesia.

D'Azevedo reminds us that the word *art* carries with it some of its earlier connotations of a special skill or technique (1973, p. 7). Non-Western societies may concentrate their creative impulses on objects of utilitarian value. But if the conception and the technique are of that high quality meant by the word *art*, then the product—basket or box, silver teapot or clay water jar—is indeed a work of art.

Dance

All human societies appear to have members who dance, although the occasions for dancing and the forms it takes vary enormously from one culture to another. Although dance is widespread as a cultural phenomenon, not all individuals participate. In numerous societies, dance is an activity for males only. Sometimes, as in parts of the Middle East, dance is performed by males for an all-male audience. More frequent perhaps is the situation in which dance is performed by women for an all-male audience (also found in the Middle East, and elsewhere). The European pattern of exclusively mixed dancing is comparatively unusual.

A culture usually has more than one kind of dance activity or, rather, dances on several different kinds of occasions. Dance most frequently appears as a component in ritual, "during religious ceremonials and community festivals of birth, maturation, courtship, marriage, harvest, death" (Lomax, 1968, p. 224). Dance is, as a repetitive series or sequence of body movements, a kind of ritualized behavior in and of itself, and even secular occasions for dance take on a ceremonial significance as a result.

Dance may be a cultural universal, but it is not an exclusively human activity, at least in the broadest sense. Mating "dances" have been described for various animal species, especially among insects and birds. As a consequence, the question may be raised as to whether the rhythmic, repetitive body movements in space that we call dance have some natural base. Perhaps dance is behavior that continues to be based on a biological drive even while its form and meaning are shaped by culture.

The approaches of anthropology to dance have followed the same sequence previously described. The evolutionist approach, responsible for some of the earliest ethnographic descriptions and influenced by Victorian morality, regarded dance as a primitive form of behavior that would be abandoned as peoples became "civilized." The personality and culture approach saw dance as a psychological safety valve for the individual within a controlling social environment. American ethnologists concentrated on cultural context, and described dance societies, dancers and their paraphernalia, and the role of dance within the culture, to the exclusion of actual choreography. European studies, more interested in folklore than in cultural context, emphasized dance forms (Royce, 1977, p. 213). Most recently, the focus has been both functionalist and structuralist, the former concerned with dance in relation to the cultural whole, the latter with dance as a communicative system, its symbolic content, and means of transmission.

A particularly ambitious study was undertaken by Lomax and several associates, who attempted to correlate dance style movements and other aspects of social life, particularly those movements utilized in work activities. His analysis of dance movements—*choreometrics*—in 43 cultures represents a cross-cultural comparison similar in order to that of the Human Relations Area Files studies. An example of the categories of dance movements the Lomax team analyzed was whether the torso is held "as a solid, block-like structure" in "one-unit" movement, or whether movement is of "two-unit" type, with "clearcut twists at the waist or undulating movements spreading from the center of the torso into other segments of the body" (Lomax, 1968, p. 237).

By comparing dance forms as seen in ethnographic films, the Lomax team noted such factors as the carry-over of posture from work stance into dancing stance. These observations led to their hypothesis that "movement style in dance is a crystallization of the most frequent and crucial patterns of everyday activity" (p. 226). They also identified seven dance-style regions that correlated closely to song-style regions previously identified. Previous analysis had shown that song performance styles were culturally related to subsistence activity. For example, "the social structures of the song teams of a society seem to resemble those of its work teams" (Lomax, 1968, p. 224). Thus, similar results in several respects were obtained for both dance and song.

It is not sufficient for *us* to define dance; we must also consider definitions from the cultures studied. Such definitions may combine music with dance, or may exclude certain categories of dance, or distinguish between ritual and secular dance (Royce, 1977, p. 10). Royce suggests that it may be more useful to consider dance events, such as weddings and festivals, than to restrict our observations to dances and dancing. A dance event may, as she shows for a Zapotec wedding, consist of a particular combination or sequence of different dances (p. 11).

The most useful studies still seem to be those that investigate dance within a particular culture with a view to the messages that are communicated. Dance may mean different things to those who create it, those who per-

An elaborately costumed and made-up dancer from Kerala, South India. The dancer will perform the *Kaliyattam,* a sacred dance originating from Shakti worship and performed to appease the gods and goddesses. (Van Bucher, Photo Researchers, Inc.)

form it, and those who view it. Dance communicates through its kinesthetic quality, unique in the arts, which evokes a sympathetic kinesthetic response in the audience (Royce, 1977). But dance communicates through other channels as well. There is the visual component—what is seen, under conditions of lighting or shadow, and by whom in what company. There are sounds, both of accompaniment and of physical exertion, such as feet against ground or stage, and there are also channels of touch and smell.

Dance may communicate by miming spirit beings or animals, as in the deer dance of the Mexican Yaqui or the kangaroo dance of indigenous Australians, or by miming activities such as war and harvesting. Dance may be metaphorical, as in the rain dance in which the Sioux circle about a container of water four times, drop to the earth, and then drink from the container. And dance may be abstract, with body movements themselves being the center of attention. The hand-movement dances of India, in which each movement represents an action or a portion of a narrative tale, and foot movement is relatively minimal, can be a combination of all three possibilities. Most cultures have dances of all three types, so that these are ways of interpreting dances but not of categorizing cultures in regard to dance.

Bateson (1972) points out that the messages communicated in dance may not always be fully conscious or clearly intended. In fact, he seems to suggest that the reason one communicates through dance rather than verbally is that there is an attempt to convey a "partly unconscious message" or perhaps "a message about the interface between conscious and unconscious" (p. 138). Thus, the meanings of dance are to be found on many levels. It is precisely this multimessage aspect of dance that gives it a unique quality and makes it attractive for study.

Music

Music, too, is found everywhere. The cross-cultural approach to this art has been undertaken by the interdisciplinary field of *ethnomusicology*—the study of music in culture (Merriam, 1968, p. 351). Within the study of music in culture, there are two distinct emphases. The first is musicological, concerned with such matters as construction, rhythm, scale, melody, instrumentation, vocalization styles, and so on. The second is more strictly anthropological, focusing on the uses and meanings of music, the performer and the audience, and the cultural context.

The role of music, as of other arts, varies from one culture to another. Music has accompanied virtually every kind of human activity in some time or place. Many cultures, such as our own, have numerous kinds of and occasions for music. The Flathead Indians have 14 distinct categories of situations calling for music, each with a number of subcategories. In the camps of African Bushmen and Pygmies, there seems always to be some music activity going on. In a Basongye village, on the other hand, many days may elapse without any kind of music being heard; indeed, the only event that requires musical accompaniment is the periodic new moon ceremonial (Merriam, 1964).

Everywhere, the human life cycle provides countless occasions for song: lullabies and puberty ceremony songs, courting and marriage songs, family and funeral songs. There are work songs, songs for war and for peace. A variety of musical expressions are associated with religious occasions everywhere; texts of prayers and myths are set to music, and there are songs for cults and for curing, for divination and for meditation. Music is often inseparable from dance as well as from drama. In our own diverse and complex society, musical preference is often a group identification symbol, which varies according to age, class, and occupational and educational status.

Among the cattle-herding Tutsi of Ruanda, there are songs for boasting, war, and greeting; songs for young women who meet to gossip; children's songs; religious songs; songs of flattery, courtship, and marriage. There is also a substantial catalogue of songs relating to cattle: songs in which two men sing competitively in praise of a particular cow or of one cow over another; songs to accompany evening cowherding; songs to sing while drawing water for cattle; songs to sing with other herders in the evening; songs in praise of the royal cattle; songs for showing cattle off to visitors, special flute songs to foil nighttime cattle thieves; and songs recounting events in which cattle figured (Merriam, 1959a, p. 50).

Music can be made in many ways; human vocalization is only one of them. Naturally occurring materials such as hollow rods or animal bones, hollow logs and reeds or grasses provided the models for numerous native instruments. But new instruments are created as new materials become available: the development of the steel drum, now the characteristic music sound of the Caribbean, dates back only

A number of different percussion instruments are represented in this group of Mangbetu musicians who are accompanying the *nebembo* **(circle dance) in Zaire.** (Photograph by Eliot Elisofon, Museum of African Art, Eliot Elisofon Archives)

Graphic art, music, and dance come together in this painted dance drum of the Montana Crow. (Photograph courtesy of the Museum of the American Indian, Heye Foundation)

to World War II. Empty oil drums left in Trinidad were found to have, with minimal shaping by humans, a most appealing tonal quality.

The world's inventory of instruments is vast. Many instruments are essentially rhythm-producing, with limited variation, if any, in pitch. Frisbie (1971) lists five kinds of rattles, sticks beaten on the ground, and a water drum for the Bushmen; seven kinds of clappers, hand bells, foot stomping and hand clapping, rattles, and hollow log drums for the Pygmies. Both of these groups have an even greater variety of pitched instruments, both wind and string varieties. Common throughout Africa is the sansa, kalimba, or thumb piano, which is both percussive and pitched. It consists of narrow metal strips of varying lengths attached to a board, played by pressing on the unattached ends of the metal strips

(Frisbie, 1971). A simple wind instrument consisting of a hollow reed or narrow piece of wood or root, with holes to be stopped by the fingers for different pitch levels, is found in some version in every part of the world.

As with his studies of dance, Lomax (1962) and colleagues (1968) has identified some correlations of musical styles with other aspects of social organization and social structure, such as work. Thus, choral music is found in conjunction with cooperative labor, whereas yodeling is characteristic of the lone herder. His conclusions have been questioned, and his particular methodology challenged, but his music studies constitute one of the most ambitious cross-cultural musicological attempts. It is interesting to note that Frisbie (1971), utilizing different techniques, arrived at conclusions similar to those of Lomax in her studies of Pygmy and Bushman music and social life. She seems to support Lomax, giving additional authority to his results. Such comparative studies are only in the formative stages, but they indicate the kinds of interrelationship which might be investigated.

The communicative power of music is well known but, contrary to romanticized popular notions, music is not a universal language. In fact, the available evidence indicates that between different music styles lie substantial barriers to communication (Merriam, 1964). In an experiment reminiscent of that of Child and Siroto with the BaKwele masks above, Morey (1950) chose selections "from Schubert, Davies, Handel, and Wagner which expressed fear, reverence, rage, and love respectively, as well as a control selection from Beethoven (which) did not express a generally acknowledged emotion" (Merriam, 1964, p. 111). Students and teachers at a mission school in Liberia for whom these selections were played did not respond. The same pieces, when played for members of a remote village, caused large portions of the audience, especially women, to get up and leave. Morey concluded that music does not convey emo-

tion to listeners whose cultural experience of music is different from that of the composer of the music (Morey, 1940, p. 354). This may seem surprising, since we respond to a wide range of music types, but then our contemporary musical upbringing has exposed us to greater variety than any people in history have experienced.

Changes in music styles and uses accompany culture change. Among the Toba of Argentina, music was primarily performed by individuals; recently, however, Pentecostal-type religious practices were introduced, and group singing during services became widely adopted. Traditionally, shamans sang to cure their patients, to control stormy weather, to appease the spirits when approaching a graveyard, and on other occasions of danger which required intervention from supernatural powers. Singing in churches in Toba communities today plays much the same role and serves to induce the ecstatic trance that is a component of the religious service.

Verbal Arts and Folklore

As speech is universal and characteristically human, so is the possession of a tradition of verbal arts. The verbal arts are a major component of folklore, which comprises also the nonverbal traditions of sports and games as well as folk dancing. All cultures have verbal art forms; among some peoples, many different forms are found. However, not every category of verbal arts is found everywhere. For example, there are many peoples, among them the Toba, who have no tradition of drama. On the other hand, drama is extremely important in many parts of the Far East— Indonesia, China, and Japan in particular— and many types of dramatic productions occur in those societies.

Dundes points out that among nonliterate peoples the verbal arts "correspond in part to the written literature of literate societies" (1968, p. 117). Dundes asserts further that oral literature should be analyzed in the same ways as are customarily applied to written literary products, in terms of structure, style, aesthetics, social and psychological content, and so on. However, this has too rarely been the case, for reasons that have to do with the ways in which oral literature has usually been collected and perceived.

Systematic collection began in early nineteenth-century Germany with the Grimm brothers, who were to a large extent motivated by a romantic view of the oral folk tradition as a link to an idealized past. As ethnology developed later in that century, quantities of folk tales, song lyrics, proverbs, jokes, and so on were transcribed. A major portion of field data has always concerned folklore, but anthropologists have not always known what to do with such materials. Usually they have been attached to anthropologists' ethnographies in the form of one or more appendices, occasionally annotated as to the identity of the singer or storyteller. Seldom was the total cultural context included; as a result, there have been far too few studies comparing the roles of particular aspects of the verbal arts among cultures.

The most useful studies of folklore describe the context in which tales are recounted or verses sung; the roles of the individual telling the tales or singing the song; the purposes they serve (entertainment, social cohesion, etc.); and the audience. Among the Toba, for example, certain tales are told only by elderly women, others only by shamans, others by any adult male. In our own culture, much of our verbal literature is told only by adults to children; another segment only by men to each other; and there is always a body of oral material told by children to one another. Elsewhere, certain songs or stories may be told only by those who have had a vision,

reached a certain age (elderly men, adolescent girls), or are members of a particular secret society. Jokes of certain kinds may be exchanged only between age mates, or only between a woman and her son-in-law, or between a young man and his uncle. Thus, who tells the stories, the content of the stories, in what context they are told, and for what purpose—all are important aspects of folklore that have seldom been adequately explored.

An additional problem crops up in the very act of translating the oral tradition into print. As Dundes shows, most published materials "have been edited to conform with the canons of written tradition and consequently the printed tale bears only a slight resemblance to the oral original" (168, p. 122). Current recording technology is of some assistance here, since it allows for preservation of the oral production, and videotaping permits the context to be preserved as well. However, the equipment itself may intrude on the spontaneity and unself-consciousness of a performance.

Folk tales probably have been told since the beginnings of culture, long before writing was developed, and they continue to be told today. Dundes (1968) distinguishes three major categories of oral folk narrative. *Myth* is a sacred narrative, set in a time span at least in part prior to creation and concerned with essential relationships of earth, humans, and the supernatural. *Folk tales* are usually set in the postcreation past ("once-upon-a-time") and deal with the adventures of an individual pursuing a personal goal. *Legends* are set in historic time and the real world, and may tell of supernaturals or provide explanations for origins of names or customs.

Products of the verbal arts—like those of dance and music but unlike those of most visual arts—are ultimately a collective effort rather than an individual one. Transmitted in oral-aural fashion ("from mouth to ear") over long periods of time, the insertion of changes becomes inevitable. Some cultures are less tolerant of variation than others: Eskimo narrators are corrected by members of their audiences if alterations are made in a tale. But because there is constant interaction between creator and appreciator while oral literature is in production, a recitation may vary in response to audience feedback or even to the composition of the audience, the particular occasion, or more personal factors. Verbal art forms must be considered always as work in progress: a tale "is *never* completed," according to Dundes (1968, p. 120). But if it does change, then the different versions may provide indications of where the culture has been and where it is going. Too often ethnologists have neglected to record variant texts and their contexts.

James L. Peacock, in a classic study (1968) of drama in Indonesia, has shown how audience response can alter the content of dramatic folklore from one community to another. These plays utilize fantasy and mockery to confront crucial aspects of social existence. Peacock's study shows how analysis of the content of folklore and the changes in its content—in this case, in a dramatic production—can identify key symbols and issues in a changing society.

Precisely because it is verbal, oral literature is readily accessible for study. It is valuable as an indication of a people's world view, of their understandings of reality, and for clues to culture contact in the far distant past. Dundes, for instance, believes that relationships between peoples, as between Asian peoples and American Indians, is attested to by numerous parallels in the folk tales in those cultures.

A number of recent studies have compared the oral traditions of African peoples with those of American blacks. Cycles of stories that in Africa featured spider or rabbit trickster characters appear widespread throughout black-settled areas of the New World. A particularly interesting black American verbal art form is "the Dozens," a verbal competition in which two or more contestants vie in hurling insulting spontaneous rhymed couplets at each other (boxer Mohammed Ali is a master of the form). Some have asserted that this game originated in the United States as an outlet for emotion in response to the cultural suppression and oppression of blacks. But Chimezie (1976) has recently pointed out significant similarities of the American game and several African versions, and sees the American form as having developed out of an African heritage. This study also interprets the content of many of the verbal exchanges, both in the African and American forms of the game, in terms of similarities between the mother-centered family units of most Africans and those of Afro-Americans.

Games and Sports

Games and sports are included in this chapter for several reasons. First, they are forms of folklore, transmitted within a culture from one generation to the next. Second, as is true for some of the verbal and dramatic acts, they provide recreation or entertainment for participants and observers. Similarly, they may be used as accompaniment to other cultural activities. Finally, they express cultural meanings and values.

Games of one sort or another are found in all cultures. Some game categories, too, are virtually universal. Many are played with materials widely available; earth or sand, beans, seeds, shells, and pebbles are to be found everywhere. As a result, counter games, such as Go, checkers, and African chess (*kala*) are widespread. Archaeologists have discovered that games and sports such as ball games appear to have been commonplace throughout the New World long before the arrival of Europeans. Thus, games are very old in human history.

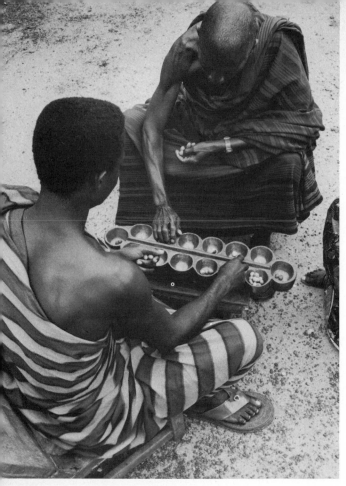

Ashanti men playing *wari* (elsewhere in Africa known as *kalah* or *mankala*) in Ghana.
(Photograph by Eliot Elisofon, Museum of African Art, Eliot Elisofon Archives)

Clearly, games are not played by children alone. In fact, children's games constitute a special subcategory; they often serve to teach adult roles and skills as well as cultural values. Games are important in reinforcing social precepts on every level. It was no accident that one of our most popular games ever invented—Monopoly, which gave practical training in the mechanics of the capitalistic society's money dealings (mortgages, manipulating interest, taxes, etc.)—caught on like wildfire during the Depression, for games also serve psychological wish-fulfillment functions.

As a human cultural universal with clear

ties to animal behavior, play has biological and psychological connotations. Our concern here, however, is with what Huizinga (1950) calls "play as a function of culture proper" (p. 5). He notes, first, that play is itself a social construction. It is everywhere separated from "ordinary" or "real" life or "serious" activity, and is voluntary.

Burridge (1968) provides a good illustration of an anthropological study of a game that serves as a model for social behavior among the Tangu of Oceania. The game is called *taketak,* the word for the spines of coconut palm fronds planted in the ground in two massed groups; opposing teams spin tops made from a dried hemisphere-shaped fruit rind with a spindle inserted into the palm fronds. The game is competitive, but not in a way familiar to us. The goal is to demonstrate the equivalence of both teams; in other words, *not* to come out ahead. Burridge describes two versions of the game. In the form played in a more acculturated area, one team may actually win. "Yet no team that loses is content to leave it at that. A return match is arranged in which every effort is made by *both* sides to come out equivalent in the series" (p. 317). In the older version, skill is required to hit the palm fronds with the top when necessary and also to miss them if it is expedient. Not outdoing the opposing team is the important thing. Similarly, in Tangu culture, "food exchanges and the rivalries that go with them can also be ended by mutual consent" at a point at which two individuals or groups are even. Thus, the values of the culture are replicated in the game.

Games and sports are cultural elements subject to borrowing and diffusion, much as are music, dance, and designs. The same form adopted in a new cultural setting may be given altogether different meaning by new participants. Toba games were not highly competitive traditionally, but they have learned to play soccer exceedingly well, and Toba teams now compete with neighboring teams. Games and sports can also be adopted because they are associated with the higher status of the group originally possessing them. Thus, rugby, cricket, polo, squash, and tennis have been widely adopted in British colonial outposts. In Barbados, for example, race tracks and cricket fields are shown with pride as "places of interest."

As with other topics discussed in this chapter, the anthropological analysis of material relating to games and sports has barely begun. Aside from the availability of certain natural materials, such as rubber for balls or wicker for baskets, why should certain types of sports develop in one cultural context and not in another? What are the differences between games traditionally played by women and those played by men? What do we know of games built around subsistence activities (fishing, planting, and the like), games that provide psychological release, games for children, games for old people? Where are sports participants an honored group? Where and under what circumstances are all members of a society expected to participate actively? The available ethnological data have seldom been

Music, dance, acrobatics, costume, and myth enhance each other, as shown in this water color, *The Delight Makers,* painted by Fred Kabotie, a twentieth century Hopi Pueblo artist. (Photograph courtesy of the Museum of the American Indian, Heye Foundation)

analyzed for their game and play materials. Only when such material has been carefully looked at and studies have been designed to investigate these problems, will we begin to fully understand the roles, now very much obscured, played by play in human cultures.

This chapter has been able to touch on only a small number of the many aspects of the arts in human societies that are (or should be) under investigation by cultural anthropologists. A point mentioned only in passing remains to be emphasized here, and that is the multidimensional nature of the artistic enterprise. Art forms are frequently used to enhance each other, creating a heightened impact that is greater than the sum of the parts. Japan provides two examples, Noh drama and the tea ceremony. Noh drama is a distinct form requiring costumes, music, dance, oral literature, makeup, architecture, and carved and painted masks. The tea ceremony involves a specified relationship between crafted objects, an interior architectural setting and furnishings; it must be fully responded to by all the senses of the performer and participants.

Similar examples can be cited for numerous other cultures. The Kwakiutl *potlatch,* at the furthest possible remove from the serenity of the tea ceremony, is equally a multisensory, multidimensional experience for participants, involving dance, music, oral narrative, carved and painted masks, costumes, food, competitions, and more. And on a miniature scale, Ashanti proverbs are frequently illustrated in tiny sculptures of animal or human figures formerly used as weights for gold dust.

It is with a feeling of awe that we observe many outstanding works of art produced in our own and other cultures. But knowledge of the varieties of artistic productions found throughout the world should instill in us an even greater awe for the vast human capacity for creativity and appreciation. It should also make us humble to realize how limited are our individual capacities, as members of one cultural tradition. Can we stretch our sensory perceptions and intellectual equipment to confront the range of human creativity with adequate comprehension of cultural relationships and appreciation of aesthetic values? The cross-cultural contribution of anthropology is a first and essential step in that direction.

Summary

1. Art is universal. It exists, and has existed, everywhere, in every culture, at every time. Anthropologists are concerned with art in relationship to culture. Art involves behavior on the part of the audience as well as of the artist. Of all aspects of culture we have examined thus far, the arts are unique in that they result in a product separable from its cultural context.

2. The separable art objects of non-European cultures were first collected as curiosities. In the nineteenth century, the primitive arts, including music and oral literature, were discovered by Europeans and Americans and hailed as representing an idealized, natural, preindustrial, uncorrupted world. By the turn of the century, these works, and especially the carved wood sculptures of Africa, were discovered by the avant garde, particularly the French artists and writers. Such works influenced the development of modern art at the same time as they were being discovered by early anthropologists. Boas and his students saw evidence of cultural contact and diffusion, especially in the visual art products of nonliterate societies.

3. Art is important as communication; but we must understand it within its cultural context in order to comprehend the full meaning of its message.

4. No category of art is overlooked by

non-Western cultures. The visual arts comprise not only graphic and sculptural productions but also production of utilitarian crafts and architecture. Many visual art objects are produced to accompany religious rituals. Some objects are status symbols, but the greatest number are the everyday items that people make for their own use.

5. Dance is found everywhere. In most cultures, there are multiple kinds of dances and occasions for dance. Anthropologists are concerned not only with how and on what occasions people dance, but also with who does the dancing and who is in the audience. There is some evidence linking dance movements to movements used in subsistence activities. Ethnomusicology investigates both such technical considerations as construction, melody, and instrumentation on the one hand, and focuses on the performers and the audience, on meanings and the functions of music within the society, on the other.

6. Oral literature, a branch of folklore, consists of tales such as myths and legends, which may be accompaniments to ritual, pure entertainment, or serve still other functions. Games and sports, also a branch of folklore, are the "play" element in cultures everywhere. Games are as old as human culture, but the spirit in which one culture plays may be very different from that of the next.

7. Not only are arts universally found, but they are also often multidimensional, with one art form being used as an accompaniment to heighten the impact of another. Everywhere, human sensory perceptions interact with the products created by talented individuals, following cultural aesthetic precepts.

PART THREE

Anthropology in the Modern World

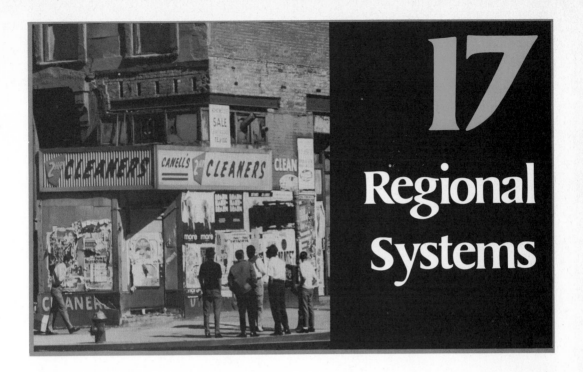

17
Regional Systems

MOST anthropological field studies, as our examples throughout this text have shown, consist of intensive investigations of local communities. The field methods and techniques described in an earlier chapter were designed to interpret data about activities and beliefs collected by participant-observers in close, day-to-day contact with their subjects. The anthropological perspective that has developed over the years is the cumulative result of generalizations from a large number of such individual local studies.

We have also seen, from the time of World War II, that there have been scattered attempts to deal with some categories of data on a national or regional scale. The national character studies of the 1940s and 1950s, mentioned earlier, were a notable exception to the otherwise pervasive local approach. However, such broad-scale investigations failed at the time to gain a permanent place in anthropological research, primarily because the conclusions often seemed simplistic and superficial.

But even earlier, soon after the turn of the century, it was becoming apparent that an alternative to the local community approach was needed—an approach that would explore the interactions of local communities and the larger regional units or systems to which they belong.

The development of the culture-area concept in the early years of this century marked the growing recognition that cultural relationships do not begin and end within the boundary of the local group. It became obvious that when there are ties of language and sharing of artifacts, diffusion of ceremonies and songs, there had to have been substantial interactions among people, both as individuals and as groups. The cultural ecology studies of the 1950s and 1960s also went beyond the locality in their focus on interactions within regions, but these studies were usually devoted primarily to economic considerations, not to the social relationships that might be associated with them.

When anthropologists began to turn their attention to the study of complex contemporary societies, they at first attempted to conduct research using what were called *community studies,* which were similar to the kind of fieldwork they had used to collect data on small-scale societies. In nearly every case the study of social relationships would stop at the edge of the village, much as it had stopped at the edge of the tribal camp. In this way, physi-

Regional systems consist of related communities; villages interact with each other and with a larger urban center. Here, roads lead in all directions from Lier (Lierre), Belgium, connecting the urban center with surrounding farm communities in a panoramic view from 1595.

cal or arbitrary political boundaries were confused with social and economic ones.

Research in village communities was displaced to some extent in the 1960s by the beginning of what has come to be called *urban anthropology*. But in most cases only the site of research had shifted. Believing that cities were the centers of activity, anthropologists continued to situate themselves in one place and study a street gang, a neighborhood, or even a whole city—as a unit in and of itself.

Again, by the 1950s it was apparent to many anthropologists that some of the assumptions inherent in the participant-observer, local community type study were due for reconsideration. The most basic of these assumptions is that intensive study of a single group or community, however small or large, will reveal all the significant dimensions of the culture as a whole. As Smith would later point out, "the standard anthropological monograph on a small community suffers theoretical limitations because of its narrow parochialism, and . . . studies of large-scale, national systems do little to illuminate the lives of people who live in small rural communities—the majority of mankind" (1976, p. 4). Thus, it was realized that in complex societies, study of contexts broader than the local community is crucial. To comprehend all of the dimensions of a *complex society* anthropologists must deal with all levels of interaction, from small-scale communities to the progressively larger units of which they are a part. The ultimate, all-encompassing level, of course, would be the entire international community, consisting of all the societies in the world. However, regional systems, consisting of related communities and their many areas of interaction, are more feasible and realistic. Here we shall discuss the development of the regional approach, which is assuming greater significance, and the application of the anthropological perspective to issues of contemporary urban society.

Toward a Regional Perspective

One of the earliest and most influential attempts to go beyond the local community was Robert Redfield's study of *The Folk Culture of Yucatán* (1941), mentioned in an earlier chapter, in which he posited the connections between what he described as rural, folk culture of a village and the urban, industrial center of which the village was a satellite. As we have pointed out, Redfield contrasted these two different social and cultural settings: He saw the *folk society* as socially satisfying; integrated and stable; and homogeneous and isolated, while he viewed the urban society as disintegrated and constantly changing; heterogeneous; and a part of a larger, even more complex social system.

In later studies Redfield posited the existence of communities halfway between these, those in which the folk society underwent "transformation" to urbanization. In *primary urbanization* the precivilized folk society becomes a peasant society attached to an urban center; the peasant and urban communities that result, however, both "share a common culture." In *secondary urbanization,* external cultural influences alter the folk, peasant, or partly urbanized society, resulting in the creation of "not only a new form of urban life in some part in conflict with local folk cultures but also new social types in both city and country" (Redfield & Singer, 1971, pp. 344–345).

Redfield's model of these different categories of communities and their interconnections—which has come to be known as the *folk-urban continuum* (1960)—stimulated much research on societies in the process of transition from one type to the other. In so doing, his model also called attention to the importance of a larger, regional perspective in anthropological study. Redfield's influence was, if anything, enhanced by the fact that his work coincided with the cultural transitions going on throughout the world in the so-called "developing societies," a fact that gave considerable impetus to support investigations of this sort.

Redfield's model has a number of limitations, however, the major one being his definition of folk and urban societies as structural opposites. In focusing on differences and describing each type in polarized terminology, structural similarities were ignored, and the interrelationships and balances between the two were overlooked. Furthermore, it was taken for granted that change was unidirectional through time, that societies were inevitably becoming more urban, and that this was an irreversible trend. Thus, what began as an analysis of the interconnections between different kinds of communities ended as an analysis of the changes that take place when folk societies become urbanized.

Edmund Leach also utilized a broader perspective in his study of the *Political Systems of Highland Burma* (1954). By lifting his sights beyond any one local community, Leach saw that two apparently contradictory ideologies —hierarchical and egalitarian—formed a framework within which he could relate the activities of all local groups at a single point in time. As Leach saw it, social groups in the Kachin Hills Area characterized by one ideology were under various social pressures to take actions that would move them towards the other ideology. These pressures worked against the establishment of complete dominance of either type in any one community. Indeed, Leach found that the local community could not be isolated. While the people of the region "may speak different languages, wear different kinds of clothes, live in different kinds of houses," they were interrelated in significant ways: "They understand one another's ritual. Ritual acts are ways of 'saying

things' about social status, and the 'language' in which these things are said is common to the whole Kachin Hills Area" (p. 279). Leach also recognized that most societies are not in a state of stability but are, rather, always in a process of change and that clear lines between local groups usually cannot be drawn: "Many . . . tribes are, in a sense, ethnographic fictions" (p. 291). Other ethnographers, in dealing with a limited area and what they perceived as a single culture, imposed unity on their material by making distinctions and choices between the "ideal" culture of which the people spoke and the actual culture in which they lived. But Leach, by focusing on the larger regional system, was able to interpret data, not as a reflection of a gap between the ideal and the real, but as part of the larger whole in which two cultural extremes were continually exerting a push-pull effect upon each other.

While we are discussing the development of a regional focus in studying societies we should mention the influence of international events. After World War II, government concern over the administration of occupied nations and territories initiated some research and led to the development of area studies, particularly in the Far East and Pacific. Such studies were later expanded to other parts of the world.

The attention paid in the late 1960s to the role of ecological factors in the formation and arrangement of social and cultural systems also prompted a regional focus in anthropology. The research of Fredrik Barth (1956, 1969) called attention to the manner in which different ethnic groups exploit distinct resources of a given environment to the extent that these groups become interdependent. In a study in Swat, North Pakistan (1956), for example, Barth showed that "different ethnic groups will establish themselves in stable co-residence in an area if they exploit different ecological niches, and especially if they can thus establish symbiotic economic relations"

(p. 1088). By focusing on the social boundaries of these groups (1969), he was able to show the degree to which one local group forms a part of the larger system made up of additional groups. According to Barth, the resulting interactions give each ethnic group its unique cultural character. As he argues, attention to one ethnic group, and not to its interactions with other groups, would lead to serious distortions.

Rappaport's analysis (1967) of the "pig culture" of the Tsembaga of Highland New Guinea, referred to previously, is another contribution in cultural ecology that utilized a regional focus. In this culture, ritual and warfare between a number of individual local groups combine to maintain ecological balance throughout a region.

While all such approaches have been useful in expanding the horizon of field research, Smith (1976) has recently argued that none of them really establishes a clear conceptual framework or a methodology for truly *regional studies*. She proposes to do this through a *level-specific regional analysis*, distinguishing the local, regional, and national as three distinct levels for research. Her own work is at the regional level, which she views as being halfway between the local and national (pp. 4–5).

Level-Specific Regional Analysis

According to Smith's model, local and regional systems are both *nodal forms of organization*, because they consist of territories peripheral to or clustering around a *node* or *central place*. The periphery may be completely rural or may comprise several smaller nodes or centers along with their peripheral territories.

One may define a nodal region at any level, to include larger or smaller areas of interdependence. Local systems are those in which both material and nonmaterial exchanges are organized around at least one higher-level node, [while] regional systems . . . include a number of levels of hierarchically organized communities . . . having a truly "urban" central place, complex linkages between communities and higher-level centers, and an organized pattern of nested local systems within them. (1976, p. 9)

The concepts of region, center, and periphery, borrowed from geography, serve to illuminate the spatial distribution of social and cultural systems. Smith argues that the view of "complex societies as nested regional systems, discrete in some aspects and overlapping in others at each level," (1976, p. 4) provides a framework that accommodates previous work so that new studies can add significantly to insights already gained.

Perhaps the best illustration of this approach is Smith's own analysis of exchange systems in agrarian societies. By concentrating on the "spatial organization of distribution" (1976, p. 314) she discerned the relationship between the distribution of goods and the organization of elites, which allowed her to demonstrate the crucial role of control over the means of exchange. She was able, on the regional level, to see that social and economic power was wielded by those who were in control of a "critical resource," which might be "a means of production, such as land, . . . a means of destruction, such as fire power, . . . a simple means of subsistence, such as salt, that cannot be locally procured or produced" (p. 311), or a means of distribution, such as transport animals or marketplaces. By stressing control over the means of exchange, rather than mere control over the means of production, Smith also was able to show the relationship between different types of stratification systems. Had she focused more narrowly, at the local community level, Smith would not have been able to see beyond the production system to the region-based distribution and stratification systems.

At about the same time, Beck utilized the same concepts of center and periphery in her analysis of the caste system of a region in southern India (1976). And Appleby used a similar regional approach in his study of an economy based on the export of a single commodity—wool—in the Puno region of southern Peru (1976). These and other analyses demonstrate Smith's point that "the *flows* of goods, services, information, and people through [a] network of centers . . . structure and maintain internodal relations" on a regional basis (1976, p. 8).

Case Studies from a Regional Perspective

In a study of regional cults, Werbner argues that Smith's "level-specific approach ignores activities overriding and not congruent with the boundaries and subdivisions of a nation. Similarly neglected are the phenomena which define international or non-national regions. Theoretically, the approach introduces a bias towards nesting relations and it does not allow for cultural variability, i.e., the variable importance of different conceptions held by the people studied themselves of their fields of relations" (1977, p. xi). Werbner goes on to propose a regional approach "without the three tiered model or its level-specific assumptions." By focusing on religious ideology and change, Werbner and his colleagues demonstrated how a religious cult can be modified by local beliefs and actions, yet integrated with divergent groups on the basis of common premises. Werbner illustrates his approach with a study of the High God cult of Mwali, or Mwari, of southern Africa. Congregations of the cult are found in spatially distinct regions scattered through Zimbabwe, Botswana, Mozambique, and the Transvaal. Each region is not continuous but rather "a set of many separated pieces" (p. 180), and each "extends over thousands of square miles across ethnic, district, and even international boundaries" (pp. 179–180). Werbner demonstrates that when faced with such material, one has no choice but to examine both the narrow range of the cult and its more in-

clusive context. In his words, "The more a cult spreads across major ethnic and political boundaries, the more its organization may have to be variable and its ritual and symbolism transcultural" (p. 179). Therefore it must be studied on multiple levels at the same time.

The value of seeing the region as a system also is shown by English (1966) in his research on settlement and economy in the Kirman basin in southeastern Iran. He points out that social scientists usually have divided society in the Middle East into three sectors: the city, the village, and the tribe.

Invariably, such authors preface their discussions by warning readers that one must *not* view these segments as discrete economic realms and cite examples to illustrate the mutual interdependence of each sphere: city dwellers depend on village-grown crops; villagers receive basic commodities . . . from the city; tribesmen supply wool and milk products to marketplaces in return for grain. Having delivered this warning, these writers proceed to discuss each segment as a self-contained system: cities are viewed as islands in a barren land, linked by networks of roads and caravan trails, and occupied by traders and processors who share in "urban" as opposed to "folk" culture; villages are isolated, self-sufficient, inward-looking peasant communities with few external relations; tribes are ethnic and/or political groups who migrate periodically in prescribed patterns. (p. xvii)

Rejecting this view, English concentrates instead on "the distribution and diversity of settlements and their functional integration in a complex regional organization" (p. xviii). As a result, he is able to make the following points:

1. The existence of Kirman City, the administrative, economic, and social capital of the region, depends on the coordination and exploitation of resources in the surrounding areas and not (as traditionally viewed) on its position on a trade route.
2. The villages in the Kirman basin, like those

in most areas of the Middle East, are not isolated, homogeneous units with bare subsistence economies, as many writers have portrayed them. They differ from each other in size, complexity, and economic basis, and some even have occupational organization structures as complex as that of Kirman City itself.

3. The economic and social arrangements made between landlord and peasant, carpet manager and weaver, and wool merchant and herder are very similar to each other and thus reflect the patterning of the regional system.

4. Modernization throughout the region has impacted more on social patterns than on economic organization.

This is an important study, as it integrates economic and social data from a regional perspective. Similarly, Cohen and Middleton (1970) focused on the political arena from a regional perspective. In our discussion of the politics of new nations in an earlier chapter, we examined the processes by which small groups are sometimes incorporated into nation-states. We see here that analysis of economic, political, religious, as well as more purely social transactions, benefits from the use of a regional perspective. Attention to the environment and ecological niches of different populations also contributes to this perspective. Thus, it is essential to include a regional aspect when analyzing local systems.

Geertz has attempted to put the regional approach into theoretical perspective. He points out that what anthropologists do best is "microsociology" (1972, p. 461), the intensive study of small-scale social systems, and urges that more attention be paid to the transition "from comprehensive ethnography in simple societies . . . to specialized microsociology in complex ones," especially in understanding the kinds of generalizations that can be made on the basis of such studies. As he puts it, anthropologists study

the same sorts of processes in micro that others study in macro. One can study metabolism at the level of the cell, the organism, or in ecology, the community of organisms. And though one gets different sorts of insights from each approach, one doesn't try to argue that a tropical forest is just a huge cell, or a cell a miniature tropical forest. Rather, one tries to make the diverse findings complementary, to shed light on one another in such a way that the general processes of metabolism are better understood. It is no different here: what one learns in Sidi Walu of a hundred souls and what one learns in the Casablanca of several hundred thousand is neither more nor less general than the other. It is just that some things can be learned about a certain problem—here politics and social change—in one place that are difficult or impossible to learn in the other, and vice versa. (1972, p. 462)

Too often anthropologists have assumed that the locality itself, and not what takes place within it, is of primary concern. Thus, the boundaries of the community have all too often become the boundaries of research.

Geertz calls also for (1) the "disaggregation" of "megaconcepts," (pp. 462–464) such as landlord-tenant and urban-rural; (2) abandonment of the tendency to validate hypotheses, often originating in other disciplines; and (3) concentration instead on deriving new conceptualizations. Geertz himself has been making useful contributions to regional studies for many years, and his early study of form and variation in a Balinese village is a classic example (1959).

All of the approaches we have been discussing represent attempts to transcend the local community in order to gain perspective and insight into the patterns and processes of more complex levels of social organization. Ultimately, however, anthropologists must return to a local community to study the influence of the regional system on its beliefs and practices. One does not solve the problem of overemphasizing the locality by overemphasizing the region, the nation, or any other organizational level. The relationships among the various levels are important and must be discerned, but the whole is more than simply the sum of its parts. In other words, while anthropologists use the regional perspective to good advantage, they cannot afford to neglect the local communities in which human beings demonstrate the real events that make up their lives.

Societies in Transition

Throughout this text, culture has been shown to be dynamic. People's designs for living change continually, and so the study of a given cultural phenomenon at one time and place does not necessarily characterize that phenomenon for all times and places. Similarly, societies are in a continual process of transition: external factors such as environmental change, culture contact, and immigration, together with internal factors such as invention, human interaction, and birth- and deathrates, continually alter the nature of any social group. But most studies have not taken the fact of continual culture change into account. However, the one key area in which such alterations have been taken for granted and have been built into every research design is peasant studies. This is because peasant societies have been considered by definition to be in a transitional state of development, somewhere between so-called folk societies and so-called urban societies. The central concept in peasant studies is that of change, frequently broadened to include the regional nature of change. For this reason, it is useful to consider such studies as examples of the kinds of contributions anthropologists have made to understanding the dynamic nature of societies, especially from the perspective of regional considerations.

Peasant Studies

The subsistence basis of *peasant society* is, of course, agriculture, which can readily be distinguished from the horticulture of tribal

In the Andes mountains of Ecuador, the trade network functions through markets held in a different village every day. Here, a bus brings vendors from the previous day's village to the marketplace of Zumbagua, where they will join people from the surrounding district in selling produce, handcrafts, and factory-produced goods. (Bob Kelly, Photo Researchers, Inc.)

societies in its greater productivity, due to more effective techniques for exploiting the environment. But in some ways peasants are not unlike many so-called "primitive" cultivators, since they, too, grow crops mostly for their own consumption. In both, too, predictable food surpluses may allow some members of the community to be non-food producing and become artisans or develop other skills, while receiving food from others in return for their services or products. Despite their often considerable productivity, peasant agriculturists cannot be considered farmers or business-minded. Their concerns are those of householders, not entrepreneurs (Wolf, 1966a, p. 2).

Some anthropologists have distinguished between the two categories, claiming, for example, that peasants constitute "part-societies with part-cultures" (Kroeber 1948, p. 284). Such a statement recognizes the fact that peasant societies form parts of larger, more complex social systems but ignores the fact that a similar case can be made for most, if not all, "primitive" cultivating societies, since very few of these are completely isolated and self-sufficient. Most participate in elaborate and long-established networks of trade and, as we have pointed out in previous chapters, many also interact with neighboring groups in such diverse fields of endeavor as warfare, marriage, and ceremony (Wolf, 1969, pp. 2–3).

How, then, do peasant societies differ from tribal societies? One key difference, it is argued, is in the kinds of interactions with outside groups and their implications for the local community. In tribal societies, as Sahlins (1960, p. 408) points out, because *"de facto* control of the means of production is decentralized, local, and familiar . . . economic relations of coercion and exploitation and the corresponding social relations of dependence and mastery"* do not arise. Any surpluses are transferred directly, usually to fulfill kinship or similar intergroup obligations.

In peasant society, on the other hand, *de facto* control of some *critical resource* (as Smith put it) is in the hands of a dominant group. Peasants must transfer their surpluses to the elite in exchange for access to the critical resource, and the ruling group can then use "the surpluses both to underwrite its own standard of living and to distribute the remainder to groups in society that do not farm but must be fed for their specific goods and services in turn" (Wolf, 1966a, pp. 3–4).

Wolf shows that, contrary to widespread notions, the development of cities is not the crucial factor in altering tribal sociopolitical organization, but rather

the crystallization of executive power. . . . Not the city but the state is the decisive criterion of civilization and it is the appearance of the state which marks the threshold of transition between food cultivators in general and peasants. Thus, it is only when a cultivator is integrated into a society with a state—that is, when the cultivator becomes subject to the demands and sanctions of power-holders outside his social stratum—that we can appropriately speak of peasantry. (p. 11)

However, because of the dynamic nature of social systems, there is no one type of peasantry. As Wolf explains, "our world contain[s] both primitives on the verge of peasantry and full-fledged peasants . . . societies in which the peasant is the chief producer of the store of social wealth and those in which he has been relegated to a secondary position" (p. 12).

Wolf's extensive study, which details both the kinds of relationships that various peasantries have with outside groups and their ways of coping with the resulting pressures, represents a significant contribution to this field. Wolf sees the interaction with outside groups as posing a crucial dilemma for peasants that ultimately is responsible for the constantly changing character of peasant societies. This dilemma is the need to synchronize the demands of the external elite with the requirements of the individual household. In the face of such vicissitudes of life as periodic changes in quantity of production (due to weather, illness, etc.) and greater demands from landlords or priests, peasants have two apparently opposite strategies for coping: increase production or curtail consumption.

An increase in production enables peasants to compete in a market; however, achieving a marketable surplus is difficult because the only real capital of peasants is the physical labor of the household, and they usually hold land under obligation to landlords. Being in an essentially subsistence economy, they also accumulate little cash or other negotiable property. However, as Wolf shows, this can be done when the economic and/or religious power structure that keeps the peasant economically encumbered is weakened, as occurred in sixteenth century England, in China, and in prerevolutionary Russia, accounting for the rise of a wealthy peasantry in those (and other) places.

By means of the alternate strategy, retrenching toward total reliance on the production of the household for all goods and services, peasants can reduce and virtually eliminate their interaction with the outside world, and thus be less subject to the pressures for change imposed from without. Wolf sees this as the explanation for the well-known conservatism of peasantry: "they fear the new as they would fear temptation: Any new novelty may undermine their precarious balance" (p. 16).

Yet even in a retrenchment situation, peasants tend to retain social and ceremonial ties within their own communities. "As long as these can be upheld, a peasant community can ward off the further penetration of outside demands and pressures, while at the same time forcing its more fortunate members to share some of their labor and goods with their less fortunate members" (pp. 16–17).

Wolf shows further that these two strategies, though apparently opposites, are not mutually exclusive. "Periods in which the first strategy is strongly favored may be followed by others when the peasant retrenches and renews his social fabric within a narrower orbit. Similarly, at any given time, there will be some individuals who will risk . . . testing the limits of traditional social ties, while others prefer the security [of] following the norm. . . . A peasantry is always in a dynamic state, moving continuously between two poles in the search for a solution to its basic dilemma" (p. 17).

Through its strategies and, as Wolf argues, supported by its ideological values, peasants interact on regional levels with other similar peasant communities and with various kinds of what Smith referred to as "central places" for religious, marketing, political, or other interactions.

Diaz and Potter similarly stress the relationships with people outside of their immediate communities as the characteristic or defining feature of peasantry. They describe peasant social institutions as "Janus-faced—looking both toward the requirements imposed by the larger political and economic order and toward the customary expectations of the peasant community" (1967, p. 154). They also point out the interrelationships between peasant communities: "People from other villages may be sources of spouses, or they may provide the aid and protection villagers need when they travel away from home," describing the different networks which serve as the axes of peasant life. The economic network, which may be "spread intricately across the countryside, spaced with markets of varied sizes and organization" is comprised "of persons to whom peasants sell their surplus handicrafts and produce, and from whom they purchase the goods that they themselves do not produce" (p. 165). There are also religious networks, such as an area served by a particular shrine or temple, or a pilgrimage route. There are marriage networks that structure kinship patterns; these may intersect the economic or religious networks, as when a marketing area provides the boundaries within which spouses must be selected, or when a ceremonial occasion provides the opportunity for courtship. Or the marriage network may set up special relationships between communities, as in the case of exogamous intermarrying villages. There may be other kinds of networks, such as mutual protection associations or irrigation societies. But above all stands the state-established administrative unit, which creates "political relationships that cut across village boundaries," such as the *municipio* of Mexico or the *mura* of Japan. Potter and Diaz conclude that:

The peasant village is thus clearly not an isolated whole; it has both vertical and horizontal ties extending from the village to the larger society and civilization. . . . it is impossible to understand the social life of any peasant community without taking state policy and its history into account. (p. 167)

Potter also has stressed the transitional nature of peasantry in his analysis of the urban, industrial impact on peasant communities (1967b). His study of rural Communist China (1967a) details the impact of a centralized administration and its revolutionary policies on a quintessentially traditional (and vast) peasantry.

Cultural Brokers

A considerable amount of attention has been paid in anthropological studies of peasantry to *cultural brokers,* the mediators who serve as bridges between the local peasant community and the outside world. This concept was originally put forth by Wolf (1956), who saw cultural brokers as those who "mediate between community-oriented groups in communities and nation-oriented groups which operate primarily through national institutions." Again, cultural brokers "stand guard over the crucial junctures or synapses of relationships which connect the local system to the larger whole." In Mexico, as he shows, historically there have been several categories of individuals who served this function—leaders of Indian communities, owners of haciendas, or political leaders in more recent times. From our own society the local political leader or ward chief in the cities certainly served in such a capacity, mediating between the immigrant ethnic groups (which had been, it must be emphasized, uprooted from peasant communities) and the new urban system of which they had become a part. Similar examples could be cited from numerous societies; however, it is important to recognize that the specific functions served by culture brokers vary with the cultures involved and the specific problems being coped with at a given time.

Silverman, for example, describes what she calls the community-nation mediator in traditional central Italy, where she found that "the concept of the mediator proved to be most pertinent for understanding the relationship of the community to the larger society during a particular period" (1967, p. 280). In the community she studied, the patrons were those individuals who had ties extending beyond the locality, and who, as the only literate members of the community, translated the national culture at the local level and in various ways served as "economic, political, social, and ideological link[s] to the larger society" (p. 289). Because of changes in "the groups which perform[ed] mediation functions" as well as structural changes in the "links between community and nation" following World War II, however, Silverman, concludes that "the mediator represents a general form of community-nation relationship which characterizes an early phase in developing nation-states, and which regularly gives way as integration of the total society advances" (p. 292).

It is not hard to understand why such a role is needed. Peasants attempt to develop relationships with individuals of superior wealth and power to gain economic and political security. In many peasant societies, particularly in Latin America and the Mediterranean, individuals involved enter into *patron-client relationships*. Patrons gain prestige and power and can call on the support due them from their clients in the event of political need. (The discussion of ritual kinship in an earlier chapter illustrated some of these relationships.) As Diaz and Potter (1967, p. 164) point out, cultural brokers "often assume leadership among peasants, exercising power and authority on the levels of society beneath the state administration." And in doing so, according to Diaz and Potter, this group also acts as a buffer, representing the interests of peasant community and state to one another, so that their brokerage is also political in nature.

Léons (1977) has described the rise of one such patron, Juan Mendoza, to a position of provincial political leadership in Bolivia. As a storekeeper, he had built up a network of creditors who became his political followers at a time of revolution and land reform. All followed his lead in voting, giving him the power to determine who would occupy local office. He became the source through which government programs, including land distribution, were delivered to the community and its people, who of course enhanced his power further as he was able to be generous to those who supported him and withhold benefits from his detractors. With a solid mass of voters behind him, Mendoza has been able to negotiate with whatever government came to national power. Léons focuses on the economic networks that made possible Mendoza's rise to power in the first place and those that he developed as his resources accumulated along with his political power. Her analyses of one individual's dealings, within as well as beyond the local community, illustrate how political and economic factors are interwoven and how a cultural—or in this case political—broker functions to relate the community to the region and the nation.

Wolf (1966a), with whom the cultural broker concept originated, applied it further in a discussion of the character of interpersonal relationships—kinship, family, friendship, and patron-client—that span a region. One of his conclusions was the possibility "that complex societies in the modern world differ less in the formal organization of their economic or legal or political systems than in the character of their supplementary interpersonal sets" and that it is these supplementary sets that make possible the functioning of the great institutions" (p. 19).

This approach points the way, for example, to a new way of viewing the family in contemporary society; instead of lamenting the passing of the traditional family, our attention should turn to understanding the ways in which new interpersonal relationships, both within and outside the family, serve to integrate individuals with the institutions of modern society.

Abandoning the "Peasant" Concept

Peasant studies have contributed significantly to the anthropological literature and have served to lift the sights of anthropologists to larger regional issues and interactions. But the question must be asked: Is "peasantry" a category like, for example, hunter-gatherers? The answer must be no. If it were, then all of the societies described as such, from Indonesia to Bolivia, and contemporary China to medieval England, would be much more similar in many more ways than they demonstrably are. These and other societies are indeed complex, in the sense that they are parts of larger economic, political, and cultural systems; but they have very few specific characteristics in common. The typologies to which peasant communities have been assigned by Wolf (1966b) and others imply that they have in common cultural form and/or content in addition to certain economic/subsistence patterns and that these differ significantly from those of other types of societies. These implications, however, are not substantiated by ethnographic evidence (Miller, 1976). For example, family farming is found in many other societies than those considered in peasant studies, including so-called folk societies, as well as both modern capitalist and communist states. Then again, the relationships of the various so-called peasant communities to regional markets, national economies, or regional or national cults and religions, have been very different in different times and places. In fact, the variability of "peasant" societies may be due as much to historical considerations as to ecological and cultural factors. Comparisons based on a limited number of similarities in economic structures may well be useful, but typologies formed on this basis are probably misleading.

In fact, many of these studies seem to show an actual bias against their subjects in applying to them such patronizing terms as *limited good, little tradition,* or *patron-client.* This would seem to represent an example of *ethnocentrism* in the very discipline that coined the term to combat such attitudes. It is almost as though the analysts are rejecting the cultural patterns they observe, perhaps reflecting the contemporary bias against people who appear to allow themselves to be exploited. If they are seeing their subjects as representatives of an earlier, less developed stage in our own civilization, it is a curious holdover of the kind of ethnocentrism that produced the evolutionary models of a century ago.

But the strongest reason for abandoning the concept of peasantry is that it is a construct that anthropologists have imposed on their data. Definitions of peasants are impossible precisely because they are arbitrarily imposed from without and not based on true similarities. Finally, the identification of peasants as part-society, part-culture can only inhibit an open-minded approach to study of the communities concerned (Miller, 1976, p. 21). No society is ever part-anything; every society

is a coherent whole to those participating in it. And since all societies are in dynamic process, there is no point in singling out so-called peasant communities as prime examples of transition.

This is not to suggest that the studies cited here have failed to contribute significantly to anthropological understanding. They certainly have contributed, as our discussion has clearly indicated. But let us call them what they truly are—studies of family-farm-based communities within regional systems. Without the imposition of arbitrary constructs, the data should speak for themselves. It is more important to understand differences, and the reasons for and implications of their existence, than it is to force data into artificial typologies.

Urban Anthropology

As anthropologists followed their objects of study from rural hinterlands into cities, and as they began to train their sights on their own culture (and on the communities surrounding their universities), there developed a subdiscipline that came by the late 1960s to be known as urban anthropology. Peasant studies played a key role in this development, since they inevitably led to studies of what Geertz calls the "post-peasant problem" (1962, p. 5). Here anthropology entered a whole new arena, the study of modernization, the coming together of old societies to form new states, and the kinds of human interactions that take place in today's ultra-complex urban communities.

However, it has never been quite clear whether the proper study of this subdiscipline should be the urbanization process itself, the comparison of different kinds of cities around the world, or the application of anthropological insight and perspective to urban problems, particularly in American culture.

Even before the peasant studies ushered in by Redfield's work, anthropological methodology was being applied to selected communities within modern, industrial nations. These community studies, as they came to be called, often crossed the boundary between anthropology and sociology, as in Warner's *Yankee City* (1963, based on work begun in 1930) or the Lynds' studies of Muncie, Indiana (1959, 1963). Later studies using similar techniques were those done in a city neighborhood by sociologists Whyte (1955) and Gans (1962), while anthropologists Vidich and Bensman (1958) applied the same methodology to a community in New York State, examining its ties to the wider regional and national scene. Community-study methods were subsequently applied to urban centers in developing nations, which continue to be an important area of investigation.

Archaeological studies of early civilizations and the earliest urban settlements, which seek to establish the relationship between the development of cities and economic and sociopolitical processes have contributed also to the anthropological understanding of urbanism.

Rethinking Urban Anthropology

A basic problem in defining the purview of urban anthropology has been, as Eames and Goode observe, "the Western ethnocentrism of many concepts dealing with the urban." As a consequence of this bias, no "universal, culture-free definition of urban centers" has been offered, and studies often suffer from an underlying anti-urbanism (1977, p. 53). (This is, of course, not peculiar to anthropologists; anti-urbanism appears to be a paradoxical, permeating, and persistent American characteristic.)

The archaeological perspective is essential to remind us that for most of pre-history and history, the city has been non- or pre-industrial. London in Shakespeare's time and Edo under the shogunate in Japan are only two cities that existed for many centuries prior to their present-day high degree of industrialization (Edo is now Tokyo). Many examples of nonindustrial cities can also be cited: Benin in Africa, "Old" Delhi in India, ancient Rome, Ur in Sumer, Tikal of the Mayans.

Sjoberg has conceived the ancient city as primarily a locus of governmental and religious functions and only secondarily as a center of economic function (1960). Traditional cities still exist, of course, in many parts of the world, and they have been and are being fruitfully studied. But Sjoberg's description of the pre-industrial city is an idealization that suffers from the same kind of problems as those noted before for peasant typologies. For most of the defining characteristics he cites, exceptions can also be cited (Keesing, 1976). Even in its pre-industrial forms, the city is too complex for simple typologies.

Cities as Subjects or Settings?

Anthropologists who use the city as their center of investigation have many different concerns. For some, cities are themselves subjects to be studied. But for others, as Keesing states, "cities [are] *settings;* one studies a neighborhood, a housing project, a street corner, as before one had studied a village or a band—as a microcosm, a social world in miniature." The city as a *setting* and understanding "how cities create new modes of human experience" (1976, p. 506) are precisely what most urban anthropology is all about.

Eames and Goode note three different types of urban studies in anthropology: the migration of peasants to cities, urban problems, and ethnographies of selected urban settings or groups—in all of which the city is used as a setting. But mention should also be made of studies in which the city itself is the

Long before the industrial urban complexes of modern times, the pre-industrial city was a sprawling, densely-populated center serving many functions, as this view of London and Westminster in 1584 demonstrates. (The Bettman Archive)

subject, such as Fox's *Urban Anthropology* (1977). The most representative example of migration-to-cities studies is that of William Mangin (1970), which contains articles on the movements of rural villagers to urban centers in the major continents of the world, with particular emphasis on Latin America. These migrations are frequently to slum areas of the city, and the life in these areas is depicted and described, along with the articulation of slums with larger urban environments.

Migration studies thus lead directly to problem-oriented research in cities. A notable example is the work of Oscar Lewis, who went from studying *Life in a Mexican Village* (1963) to studying the urban poor. Lewis conceptualized a "culture of poverty" based on his studies of Mexican and Puerto Rican families, which he held was characteristic of urban poor in many parts of the world. As a scheme for viewing similarities that cross-cut cultural boundaries, Lewis's concept has been useful, but it has also been controversial with respect to both topic and method. Valentine, for example, criticizes both Lewis's notions that urban poverty is inevitably self-perpetuating and the idea that there is a distinct poverty culture that transcends national/cultural boundaries. In *Culture and Poverty* (1968) Valentine provides alternative ways of viewing poverty and the poor.

Undoubtedly, many of today's urban problems, not only in the United States but throughout the world, are a direct result of

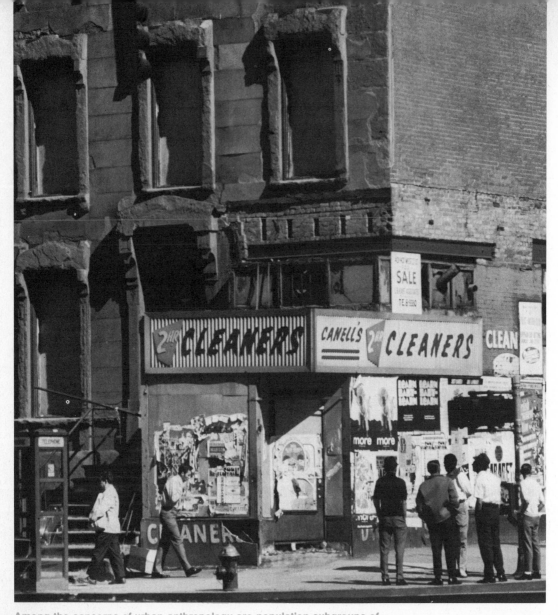

Among the concerns of urban anthropology are population subgroups of the city. The world of unemployed black men who spend their days "hanging out" on street corners, such as in this scene, is explored in *Tally's Corner,* a classic ethnography. (Jim Cron, Monkmeyer)

rural-to-urban migration. Uprooted from the relatively homogeneous societies with simpler social and economic structure and thrust into urban settings, individuals discover that familiar rules and relationships no longer apply. With traditional networks disrupted, new support systems must be devised. The language barrier is only one of many cultural hurdles that must be crossed by most such migrants. Their accustomed techniques for manipulating available resources are no longer workable. (They were often no longer workable in the traditional setting either; an extensive period of economic malfunctioning—due to population pressures, weather conditions, or other factors—is the customary prelude to rural-to-urban migration.)

The third type of urban study identified by Eames and Goode, ethnography applied to a selected urban subgroup, is well illustrated by Elliot Liebow's work among unemployed black men in Washington, D.C., *Tally's Corner* (1967). Another classic urban ethnography is that of James Spradley, who studied alcoholics, primarily in Seattle. His work, entitled *You Owe Yourself a Drunk* (1970), attracted a lot of attention not only in anthropology but in other disciplines as well. Both of these studies were based on *intensive interviewing* and on extensive participant-observation. Both attempted to grasp the participants' point of view (the "native" point of view as we describe it in traditional anthropological studies), and both succeeded to

the extent that order and rationality became apparent where disorder and irrationality had appeared before to an outside observer. Both studies also identified the structures of interaction between the populations concerned and particular elements of the broader society of which these participants formed a part. And both call for a new perception of the world as lived by the people they studied, identifying the external constraints that give life among these natives its distinctive character.

Urban anthropology is itself developing subfields. Two that are assuming particular importance at present are ethnic studies and the related development of medical anthropology. Urban ethnic studies developed from studies of migrations to cities, since the ethnic subgroups clustered in urban settings originated as transplanted "peasant" or "folk" groups. A key example of how traditional anthropological subject matter became a subject for urban anthropology is the case of Ameri-

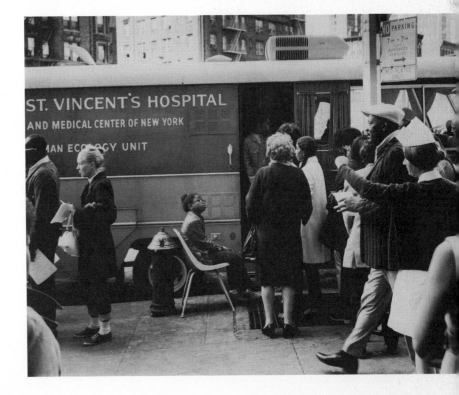

The anthropological perspective can enhance our understanding of the components of urban problems and assist in devising solutions. Providing preventive medical care for all segments of a diverse population is one such problem. Here, residents of a New York City neighborhood wait for free medical tests given in a mobile van. (Irene Bayer, Monkmeyer)

can Indians. And so-called ethnic studies have been spurred by government policies of funding programs for minority groups and by minority competition for this attention. The anthropological perspective has made a great contribution to understanding in this area.

Medical anthropology is concerned with provision of modern medical care to the various ethnic groups comprising contemporary (although not necessarily urban) society, and it is thus problem oriented. But studies of the perception of illness, reactions to medical intervention, the expression of pain, and how illness is managed in the native cultural setting must be drawn from traditional ethnographic materials or investigated directly using ethnographic techniques (Grossman, 1976).

Similarly problem-oriented is the exploration of food habits and nutrition from an anthropological perspective. In part this, too, is an outgrowth of ethnic studies, but it has important application to problems of world nutrition and food supply. The relationship of food habits to a variety of ecological and social factors has been touched on earlier in this text.

Current issues, rather than social problems as such, are also leading to new areas for urban anthropological investigation. The theorizing and publications that have come out of the women's movement have led to the realization that in every society women are enculturated differently from men, and that cultures in effect consist of subcultures in respect to the two sexes. Lakoff's study of women's language in our society (1973) is a case in point. Women anthropologists today are bringing a new perspective to traditional topics and are, for example, engaged in such projects as comparison of women's roles in traditional societies. An early woman-centered study was Laura Bohannan's (1949) analysis of Dahomeyan marriages, which focused on rights to women and the status of women (and their children) as a consequence of different marital situations. Even earlier, of course,

were Mead's studies of child-rearing and adolescence, which gave full emphasis to female development and women's roles (1928, 1930).

Similarly, the development of interest in gerontology in recent years has led to ethnographic studies of the elderly, such as that of Myerhoff and Tufte in a community center for Jewish senior citizens in Venice, California (1975). An early antecedent was the extensive cross-cultural compilation and analysis of Simmons (1970) on *The Role of the Aged in Primitive Society.*

From Urban to Global Perspective

Studies in and of the city inevitably have multidisciplinary implications; sociology, psychology, and economics are brought to bear along with anthropology. Anthropology in its urban focus can serve as a synthesizing agent, marshaling the whole range of social science approaches without restriction. There is no particular virtue in maintaining distinctions between disciplines. As Eames and Goode state, "There will be an overlap in those segments of all social science disciplines focused on the city. The mature development of anthropology as well as urban anthropology demands that we not waste so much energy on concern over our domain or turf" (1977, p. 17).

The important point is that, no matter what the subject of study, the anthropological perspective is crucial. The recent emergence of urban anthropology may seem to be a variety of things, with no clearly defined area of study, but it can lead to fruitful insights. As Keesing says, "An anthropology that studies urban life in comparative perspective can perhaps fulfill in this new realm the historical role of anthropology in the social sciences: sorting the culture-bound from the universal, and hence pushing toward a genuinely comparative understanding of human ways" (1976, p. 506).

But it is becoming increasingly obvious that in shifting the focus from local, rural communities to large urban centers, anthropologists can repeat the same mistake of myopia. Rather than make cities themselves the center of study, human populations of cities, along with their ties to rural homelands or foreign countries, should constitute the field of study. Extension of study to fill a regional framework would be valid whether the site of the study is the United States, Latin America, Europe, Africa, Asia, or Oceania.

The regional and world perspective proposed here would locate any study in a larger framework incorporating all the factors that play a role in the lives of the people concerned. It is not the focus of study that should necessarily be changed, but rather the scope of interpretation. The methodology would continue to be what Geertz calls *microsociology*, carried out with participant-observer techniques, but the data elicited would be interpeted in broader terms than is generally now being done. As Redfield said in 1956: "I

361

Toward a global perspective . . . (Marylin Yee, *The New York Times*)

362 think we shall come to study regional systems. We shall study such systems, not, as we now tend to do, from the viewpoint of some one small local community looking outward, but from the viewpoint of an observer who looks down upon the whole larger regional system" (cited in Smith, 1976, p. 3). It is time that this prophetic vision of the potentialities of anthropological research in today's world be realized.

studies of various kinds have been applied productively to analyses of religious cults, economic systems, political organization, and social stratification.

Summary

1. In recent years anthropological studies have moved beyond their traditional focus on a local community to the larger region with which the community is integrated.

2. Redfield's *The Folk Culture of Yucatán,* an early study emphasizing links between a village and its region, contrasted the homogeneous, stable folk culture of the village with the heterogeneous, disintegrated urban culture of the city that served as its political, religious, and commercial center. Redfield's concept of a folk-urban continuum held that there was a definite tendency toward urbanization, and that peasant societies were in an intermediate stage of transition from one to the other. This model inspired a number of so-called "peasant studies," which detailed the networks by which peasant communities in different parts of the world are tied to the regions in which they are situated.

3. Level-specific regional analysis has been proposed by Smith as a methodological approach, the levels being local, regional, and national. This approach views communities in terms of their spatial arrangement vis-à-vis a "central place" that serves as hub to a number of interconnected satellite localities. Regional

4. Peasant societies have been studied as agricultural, family-farm-based, and held in a dependent relationship to an external dominant group that has control over a critical resource such as land or access to markets. Peasants have been described as "Janus-faced," looking both to the impositions by the outside forces and to the requirements of their own community.

5. The interactions of peasants and the dominant elite has been described as a client-patron relationship. Cultural brokers are individuals who mediate between the peasant community and the outside world, usually in such areas as commerce and politics.

6. However, in all other respects, so-called peasant communities are quite varied in different places and at different times in the human past, and thus there is really no one socio/political/economic system that can be singled out as "peasantry." So-called peasant societies coexist within modern industrial states, both capitalist and communist, as well as in developing nations. Because much of the terminology applied to peasant societies seems to reflect an ethnocentric bias on the part of researchers, and because categories are artificial constructs imposed from without, the concept of *peasantry* as an economic/social cultural unit should be abandoned.

7. The subdiscipline of urban anthropology developed out of community studies, as anthropologists followed the migrations of their traditional subjects of study from rural hinterlands into cities and as they turned their attention to the societies of which they themselves are a part. New perspectives and areas of investigation are still in the process of development.

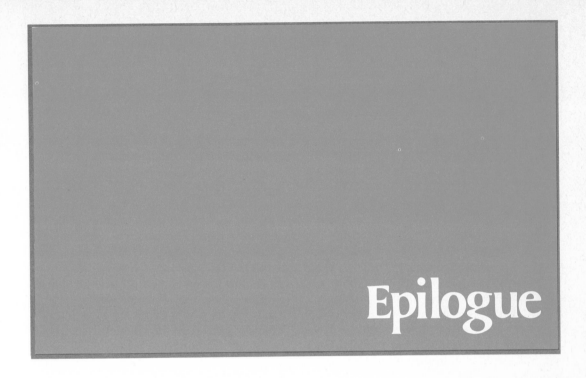

Epilogue

I N an earlier chapter we discussed the two crises for anthropology identified by Claude Lévi-Strauss in 1967. The first stems from a drastic change in the anthropologist's laboratory. Since World War II, small isolated groups of primitive people, once favorite objects of study, have nearly disappeared. Some of these primitive groups were reduced by maltreatment on the part of colonial powers or by infectious diseases introduced from the outside world. But even the survivors among these peoples have not emerged unaltered from their encounters with representatives of more technologically developed societies. As Lévi-Strauss notes, the result of Western contact with primitive groups has been a transformation in these once isolated cultures. In effect, all humans now seem close to becoming members of one civilization based on Western technology.

The second crisis facing anthropologists today is the increasing hostility shown them by third and fourth world peoples. This crisis is a product of anthropology's history. In the past, anthropologists came to be identified with colonial powers, even as they sought to avoid this identification. Furthermore, they sometimes treated the people they had come to study as "scientific objects" rather than as independent human beings with sensitive feelings. Viewed in this light, one can readily understand how resentment toward anthropological fieldwork developed.

Both of these crises have affected anthropologists' ability to gather data for analysis. But there also exists a crisis in anthropology at a more theoretical level; that is, at the level of analysis. The approaches of holism (seeing an overall picture), fieldwork, and comparison, once the distinct characteristics of anthropology, have now been adopted by such other disciplines as economics, sociology, and psychology. As researchers in the social sciences came to recognize the interrelationship of economic, social, and political processes, the idea of anthropology as a separate, well-defined field has been called into question (Kaplan & Manners, 1972). In fact, many studies published by anthropologists today include strong doses of related fields, from economics to political science, in their analyses (Needham, 1970).

With primitive societies practically vanished, many anthropologists have changed the focus of their studies in recent years. Some have begun to investigate small units within large industrial societies, such as urban neighborhoods or workers in a factory or hospital. Others have attempted to analyze larger units, even whole nations or regions, while continuing to use the same holistic approach once employed to study small communities. And still other researchers have focused on important or powerful groups within a complex society, hoping in this way to understand many of the hidden factors controlling large-scale systems (Kaplan & Manners, 1972).

Thus, anthropologists have shifted the directions of their studies both as a result of changes in field conditions and in response to changes in their adoption of theory from other social sciences. They have also altered their research techniques in response to the resentment shown to them by new nations. In general, anthropologists have become more concerned with the way in which their fieldwork may disrupt or harm the cultures they are investigating.

One of the most important ethical difficulties anthropologists have faced in recent years is related to the question of work undertaken for government agencies. On occasion, governments have used the results of anthropological fieldwork as a source of intelligence information. Once gathered, this information has been kept secret and used to direct political and military operations in foreign countries. In 1971, the American Anthropological Association responded to this problem by adopting the Principles of Professional Responsibility, insisting that all research results obtained by anthropologists be available to the public (American Anthropological Association, 1973, p. 1). This position taken against secrecy may demonstrate to the developing world that anthropologists today do not intend to be used as representatives of colonial powers.

Besides recognizing the rights and independence of nations in the process of modernization, the 1971 statement of principles also emphasizes the rights of individuals under investigation. According to the guidelines of the statement, anthropologists have a duty to explain the purpose of their studies to subjects and to respect their privacy. Of course, such guidelines are not always easy to apply in fieldwork, as a recent book on the ethical dilemmas of anthropology (Rykiewich & Spradley, 1976) demonstrates. For example, one researcher found many difficulties in studying marriage and family behavior in a small elite group in Western Africa. The topic she was interested in was itself very sensitive and required keeping information confidential. When writing a report on her fieldwork, she realized that many of her subjects would eventually read the results, and so she felt obligated to not only disguise identities but also tone down her findings (Harrell-Bond, 1976).

Another ethical problem in anthropological fieldwork arises when the researcher takes a political or moral position on the events he or she is in the process of recording. For example, an anthropologist studying the inhabitants of the Marshall Islands in the Pacific found himself increasingly drawn into disputes about whether the islands should seek independent status or permit the development of large American military installations. Although, as a professional researcher, he felt it would be best to remain neutral, he did develop strong opinions against the American military presence. Later, he felt that he could have helped the Marshallese make a wise decision by discussing politics more openly with them (Rynkiewich, 1976). Thus, while it is possible to state as a general principle that anthropologists should not interfere in the internal affairs of the societies they study (Beals, 1969), in practice, neutrality is not always easy to maintain.

Working under government contract, maintaining the confidentiality of sources, and dealing with one's own political opinions in the field—these are day-to-day ethical problems for an anthropologist. On a more theoretical level, the ethical problems posed by the practice of anthropology and the other social sciences have recently come under discussion. As noted by Lévi-Strauss, anthropologists have often tended to treat the people they study as "scientific objects," and not as human beings involved in a struggle for existence. As one remedy for this prejudiced outlook, he recommended that third world anthropologists come to study Western cultures. Certainly such a program would reverse the traditional situation of Westerners as observers and third world people as objects studied. Similarly, one sociologist recently stated that researchers in his field need to stop considering humans as two different and unequal breeds: those who investigate and those who are the objects of the investigations. He adds that every study in the social sciences involves the interaction between the researcher and those who are studied. Thus, the results of a research project in the social sciences can reveal as much about the culture and the values of the investigator as about the culture and values of those under examination (Gouldner, 1970).

Furthermore, if all research results are influenced by the values of the investigator, then it should be the investigator's responsibility to understand exactly how his or her views affect what is seen. This idea of social sciences committed to values is of course sharply different from traditional notions about the possibility and desirability of a completely value-free or objective approach (Gouldner, 1970).

In some respects, the recognition that their findings are often colored by their own views may make anthropologists less convinced that they can offer the right answers to political or social problems that involve conflicting values. On the other hand, there is no reason why this recognition of a commitment to values should prevent anthropologists from contributing to the discussion of public policy. In fact, the principles adopted by the American Anthropological Association in 1971 affirm that anthropologists have a duty to help develop an "adequate definition of reality" on which public policy can be based. (When offering advice, of course, anthropologists need to be honest about the limitations in their knowledge and in the methodology of their discipline.)

One of the ways in which anthropologists have undertaken to help formulate policies is through the analysis of future trends. Naturally, there are difficulties involved in attempting to describe the future on the basis of anthropological insights gained through research. A student of the future must be able to focus on those present trends that will have the most importance for later events, and these are not easy to recognize. A second type of difficulty arises when anthropologists or other social scientists are asked to help formulate plans to improve social conditions, such as poverty, unemployment, or white-collar crime. Such planning often involves the adoption of a specific value system. In effect, anthropologists may be asked to set cultural goals for societies whose members hold a wide variety of beliefs. Of course, the ability and the right of any one person or group of persons to define such goals is frequently questioned (Kaplan & Manners, 1972).

On the other hand, it seems likely that people will always spend a significant amount of time and energy planning for the future, and there is no reason why anthropologists should not play an important role in this endeavor. In fact, as Margaret Mead has pointed out, anthropological knowledge has some special contributions to make to *futuristics,* the science of the future. Anthropologists, she writes, have studied humankind over very long periods of time and thus have gained insight into the way innovation has changed pace. The rapid population growth following the development of agriculture and the accelerating rate of technological change since the beginning of the Industrial Revolution two centuries ago are both familiar phenomena to the anthropologist. By a process of comparison or analogy, anthropologists may be able to develop a similar understanding of the rapidly accelerating changes that may occur in the future. Second, the ability of anthropologists to deal with an entire culture at once, considering all its aspects, may make them particularly suited to analyze the global problems of the future (Mead, 1971).

The publication of Alvin Toffler's *Future Shock* in 1970 marked the beginning of a widespread awareness of the special qualifications of social scientists for the analysis of the future. Yet, at the same time, there are researchers who dispute the idea that futuristics can merely borrow methods from such existing disciplines as anthropology. According to this view, future rates of change *cannot* be studied simply on the basis of the past, as proposed by Margaret Mead. Margoroh Maruyama, for example, argues that it is the unprecedented event that determines the future. Thus, researchers in futuristics must be occasionally capable of abandoning all assumptions in order to imagine completely different rates and types of development. Nevertheless, this capacity for imagination cannot become just a tendency toward fantasy. The imaginative predictions and solutions to future problems need to be grounded in a scientist's and experimentalist's ability to develop realistic accounts of events. It is perhaps not surprising then that most early studies of the future have dealt with technological and economic trends. It is only recently that topics with less technical content and greater value orientation, such as cultural aspects of future society, have been investigated (Maruyama, 1971).

Confronting the ethical problems of fieldwork and focusing their analytical skills on future trends and problems are two important responses on the part of anthropologists to the crises in their discipline. But it may be safely predicted that while anthropology will continue to change its focus and its techniques, its basic aims will not be discarded. As Lévi-Strauss wrote in 1967, anthropology has always helped to expand our comprehension of humanity. There will no doubt continue to be a need for anthropologists to aid in the processes of communication and interpretation.

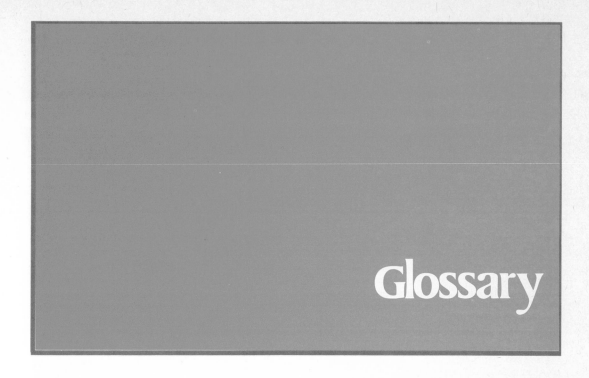

Glossary

adaptation   the ability of a living organism to maintain or regain stability under conditions of environmental change.

administration   the conducting of public affairs by those who have gained that power.

aesthetics   the study of beauty and of psychological responses to it.

affinal kin   individuals who are legally related through marriage.

affinity   relationship by marriage.

age grade   a category of persons arranged according to age only.

age set   a group of members of a given age grade who pass together through various life stages.

agnatic descent   *see* patrilineal descent.

agriculture   intensive plant cultivation using technological means such as plows.

ambilocal residence   a pattern in which a newly married couple is expected to live for a period of time with or near the bride's parents and for another period of time with or near the groom's parents.

ancestor-focused group   descent group that traces descent to a common ancestor.

anthropology   the organized study of human beings.

authority   the institutionalized right to take control and to take certain actions; it represents rules, procedures, and accepted actions considered binding when applied within a given society.

avunculocal residence   the pattern of residence in which the newly married couple lives with or near the groom's mother's brother.

basic personality structure   the cluster of tendencies common to the personalities of individuals who shared early experiences as a result of being brought up in the same culture.

balanced reciprocity   an exchange transaction in which one expects goods or services of roughly equal value in return for what one gives.

band   a small group of families, numbering 50 to 100 persons, with simple political organization.

belief   statements that are generally held to be true by the members of a given society.

bilateral descent   the rule of descent, used in our society, in which the individual traces his or her ancestry through lineal relatives of both sexes.

bilocal residence   the pattern of residence in which the newly married couple has a choice of living with or near the parents or kin group of either the bride or groom.

bridewealth goods and/or valuables given to the bride's kin group by the groom or his kin group.

capital equipment and supplies used to produce more goods.

caste a culturally and socially distinct group whose membership is determined by birth and that is assigned a particular position in the social hierarchy.

childhood determinism the notion that childhood training shapes adult personality.

clan a unilineal descent group in which relationships between members cannot be demonstrated and are simply assumed; clans often trace their descent to an ancestor in the distant past.

class a group that shares the same social or economic status.

coercion model of social order model based on the belief that order is a product of force and constraint of conflicting elements in society.

cognitive anthropology *see* ethnoscience.

cognitive dissonance inconsistency between an individual's outlook or self-image and new experiences or situations.

collateral relatives kin who are not related in a direct biological line, such as father's brother or mother's sister.

complementary filiation kin relationships through the parent who does not determine descent.

conjugal family family arrangement consisting of two mates of opposite sex and their offspring.

consanguineal kin individuals who are biologically related by "blood."

consensus model of social order model based on the belief that order results from the general agreement of the members of society on a set of values that are more important to them than any differences of opinion among them.

controlled comparison a comparative method of study that considers together only groups that show strong social or cultural similarities.

cross cousins children of the opposite-sex siblings of one's parents—the children of one's mother's brothers and one's father's sisters.

cross-cultural comparison a study that compares features of one culture with those of another to see if there are regularities in the ways humans approach various facets of social life.

cultivators people who practice some method of raising crops.

cultural brokers mediators who serve as bridges between the local peasant community and the outside world.

cultural ecology the study of the relationship of specific cultural features to a group's adaptation to its total habitat.

cultural relativism the attempt to understand and evaluate each cultural system in terms of its own internally consistent logic.

culture something shared by everyone in a particular society, learned from one another and from past generations, that influences the way we think and act; that which is learned and shared rather than genetically transmitted.

culture and personality school *see* psychological anthropology.

culture core according to Steward, the economic and subsistence activities that seem most directly involved with enabling people to survive in their particular environment.

culture shock a psychological response to an unfamiliar culture; characterized by disorientation, anxiety, and sometimes mental breakdown, depression, or even suicide.

customary control *see* informal control.

deep structure in transformational grammar, the underlying meaning of a sentence.

descent the principle that links one generation to another in a systematized manner.

descent group a group of kin related by common descent—by certain specified rights and obligations across generations.

diffusion the spread of culture traits from one culture to another by historical contacts.

distinctive features the differences in sound that speakers recognize unconsciously in minimally different words.

divination the manipulation of the supernatural to discover concealed information.

divorce the lawful dissolution of the legal ties established at marriage.

double descent the rule of unilineal descent that traces ancestry through *both* father's and mother's lines.

dowry goods given to the bride or the newly married couple by the bride's kin group.

ecology the study of the ways in which all living organisms interact within the environment.

economic activity the choices people make in determining how available resources are to be used in producing, distributing, and consuming material goods and services.

egalitarian society a society in which occupational alternatives are few.

ego-focused group descent group that consists of people closely related to oneself (Ego) rather than to an ancestor.

enculturation the process whereby members of a society acquire the characteristics of a given culture, learning its language and generally acquiring competence in the culture.

endogamy the expectation that a marriage partner will be chosen from within the social group of which one is a member.

environmental determinism the belief that the reason for the presence of a specific cultural feature could be traced to the habitat in which it occurred; also called environmentalism.

environmentalism *see* environmental determinism.

environmental possibilism the belief that environmental factors limit the adaptive possibilities for a given culture but do not determine which adaptations or choices a society/culture makes.

ethnic group a population that is biologically self-perpetuating; shares fundamental cultural values expressed in unified forms; is characterized by internal communication and interaction; and considers itself to have particular identity.

ethnocentrism the tendency to judge other cultures by the standards of one's own culture.

ethnography a detailed and noninterpretive description of the social life, values, and thought of a given social group.

ethnology a study of culture that compares different cultures, often on a theoretical basis.

ethnomusicology the study of music in culture.

ethnoscience an approach to studying other cultures that claims that use of native language categories enables one to identify native points of view; also called cognitive anthropology.

exogamy the expectation that the choice of a marriage partner will be from a social group of which one is not a member.

extended family family arrangement consisting of the oldest male and his wife, the married sons with their wives, all the unmarried daughters, and the young dependent children of all the married pairs.

fission the permanent division of a clan or lineage into two or more segments.

folk-urban continuum Redfield's model of certain specific categories of communities and their interconnections.

formal control social control characterized by a systematized set of rules and procedures for managing disputes.

fraternal polyandry the marriage of a woman to two or more brothers at the same time.

fusion the recombination, usually temporary and in response to a specific need, of segmented lineages.

generalized other according to G. H. Mead, a person's mental representation of the expectations of society; an abstract entity that enables a person to see things from the perspective of his or her entire group.

generalized reciprocity an exchange transaction in which goods, services, or assistance is freely given to kin, friends, and neighbors without any open statement that anything is expected in return.

gift exchange exchange of gifts or payments by each of the two kin groups being linked to each other by a marriage.

grammar linguistic rules dealing with the ways language is structured into larger units of meaning.

grammatical transformations a set of "rewrite rules" that breaks units of the deep structure of a sentence into noun and verb phrases and transforms them into the surface structure of the sentence.

group marriage the marriage of two or more women to two or more men at a time.

holism the attempt in anthropology to incorporate various fields of knowledge into a meaningful understanding of humanity.

horticulture plant cultivation using simple tools and, mostly, human muscle power.

hunters-and-gatherers peoples who forage for food by hunting animals, by fishing, and by gathering wild fruits, vegetables, and nuts.

incest taboo the prohibition of sexual access to certain categories of kin.

informal control social control that consists of traditional or customary rules, beliefs, and procedures that are not arranged systematically; also called customary control.

integration the modification of borrowed culture traits to fit local cultural, social, or environmental factors.

joint family *see* extended family.

kindred any group of close consanguineal relatives, without reference to either maternal or paternal line of descent.

kinesics the study of body movement and gesture as means of communication.

kinship the relationships between individuals based on descent and marriage.

***kula* system** a special system of trade in New Guinea that consists of the circulation of shell armbands and shell necklaces for ceremonial purposes.

legal pluralism the existence within a society of more than one legal system at the same time, some of which may actually be in conflict with one another.

leisure preference the desire of people in industrial economies to work shorter hours rather than earn more money.

level-specific regional analysis method of research that distinguishes the local, regional, and national as three distinct levels.

levirate the practice requiring or permitting a man to marry the wife of his deceased brother.

lineage a unilineal descent group in which relationships among members are known and demonstrable; members of lineages often trace their descent to a common ancestor of several generations back.

lineal relatives kin related in a direct biological line.

linguistic universals *see* universal grammar.

market exchange an exchange transaction in which the parties to the exchange bargain to reach a price that is acceptable to both.

marriage a socially recognized and stable union providing sexual access, legitimating offspring, and establishing other rights and obligations between the marriage partners and other units of society.

matrilateral belonging to one's mother's side.

matrilineal descent the rule of unilineal descent that traces ancestry through the female line; also called uterine descent.

matrilocal residence the pattern of residence in which the groom goes to live with the bride in the household headed by her mother.

metacommunication a message that tells the receiver how another message is to be interpreted.

minimal pairs pairs of words that differ in only one sound, such as *pat* and *bat* in English.

modal personality proposed by Du Bois, the characteristics or tendencies shared by *most* members of a given culture.

model a system of relations that is thought to be parallel to, or a simulation of, a set of relations under study.

modernizing oligarchy a form of government in which ruling power belongs to only a few persons.

moieties the two groups into which a society may divide, in order to exchange women through marriage; each moiety consists of a number of either clans or phratries.

monogamy the marriage of one man to one woman at a time.

morph the smallest unit of meaning in a given language.

morphology the study of the ways in which morps in a given language combine to make words.

myth the verbal rationale for religion, differing from other kinds of verbal material in having the connotation of the sacred.

natives indigenous people; those belonging to a region.

natolocal residence a pattern of residence in which an individual resides in the house in which he or she was born.

negative reciprocity an exchange transaction in which goods or services are obtained through force or deception.

neolocal residence the pattern of residence in which the newly married couple establishes its residence without regard to the residence of either partner's family of origin.

nuclear family *see* conjugal family.

ostracism the rejection or exclusion of an individual by the general consent of the group of which he or she is a member.

parallel cousins children of the same-sex siblings of one's parents—the children of one's mother's sisters and father's brothers.

parallel descent the rule of unilineal descent in which males trace ancestry through males and females through females.

participant observation a method of fieldwork in which the anthropologist lives for a period of time among the subjects of his or her study.

pastoralism raising and herding animals for meat, milk, and the products derived from them.

patrilateral belonging to one's father's side.

patrilineal descent the rule of unilineal descent that traces ancestry through the male line; also called agnatic descent.

patrilocal residence the pattern of residence in which the bride goes to live with the groom in the household headed by his father.

personality the collective response patterns within every human being that determine the behaviors, thoughts, and feelings of the individual.

phonemes the distinctive but meaningless sounds heard by native speakers of a language.

phonemics the study of the manner in which sounds are used to communicate meaningfully in a given language.

phonetics the study of speech sounds from a physiological point of view.

phonology the study of human speech sounds.

phratry the several clans that claim common descent from the original common ancestor.

political democracy a system in which the central element is an elected legislative body whose laws are carried out by an executive with the help of an organized bureaucracy; political parties are accepted and active.

political system a system that applies to societies that have governments, politics, and administration.

politics   the contest to gain power within an authoritative political system.

polyandry   the marriage of one woman to two or more men at a time.

polygamy   plural marriage; polygyny, polyandry, and group marriage are forms of polygamy.

polygyny   the marriage of one man to two or more women at a time.

potlatch   a ceremonial feast of the northwest Pacific coast Indians at which a chief gave away goods to another chief in order to gain prestige.

power   the capacity to take independent action in the face of resistance from persons, groups, or rules.

prescriptive marriage rules   obligations that require individuals to marry certain relatives.

priests   religious specialists associated with organized churches and characteristically found in more formally structured societies.

primary institutions   according to Kardiner, those institutions that shape basic personality structure, including family and kinship arrangements, subsistence patterns, and institutionalized activities associated with feeding, weaning, and sex training.

primary urbanization   stage during which precivilized folk society becomes a peasant society attached to an urban center.

production   the various modes used by members of society to procure their material means of existence.

production organizations   groups engaged in the production of some type of material goods.

prophets   religious specialists who receive visions and communicate directly with supernatural powers on an individual basis; they are generally called upon to criticize the existing social order and to point the way to a better way of life.

proxemics   the study of the ways in which various societies use physical space in human interaction.

psychological anthropology   an area of study in anthropology that analyzes culture as expressed in the behaviors, thoughts, and feelings (or personality) of its individual members; also known as "culture and personality school."

rank society   a society characterized by a formalized system of graduated social statuses.

reciprocity   an exchange transaction that involves direct movement of goods or services between two parties.

redistribution   an exchange transaction in which goods are collected from the members of a group by a central authority and then divided up among the group.

reference group   a group with which individuals identify themselves as members or aspire to be identified.

reliability   the degree to which the results of an experiment or a set of scientific observations can be obtained on another trial.

religion   the system of social interactions consisting of those beliefs and activities that order human life by relating humans to spiritual beings and/or powers.

ritual   the demonstration of religious belief through performance of specific acts by the members of a society.

ritual kinship   the formalized relationship modeled on kin relations that one may have with a nonkin individual.

role models   members of society already engaged in a role that an individual can later expect to assume.

role theory   the theory that individuals learn from observing those around them.

sanctions   means of dealing with or controlling deviant or socially unacceptable behavior.

Sapir-Whorf hypothesis   the theory that language reflects the way in which speakers of the language perceive and think about the world.

secondary institutions   according to Kardiner, those institutions through which basic personality structure is expressed, including taboo systems, religion and rituals, folktales, and art.

secondary urbanization   stage in which external cultural influences alter the folk, peasant, or partly urbanized society.

segmentation   the subdivision of a clan or lineage into subgroups.

semantics   the study of meaning.

serial monogamy   a form of monogamy that consists of a series of monogamous marriages, one after another.

shamans   religious specialists whose primary function is healing the sick and protecting the community from harm; their healing proceeds by supernatural intervention.

significant others   according to G. H. Mead, individuals in one's life with whom one deals most intensively, parents, siblings, teachings, peers—and from whom one learns social roles.

slash-and-burn   technique of cultivation that involves slashing trees and underbrush, burning off the refuse, and planting in the cleared area.

slavery   a hierarchical system in which one group of people owns the labor and the products of the labor of another group of people.

social group   a group of individuals who come together for the purpose of achieving certain common goals and who interact in predictable ways that serve the interests of the group over a period of time.

socialization the process whereby an individual new to a society learns to function as a member of that society, including the learning of social roles.

social stratification the arrangement of status within a society into a hierarchy of socially superior and inferior ranks.

sociolinguistics the study of language use within a speech community.

sorcerers religious specialists who can cause harm and kill enemies.

sororal polygyny the marriage of a man to two or more sisters at the same time.

sororate the practice requiring or permitting a man to marry the sister of his deceased wife.

structural-functionalism an approach to the study of culture that assumes that every relationship or institution has a function and is understood as a part of a larger whole, called society.

subsistence economy an economic system in which people use what they themselves produce in order to meet their own needs.

suitor service a period during which a groom lives with and works for the kin group of the bride.

surface structure in transformational grammar, the outward appearance of a sentence; the sounds we hear.

syntax the study of the rules for combining words into larger units of meaning, such as phrases or sentences.

technology the tools and processes by means of which material goods can be produced in greater quantity and with less physical effort.

thick description understanding the meaning of social patterns to those who take part in them.

totem a plant or animal considered sacred and claimed as a symbol or emblem by a clan.

transformational grammar a grammar, introduced by Chomsky, that explains the *surface structure* of a sentence as the result of transformational operations on the *deep structure* of the sentence.

transhumance seasonal movement of livestock and people between two regions.

tutelary democracy a system in which the power of the legislature and the political parties and freedom of expression is reduced.

unilineal descent the most common rule of descent, which traces relations through one line of parentage.

universal grammar according to Chomsky, a substructure of rules or principles common to all languages.

uterine descent *see* matrilineal descent.

uxorilocal residence the pattern of residence in which the groom goes to live with the bride in the vicinity of her kin group or family of origin.

validity the degree to which scientific observations record the facts and values they claim to record.

virilocal residence a pattern of residence in which a married couple lives with or near the husband's family.

voluntary association any group that one joins by choice in order to accomplish a common purpose.

Bibliography

ABERLE, D. F., BRONFENBRENNER, U., HESS, E. H., MILLER, D. R., SCHNEIDER, D. M., & SPUHLER, J. N. The incest taboo and the mating behavior of animals. *American Anthropologist,* 1963, *65,* 253–264.

APPLEBY, G. Export monoculture and regional social structure in Puno, Peru. In C. A. Smith (Ed.), *Regional analysis. Vol. II: Social systems.* New York: Academic Press, 1976.

AMERICAN ANTHROPOLOGICAL ASSOCIATION. *Professional ethics: Statements and procedures of the American Anthropological Association.* Washington, D.C., 1973.

BAILEY, F. G. *Caste and the economic frontier.* Manchester: Manchester University Press, 1957.

BALANDIER, G. *Political anthropology* (A. M. S. Smith, Trans.). London: Penguin, 1970.

BALIKCI, A. Shamanistic behavior among the Netsilik Eskimos. *The Southwestern Journal of Anthropology,* 1963, *19*(4), 380–396.

BAMBERGER, J. *Kayapó age grades: A case of political development in central Brazil?* Paper presented at the 75th Annual Meeting of the American Anthropological Association, Washington, D. C., 1976.

BANTON, M. Voluntary associations: Anthropological aspects. In D. Sills (Ed.), *International encyclopedia of the social sciences.* Vol. 2 New York: Macmillan, 1968.

BARNOUW, V. *Culture and personality* (Rev. ed.). Homewood, Ill.: Dorsey, 1973.

BARTH, F. Ecological relationships of ethnic groups in Swat, North Pakistan. *American Anthropologist,* 1956, *58,* 1079–1089.

BARTH, F. (Ed.). *Ethnic groups and boundaries: The social organization of culture difference.* Boston: Little, Brown, 1969.

BASSO, K. H. Ice and travel among the Fort Norman Slave: Folk taxonomies and cultural rules. *Language in Society, 1,* 31–49.

BATESON, G. *Naven.* Stanford: Stanford University Press, 1936.

BATESON, G. Morale and national character. In G. Watson (Ed.), *Civilian morale.* Boston: Society for the Psychological Study of Social Issues, Second Yearbook, 1942.

BATESON, G. The message "This is play." In J. B. Schaffner (Ed.), *Group processes.* New York: Josiah Macy Foundation, 1956.

BATESON, G. *Steps to an ecology of mind.* New York: Ballantine, 1972.

BEALS, R. L. *Politics of social research: An inquiry into the ethics and responsibilities of social scientists.* Chicago: Aldine, 1969.

BECK, B. E. F. Centers and boundaries of regional caste systems: Toward a general model. In C. A. Smith (Ed.), *Regional analysis. Vol. II: Social systems.* New York: Academic Press, 1976.

BENDER, D. R. Agnatic or cognatic? A reevaluation of Ondo descent. *Man,* 1970, *5*(1), 71–87.

BENDIX, R. Tradition and modernity reconsidered. In L. Plotnicov & A. Tuden (Eds.), *Essays in comparative social stratification.* Pittsburgh: University of Pittsburgh Press, 1970.

BENEDICT, B. Capital, saving and credit among Mauritian Indians. In R. W. Firth & B. S. Yamey (Eds.), *Capital, saving and credit in peasant societies.* Chicago: Aldine, 1964.

BENEDICT, R. *Patterns of Culture.* New York: Houghton Mifflin, 1934. (New American Library Mentor paperback edition, 1948.)

BENEDICT, R. *The chrysanthemum and the sword.* New York: Houghton Mifflin, 1946.

BENEDICT, L. W. People who have two souls. 1916. In M. Mead and N. Calas (Eds.), *Primitive heritage.* New York: Random House, 1953.

BERREMAN, G. D. The concept of caste. In D. Sills (Ed.), *International encyclopedia of the social sciences* (Vol. 2). New York: Macmillan, 1968.

BOAS, F. *Race, language, and culture.* New York: Free Press, 1940.

BOGORAS, W. The Chuckchee. In M. Mead & N. Calas (Eds.), *Primitive heritage.* New York: Random House, 1953. (pp. 425–428.)

BOHANNAN, L. Dahomean marriage: A reevaluation. *Africa,* 1949, *19*(4), 273–287.

BOHANNAN, P. The impact of money on an African subsistence economy. *The Journal of Economic History,* 1959, *19*(4), 491–503.

BOHANNAN, P. Kinship networks and kinship terminology. In *Social anthropology.* New York: Holt, Rinehart & Winston, 1963.

BOHANNAN, P. Artist and critic in an African society. In C. M. Otten (Ed.), *Anthropology and art.* Garden City, N.Y.: Natural History Press, 1971.

BORDERS, W. At farm in the Great Indian desert, the camel is man's best friend. *The New York Times,* April 23, 1978, p. 15.

BOURGUIGNON, E. Dreams and altered states of consciousness in anthropological research. In F. L. K. Hsu (Ed.), *Psychological anthropology* (Rev. ed.). Cambridge, Mass.: Schenkman, 1972. (pp. 403–430.)

BOURGUIGNON, E. Psychological anthropology. In J. J. Honigman (Ed.), *Handbook of social and cultural anthropology.* Skokie, Ill.: Rand McNally, 1973.

BOURGUIGNON, E., & GREENBAUM, L. S. *Diversity and homogeneity in world societies.* HRAF Press, 1973. (pp 51–56.)

BRAIN, R. *The last primitive peoples.* New York: Crown, 1976.

BROWN, R. *Words and things.* Glencoe, Ill.: The Free Press, 1957.

BROWN, R. (Ed.) *Psycholinguistics.* New York: Free Press, 1970.

BUNZEL, R. L. Psychology of the Pueblo potter. 1929. In M. Mead & N. Calas (Eds.), *Primitive heritage.* New York: Random House, 1953. (pp. 270–275.)

BURLING, R. Cognition and componential analysis: God's truth or hocus pocus? *American Anthropologist,* 1964, *66,* 20–28.

BURRIDGE, K. O. L. A Tangu game. *Man,* 1957, *57,* 88–89.

CARPENTER, E. The Eskimo artist. In C. M. Otten (Ed.), *Anthropology and art.* Garden City, N. Y. Natural History Press, 1971.

CHAGNON, N. A. *Studying the Yanomamö.* New York: Holt, Rinehart & Winston, 1974.

CHAGNON, N. A. *Yanomamö: The fierce people.* New York: Holt, Rinehart & Winston, 1977.

CHILD, I. L., & SIROTO, L. BaKwele and American aesthetic evaluations compared. In C. F. Jopling (Ed.), *Art and aesthetics in primitive societies.* New York: Dutton, 1971.

CHILDE, V. *Man makes himself.* New York: Mentor Books, 1951.

CHIMEZIE, A. The dozens: An African-heritage theory. *Journal of Black Studies,* 1976, *6*(4), 401–419.

CHOMSKY, N. *Aspects of the theory of syntax.* Cambridge, Mass.: M.I.T. Press, 1965.

CHOMSKY, N. *Language and mind.* New York: Harcourt Brace Jovanovich, 1972.

CODERE, H. Fighting with property. *Monographs of the American Ethnological Society,* 1950, No. 18.

COHEN, R. Generalizations in ethnology. In R. Naroll & R. Cohen (Eds.), *A Handbook of Method in Cultural Anthropology.* New York: Columbia University Press, 1970. (pp. 31–50.)

COHEN, R., & Middleton, J. (Eds.). *From tribe to nation in Africa: Studies in incorporation processes.* Scranton, Pa.: Chandler, 1970.

COHEN, Y. A. (Ed.) *Man in adaptation:* The institutional framework. Chicago: Aldine, 1971.

COLUM, P. *Myths of the world.* New York: Grosset & Dunlap, 1930.

COOK, S. Economic anthropology: Problems in theory, method, and analysis. In J. J. Honigmann (Ed.), *Handbook of social and cultural anthropology.* Skokie, Ill.: Rand McNally, 1973.

DAHRENDORF, R. *Class and class conflict in industrial society.* Stanford: Stanford University Press, 1959.

DALTON, G. Primitive money. *American Anthropologist,* 1965, *67,* 44–65.

DALTON, G. (Ed.). Traditional production in primitive African economies. In *Tribal and peasant economies: Readings in economic anthropology.* Garden City, N.Y.: Natural History Press, 1967.

d'AZEVEDO, W. L. (Ed.). Introduction. In *The traditional artist in African societies*. Bloomington: Indiana University Press, 1973.

DARK, P. J. C. The study of ethno-aesthetics: The visual arts. In J. Helm (Ed.), *Proceedings of the 1966 Annual Spring Meeting of the American Ethnological Society*, 1967. (pp. 131–148.)

DIAZ, M. N., & POTTER, J. M. Introduction: The social life of peasants. In J. M. Potter, M. N. Diaz, & G. M. Foster (Eds.), *Peasant society: A reader*. Boston: Little, Brown, 1967.

DOUGLAS, M. Raffia cloth distribution in the Lele economy. *Africa*, 1958, *28*, 109–122.

DRUCKER, P. Rank, wealth, and kinship in Northwest Coast society. *American Anthropologist*, 1939, *41*, 55–65.

DRUCKER, P. *Indians of the Northwest Coast*. Garden City, New York: Natural History Press, 1963.

DRUCKER, P. *Cultures of the North Pacific coast*. San Francisco: Chandler, 1965.

DU BOIS, C. *The people of Alor: A social-psychological study of an East Indian island*. Minneapolis: University of Minnesota Press, 1944.

DUNDES, A. (Ed.). *Every man his way: Readings in cultural anthropology*. Englewood Cliffs, N.J.: Prentice-Hall, 1968a.

DUNDES, A. Oral literature. In J. A. Clifton (Ed.), *Introduction to cultural anthropology: Essays in the scope and methods of the science of man*. Boston: Houghton Mifflin, 1968b.

DYSON-HUDSON, R., & DYSON-HUDSON, N. Subsistence herding in Uganda, *Scientific American*, 1969, *220*, 76–89.

EAMES, E., & GOODE, J. G. *Anthropology of the city: An introduction to urban anthropology*. Englewood Cliffs, N.J.: Prentice-Hall, 1977.

EGGAN, D. Hopi dreams in cultural perspective. In G.E. von Grunebaum & R. Callois (Eds.), *The dream and human societies*. Berkeley: University of California Press, 1966.

EGGAN, F. Social anthropology and the method of controlled comparison. *American Anthropologist*, 1954, *56*, 743–763.

EISENSTADT, S. N. Transformation of social, political, and cultural orders in modernization. In R. Cohen & J. Middleton (Eds.), *Comparative political systems: Studies in the politics of pre-industrial societies*. Garden City: Natural History Press, 1967.

ELGIN, S. H. *What is linguistics?* Englewood Cliffs, N.J.: Prentice-Hall, 1973.

EMBER, M., & EMBER, C. R. The conditions favoring matrilocal versus patrilocal residence. *American Anthropologist*, 1971, *73*, 571–594.

ENGLISH, P. W. *City and village in Iran: Settlement and economy in the Kirman basin*. Madison: University of Wisconsin Press, 1966.

ESCH, H. The evolution of bee language. *Scientific American*, 1967, *216*, 97–103.

EVANS-PRITCHARD, E. E. The Nuer of the Southern Sudan. In M. Fortes and E. E. Evans-Pritchard (Eds.), *African political systems*. London: Oxford University Press/African Institute, 1970. (pp. 272–297.)

EVANS-PRITCHARD, E. E. (Ed.). The notion of witchcraft explains unfortunate events. In *Witchcraft, oracles, and magic among the Azande*. Oxford: Clarendon Press, 1976.

FALLERS, L. A. Equality and inequality in human societies. In S. Tax & L. G. Freeman (Eds.), *Horizons of anthropology* (2nd ed.). Chicago: Aldine, 1977.

FARB, P. *Man's rise to civilization as shown by the Indians of North America from primeival times to the coming of the industrial state*. New York: Dutton, 1968.

FERNEA, E. *A street in Marrakech*. New York: Doubleday, 1975.

FIRTH, R. *We, the Tikopia: A Sociological Study of Kinship in Primitive Polynesia*. Boston: Beacon Press, 1963.

FISHMAN, J. A. Bilingual attitudes and behavior. *Language Sciences*, 1969, *5*, 5–11.

FISHMAN, J. A. *Sociolinguistics: A brief introduction*. Rowley, Mass.: Newbury House, 1970.

FORD, C. S., & BEACH, F. A. *Patterns of sexual behavior*. New York: Harper, 1951.

FORDE, C. D. *Habitat, economy and society: A geographical introduction to ethnology*. New York: Dutton, 1934.

FORGE, A. *Primitive art and society*. New York: Oxford University Press, 1973.

FORTES, M. (Ed.). *Marriage in tribal societies*. Cambridge Papers in Social Anthropology, No. 3. Cambridge: Cambridge University Press, 1962.

FORTES, M. Pietas in ancestor worship. In Y. A. Cohen (Ed.), *Man in adaptation: The institutional framework*. Chicago: Aldine, 1971.

FOSTER, B. L. Ethnicity and commerce. *American Ethnologist*, 1974, *1*, 437–448.

FOULKS, E. F. *The Arctic hysterias of the North Alaskan eskimo*. Washington, D.C.: American Anthropological Association, 1972.

FOX, R. *Kinship and marriage*. Harmondsworth, Middlesex, England: Penguin, 1967.

FOX, R. *Urban anthropology: Cities in their cultural setting*. Englewood Cliffs, N. J.: Prentice-Hall, 1977.

FRAKE, C. O. The diagnosis of disease among the Subanun of Mindinao. *American Anthropologist*,

1961, *63*, 113–132.

FRAKE, C. O. Cultural ecology and ethnography. *American Anthropologist,* 1962, *64*, 53–59.

FRAKE, C. O. How to ask for a drink in Subanun. In J. Gumpery & D. Hymes (Eds.), *The ethnography of communication.* American Anthropologist Special Publication, 1964a, *66*(6), part 2.

FRAKE, C. O. A structural description of Subanun "religious behavior." In W. Goodenough (Ed.), *Explorations in cultural anthropology.* New York: McGraw-Hill, 1964b.

FRAZER, J. G. *Anthologia anthropologia: The native races of Africa and Madagascar.* London: Lund Humphries, 1938.

FREEMAN, L. C. Conflict and congruence in anthropological theory. In R. Manners & D. Kaplan (Eds.), *Theory in anthropology.* Chicago: Aldine, 1968. (pp. 193–195.)

FREILICH, M. (Ed.). *Marginal natives: Anthropologists at work.* New York: Harper & Row, 1970.

FRIED, M. H. *The evolution of political society: An essay in political anthropology.* New York: Random House, 1967.

FRIED, M. H. *The study of anthropology.* New York: Thomas Y. Crowell, 1972.

FRISBIE, C. J. Anthropological and ethnomusicological implications of a comparative analysis of Bushmen and African Pygmy music. *Ethnology,* 1971, *10*, 265–287.

FROMKIN, V. & RODMAN, R. *An introduction to language.* New York: Holt, Rinehart & Winston, 1974.

GANS, H. *The Levittowners.* New York: Pantheon, 1967.

GEERTZ, C. Ritual and social change: A Javanese example. *American Anthropologist,* 1957, *59*, 32–54.

GEERTZ, C. Form and variation in Balinese village structure. *American Anthropologist,* 1959, *61*(6).

GEERTZ, C. *The religion of Java.* Glencoe, Ill.: The Free Press, 1960.

GEERTZ, C. Studies in peasant life, community, and society. In B. J. Siegel (Ed.), *Biennial review of anthropology.* Stanford: Stanford University Press, 1962.

GEERTZ, C. (Ed.). The integrative revolution: Primordial sentiments and civil politics in the new states. In *Old societies and new states: The quest for modernity in Asia and Africa.* Glencoe, Ill.: The Free Press, 1963. (pp. 105–145)

GEERTZ, C. Religion as a cultural system. In Michael Banton (Ed.), *Anthropological approaches to the study of religion.* London: Tavistock, 1966.

GEERTZ, C. (Ed.). The integrative revolution: Primordial sentiments and civil politics in the new states. In *Old societies and new states.* Chicago: University of Chicago Press, 1968a.

GEERTZ, C. Religion. I.: Anthropological study. In D. Sills (Ed.), *International encyclopedia of the social sciences* (Vol. 13). New York: Macmillan, 1968b.

GEERTZ, C. Ethos, world-view and the analysis of sacred symbols. In E. A. Hammel & W. S. Simmons (Eds.), *Man makes sense: A reader in modern cultural anthropology.* Boston: Little, Brown, 1970.

GEERTZ, C. The wet and the dry: Traditional irrigation in Bali and Morocco. *Human Ecology,* 1972a, *1*(1), 23–39.

GEERTZ, C. Summary comments. In R. Antoun & Iliya Harik (Eds.), *Rural politics and social change in the Middle East.* Bloomington: Indiana University Press, 1972b.

GEERTZ, C. *The interpretation of cultures.* New York: Basic Books, 1973.

GEERTZ, C. On the nature of anthropological understanding. *American Scientist,* 1975, *63*, 47–48.

GEERTZ, C. Art as a culture system. *MLN,* 1976, *91*, 1473–1499.

GIBBS, J. L., Jr. Poro values and courtroom procedures in a Kpelle chiefdom. *Southwestern Journal of Anthropology,* 1962, *18*(4), 341–350.

GIBBS, J. L., Jr. Marital instability among the Kpelle: Toward a theory of epainogramy. *American Anthropologist,* 1963, *65*, 552–559.

GIFFORD, E. W. Miwok lineages and the political unit in California. *American Anthropologist,* 1926, *28*, 389–401.

GILMORE, D. Varieties of gossip in a Spanish rural community. *Ethnology,* 1978, *17*, 89–99.

GLICK, P. B. Melanesian mosaic: The plural community of Vila. In L. Plotnicov & A. Tuden (Eds.), *Essays in comparative social stratification.* Pittsburgh: University of Pittsburgh Press, 1970.

GLUCKMAN, M. Kinship and marriage among the Lozi of northern Rhodesia and the Zulu of Natal. In A. R. Radcliffe-Brown & D. Forde (Eds.), *African systems of kinship and marriage.* Oxford: Oxford University Press, 1950.

GLUCKMAN, M. (Ed.). Les rites de passage. In *Essays on the ritual of social relations.* Manchester: Manchester University Press, 1962.

GLUCKMAN, M. *Order and rebellion in tribal Africa.* London: Cohen and West, 1963.

GLUCKMAN, M. Inter-hierarchical roles: Professional and party ethics in tribal areas in South and Central Africa. In M. J. Swartz (Ed.), *Local-level politics: Social and cultural perspectives.* Chicago: Aldine, 1968.

GOLDSCHMIDT, W. *Sebei law*. Berkeley: University of California Press, 1967. (pp. 245–260)

GOLDWATER, R. Art history and anthropology: Some comparisons of methodology. In A. Forge (Ed.), *Primitive art and society*. New York: Oxford University Press, 1973.

GOODALE, J. C., & KOSS, J. D. The cultural context of creativity among Tiwi. In C. M. Otten (Ed.), *Anthropology and art*. Garden City, N.Y.: Natural History Press, 1971.

GOODENOUGH, W. H. A problem in Malayo-Polynesian social organization. *American Anthropologist*, 1955, *57*, 71–83.

GOODENOUGH, W. H. Residence rules. *Southwestern Journal of Anthropology*, 1956, *12*, 22–37.

GOODENOUGH, W. H. *Description and comparison in cultural anthropology*. Chicago: Aldine, 1970.

GOODY, J. Bridewealth and dowry in Africa and Eurasia. In J. Goody & S. J. Tambiah (Eds.), *Bridewealth and dowry*. Cambridge: Cambridge University Press, 1973.

GORER, G., & RICKMAN, J. *The people of Great Russia: A psychological study*. New York: Chanticleer, 1950.

GOUGH, E. K. The Nayars and the definition of marriage. *Journal of the Royal Anthropological Institute*, 1959, *89*, 23–34.

GOULD, H. A. Castes, outcastes, and the sociology of stratification. *International Journal of Comparative Sociology*, 1960, *1*,(2).

GOULD, H. A. *Caste and class: A comparative view*. A McCaleb Module in Anthropology. Addison-Wesley Modular Publications, 1971.

GOULDNER, A. W. *The coming crisis of Western sociology*. New York: Basic Books, 1970.

GRABURN, N. H. H. (Ed.). Introduction: Arts of the Fourth World. In *Ethnic and tourist arts: Cultural expressions from the Fouth World*. Berkeley: University of California Press, 1976.

GRANQVIST, Hilma. *Marriage Conditions in a Palestinian Village*. Helsingfors: Akademische Buchhandrung, 1931.

GRINNELL, G. B. *The Cheyenne Indians: Their history and way of life* (Vol. 1). New York: Cooper Square Publishers, 1962.

GROSSMAN, L. Ethnicity and health delivery systems. In P. S. J. Cafferty & L. Chestang (Eds.), *The diverse society: Implications for social policy*. Washington: National Association of Social Workers, 1976.

GULLIVER, P. H. The Jie of Uganada. In J. L. Gibbs, Jr. (Ed.), *Peoples of Africa*, New York: Holt, Rinehart & Winston, 1965.

HALL, E. T. Proxemics. *Current Anthropology*, 1968, *9*, 83–95.

HARDESTY, D. L. *Ecological anthropology*. New York: Wiley, 1977.

HARRELL-BOND, B. Studying elites: Some special problems. In M. A. Rynkiewich & J. P. Spradley, *Ethics and anthropology: Dilemmas in fieldwork*. New York: Wiley, 1976.

HARRIS, M. *Cows, pigs, wars, and witches*. New York: Vintage/Random House, 1974.

HARRISON, S. The challenge to Indian nationalism. *Foreign Affairs*, 1956, *34*.

HAUSER, P. M., & SCHNORE, L. F. (Eds.). *The study of urbanization*. New York: Wiley, 1965.

HERSKOVITS, M. J. *Economic anthropology: The economic life of primitive peoples*. New York: Norton, 1965.

HIMMELHEBER, H. The present status of sculptural art among the tribes of the Ivory Coast. In J. Helm (Ed.), *Proceedings of the 1966 Annual Spring Meeting of the American Ethnological Society*, 1967. (pp. 192–197.)

HOOTON, E. A. *Crime and the man*. Cambridge, Mass.: Harvard University Press, 1939.

HOSTETLER, J. A., & HUNTINGTON, G. E. *Children in Amish society: Socialization and community education*. New York: Holt, Rinehart & Winston, 1971.

HUIZINGA, J. *Homo ludens: A study of the play-element in culture*. Boston: Beacon Press, 1955.

HUNTER, D. E., & WHITTEN, P. *Encyclopedia of anthropology*. New York: Harper & Row, 1976.

HUNTINGFORD, G. W. B. *The Nandi of Kenya: Tribal control in a pastoral society*. London: Routledge & Kegan Paul, 1953.

HYMES, D. Linguistic method in ethnography: Its development in the United States. In P. Garvin (Ed.), *Method and theory in linguistics*. The Hague: Mouton, 1971a.

HYMES, D. Sociolinguistics and the ethnography of speaking. In E. Ardener (Ed.), *Social anthropology and linguistics*. ASA Monographs, 10. London: Tavistock, 1971b.

HYMES, D. *Foundations in Sociolinguistics: An ethnographic approach*. Philadelphia: University of Pennsylvania Press, 1974.

KAPLAN, D., & MANNERS, R. A. *Culture theory*. Englewood Cliffs, N. J.: Prentice-Hall, 1972.

KARDINER, A. *The individual and his society*. New York: Columbia University Press, 1939.

KARDINER, A., & PREBLE, E. *They studied man*. New York: Crown, 1961.

KEESING, R. M. Theories of culture. In B. Siegel, A. Beals, & S. Tyler (Eds.), *Annual review of anthropology* (Vol. 3). Palo Alto, Calif.: Annual Reviews, Inc., 1974. (pp. 73–97.)

KEESING, R. M. *Cultural anthropology: A contemporary perspective*. New York: Holt, Rinehart & Winston, 1976.

KEESING, R. M., & KEESING, F. M. *New perspectives in cultural anthropology.* New York: Holt, Rinehart & Winston, 1971.

KLUCKHOHM, C. Myths and rituals: A general theory. *Harvard Theological Review,* 1942, *35,* 45–79.

KLUCKHOHN, C. & KELLY, W. H. The concept of culture. In R. Linton (Ed.), *The science of man in the world crisis.* New York: Columbia University Press, 1945.

KLUCKHOHN, C., & LEIGHTON, D. C. *The Navaho.* Cambridge, Mass.: Harvard University Press, 1946.

KLUCKHOHN, C., & MURRAY, H. A. (Eds.). *Personality in nature, society, and culture* (2nd ed.). New York: Knopf, 1962.

KOPYKOFF, I., & MIERS, S. African "slavery" as an institution of marginality. In S. Miers & I. Kopykoff (Eds.), *Slavery in Africa.* Madison: University of Wisconsin Press, 1977.

KRADER, L. *Formation of the state.* Englewood Cliffs N. J.: Prentice-Hall, 1968.

KROEBER, A. L. Classificatory systems of relationship. *Journal of the Royal Anthropological Institute,* 1909, *39,* 77–84.

KROEBER, A. L. *Anthropology.* New York: Harcourt, 1923.

KROEBER, A. L. *Anthropology* (rev. ed.). New York: Harcourt, 1948.

KROEBER, A. L., & Kluckhohn, C. (Eds.). *Culture, a critical review of concepts and definitions.* New York: Random House, 1952.

LABARRE, W. Some observations on character structure in the Orient: The Japanese. *Psychiatry,* 1945, *8,* 326–342.

LABARRE, W. *The human animal.* Chicago: University of Chicago Press, 1954.

LABOV, W. *Sociolinguistic patterns.* Philadelphia University of Pennsylvania Press, 1972.

LAKOFF, R. Language and women's place. *Language in Society,* 1973, *3,* 45–80.

LEACH, E. R. *Political systems of highland Burma: A study of Kachin social structure.* Boston: Beacon Press, 1954.

LEACH, E. R. Polyandry, inheritance and the definition of marriage. *Man,* 1955, *54,* 182–186.

LEACH, E. R. Golden bough or gilded twig? *Daedalus,* 1961, *90,* 371–387.

LEACH, E. R. Ritual. In D. Sills (Ed.), *International encyclopedia of the social sciences* (Vol. 13). New York: Macmillan, 1968.

LEACH, M. (Ed.). Swastika. In *Standard dictionary of folklore, mythology, and legend.* New York: Funk & Wagnalls, 1950.

LEE, R. B. !Kung bushman subsistence: An input-output analysis. In A. P. Vayda (Ed.), *Environment and cultural behavior.* Garden City, N.Y.: Natural History Press, 1969.

LEE, R. B., & DEVORE, I. (Eds.). Problems in the study of hunters and gatherers. In *Man the hunter.* Chicago: Aldine, 1968.

LÉONS, M. B. The economic networks of Bolivian political brokers: Revolutionary road to fame and fortune. In R. Halperin & J. Dow (Eds.), *Peasant livelihood: Studies in anthropology and cultural ecology.* New York: St. Martin's, 1977.

LESSA, W. A. The decreasing power of myth on Ulithi. In W. A. Lessa & E. Z. Vogt, *Reader in comparative religion: An anthropological approach* (2nd ed.). New York: Harper & Row, 1965.

LESSA, W. A., & VOGT, E. Z. *Reader in comparative religion: An anthropological approach* (2nd ed.). New York: Harper & Row, 1965.

LEVINE, R. A., & LEVINE, B. B. *Nyansongo: A Gusii community in Kenya.* Six Cultures Series (Vol. 2). New York: Wiley, 1966.

LÉVI-STRAUSS, C. The social and psychological aspects of chieftainship in a primitive tribe: The Nambikuara of northwestern Mato Grosso. *Transactions of the New York Academy of Sciences,* 1944, 16–32.

LÉVI-STRAUSS, C. Social structure. In A. L. Kroeber (Ed.), *Anthropology today.* Chicago: University of Chicago Press, 1953.

LÉVI-STRAUSS, C. *Structural anthropology.* New York: Basic Books, 1963.

LÉVI-STRAUSS, C. Today's crisis in anthropology. In S. Rapport & H. Wright (Eds.), *Anthropology.* New York: Washington Square Press, 1967.

LÉVI-STRAUSS, C. The concept of primitiveness. In R. Lee & I. DeVore (Eds.), *Man the hunter.* Chicago: Aldine, 1968. (pp. 349–352.)

LEWIS, I. M. *Ecstatic religion.* Baltimore: Penguin, 1971.

LEWIS, O. *Life in a Mexican village: Tepoztlan restudied.* Urbana: University of Illinois Press, 1951.

LIEBOW, E. *Tally's corner: A study of Negro street-corner men.* Boston: Little, Brown, 1967.

LITTLE, K. L. The role of the secret society in cultural specialization. *American Anthropologist,* 1949, *51,* 199–212.

LITTLE, K. L. Voluntary associations in urban life: A case study of differential adaptation. In M. Freedman (Ed.), *Social organization: Essays presented to Raymond Firth.* Chicago: Aldine, 1967.

LITTLE, M. A., & MORREN, G. E. B., Jr. *Ecology, energetics, and human variability.* Dubuque, Iowa: Brown, 1976.

LLOYD, P. C. Divorce among the Yoruba. *American Anthropologist,* 1968, *70* (1), 67–81.

LOMAX, A. Song structure and social structure.

Ethnology, 1962, *1*(4), 425–451.

LOMAX, A. *Folk song style and culture.* Washington: American Association for the Advancement of Science, 1968. (No. 88.)

LOWIE, R. *The history of ethnological theory.* New York: Rinehart, 1937.

LYND, R. S., & LYND, H. M. *Middletown: A study in contemporary American culture.* New York: Harcourt, 1959.

LYND, R. S., & LYND, H. M. *Middletown in transition.* New York: Harcourt, 1963.

MADDI, S. R. *Personality theories: A comparative analysis.* Homewood, Ill.: Dorsey, 1968.

MAIR, L. *Primitive government.* Baltimore: Penguin, 1962.

MAIR, L. *An introduction to social anthropology* (2nd ed.). Oxford: Clarendon, 1972.

MALEFIJT, A. De Waal. *Images of man: A history of anthropological thought.* New York: Knopf, 1974.

MALINOWSKI, B. Kula; the circulating exchange of valuables in the archipelagoes of eastern New Guinea. *Man,* 1920 (No. 51), 97–105. (In George Dalton (Ed.), *Tribal and peasant economies. Readings in economic anthropology.* Garden City, N.Y.: The Natural History Press, 1967.)

MALINOWSKI, B. *Argonauts of the Western Pacific.* London: Routledge & Kegan Paul, 1922.

MALINOWSKI, B. *Coral gardens and their magic.* London: Allen & Unwin, 1935.

MALINOWSKI, B. *A diary in the strict sense of the term.* London: Routledge & Kegan Paul, 1967.

MANDLEBAUM, D. G. (Ed.). *Selected writings of Edward Sapir in language, culture and personality.* Berkeley: University of California Press, 1949.

MANGIN, W. *Peasants in cities: Readings in the anthropology of urbanization.* Boston: Houghton Mifflin, 1970.

MARETZKI, T. W., & MARETZKI, H. *Taira: An Okinawan village.* Six Cultures Series. (Vol. 7). New York: Wiley, 1966.

MARSHALL, G. Marriage: Comparative analysis. In D. Sills (Ed.), *International encyclopedia of the social sciences* (Vol. 10). New York: Macmillan, 1968. (pp. 8–19.)

MARSHALL, L. !Kung bushman bands. *Africa,* 1960, *30*(4), 26–43.

MARUYAMA, M. Toward human futuristics. In M. Maruyama & J. A. Dator (Eds.), *Human futuristics.* Honolulu: Social Science Research Institute, University of Hawaii, 1971.

MAYBURY-LEWIS, D. *Akwe̅-Shavante society.* New York: Oxford University Press, 1974.

MEAD, G. H. *Mind, self, and society.* Chicago: University of Chicago Press, 1934.

MEAD, M. *Coming of age in Samoa.* New York: Morrow, 1928.

MEAD, M. *Growing up in New Guinea.* New York: Morrow, 1930.

MEAD, M. *Sex and temperament in three primitive societies.* New York: Morrow, 1935.

MEAD, M. The study of national character. In D. Lerner & H. D. Lasswell (Eds.), *The policy sciences.* Stanford: Stanford University Press, 1951. (pp. 70–85.)

MEAD, M. A note on contributions of anthropology to the science of the future. In M. Maruyama & J. A. Dator (Eds.), *Human futuristics.* Honolulu: Social Science Research Institute, University of Hawaii, 1971.

MEAD, M. & METRAUX, R. (Eds.). *The study of culture at a distance.* Chicago: University of Chicago Press, 1953.

"Mennonite Dissident Shunned by Church and Wife," *The New York Times,* July 23, 1973.

MERRIAM, A. P. Purposes of ethnomusicology: An anthropological view. *Ethnomusicology,* 1963, *7,* 206–213.

MERRIAM, A. P. *The anthropology of music.* Evanston, Ill.: Northwestern University Press, 1964a.

MERRIAM, A. P. The arts and anthropology. In S. Tax (Ed.), *Horizons of anthropology.* Chicago: Aldine, 1964b.

MEZZROW, M. & WOLFE, B. *Really the blues.* New York: Random House, 1946. (pp. 71–77.)

MIDDLETON, J. *Lugbara religion: Ritual and authority among an East African people.* New York: Oxford University Press, 1960.

MILLER, E. S. The Christian missionary, agent of secularization. *Anthropological Quarterly,* 1970, *43*(1), 14–22.

MILLER, E. S. *Rethinking the concept "peasantry."* Unpublished manuscript prepared for presentation at the Third Annual Meeting of the Working Group in Social Articulation, Quito, Ecuador, December 1976. (Available from author, Department of Anthropology, Temple University.)

MINTZ, S. W., & WOLF, E. R. An analysis of ritual co-parenthood (compadrazgo). *Southwestern Journal of Anthropology,* 1950, *6,* 54.

MITCHELL, J. C. Marriage, matriliny, and social structure among the Yao of southern Nyasaland. *International Journal of Comparative Sociology,* 1962, *3,* 29–32; 35–37; 39–40.

MITCHELL, J. C. On quantification in social anthropology. In A. L. Epstein (Ed.), *The craft of anthropology.* London: Tavistock, 1967. (pp. 17–45.)

MOONEY, J. An Indian messiah. 1892. In M. Mead & N. Calas (Eds.), *Primitive heritage.* New York: Random House, 1953. (pp. 412–424.)

MUNN, N. D. Visual categories: An approach to the study of representational systems. In C. F.

Jopling (Ed.), *Art and aesthetics in primitive societies.* New York: Dutton, 1971.

MUNN, N. D. The spatial presentation of cosmic order in Walbiri iconography. In A. Forge (Ed.), *Primitive art and society.* New York: Oxford University Press, 1973.

MURDOCK, G. P. *Our primitive contemporaries.* New York: Macmillan, 1934.

MURDOCK, G. P. Double descent. *American Anthropologist, 42*(4), 1940, 555–561.

MURDOCK, G. P. *Social structure.* New York: Macmillan, 1949.

MYERHOFF, B. G., & TUFTE, V. Life History as integration: An essay on an experimental model. *Gerontologist* 1975, *15,* 541–543.

NADEL, S. F. Witchcraft in four African societies: An essay in comparison. In S. Ottenberg & P. Ottenberg (Eds.), *Cultures and societies of Africa.* New York: Random House, 1960. (pp. 407–419.)

NASH, M. The social context of economic choice in a small society. *Man,* 1961a (219), 186–191

NASH, M. Witchcraft as social process in a Tzeltal community. *American Indigena,* 1961b, *20,* 121–126.

NASH, M. *Primitive and peasant economic systems.* San Francisco: Chandler, 1966.

NASH, M. The organization of economic life. In S. Tax & L. G. Freeman (Eds.), *Horizons of anthropology* (2nd ed.). Chicago: Aldine, 1977.

NEEDHAM, R. The future of social anthropology: Disintegration of metamorphosis? In *Anniversary contributions to anthropology: Twelve essays.* Leiden: E. J. Brill, 1970.

NEEDHAM, R. *Rethinking kinship and marriage.* London: Tavistock, 1971.

NEETING, R. McC. The ecological approach in cultural study. Addison-Wesley Modular Publications, 1971, (Module 6). (pp. 1–30.)

OAKLEY, K. P. *Man the tool-maker.* Chicago: University of Chicago Press, 1959.

OLIVER, O. O. In M. Herskovits, *Economic Anthropology:* The economic life of primitive peoples. New York: Norton, 1965.

OTTENBERG, S., & OTTENBERG, P. (Eds.). *Cultures and societies of Africa.* New York: Random House, 1960.

PARK, G. K. Divination and its social contexts. In J. Middleton (Ed.), *Magic, witchcraft, and curing.* Garden City, N.Y.: Natural History Press, 1967.

PATAI, R. *Sex and family in the Bible.* New York: Doubleday, 1959.

PEACOCK, J. L. *Rites of modernization.* Chicago: University of Chicago Press, 1968.

PELTO, P. J. *Anthropological research: The structure of inquiry.* New York: Harper & Row, 1970.

PELTO, P. J., & PELTO, G. H. Ethnography: The fieldwork enterprise. In J. J. Honigman *(Ed.), Handbook of social and cultural anthropology.* Skokie, Ill.: Rand McNally, 1973. (pp. 241–281.)

PETERS, E. L. Some structural aspects of the feud among the Bedouin of Cyrenaica. In J. G. Peristiany (Ed.), *Contributions to Mediterranean Sociology.* The Hague: Mouton, 1963a.

PETERS, E. L. The tied and the free. In J. G. Peristiany (Ed.), *Contributions to Mediterranean sociology.* The Hague: Mouton, 1963b. (pp. 167–188.)

PFEIFFER, J. E. *The emergence of man* (2nd ed.). New York: Harper & Row, 1972.

PITT-RIVERS, J. The kith and the kin. In J. Goody (Ed.), *The character of kinship.* Cambridge: Cambridge University Press, 1973. (pp. 89–105.)

POLYANI, Karl, et al. (Eds.). The economy as institutional process. In *Trade and market in the early empires.* New York: The Free Press, 1957.

POLYANI, Karl, et al. 1957

POTTER, J. M. From peasants to rural proletarians: Social and economic change in rural Communist China. In J. M. Potter, M. N. Diaz, & G. M. Foster (Eds.), *Peasant society: A reader.* Boston: Little, Brown, 1967a.

POTTER, J. M. Introduction: Peasants in the modern world. In J. M. Potter, M. N. Diaz, & G. M. Foster (Eds.), *Peasant society: A reader.* Boston: Little, Brown, 1967b.

PREMACK, A. J., & PREMACK, D. Teaching language to an ape. *Scientific American,* 1972, *227*(14), 92–99.

QUEEN, S. A., & HABENSTEIN, R. W. *The family in various cultures* (4th ed.). Philadelphia: Lippincott, 1974.

RAPPAPORT, R. A. *Pigs for the ancestors: Ritual in the ecology of a New Guinea people.* New Haven, Conn.: Yale University Press, 1967.

RAPPAPORT, R. A. Ritual regulation of environmental relations among a New Guinea people. In Y. A. Cohen (Ed.), *Man in adaptation: The institutional framework.* Chicago: Aldine, 1971.

RATTRAY, R. S. *Ashanti.* Oxford: Oxford University Press, 1923.

REDFIELD, R. *Tepoztlan—A Mexican village.* Chicago: University of Chicago Press, 1930.

REDFIELD, R. *The folk culture of Yucatan.* Chicago: University of Chicago Press, 1941.

REDFIELD, R. *The little community and peasant society and culture.* Chicago: University of Chicago Press, 1960.

REDFIELD, R., & M. B. SINGER. City and countryside: The cultural independence. In T. Shanin (Ed.), *Peasants and peasant societies: Selected read-*

ings. Baltimore: Penguin Books, 1971.

REID, R. M. Effects of consanguineous marriage and inbreeding on couple fertility and offspring mortality in rural Sri Lanka. In B. A. Kaplan (Ed.), *Anthropological studies of human fertility.* Detroit: Wayne State University Press, 1976. (pp. 139–146.)

RENSBERGER, B. The world's oldest works of art. *The New York Times Magazine,* May 21, 1978, 27–29; 32; 37; 40; 42.

RHEINSTEIN, M. Problems of law in the new nations of Africa. In C. Geertz (Ed.), *Old societies and new states: The quest for modernity in Asia and Africa.* Glencoe, Ill.: The Free Press, 1963. (pp. 220–246.)

RICHARDS, A. I. Land labor and diet in Northern Rhodesia (2nd ed.). London: Oxford University Press, 1961.

RIVIERE, P. G. Marriage: A reassessment. In R. Needham (Ed.), *Rethinking kinship and marriage.* London: Tavistock, 1971.

ROYCE, A. P. *The anthropology of dance.* Bloomington: Indiana University Press, 1977.

RYNKIEWICH, M. A. The underdevelopment of anthropological ethics. In M. A. Rynkiewich & J. P. Spradley (Eds.), *Ethics and anthropology: Dilemmas in fieldwork.* New York: Wiley, 1976.

RYNKIEWICH, M. A., & Spradley, J. P. *Ethics and anthropology: Dilemmas in fieldwork.* New York: Wiley, 1976.

SAFER, J. Parallel descent and mother/daughter marriage among the Saha. Paper presented at the Annual Meeting of the American Anthropological Association, Mexico City, November 1974.

SAFER, J. Parallel descent: Does it exist? Paper presented at the Annual Meeting of the American Anthropological Association, San Francisco, December 1975.

SAHLINS, M. D. *Social stratification in Polynesia.* Seattle: University of Washington Press, 1958.

SAHLINS, M. D. Political power and the economy in primitive society. In G. E. Dole & R. L. Carneiro (Eds.), *Essays in the science of culture in honor of Leslie A. White.* New York: Crowell, 1960.

SAHLINS, M. D. The segmentary lineage: An organization of predatory expansion. *American Anthropologist,* 1961, 63(2), 332–345.

SAHLINS, M. D. Culture and environment; The study of cultural ecology. In S. Tax (Ed.), *Horizons of anthropology.* Chicago: Aldine, 1964. (pp. 132–147.)

SAHLINS, M. D. *Stone age economics.* London: Tavistock, 1972.

SAPIR, E. *Language.* New York: Harcourt Brace Jovanovich, 1921.

SAPIR, E. Culture, genuine and spurious. In D. Mandelbaum (Ed.), *Selected writings of Edward Sapir in language, culture and personality.* Berkeley: University of California Press, 1949. (pp. 308–312.)

SHEFFLER, H. W. Structuralism in anthropology. In J. Ehrmann (Ed.), *Structuralism.* New York: Anchor Books, 1970. (pp. 56–79.)

SCHNEIDER, D. & SHARP, L. The dream life of a primitive people: The dreams of the Yir Yoront of Australia. W. H. Goodenough (Ed.). American Anthropology Association. Ann Arbor: University Microfilms, 1969.

SCHWAB, W. B. Kinship and lineage among the Yoruba. *Africa,* 1955, 25 352–373.

SERVICE, E. R. *The hunters.* Englewood Cliffs, N.J.: Prentice-Hall, 1966.

SHELDON, W. H. *The varieties of human physique.* New York: Harper, 1940.

SHELDON, W. H. *The varieties of temperament.* New York: Harper, 1942.

SHILS, E. Political development in the new states: I, II. *Comparative studies in society and history,* 1960, 2(4), 266–292; 379–411.

SIEBER, R. The aesthetics of traditional African art. In C. F. Jopling (Ed.), *Art and aesthetics in primitive societies.* New York: Dutton, 1971.

SILVERSTEIN, M. Language as a part of culture. In S. Tax & L. G. Freeman (Eds.), *Horizons of anthropology* (2nd ed.). Chicago: Aldine, 1977. (pp. 119–131.)

SILVERMAN, S. F. The community-nation mediator in traditional Central Italy. In J. M. Potter, M. N. Diaz, & G. M. Foster (Eds.), *Peasant society: A reader.* Boston: Little, Brown, 1967.

SIMMONS, L. W. *The role of the aged in primitive society.* Hamden, Conn.: Shoe String Press, 1970.

SINGER, M. A survey of culture and personality theory and research. In B. Kaplan (Ed.), *Studying personality cross-culturally.* New York: Harper & Row, 1961.

SJOBERG, G. *The preindustrial city.* New York: Free Press, 1960.

SMELSER, N. J. Mechanisms of change and adjustment of changes. In W. E. Moore & B. F. Hoselitz (Eds.), *The impact of industry.* Paris: International Social Science Council, 1963.

SMELSER, N. J., & LIPSET, M. Social structure, mobility, and development. In N. J. Smelser & M. Lipset (Eds.), *Social structure and mobility in economic development.* Chicago: Aldine, 1966.

SMITH, C. A. (Ed.), *Regional analysis Vol. II: Social systems.* New York: Academic Press, 1976.

SMITH, M. G. Pre-industrial stratification systems. In N. J. Smelser & S. M. Lipset (Eds.), *Social structure and mobility in economic development.* Chicago: Aldine, 1966.

SMITH, M. G. Political organization. In D. Sills (Ed.), *International encyclopedia of the social sciences* (Vol. 12). New York: Macmillan, 1968a.

SMITH, M. G. Secondary marriage in northern Nigeria. In P. Bohannan & J. Middleton (Eds.), *Marriage, family, and residence*. Garden City, N.Y.: The Natural History Press, 1968b. (pp. 298–323.)

SOUTHALL, A. W. Stratification in Africa. In L. Plotnicov & A. Tuden (Eds.), *Essays in comparative social stratification*. Pittsburgh: University of Pittsburgh Press, 1970.

SPENCER, R. F. The North Alaskan Eskimo: A Study in ecology and society. Smithsonian Institute of American Ethnology. Bull. 171. Washington, D.C.: U.S. Government Printing Office, 1959.

SPRADLEY, J. *You owe yourself a drunk: An ethnography of urban nomads*. Boston: Little, Brown, 1970.

STEWARD, J. *Theory of culture change*. Urbana: University of Illinois Press, 1955.

STOCKING, G. W., Jr. (Ed.). *The shaping of American anthropology, 1883–1911: A Franz Boas reader*. New York: Basic Books, 1974.

STOUT, D. B. Aesthetics in "primitive societies." In C. F. Jopling (Ed.), *Art and aesthetics in primitive societies*. New York: Dutton, 1971.

SWANSON, G. *The birth of the Gods: The origin of primitive beliefs*. Ann Arbor: University of Michigan Press, 1960.

SWARTZ, M. J., Turner, V. W., & TUDEN, A. (Eds.). *Political anthropology*. Chicago: Aldine, 1966.

TAMBIAH, S. J. Dowry and bridewealth, and the property rights of women in South Asia. In J. Goody & S. J. Tambiah (Eds.), *Bridewealth and dowry*. Cambridge: Cambridge University Press, 1973.

THOMAS, E. M. Leadership in the Bushman band. In P. K. Bock (Ed.), *Culture shock*. New York: Knopf, 1970.

THOMPSON, R. F. Aesthetics in traditional Africa. *Art News*, 1968, 66(9), 44–45; 63–66.

TURNER, V. W. *Schism and continuity in an African society*. Manchester: Manchester University Press, 1957.

TURNER, V. W. *The drums of affliction*. Oxford: Clarendon, 1968.

TYLOR, E. B. *Origins of culture*. (Primitive Culture, Part I.) New York: Harper & Row, 1958.

UDY, S. H. *Work in traditional and modern society*. Englewood Cliffs, N.J.: Prentice-Hall, 1970.

VALENTINE, C. *Culture and poverty*. Chicago: University of Chicago Press, 1968.

VAYDA, A. P., & RAPPAPORT, R. A. Ecology, cultural and noncultural. In J. A. Clifton (Ed.), *Introduction to cultural anthropology*. Boston: Houghton Mifflin, 1968. (pp. 447–497.)

VIDICH, A., & BENSMAN, J. *Small town in mass society*. Princeton: Princeton University Press, 1958.

VOGT, E. Z. Structural and conceptual replication in Zinacantan culture. *American Anthropologist*, 1965, 67.

WALLACE, A. F. C. *Culture and personality*. New York: Random House, 1961.

WARNER, W. L. *Yankee City*. New Haven, Conn.: Yale University Press, 1963.

WEBER, M. *The theory of social and economic organization* (A. M. Henderson & T. Parsons, Trans.). Glencoe, Ill.; The Free Press, 1947.

WERBNER, R. P. *Regional cults*. New York: Academic Press, 1977.

WHITE, L. A. *The science of culture*. New York: Farrar, Straus & Girous, 1949.

WHITE, L. A. *The evolution of culture*. New York: McGraw-Hill, 1959.

WHORF, B. L. The relation of habitual thought and behavior to language. In J. B. Carroll (Ed.)., *Language, thought and reality; selected writings of Benjamin Lee Whorf*. Cambridge, Mass.: M.I.T. Press, 1956.

WHYTE, W. F. *Street corner society: The social structure of an Italian slum*. Chicago: University of Chicago Press, 1955.

WOLF, A. P. Childhood association and sexual attraction: A further test of the Westermarck hypothesis. *American Anthropologist*, 1970, 72, 503–515.

WOLF, E. R. Aspects of group relations in a complex society: Mexico. *American Anthropologist*, 1956, 58(6), 1065–1078.

WOLF, E. R. *Peasants*. Englewood Cliffs, N.J.: Prentice-Hall, 1966a.

WOLF, E. R. Kinship, friendship, and patron-client relations in complex societies. In M. Banton (Ed.), *The social anthropology of complex societies*. New York: Tavistock, 1966b.

WOLFENSTEIN, M. French parents take their children to the park. In M. Mead & M. Wolfenstein (Eds.), *Childhood in contemporary cultures*. Chicago: University of Chicago Press, 1955. (pp. 114–115.)

WORSLEY, P. M. Millenarian movements in Melanesia. In J. Middleton (Ed.), *Gods and rituals; Readings in religion, beliefs and practices*. Garden City, N. Y.: Natural History Press, 1967.

WRIGHT, G. E. *Biblical archaeology*. Philadelphia: Westminster Press, 1960.

YERGIN, D. The Chomskyan revolution. *The New York Times Magazine*, Dec. 3, 1972, 42–43ff.

Indexes

Name Index

Aberle, D., 137
Appleby, G., 347–348

Bailey, F. G., 249
Balandier, G., 262, 265
Bamberger, J., 168
Banton, M., 174
Barnouw, V., 85–86, 94
Barth, F., 176–177, 346–347
Basso, 9, 50
Bateson, G., 59, 92, 331
Beach, F. A., 133–135, 144
Beck, B. E. F., 347
Bender, D. R., 128, 129
Bendix, 261, 264, 265
Benedict, B., 249
Benedict, L. W., 96
Benedict, R., 47–49, 58, 93, 289
Bensman, J., 356
Berreman, G. D., 258, 260
Birdwhistell, R., 74
Bloomfield, L., 63, 64
Boas, F., 21, 43–44, 64
Bogoras, W., 135

Bohannan, P., 128, 246, 321, 323–324, 360
Borders, W., 202
Bourguignon, E., 89, 95, 98, 144, 146, 148, 262
Brain, R., 50
Brown, R., 65
Bunzel, R. L., 95
Burling, R., 51
Burridge, K. O. L., 336

Carpenter, E., 324
Chagnon, N. A., 26–27, 279
Child, I. L., 318, 332
Childe, V.G., 201–202
Chimezie, A., 335
Chomsky, N., 63, 68–69
Codere, H., 281
Cohen, R., 30, 349
Cohen, Y. A., 182, 185–186, 209–210, 298, 300
Colum, P., 38
Cook, S., 215, 233

Dahrendorf, R., 181–182
Dalton, G., 231, 245
Dark, P. J. C., 323
d'Azevado, W. L., 315–316, 324, 328
De Vore, I., 221
Diaz, M. N., 352–353, 354

Douglas, M., 245
D'Oyly, 146
Dundes, A., 187
Drucker, P., 197, 242–244, 256–257, 263–264
Du Bois, C., 91–92
Dundes, A., 334–335
Durkheim, E., 286, 291–292
Dyson-Hudson, N., 56–57
Dyson-Hudson, R., 56–57

Eames, E., 356, 359, 360
Eggan, F., 32, 97
Eisenstadt, 264
Elgin, S. H., 69
Ember, C. R., 149
Ember, M., 149
English, P. W., 348–349
Evans-Pritchard, E. E., 113, 135, 143, 156–157, 304–305

Fallers, L. A., 253, 255
Farb, P., 97
Fernea, E., 22
Firth, R., 49
Fischer, J., 28, 149
Fishman, J. A., 70, 72
Ford, C. S., 133–135, 144
Forde, C. D., 222–223, 225–226, 228–229

383

Subject Index